NEW DIRECTIONS IN ORAL THEORY

MEDIEVAL AND RENAISSANCE
TEXTS AND STUDIES

VOLUME 287

NEW DIRECTIONS IN ORAL THEORY

edited by

Mark C. Amodio

Arizona Center for Medieval and Renaissance Studies
Tempe, Arizona
2005

© Copyright 2005
Arizona Board of Regents for Arizona State University

Library of Congress Cataloging-in-Publication Data

New directions in oral theory : essays on ancient and medieval literatures / edited by Mark C. Amodio.
    p. cm. — (Medieval and renaissance texts and studies ; v. 287)
    Includes bibliographical references and index.
    ISBN 0-86698-330-9 (alk. paper)
    1. Literature–History and criticism. 2. Oral-formulaic analysis. 3. Oral tradition. I. Amodio, Mark. II. Arizona Center for Medieval and Renaissance Studies. III. Series: Medieval & Renaissance Texts & Studies (Series)

PN511.N42 2005
809–dc22

2005002118

∞
This book is made to last.
It is set in Goudy Old Style, smythe-sewn, and printed
on acid-free paper to library specifications.

Printed in the United States of America

CONTENTS

Acknowledgments — vii

Abbreviations — ix

Introduction: Unbinding Proteus — 1
   Mark C. Amodio, Vassar College

Part I: Ancient Greek and Latin

Fieldwork on Homer — 15
   John Miles Foley, University of Missouri, Columbia

Homer's *Iliad* and *Odyssey*: From Oral Performance to Written Text — 43
   Steve Reece, St. Olaf College

Orality and Aristotle's Aesthetics — 91
   Daniel F. Melia, University of California, Berkeley

Proteus in Latin: Vernacular Tradition and the Boniface Collection — 107
   Alexandra Hennessey Olsen, University of Denver

Oral-Formulaic Tradition and the Composition of Latin Poetry
from Antiquity through the Twelfth Century — 125
   Jan M. Ziolkowski, Harvard University

Part II: Old English, Middle English, and Middle Welsh

Deaths and Transformations: Thinking through the 'End' of
Old English Verse — 149
   Katherine O'Brien O'Keeffe, University of Notre Dame

Res(is)ting the Singer: Towards a Non-Performative Anglo-Saxon
Oral Poetics   179
    Mark C. Amodio

Writing Out "Óðinn's Storm": The Literary Reception of an
Oral-Derived Template in the Two Versions of Laȝamon's *Brut*   209
    Jonathan Watson, Manchester College

A Leash and an *Englyn* in the Medieval Welsh Arthurian Tale
Culhwch ac Olwen   237
    Joseph Falaky Nagy, University of California, Los Angeles

The Role of Proverbs in Middle English Narrative   255
    Lori Ann Garner, University of Illinois, Champaign-Urbana

Writing the Failure of Speech in *Pearl*   279
    Tim William Machan, Marquette University

Bibliography   307

About the Contributors   339

ACKNOWLEDGMENTS

I would like, first of all, to thank the contributors to this collection for their commitment to this project as it wound its way to press. I would also like to express my thanks to Bob Bjork at ACMRS for his enthusiasm for this volume. The anonymous readers for the press offered many helpful suggestions and I am grateful for the care with which they read the manuscript. Finally, I would like to offer special thanks to Katrina Bartow, '03, and Jaji Crocker, '04, the student assistants who worked with me on this project and who provided invaluable help at every stage of its production.

ABBREVIATIONS

AJP   *American Journal of Philology*
ASE   *Anglo-Saxon England*
ASPR   Anglo-Saxon Poetic Records

BJRL   *Bulletin of the John Rylands University Library*
BMCR   *Bryn Mawr Classical Review*

CA   *Classical Antiquity*
CCCC   Cambridge, Corpus Christi College
CL   *Comparative Literature*
CMERS   Center for Medieval and Early Renaissance Studies
CP   *Classical Philology*
CQ   *Classical Quarterly*
CR   *Chaucer Review*
CSASE   Cambridge Studies in Anglo-Saxon England

EETS   Early English Text Society

HSCP   *Harvard Studies in Classical Philology*

JAF   *Journal of American Folklore*
JHS   *Journal of Hellenic Studies*

LCL   Loeb Classical Library

MÆ   *Medium Ævum*
MGH   Monumenta Germaniae Historica

MH	*Museum Helveticum*
MJ	*Mittellateinisches Jahrbuch*
MRTS	*Medieval and Renaissance Texts and Studies*
NLH	*New Literary History*
NM	*Neuphilologische Mitteilungen*
OEN	*Old English Newsletter*
OT	*Oral Tradition*
PAPS	*Proceedings of the American Philosophical Society*
PCP	*Pacific Coast Philology*
PCPS	*Proceedings of the Cambridge Philological Society*
PL	*Patrologia Latina*
PMLA	*Publications of the Modern Language Association*
RES	*Review of English Studies*
SN	*Studia Neophilologica*
SO	*Symbolae Osloenses*
TAPA	*Transactions of the American Philological Association*
TRHS	*Transactions of the Royal Historical Society*
TSE	*Tulane Studies in English*
TSLL	*Texas Studies in Literature and Language*

MARK C. AMODIO

Introduction: Unbinding Proteus

The theory of oral-formulaic composition first articulated by Milman Parry and later refined and developed by Albert Bates Lord during his long and remarkably productive scholarly career has played a prominent role in classical studies since the early decades of the last century, and it has played an equally important role in medieval studies for what is now nearly fifty years.[1] From its early and highly influential articulations onwards, this theory, known more familiarly as the Parry-Lord theory, helped establish the terms of inquiry for what today has become the discipline of oral studies, a vibrant field of investigation that encompasses the verbal art produced by a great many cultures from antiquity to the present day. Because the Parry-Lord theory challenged a great many closely held and largely unexamined assumptions about the production, dissemination, and reception of works of verbal art in pre-literate and literate cultures, it engendered strong reactions, among both those who accepted its premises and those who rejected them. During the late 1970s and throughout much of the 1980s, the positions of oralists and non-oralists became more and more firmly entrenched, with oralists somewhat paradoxically stressing the orality of many ancient and medieval works that survive only as texts and non-oralists pointing to the textuality of the very same works, and the theory seemed headed for an impasse. But over the

---

[1] Parry's writings are collected in A. Parry, *Making of Homeric Verse*; a comprehensive bibliography of Lord's writings can be found in the obituary Foley wrote in *JAF*. To the thorough list Foley offers we can now add Lord, *Singer Resumes the Tale*, a volume that was published several years after Foley's obituary of Lord appeared.

past fifteen years, oral theory has been undergoing what is proving to be both the most productive and the most important reconfiguration in its history, one that is simultaneously strengthening its foundations and expanding its applicability. In working to articulate an oral theory that is more nuanced and more flexible than the oftentime programmatically presented Parry-Lord theory proved to be, a number of oral theorists have been reassessing oral-formulaic theory's central tenets and have begun to map out profitable and important new directions for the broad field of oral studies. In doing so, they have not only demonstrated to oralists and non-oralists alike just what a supple and far-reaching hermeneutic tool oral theory is and just how profitably it can be applied to a wide range of verbal art, but they have also begun to free oral tradition itself from the bonds oral-formulaic theory's formalist emphasis unintentionally placed upon it.[2]

Because space does not allow a detailed accounting of the emergence of oral studies as a discipline, I offer here a highly selective, chronological list of some works that have played especially critical roles in the recent development of oral theory.[3] At the forefront stands Eric Havelock's *The Muse Learns to Write: Reflections on Orality and Literacy from Antiquity to the Present* (1986), one of the first works of oral theory to question the Parry-Lord theory's assumption that the worlds of orality and literacy were necessarily mutually exclusive. In an important challenge to those who posited a so-called Great Divide between these worlds, Havelock argued that their relationship is far more complex, intertwined, and interdependent than it had previously been thought to be. In *A Key to Old Poems: The Oral-Formulaic Approach to the Interpretation of West-Germanic Poetry* (1988), Alain Renoir examined the rhetorical and affective dynamics of oral and oral-derived poetry, areas that the largely formalist Parry-Lord theory was not well suited to explore. Richard Martin's *The Language of Heroes: Speech and Performance in the Iliad* (1988) helped further broaden the field's critical foundations by bringing ethnographic and sociolinguistic approaches to bear on the ancient Greek oral tradition. In *Traditional Oral Epic: The Odyssey, Beowulf, and the Serbo-Croatian Return Song* (1990), John Miles Foley

---

[2] See, for example, the clusters of essays recently edited by the editor of this collection in *Oral Tradition* 17.1 (2002) and 17.2 (2002), among which are ones that bring oral theory into dialogue with, among other theories and texts, hypertext theory, romanticism, and E. M. Forster's *A Passage to India*.

[3] For a lucid and succinct history of the field's development through the 1980s, see Foley, *Theory of Oral Composition*.

offered what remains the most thorough and most important study yet to appear of the tectonics of traditional oral expression in the ancient Greek, Anglo-Saxon, and South Slavic traditions and in the companion piece to this volume, *Immanent Art: From Structure to Meaning in Traditional Oral Epic* (1991), he embarked upon a pioneering study of a dimension of traditional oral poetry, its aesthetics, that had previously received scant critical attention. And finally, in *Visible Song: Transitional Literacy in Old English Verse* (1990), Katherine O'Brien O'Keeffe broke important new ground by considering what the materiality of the Anglo-Saxon manuscript records reveals about the oral and literate compositional practices of the poets and scribes who produced and in some cases physically encoded Old English poetry. Togethert these works – several of which appeared virtually simultaneously and all of which appeared within a few years of each other –, along with a number that have subsequently appeared, have moved oral theory beyond the limitations its early articulators inadvertently placed upon it and have helped anchor it securely to the firmer ground upon which it now rests.[4]

Focusing on a wide variety of genres, ranging from ancient Greek epic to late medieval English dream vision, and on texts produced across several millennia in a variety of different ancient and medieval languages and cultures, the essays in this volume revisit and reimagine the central, oftentimes tangled, and still not fully understood relationship between those large and extraordinarily complex cultural forces that scholars have, for the sake of convenience, reductively come to label 'orality' and 'literacy.' But despite the diversity of texts and genres upon which they focus and despite the breadth of their critical perspectives, the essays collected here all challenge, in some cases explicitly, in others implicitly, the notion that orality and literacy are exclusive and contradictory epistemes whose contact radically alters the former and inevitably signals its end. Far from accepting the mutual exclusivity of the oral and the literate worlds, the essays gathered here collectively work to develop instead a more responsive theory of the oral-literate nexus, one that sees orality and literacy not as dis-

---

[4] Other important works to have appeared within the last decade include Foley, *Singer of Tales in Performance*, *Homer's Traditional Art*, and *How to Read an Oral Poem*; G. Nagy, *Homeric Questions* and *Poetry as Performance*; Lord, *Singer Resumes the Tale*; and Stock, *Listening for the Text*. For the most comprehensive bibliography of research in oral theory, see Foley, *Oral-Formulaic Theory and Research*, available in searchable form, with updates, at www.oraltradition.org.

crete, competing cultural forces but as subtly — and necessarily — intertwined and deeply interdependent ones. Orality and literacy, we are coming to understand with ever-increasing clarity, exist not in conflict with each other but as constituents of a continuum whose termini, what we might label 'pure orality' and 'pure literacy,' exist only as theoretical constructs. These termini are useful heuristics in that they provide us with touchstones against which to situate various cultures and their practices along the oral–literate continuum, but they do not reflect real world states.

There is, of course, tension between the oral and literate worlds, tension that even now at the beginning of the twenty-first century we continue to experience every day all around us; but it is a necessary, enriching, and perhaps even sustaining tension, not the debilitating or distracting one it was sometimes thought to be.[5] To put this another way, even in our highly literate Western culture literacy is far from universal, and even the most highly literate members of our culture must nevertheless continually navigate their way through the layers of oral/aural culture that surround, inform, and help define contemporary Western (literate) culture. From our literate perspective it is easy to forget that the same holds true of oral culture, however broadly or narrowly one wishes to define it:[6] literates may have easier and more direct access to the world of orality than non-literates have to the world of literacy,[7] but non-literates encounter literate culture

---

[5] Pearsall's comment in *Old and Middle English*, 155, that "oral tradition in a literate society is inevitably 'low' and inevitably makes wretched what it touches," remains perhaps the most succinct articulation of this latter view, one that is no longer current but that enjoyed wide currency through the 1980s.

[6] For a broadly inclusive definition of orality and oral literature, see Finnegan, *Oral Poetry*, esp. 1–29.

[7] Members of literate culture engage the world of orality every single day. A mother who recounts to her family over the dinner table something funny that happened to her at work that day, a boy who puts down his book to listen to his grandfather tell about his experiences as a B-17 pilot, or a college freshman who takes copious notes during a lecture on the *Iliad* are all participating — in various ways — in oral culture. Non-literates by definition have more difficulty entering into literate culture without the aid of some sort of mediator, but they can and do engage it in any number of ways: to cite but two examples, thumbprints have long been accepted by many banks and other institutions as a legal means of establishing identity and we are surely approaching the day when submitting to a retinal scan as a means of establishing one's identity will be as common a practice as displaying one's driver's license or passport is now.

everywhere and the (oral) world they inhabit is necessarily infused with and to a considerable extent shaped by literacy and its attendant practices and habits of mind.[8]

Taken as a whole, the essays in this collection constitute a series of discussions by a leading group of scholars on some of the most pressing issues facing oralists today, among which are the interplay between oral and literate culture in the ancient and medieval worlds; the role of texts and textuality in cultures positioned at various points along the oral–literate continuum; the place of the performer and the varying importance of performativity in different traditions; the survival of traditional oral poetics – the specialized constellations of traditional metrics, formulas, and story patterns that developed in different oral cultures – in textualized, not performative environments; and the influence that oral poetics continues to exert on authors composing in literate cultures. These essays do not seek to classify ancient and medieval texts as either 'oral' or 'literate' but rather attempt to discover what the unique mix of oral *and* literate poetics evident in the text(s) each author focuses upon reveals about the oral–literate matrices within which these texts were produced, disseminated, and received. In so doing, the authors – individually and collectively – strive to define and to illuminate further the oral poetics that is emerging as a cornerstone of contemporary oral theory.

In exploring how oral poetics functions in various traditions, scholars have begun to question and to recalibrate the emphasis that oral-formulaic theory placed on the necessarily performative aspects of oral and oral-derived poetry. As a result, oralists now address directly what was long seen to be oral-formulaic theory's crippling paradox: namely, that putatively oral (and oral-derived) works such as the *Iliad* and *Beowulf*, to take just two well-known examples, have come down to us not as shared, flexible, and protean oral texts but as unique, indisputably fixed, written ones.[9]

---

[8] Stock was among the first to call attention to this in *Implications of Literacy*, where he developed the notion of "textual communities" (see esp. 88–240). For a startling example of just how complex the relationship between oral and literate cultures is even in cultures that are highly non-literate, one need look no further than the photograph of the Tibetan paper singer Grags-pa seng-ge that graces the cover of Foley, *How to Read an Oral Poem*. See also Foley's discussion of this singer, 1–3. The photograph can be viewed online at www.oraltradition.org/hrop/.

[9] Cf. Benson, "Literary Character," for an early and still influential articulation of this view.

Performance remains a demonstrably central component of many contemporary oral traditions and before the advent of literacy in, for example, ancient Greece, it no doubt functioned much as the Parry–Lord theory posits it did:[10] that is, singers/poets engaged their tradition's performative oral poetics to (re-)compose poetry in the crucible of performance, for, as Lord succinctly puts it, "An oral poem is not composed *for* but *in* performance."[11] Many questions remain to be answered and many more still need to be formulated regarding the relationships between and among singers, performers, authors, scribes, listeners, readers, performances, and texts and regarding the universal and/or tradition-specific dynamics of what Foley has labeled the "performance arena";[12] but in building upon and extending the project of oral-formulaic theory, contemporary oral theorists have begun to uncover and to understand more fully the aesthetics that underlie traditional oral poetries, aesthetics that had proved largely resistant to the literate interpretive strategies that had habitually, and with predictably unsatisfactory results, been brought to bear on them. Rather than imposing what are often simply impertinent interpretive strategies upon ancient, medieval, and modern oral and oral-derived literatures, we must instead determine as best we can the contours and shared/unique features of each tradition's aesthetics before we attempt to investigate any tradition's verbal art.

The collection opens with a cluster of essays on the ancient Greek tradition. In "Fieldwork on Homer," John Miles Foley argues that the only way investigators can gain sufficiently deep and rewarding perspectives into oral traditions is to become as fluent as possible in the specialized language of lexical, phrasal, thematic, and narrative "words" through which cultures articulate verbal art.[13] In the case of a living tradition, such fluency entails not just immersing oneself in the language but experiencing the culture as deeply as possible through fieldwork. But what of those oral traditions that we can no longer experience firsthand but only through the mute witness of the manuscript page? Does their inaccessibility to the con-

---

[10] See esp. Foley, *How to Read an Oral Poem*.

[11] Lord, *Singer of Tales*, 13; Lord's emphasis. For his full and still important articulation of this model, see 13–29 and 99–123.

[12] Foley, *Singer of Tales in Performance*, 47–9, et passim.

[13] On the specialized sense of "word," see further Foley, *How to Read an Oral Poem*, 11–21.

temporary fieldworker forestall all possibility of understanding them? As a way into this knotty problem, Foley employs the trope of fieldwork to interrogate the specialized *Kunstsprache* of the Homeric epics. To become effective 'fieldworkers' of entexted oral traditions requires a significant reorientation on our part because we must proceed not from the outside in, as we logically and habitually do when investigating living oral traditions, but rather from the inside out: the ancient and medieval manuscript page may be an imperfect, silent witness to a once vibrant oral tradition, but it is one that, as Foley demonstrates, responds readily, and at times even somewhat surprisingly, to our inquiries once we approach it on its own terms and no longer try to impose upon it interpretive strategies that evolved as tools for understanding a very different sort of verbal art. Foley's 'fieldwork' on Homer does not seek to recover the unrecoverable — who Homer was, or if indeed he ever existed — but rather reveals that the specialized idioms of oral traditions and their highly charged modes of meaning survive even when verbal art comes to us not through the mouth of a living, breathing singer/poet but through words written on a page.

In "Homer's *Iliad* and *Odyssey*: From Oral Performance to Written Text," Steve Reece revisits one of the most fundamental issues in Homeric studies — the vexed and oftentimes vexing relationship between the inherited texts of the Homeric epics and their relationship to the active, dynamic oral tradition from which they emerged. Two perspectives have dominated this issue: the evolutionary model and the oral-dictation model. Those who favor an evolutionary model of the Homeric texts' composition contend that any number of singers/poets (and perhaps even scribes) all played a role, through their (re-)composition and transmission of the epics over the course of several millennia, in shaping the contours of the epics before they came to be crystallized in the written forms through which they are still best known. While the evolutionary model has much to recommend it and while it offers attractive explanations to a number of important issues, including the process through which the texts were transmitted and the ways in which they are used by classical authors, Reece suggests that the theory of oral dictation, a theoretical model that in recent years has been largely supplanted by the evolutionary model, in fact offers more plausible answers to these and other pressing questions. In a broad-ranging discussion, Reece questions the primacy of the evolutionary model and urges us to consider rather that the texts of the Homeric epics are just what they had for a long time been thought to be: the products of an individual poet, one of whose real, historical performances, at a specific time and a specific place, was textualized by a scribe (or several scribes).

Daniel F. Melia rounds out the cluster on ancient Greek literature with "Orality and Aristotle's Aesthetics," an essay that considers how the world of orality may have helped shape the ways in which Aristotle, whom Melia accurately — and wittily — labels "the poster boy of literacy," conceptualized the very literate skills he was instrumental in explaining and defining in the seminal *Art of Rhetoric* and *Poetics*. Because Aristotle stands as a paragon of literate thought and praxis, it has been easy to overlook that he lived during a time when the technology of literacy was still in its formative stages and when only a very small percentage of the population would have been able to participate directly in literate culture. In arguing that Aristotle's method of inquiry and explanation emerges from his attention to what can be labeled the "surface of abstraction," Melia offers us a new perspective on what differentiates the "mental culture of writing from the mental culture of orality" and argues that Aristotle's sense of aesthetic congruity derives from his absorption — conscious or otherwise — of the oral tradition to which he and his contemporaries were exposed throughout their lives.

In the second cluster of essays in part I, Alexandra Hennessey Olsen and Jan M. Ziolkowski turn their attention to Latin culture and its relationship to the oral culture(s) with which it co-existed throughout the diglossic Latin Middle Ages. While it is widely acknowledged that Latin, the language of literate culture, exerted considerable influence over the Germanic vernaculars, the degree to which the vernacular helped shape Latin texts composed in the Germanic-speaking countries has not yet received sufficient or sustained attention.[14] In "Proteus in Latin Prose: Vernacular Tradition and the Boniface Collection," Olsen focuses on a group of epistles written by Boniface and his circle in eighth-century England and argues that just as Aldhelm's frequent use of alliteration and his creation of phrases reminiscent of vernacular formulas in his Latin writings witness his familiarity with Anglo-Saxon poetics, so, too, do the epistles reveal just how central traditional Anglo-Saxon thematics is to their authors' expressive economy. Olsen discovers running through the Boniface Collection several well-known traditional themes — the Journey to Trial, the

---

[14] Among the important exceptions to this general trend are Orchard, *Poetic Art*, and Ziolkowski, "Cultural Diglossia."

Sea Voyage, and Exile — and demonstrates that they retain their traditional framework and their traditional affective dynamics despite being deployed in a non-narrative, demonstrably inter-textual genre and despite being expressed in a language different from the one within which they originally developed. Writing in Latin, the authors of the epistles seamlessly weave the expressive economy that is Anglo-Saxon oral poetics into both their prose compositions and the poetry that appears on occasion in the collection.

In the essay that closes part I of the collection, "Oral-Formulaic Tradition and the Composition of Latin Poetry from Antiquity through the Twelfth Century," Jan M. Ziolkowski focuses on the Latin poetic tradition, one that has to date not received much attention from oral theorists largely because it and the poets who worked within it have always been ineluctably associated with the world of letters. In his essay, Ziolkowski explores largely uncharted territory by asking not what impact the intensely literary Latin tradition had upon the composition of vernacular poetry but rather what impact oral culture and oral poetics had upon the composition of Latin poetry. Even though this poetry was indisputably composed in writing by authors whose compositional practices closely mirror our own contemporary ones, the poets who composed it were not in any way cut off from the world of orality but remained vitally connected to it. In considering reports of extemporaneous composition contained in texts ranging from the *Vitae Virgilianae*, to Bede's *Historia ecclesiastica*, to a late twelfth-century manuscript from Aulne, among others, Ziolkowski reassesses the position orality occupies in literate Latin culture. The instances upon which he focuses are not, as he stresses, moments of oral-formulaic composition in the Parry–Lord sense of the term, but they nevertheless reveal the close connection between the scholastic practices upon which the study and composition of Latin literature were predicated and those fundamental to the composition of oral poetry.

The essays in part II focus upon one literature to which oral theory has long been profitably applied, Old English, and upon two others, medieval Welsh and Middle English, that have yet to receive much scrutiny from oral theorists. In "Deaths and Transformations: Thinking through the 'End' of Old English Verse," Katherine O'Brien O'Keeffe explores the viability of Old English verse in the eleventh century by focusing upon two of the latest poems contained in the Anglo-Saxon Chronicle, the *Death of Alfred* (1036) and the *Death of Edward* (1065). Although these poems have never been numbered among the masterpieces of Old English verse and although they continue to attract little critical attention, O'Brien O'Keeffe argues that they reveal much about the past and future of Old English verse, as well as about the very different types of work that traditional verse forms continued to perform in the decades before the Norman Conquest changed forever the linguistic, cultural, and political landscapes of England. The metrical irregularities and sporadic rhyming of the *Death of Alfred* that led many of its editors to emend the poem, often rather freely, to bring its formal features more into line with what we know of so-called classical Old English verse do not so much mark the end of the tradition of Old English verse as stand as signposts of the tradition's continuing development. And even in its fractured form, the poem continues to perform significant political work by finding a new, politically more acceptable way to present the King's death. *The Death of Edward* also offers us a glimpse of how the Anglo-Saxon poetic tradition continued to be put into the service of contemporary political ends, although it does so by consciously evoking the heroic dynamics of Anglo-Saxon poetics in verse that is highly regular. As O'Brien O'Keeffe contends, the appearance of classical Old English verse in the twelfth century and the immediate and pressing political ends to which it is put in the Chronicle point both to the Anglo-Saxon tradition's continued survival and to its continued vitality.

In "Res(is)ting the Singer: Towards a Non-Performative Anglo-Saxon Oral Poetics," the present editor suggests that the entexted performances and the reports of poetic activity contained in our ancient and medieval manuscript records do not necessarily signal the presence of an active oral tradition. Rather than approaching them as if they were the equivalent of an observer's field notes on contemporary Anglo-Saxon poetic praxis, I argue that the instances of scopic activity that survive in the extant Old English poetry need to be seen instead as the written, fictional, and perhaps even highly idealized (re)presentations of past poetic practices that they are. Separating Anglo-Saxon oral poetics from the strictly performative model to which it has been wed since the mid 1950s does not, however, mean that we must also reject the possibility (probability, really) that Old English poetry was at some point in its history (re)composed orally by singers during performance; rather, approaching this poetry from the perspective of a non-performative oral poetics enables us better to understand the complex mix of oral *and* literate poetics found throughout the Old English poetic corpus.

In "Writing Out 'Óðinn's Storm': The Literary Reception of an Oral-Derived Template in the Two Versions of Laȝamon's *Brut*," Jonathan Watson investigates the complex intermingling of oral and written compositional practices in the early Middle English period. Because it is one of the earliest poems to appear in English after the Norman Conquest and because it survives in two manuscript versions — London, British Library, Cotton Vitellius A. ix and the later London, British Library, Cotton Caligula C. xiii — the *Brut* affords Watson the opportunity to trace the shifting dynamics of the traditional compositional unit he labels "Óðinn's Storm" as it is put to use by the poem's thirteenth-century scribes/poets. Despite their being separated by perhaps as little as fifty years, the scribes/poets responsible for producing the two extant versions of the *Brut* nevertheless have sharply different relationships to the medieval English oral tradition and its specialized idiom of lexeme, phrase, theme, and story-pattern. In so focusing on the two extant versions of the *Brut*, Watson reveals that post-Conquest scribes/poets were able to deploy oral poetics — to varying degrees — even as their literate sensibilities led them to reconfigure their traditional, inherited material.

In "A Leash and an *Englyn* in the Medieval Welsh Arthurian Tale *Culhwch ac Olwen*," Joseph Falaky Nagy examines the complex relationship between poetry and prose in one of the eleven tales of what we know collectively as the *Mabinogion*. In arguing that the combination of poetry and prose in *Culhwch ac Olwen* results not only in formal tension on the surface of the manuscript page but also in thematic tension within the poem's narrative, Nagy offers a corrective to the view that sees prose frames and embedded poetry as harmonious components of a text which function cooperatively in the production of that text. For Nagy, the voice raised in song within the confines of a prose text is one that is often sharply at odds with the text and that further signals its mistrust of the very process of textualization. Voiced by Arthur in a spontaneous oral performance, the *englyn* — a rhyming, three- or four-line verse form with a fixed number of syllables used for epigrammatic or gnomic comment — that is the focus of Nagy's discussion strikes a powerfully discordant note in the tale and offers a reminder of the power of oral performance and of oral poetics to disrupt, rather than harmonize with, the prose contexts in which they are so frequently embedded in the Middle Ages.

Focusing on two texts that are positioned at very different spots along the oral–literate continuum, the thirteenth-century *Havelok the Dane* and

Chaucer's late-fourteenth century *Troilus and Criseyde*, Lori Ann Garner investigates what proverbs and the textualized acts of their performance reveal about a text's participation in the medieval English oral and written traditions. As they do in living oral traditions, the proverbs that appear in *Havelok* validate actions and events by situating them within a highly traditional framework, a framework that both calls forth and directs the audience's response. One of the defining features of the proverbs in *Havelok* is that they always speak with the authority the oral tradition invests in them, even when characters apply them inappropriately. By way of contrast, in *Troilus*, a text positioned far closer to the literate end of the oral-literate continuum than *Havelok*, proverbs are often put to highly non-traditional uses by characters who do not engage the proverbs' rich web of traditional, associative meaning(s) but rather employ them to *confer* authority upon and so legitimize their present narrative purposes.

As does the essay that opens this collection, the one that closes it, Tim William Machan's "Writing the Failure of Speech in *Pearl*," productively stretches the boundaries of the field by asking us to adopt a sharply different perspective. In resituating the dream vision *Pearl*, one of the masterpieces of Middle English literature, in a gray area along the oral-literate continuum despite its being universally acknowledged as a highly literate, learned, and overtly doctrinal poem, Machan reveals it to be an aesthetically transitional work with roots in both medieval textual and oral culture. Through the direct discourse of the Dreamer and Pearl Maiden, which comprises more than one-half of the poem's 1212 lines, Machan explores the ways in which *Pearl*'s larger, oral context serves to inform its remarkable aesthetic achievement. Approaching the poem from the perspective of contemporary discourse analysis reveals that the miscommunication between the Dreamer and Pearl Maiden is more extensive than critics have recognized, and it also allows the sociolinguistic implications of their miscommunication to come more fully into focus. While the poem's textualized conversational features are significant because they are survivals of earlier cultural praxis and because they offer residual evidence of such praxis, they also provide important evidence of oral culture's intimate, extensive, and ongoing interaction with textual culture.

Pointing suggestively, and perhaps at times controversially, towards new avenues of investigation, each of the contributors to this volume continues the important and necessary project of allowing the various lexical, metrical, and thematic multiformities that comprise oral traditional verbal art to come more sharply into focus. Binding oral tradition to any set of fixed interpretive strategies can give us, as it has in the past, only a partial and distorted glimpse of its richly complex nature; unlike even that most famously metamorphosic of Greek gods, Proteus, who ultimately reverts to his true form after being pinned down by Menelaus, oral tradition can neither be captured by any single, monolithic theory nor reduced to any single avatar.

JOHN MILES FOLEY

Fieldwork on Homer

The rationale for fieldwork
Fieldwork has always entailed much more than collecting, examining, and reporting on items. As a matter of procedure it has always involved recovering and recreating contexts, re-weaving as completely as possible the web of assumption and expressive potential in which any culture's "items" are necessarily suspended. Anthropologists and folklorists engaged in on-site study of a culture's verbal art have consistently sought not simply the utterance itself, comfortably disengaged from the complexities of real life, but rather the whole, situated phenomenon — warts and all. Recent explorations have even gone so far as to take note of the undeniable contributions of (inevitably non-objective) observers, moving us even further away from construing verbal art in a vacuum. Later on, of course, when it was time to present the fruits of their labor to a bookish, armchair readership, folklorists have usually configured their results in the familiar medium of texts, settling for editorial reductions that plug easily into the scholarly network of exchange. But such flattening of experience to object has more to do with available, approved avenues for presentation and publication than with actively misunderstanding and reworking contextualized acts of expressive art.[1] The distance between experienced process and extruded

---

[1] On various approaches to editing oral traditions, see Fine, *Folklore Text* and Foley, "Folk Literature" and "Textualization."

product – between the phenomenon and its shallow, one-dimensional reflection on the page – amounts to a casualty of media translation.[2]

To gain deeper perspective on oral traditions, fieldworkers must commit themselves to a goal that is at once more realistic and more difficult to achieve: fluency in the specialized language of whatever verbal art they are investigating. This commitment goes far beyond acquiring basic knowledge of the standard language (although that is of course an obligatory first step that will continue to reap benefits during subsequent cultural negotiations). It entails a grasp of *idiom*, that is, of all of the expressive strategies one doesn't find conveniently lemmatized in standard dictionaries and lexicons. Does a storyteller begin a tale with some character "crying out in prison," for example? In most traditions this phrase harbors no value-added meaning whatsoever, and we are left to see what develops as the story evolves. But in South Slavic epic this modest signal unfolds the map of the Return Song, an *Odyssey*-type story complete with captivity, a flashback tale of prior adventures, suitors who serve as rivals, a wife or fiancée who may be either faithful or dangerous, and a dénouement based on a secret trick.[3] Or consider the case of the village healer from the same area, whose medical intervention depends upon the rapid-fire whispering of highly organized, eight-syllable verses into her patient's ear. Unless ethnographers take seriously the somatic reality of her closing verse – "Out of my *speaking* has come the cure" – they will miss the enabling force of the very sounds she utters, so full of rhymes, plosive consonants, rhythmic appeals to denizens of the other world, and other acoustic dimensions the expressive impact of which falls viscerally upon the ear.[4] While no dictionary glosses "crying out in prison" as the single, idiomatic word it proves to be, and while no lexicon explains the acoustic content of the phonological and prosodic codes that make up the living fabric of the South Slavic charms, both kinds of features are real and crucial aspects of

---

[2] On using hypertext media for more fruitful representation of oral poetry than the book medium can manage, see Foley, *How to Read an Oral Poem*, 219–25 ("Post-Script") and "Challenge of Translating."

[3] See further Foley, *Homer's Traditional Art*, esp. 137–67, and *How to Read an Oral Poem*, esp. 166–8.

[4] See further Foley, *Singer of Tales in Performance*, 99–135, and *How to Read an Oral Poem*, 190–5.

the communication; effective fieldworkers must make it a point to factor their idiomatic contribution into construal of the overall speech-act.

But how do fieldworkers spot such crucial features and how do they assess their role in the composition and reception of verbal art? We might put it even more directly — how do non-native speakers go about learning the specialized idiom? In actual ethnographic research the answer is simple enough, even if the road is long: listen carefully, ask questions, and remain ever-ready to reshuffle assumptions that have never been challenged before. All fieldworkers eventually become aware (sometimes to their consternation but always to their edification) that apprehending the strategies associated with any genre of verbal art is a gradual and ongoing process.[5] It necessarily entails false starts, blind alleys, and mid-course corrections; it requires recurrent experiences, many series of questions (that regularly lead to further questions), and an openness to rethinking our most cherished opinions. Clinging to presuppositions — whatever their usefulness in other arenas — is the death-knell of fieldwork-based inquiry because it inhibits language-learning by erecting a barrier of unintelligibility between even the most well-intentioned observer and the tradition of verbal art under scrutiny. Indeed, the realistic fieldworker can glean unsought knowledge even when an informant fails to answer the carefully posed question; an "irrelevant response" may reveal a new area of concern even as the exchange seems to founder. Anyone who has engaged in this sort of investigation knows what it means to ask a question and receive a reply that, while initially a disappointment, ends up elucidating a much more interesting point. Nor must we forget the inevitable shortfall that is also a standard feature of this process. Since the distance between the outsider and the insider never entirely disappears, outsiders can never fully translate themselves into native speakers of an idiom. That's what it means to conduct on-site fieldwork: be ready to learn the language of oral tradition from the inside out, on its own terms, as thoroughly as you can. Be aware that context is a full partner to any utterance, and that even partial fluency is far preferable to speaking the wrong language.

---

[5] Because this process resembles nothing so much as learning a language, I have elsewhere argued in the form of a homemade proverb, Foley, *How to Read an Oral Poem*, esp. 127–8, that "Oral poetry works like language, only more so." For a full explanation of this and other such facsimile aphorisms about oral poetry, see 125–45.

Prospects for interviewing Homer

Homer presents us with an enormous added challenge, of course, since we can't actually interview him. Indeed, all that we have to work with are two texts of frankly uncertain provenience. Moreover, ancient testimony on the *Iliad* and the *Odyssey* and their background is famously ambiguous or opaque, not to mention the multiple uncertainties surrounding their apparent recording in the sixth century B.C.E. (?) through their possible edition in Alexandria and their first appearance as whole poems (after the effects of Byzantine scholarship?) in the tenth century C.E.[6] In fact, it seems quite probable that in the ancient world the name "Homer" designated not a flesh-and-blood individual but rather the collective tradition of poets that produced these poems – and other poems now lost to us – and thus does not fit the comfortably modern concept of authorship that we anachronistically force upon fragmentary traces of an ancient legend.[7] Doing fieldwork on the *Iliad* and *Odyssey* appears to be blocked not only by the circumstances of time and place, but also by our inability to penetrate behind these two mysterious (and very late) texts to the tradition that produced them almost two millennia beforehand. Likewise, doing fieldwork on "Homer himself" seems to be ruled out not only by those same historical and geographical factors, but also by the inescapable fact that interviewing an anthropomorphization of tradition just isn't feasible.[8]

Or is it? Granted that more than 2500 years separate us from the ancient Greek oral epic tradition, and further that hard data on the role of actual individual *aoidoi* [epic poets] is forever beyond our reach, we may still be able to recover some of the information and perspective – some of the idiomatic context – at which on-site fieldwork aims. More specifically, we may be able to revivify the two extruded texts to some extent by interviewing the poet about his specialized language, by enrolling in a brief tutorial on the traditional poetic idiom, what an anthropologist would call

---

[6] On the transmission of the text, see esp. the magisterial work of Haslam, "Homeric Papyri."

[7] On Homer as an anthropomorphization of the epic tradition, see Foley, "Individual Poet," and *Homer's Traditional Art*, 50, 56-8.

[8] Although he was not aware of it, this was the source of the early twentieth-century investigator Alois Schmaus's consternation over not being able to directly contact the (legendary) South Slavic *guslar* known as Ćor Huso. See further Schmaus, "Ćor Huso."

the Homeric "register" or "way of speaking."[9] In other words, our goal is to figure out how this verbal art works by asking the poet to explain it. Since we have access to that poet — or, better, to that tradition of poets — only through the records he or they have left behind, our interview must start with those silent, decontextualized artifacts. But in an act of "text-ethnography" we will also be reaching beyond those mute records, trying to hear the voice and understand the artistic process behind them.

In that sense, our investigation will entail just the sort of questioning and sifting of accumulated evidence that fieldworkers use to reconstruct a realistic context for the individuals and verbal art they study. Since we cannot directly query individual poets about their units of utterance and meaning (and since fieldwork on living oral traditions has illustrated that poets aren't aware of our categories — and why should they be?), we will apply what has been uncovered by prior research on the fundamental structural bytes termed "formulas," "themes," and "story-patterns." These "larger words" — rather than the philologically canonized increments we enshrine in reference books and assume to be at the basis of all verbal art — will serve as our entry-point.[10] Since we do not have access to the multiple performances that fieldworkers customarily elicit to test and probe compositional habits, we will consider multiple instances of a few selected traditional "words" within the two poems as we have them. After collating these instances we will ask some simple but far-reaching questions: What idiomatic implications do the "words" convey that we will not find attested in any lexical source? What value-added, complementary meaning do they encode and contribute to the negotiation of verbal art? This context of implication, to which I have elsewhere applied the term *traditional referentiality*,[11] often proves crucial to reading a traditional oral poem.

The interview I plan for Homer will thus amount to a kind of fieldwork. We seek to get behind the decontextualized utterance, to restore at

---

[9] Hymes, "Ways of Speaking," 440, defines "registers" as "major speech styles associated with recurrent types of situations." On registers in oral poetry, see Foley, "Folk Literature," 49-53, *Homer's Traditional Art*, 22-55, and *How to Read an Oral Poem*, 114-17.

[10] On formula, theme, and story-pattern in ancient Greek, Old English, and South Slavic epic, see Foley, *Traditional Oral Epic*; on singers' own conception of a "word" as a unit of utterance, see Foley, *How to Read an Oral Poem*, 11-21.

[11] See Foley, *Immanent Art*, xiv, 6-8; exemplified at Foley, *How to Read an Oral Poem*, 114-22.

least something of what textualization has eliminated, to learn the language in which the *Iliad* and *Odyssey* are composed and meant to be received rather than forcibly to dislocate them into our language and frame of reference.[12] If we're successful in this enterprise, we stand to make substantial gains. Like the anthropologist who offers a fuller perspective on a ritual or custom by exposing its cultural matrix, and like the folklorist whose firsthand experience with verbal art opens up levels of meaning that literary analysis can never unearth, we can restore at least a fraction of the idiom on which "Homer" and his audience(s) depended for fluent communication. Two millennia and more after the fact, we can indeed conduct a kind of on-site investigation into the cultural poetics of these ancient texts.

Three formidable challenges
Any ethnographic protocol worth the name calls for setting the ground rules for the interview, and so our first challenge is to sketch an outline of the specialized language under consideration. Scholars have long realized that Homer — and for the sake of convenience let us follow the ancient practice of calling the tradition "Homer" — composed in a nonstandard variety of ancient Greek. That is, the language of the *Iliad* and *Odyssey* was hardly the street talk of archaic Greece, but rather a unique register or way of speaking that drew its vocabulary and morphology from different dialects and different historical eras. Like the specialized poetic diction employed by the South Slavic *guslari* [epic singers], it combined forms from various places and times, sometimes even in the very same line of verse.[13] While everyday language counts such juxtapositions as errors or infelicities and regularly replaces out-of-dialect or archaic forms with localized, up-to-date equivalents, Homer and the *guslar* actually depended on these features to identify and distinguish epic phraseology, as well as to cue the audience. This is one way in which the language of the *Iliad* and *Odyssey* does not match our modern, textual model, and a major challenge that the prospective interviewer of Homer must face.

---

[12] Proverbially speaking, "True diversity demands diversity in frame of reference." See further, Foley, *How to Read an Oral Poem*, 141-4.

[13] For explanation and examples in South Slavic and ancient Greek, see Foley, *Homer's Traditional Art*, 76-80.

Fieldwork on Homer 21

A second challenge is the formulaic and thematic structure of the ancient Greek epics. As alluded to above, the taletelling language is configured not in our words — defined as morphemes, or as sequences of letters bounded by white spaces, or in some other conventional fashion — but in the larger "words" of phrase, scene, and story-pattern. The research and scholarship of Milman Parry and Albert Lord provided us an initial awareness of the byte-sized texture of Homeric diction and narrative, and further investigation has buttressed their conclusions.[14] We now know that phraseological "words" have minimal size, for example, so that dissecting traditionally coherent phrases like "swift-footed Achilles" or the South Slavic "Mustajbey of the Lika" will produce meaningless shards of verbiage. We can no more segregate epithets from their noun partners than we can subdivide one of our own words: say "ship" and you've voiced a recognizable, meaningful combination of sounds in modern English, but its acoustic components "sh" and "ip" cannot stand alone. If we want to foster a coherent exchange with Homer, we'll need to interview him in his own "words," not in ours.

This simple principle has some important ramifications. Because the larger "word" of formula — and not each of its parts — serves as the minimal meaning-bearing unit, epithets cannot be situationally attuned to individual narrative moments. Achilles may (and does) remain fleet of foot while sulking in his tent, Mustajbey will retain his geographical and mythical identity wherever he turns up and whether or not the Lika borderland and its mystery are specifically invoked. To put it another way, as effective interviewers we will need to be alive to what actually constitutes a word, rather than try to manufacture meaning from what amounts to a syllable. Just as in face-to-face communication, if we ask Homer what half of a "word" means we had better be prepared for a confusing answer. Just as our dictionaries warehouse their contents in approved, archetypal units that correspond to everyday textual structure and usage, so as fieldworkers we must be attentive to Homer's logical units of utterance. Whether at the level of phrases, scenes, or whole stories, we must be sure we're asking him about *his* "words" rather than our words. The second step, then, consists

---

[14] In addition to the classic writings of Parry, *Making of Homeric Verse*, and Lord, esp. *Singer of Tales*, *Epic Singers*, and *Singer Resumes the Tale*, see Foley, *Oral-Formulaic Theory*, available in searchable electronic form (with updates) at www.oraltradition.org.

of code-switching to Homer's linguistic categories and learning to ask the right kind of question.

With these two challenges faced, we encounter a third and extremely daunting one. Most straightforwardly put, fieldwork on Homer must engage traditional referentiality, the idiomatic meaning attached — always implicitly, of course — to larger "words." This kind of signification differs in nature from discursive, metaphorical, or symbolic meaning in that it inheres in the specialized language used by generations of poets and audiences to negotiate what Homer calls the "pathways" [*oimai*] of epic song.[15] It's part of their way of transacting epic. Just as "birds of a feather flock together" has pertinence far beyond any ornithological application, so the idioms that populate Homeric diction and narrative carry with them added implications that enrich whatever individual situation they help to describe. Elsewhere I have explained how "green fear" [*chlôron deos*] has little to do with the color green but instead collectively expresses the traditional idea of supernatural fear that grips a person and leaves him or her helpless. The small phrase "But come" [*all' age*, etc.] serves as a recognizable rhetorical fulcrum that leads to either a prayer or a command. On the larger canvas, recurrent and multiform Feast scenes not only support the storytelling task; they also forecast mediation of an existing dilemma, whatever that dilemma may be. At the largest level of all, the Return Song pattern sets up an Odyssean sequence of absence, devastation, return, vengeance, and wedding just as dependably and economically as the smaller "words" do their expressive job.[16]

This third challenge highlights the insufficiency of settling for a merely structural profile of the *Iliad* and *Odyssey*. Although attention to structure is a necessary preliminary (else we risk asking impertinent questions), simply parsing traditional poetry will not reveal its dynamism or its verbal artistry, any more than a standard grammar and dictionary will exhaust the riches of Shakespeare. Even a thorough awareness of formulas, typical scenes, and story-patterns will amount to little if we persist in compromising their ability to mean by continuing to resort to an irrelevant

---

[15] Homer's usages of the word occur at *Odyssey* 8.74, 8.481, and 22.347. On *oimê* as both a traditional singer's pathway and an analogue to links on the Internet, see Foley, "Impossibility of Canon."

[16] See further Foley, *Homer's Traditional Art*: 216-18 ("green fear"), 224-5 ("But come"), 171-87 (Feast scenes), and 137-67 (Return story-pattern).

lexicon. From establishing the increments we must move on to their idiomatic implications, to "word"-definitions not found in the standard resources but nonetheless fundamental to the way Homer and his audience think. In interviewing Homer we must be ready to ask not merely what his "words" are, but also and more crucially *what they mean in their traditional context*.

With these preliminaries firmly in mind, I now turn to the interview itself, which will consist of two questions together with the best answers I can elicit from Homer based on the available evidence. Each query addresses the meaning of a short phrase in either the *Iliad* or the *Odyssey*, and each one asks our informant to consider both the structural and the idiomatic dimensions of the phrase. Just as in fieldwork on living traditions, the questions themselves are heuristic rather than determinative. That is, they open up areas of inquiry rather than point reductively toward simplex responses. Each one amounts to pulling a single thread from a larger fabric, as it were, in order to gain perspective on the fabric as a whole. One caveat: our interview will take us in heretofore unmapped directions. In other words, Homer has some surprises in store for us.

Two Questions for Homer
   I. What does the phrase – and single "word" – "boundless ransom" [*apereisi' apoina*] mean?
We start with a few text-ethnographic observations about the structural profile of this "word," so that we can be confident that we are speaking Homer's specialized language. The phrase "boundless ransom" occurs eleven times in the available sample of epic, and its instances involve many different characters and situations.[17] Second, the phrase is consistently located at line-end, where it regularly occupies a particular metrical site. Third, this single "word" shows considerable variety in its combination with other diction, existing both as an increment in its own right and as a part of several larger units. Fourth, we find "boundless ransom" exclusively in the *Iliad*; there are no occurrences in either the *Odyssey* or the *Homeric Hymns*.[18]

---

[17] For the record, the eleven instances occur at *Iliad* 1.13, 1.372, 6.49, 6.427, 9.120, 10.380, 11.134, 19.138, 24.276, 24.502, and 24.579.

[18] These observations, as well as those reported below for other "words," derive from Pandora searches of the *Thesaurus Linguae Graecae* (see www.tlg.uci.edu).

These few facts suggest some conclusions about the shape and dynamics of this integral item of epic vocabulary. Like so many other traditional units, "boundless ransom" is apparently applicable to a broad spectrum of narrative situations. At *Iliad* 1.13 Chryses bears innumerable gifts to Agamemnon as the price for releasing his captive daughter Chryseis; at 6.49, in a futile effort to save his skin, Adrestos promises Menelaos ransom from his father; at 6.427 Andromache tells how Achilles accepted *apereisi' apoina* to release her captured mother; and at 19.138 Agamemnon pronounces himself deluded and pledges again to make things good by presenting gifts to Achilles. The other seven instances involve Dolon, Diomedes, Odysseus, Peisandros, Hippolochos, Priam and his living sons, Hektor's corpse, Automedon, and Alkimos in a wide selection of attempted and successful ransoms. From a purely utilitarian standpoint, this "word" is clearly a valuable structural tool in Homer's taletelling kit. In that sense we can understand it as useful.

But Homer and his poems tell us a good deal more. As an item in traditional epic vocabulary, *apereisi' apoina* happens to occupy the most stable portion of the hexameter verse-form, the final colon. This same slot houses many of the noun-epithet formulas in the *Iliad* and *Odyssey*, such as "grey-eyed Athena" [*glaukôpis Athênê*] and "glancing-helmed Hektor" [*koruthaiolos Hektôr*].[19] In accordance with the general Homeric rule of right justification, which accounts for the increasing size of metrical units and increasing conservatism of diction as one moves from the beginning toward the end of the line (from left to right), it is localized *as a single "word"* exclusively at that site. In broader perspective, "boundless ransom" serves as an example of how Homer and his tradition think from right to left.[20] Within the ever-malleable language of composition and reception stand structural supports like this one, valuable both for their individual steadfastness and their protean adaptability to many situations.

The rich morphology of *apereisi' apoina* — its ability to combine with many other partners in Homer's line-making and its identity as both a

---

[19] Note that, typically for this flexible phraseology, both "words" can be "inflected" to a metrically more expansive form by adding an optional two-syllable increment *before* the phrase: thus, "<u>goddess</u> grey-eyed Athena" [<u>thea</u> *glaukôpis Athênê*, e.g., *Od.* 1.44] and "<u>great</u> glancing-helmed Hektor" [<u>megas</u> *koruthaiolos Hektôr*, e.g., *Il.* 2.816], both of them hemistich (or half-line) units.

[20] For discussion and examples of right justification in Homer, see Foley, *Traditional Oral Epic*, 127ff.

member of larger units and an increment by itself — only increases its utility and broad applicability. Twice it rounds off a whole-line phrase (*Il.* 1.13, 372):

> *intending to free his daughter and bearing* <u>*boundless ransom*</u>
> *lusomenos te thugatra pherôn t'* <u>*apereisi' apoina*</u>

and a third time it participates in a nearly identical verse (*Il.* 24.502):

> *intending to free [my son] from you, and I bear* <u>*boundless ransom*</u>
> *lusomenos para seio, pherô d'* <u>*apereisi' apoina.*</u>

Interestingly, though, these close relationships do not exhaust the correspondences among the three phrases and lines. The first two verses are part of yet larger clusters detailing the priest Chryses' futile approach to Agamemnon, described in the opening scene of the poem by the narrator and later by a frustrated Achilles. With these two instances, as so often in Homeric epic and other oral and oral-derived poetry, we have three levels of "word" in a Chinese-box kind of arrangement: the formula *apereisi' apoina*, the line that contains it, and the four-line increment that houses the recurrent line. Lest we think that mindless repetition (rather than pliable traditional language) is at the root of this systemic correspondence, Homer responds to our query with another sort of variant in the third instance: by using it to help frame Priam's ransom of Hektor's corpse, he shows how generative his traditional phraseology can be. Not only are there line-internal differences — controlled as always by traditional rules — but line 24.502 stands alone rather than as part of a multi-verse capsule.[21] Such is the flexibility of Homer's "words," as he himself attests.

The same sort of variation within limits, with the emphasis on rule-governed pliability, is evident in the other whole-line unit involving "boundless ransom." Here are the three lines Homer has given us:

---

[21] On traditional rules for Homeric phraseology, see Foley, *Traditional Oral Epic*, 128–55. Note that I do not count *néas Achaiôn* (1.12 and 24.501) as a correspondence because the colonic structure in which they participate is fundamentally different (the former, with proclitic *epi*, subtending a C1+ colon; the latter, C2+ with C1 blocked). Moreover, the lines do not otherwise match.

for these things my father would bestow upon you (sing.) <u>boundless ransom</u>
tôn ken toi charisaito patêr <u>apereisi' apoina</u> (Il. 6.49)

from these things my father would bestow upon you (pl.) <u>boundless ransom</u>
tôn k' ummin charisaito patêr <u>apereisi' apoina</u> (Il. 10.380)

from these things my father would bestow upon you (sing.) <u>boundless ransom</u>
tôn ken toi charisaito patêr <u>apereisi' apoina</u> (Il. 11.134)

In this case the range of variation is narrower, while each verse also participates in the same three-line capsule describing the father's wealth and the condition placed on the ransom.[22] Although the three instances portray interactions involving Adrestos vs. Menelaos, Dolon vs. Diomedes and Odysseus, and Peisandros and Hippolochos vs. Agamemnon, the same three-tiered structure harmonizes their natural incongruities. The remaining five uses of "boundless ransom" each seems *sui generis*, occurring without any additional regularities of line or multi-line unit and illustrating another dimension of the flexibility of the phraseology surrounding this "word."

The initial stage of our interview with Homer has turned up one final physical characteristic of *apereisi' apoina* – its limitation to the *Iliad*. At first sight this might seem merely a manifestation of its pertinence to that epic's story-line, the natural result of ransoms being more appropriate to the martial content and tenor of the *Iliad* than to the adventure, discovery, and fantasy of the *Odyssey*. Perhaps, we might be tempted to conclude, Homer and his tradition simply have no need for this "word" in telling the story of Odysseus. But, leaving aside that dubious thesis (recalling, for instance, the many inset tales in the *Odyssey* that could entail ransoms), we should emphasize the often overlooked fact that the two epics simply do not share an identical store of phraseology. Some "words" are peculiar to one or the other epic, mirroring the situation in South Slavic oral epic in which one can track both idiolectal and dialectal versions of formulaic and

---

[22] 6.48-50=10.379-81=11.133-5. Note also the end-line correspondence between 6.47 and 11.132.

narrative increments across the community of singers.[23] Although our received texts of Homer — and here the composite code-name *Homêros* is stretched to the breaking point — have undergone untold editorial modification on the long and tortuous journey from recording to the first tenth-century C.E. exemplars, they still reveal some small but tell-tale differences between them. When we add in the *Homeric Hymns*, the variations across poems become more dramatic.[24] In explaining the nature of "boundless ransom" as a solely Iliadic "word," we must at least entertain the possibility that such exclusivity results from the *Iliad* and *Odyssey* stemming ultimately from different poets or different regions.

So much for the structure and dynamics of the sign or *sêma*.[25] Let's now ask Homer the truly important question: can he say something about the traditional referentiality, the idiomatic yield of "boundless ransom"? We recall that our fieldwork methodology prescribes a procedure for posing such queries: collect all instances of the contextually embedded byte of diction, collate the individual witnesses fairly, and evaluate what (if any) contextual meaning they share in addition to their literal denotation. In short, we will be asking Homer what he means beyond what we can glean from lexicons, which as text-derived and text-oriented instruments can never help us with his traditional, idiomatic implications.[26] The initial steps in our investigation — the background interviews, so to speak — now give way to a focus on the contextual significance of the "word" within its expressive ecology.

---

[23] On idiolectal and dialectal levels in South Slavic oral epic language, see Foley, *Traditional Oral Epic*, chaps. 5 (phraseology) and 8 (narrative patterning).

[24] On diachronic differences among the epics, the hymns, and the Hesiodic poems, see Janko, *Homer, Hesiod, and the Hymns*.

[25] See further Foley, *Homer's Traditional Art*, 13-34, *et passim*.

[26] Compare the information-gathering process that underlies the formulation of modern dictionaries and lexicons. Even for ancient languages, scholars customarily sample multiple genres, authors, and periods in order to chart the lexical spectrum of any given word over time, place, and usage. In the present case our lexicography focuses on a single, well-defined, and idiomatic variety of the language used for one purpose only: to compose epic. The same sort of difference marks the distance between the (marked) South Slavic oral epic dialect and the (unmarked) contemporary spoken and written language; see further Foley, *Homer's Traditional Art*, 66-83.

To begin, I list Homer's opening responses to our query: the first eight occurrences of *apereisi' apoina* by book and line number, adding brief notes on the events and results he has linked with each instance:

Site   Event   Result

1.13   Chryses ransoming his daughter Chryseis > Ag. refuses; Achilles withdraws
intending to free his daughter and bearing boundless ransom
lusomenos te thugatra pherôn t' apereisi' apoina

1.372   Chryses ransoming his daughter Chryseis > Ag. refuses; Achilles withdraws
intending to free his daughter and bearing boundless ransom
lusomenos te thugatra pherôn t' apereisi' apoina

6.49   Adrestos ransoming his own life > Agamemnon refuses; kills him
from these things my father would bestow upon you (sing.) boundless ransom
tôn ken toi charisaito patêr apereisi' apoina

6.427   Andromache's mother ransomed > Achilles accepts; she commits suicide
He released her in turn, accepting boundless ransom
aps ho ge tên apeluse labôn apereisi' apoina

9.120   Ag. promises ransom to Achilles > Achilles refuses; does not rejoin war
I wish to make atonement in turn and give him boundless ransom
aps ethelô aresai domenai t' apereisi' apoina

10.380   Dolon ransoming his own life > Diomedes refuses; kills him
from these things my father would bestow upon you (pl.) boundless ransom
tôn k' ummin charisaito patêr apereisi' apoina

11.134   Peisandros and Hippolochos ransoming their own lives > Agamemnon refuses; kills them
from these things my father would bestow upon you (sing.) boundless ransom
tôn ken toi charisaito patêr apereisi' apoina

19.138 Ag. promises ransom to Achilles > Achilles pronounces himself
doomed
I wish to make atonement in turn and give him <u>boundless ransom</u>
aps ethelô aresai domenai t' <u>apereisi' apoina</u>

Collating Homer's initial set of responses makes one thing crystal clear: whatever the narrative context of "boundless ransom," it regularly involves a life-or-death scenario. The first two instances, already mentioned above, describe Chryses' appeal to Agamemnon to relinquish his daughter in exchange for the proverbial ransom. The Achaean chief's surly dismissal not only imperils the young woman and insults the priest of Apollo; it also kindles the flame of quarrel between the Greek leader and his most accomplished warrior, the semi-divine Achilles. As a direct result of the imperious commander's wrongheaded actions, a great many of his army will die. The third occurrence, in Book 6, frames another of Agamemnon's refusals; although Menelaos is ready to accept Adrestos's negotiated plea, his brother overrides him and dispatches Adrestos with his spear. The sixth and seventh instances are parallel: first Dolon and then Peisandros and Hippolochos pledge their fathers' *apereisi' apoina*, but they win only their own execution, by Diomedes and Agamemnon respectively. On the basis of Homer's own "words" we begin to sense the futility of such attempted bargains, keyed by the recurrent traditional signal of "boundless ransom." Although none of our lexicons report the connection (or even house the whole "word"), this phrase seems to prescribe a horizon of expectation. Or so Homer would have us believe.

The idiomatic pathway from proposed ransom to death and futility frames the other three of these eight occurrences as well. At 6.427, within Andromache's plea for Hektor to remain inside Troy (a plea that is also a lament for the hero destined to die),[27] we hear that her mother was taken captive by Achilles. Although she was later freed by supplying her captor with *apereisi' apoina*, the old woman eventually committed suicide in her halls. Twice more, at 9.120 and 19.138, a proffered ransom ends in dys-

---

[27] On the aesthetic role of the typical scene of Lament as an aspect of Andromache's plea, see Foley, *Homer's Traditional Art*, 187-98; cf. Dué, *Homeric Variations*, 67-81.

function, although the narrative embedding is interestingly different. Book 9 portrays the failed embassy to Achilles, which cannot repair the damage done the great hero's honor no matter how magnificent the gifts brought to propitiate him. Even when in Book 19 Agamemnon pronounces himself deluded and promises "boundless ransom" to make things right with the "best of the Achaeans," that promise has little or nothing to do with Achilles' motivation or actions. In fact, he denies the offer just as he refuses his fellow Achaeans' insistence on a recuperative rest and dinner, having already renounced his withdrawal and now fixated only on revenging Patroklos's death. Once again, *apereisi' apoina* is distinguished most centrally by its fundamental inefficacy. Homer is in effect telling us that he uses this phrase as a proleptic signal to indicate that whatever the prospective giver aims at will dependably go awry. As fieldworkers who in interviewing Homer look beyond our isolated words to his contextualized "words," we can count on that reversal as an idiomatic reflex.

Or at least that's what our informant's first eight responses indicate. Now consider the last three of his eleven answers to our question, all of them involved with Priam's sorrowful but remarkably brave journey behind enemy lines:

<u>Site</u> <u>Event</u>   <u>Result</u>
24.276 Priam's sons load ransom for corpse > ***
    They piled up <u>boundless ransom</u> for Hektor's person
    nêeon Hektoreês kephalês <u>apereisi' apoina</u>

24.502 Priam urges Achilles to accept ransom > ***
    intending to free [my son] from you, and I bear <u>boundless ransom</u>
    lusomenos para seio, pherô d' <u>apereisi' apoina</u>

24.579 Automedon and Alkimos unload ransom > ***
    They took the <u>boundless ransom</u> for Hektor's person
    hêireon Hektoreês kephalês <u>apereisi' apoina</u>

On the face of it, these three verses and their implications seem to contradict Homer's earlier testimony. Instead of leading to futility and death, this attempt at ransoming accomplishes the impossible: the person petitioned, Achilles, actually agrees to the bargain, breaks bread with the fallen champion's father, and pledges to delay the Achaean assault in order to give Priam and the Trojans sufficient time to conduct Hektor's funeral. What has happened here? Are Homer's first eight responses misleading? Is the apparently well-worn pathway illusory? Is *apereisi' apoina* not the idiomatic signal we thought it was?

Homer's responses are in fact not at all contradictory. Very often in traditional oral poetry an especially momentous effect is realized not by fulfilling an idiomatic expectation but rather by frustrating or reversing it. Although readers of *Beowulf* expect that hero to arm himself ritually before entering battle, his direct refusal to do so in the fight against Grendel sets that encounter into dramatic relief: because Beowulf seeks fair combat, the only possible venue for earning renown within Anglo-Saxon poetry, he must forsake weapons that the monster lacks. He must *dis*-arm.[28] Likewise, in a famous song from the nineteenth-century field collections of Vuk Karadžić, the Serbian hero Prince Marko also reverses his customary actions by disarming, in his case to prepare himself for death; one by one he destroys his weapons and slaughters Šarac, his faithful horse and companion. What the singer Filip Višnjić is doing at this juncture is to use the traditional pattern of Arming the Hero, heavily freighted with implications, to describe Marko's demise in a strikingly counter-traditional way.[29] Similarly, although anointment scenes in the *Odyssey* almost always lead to feasts and eventual mediation of conflicts, one such scene forecasts a different sort of celebration: the rapprochement of Penelope and Odysseus in a long-deferred "feast" of reunion.[30] In these and many more instances, it is the power of the idiomatic frame of reference that highlights the unusual nature of the moment at hand. Precisely because the audience — and the competent reader — learn to expect a certain result, the reversal or departure is that much more striking. This is one particularly dramatic twist on a cardinal expressive strategy in traditional poetry: melding the unique with the expected, setting the unprecedented off against the idomatic.[31]

As we shall see, this strategic twist perfectly suits the highly charged situation in Book 24. Priam has no business undertaking what appears to

---

[28] See Foley, *Immanent Art*, esp. 233-4.

[29] See Foley, *Immanent Art*, 124-33.

[30] See Foley, *Traditional Oral Epic*, 265-76, and *Homer's Traditional Art*, 171-87.

[31] Proverbially speaking, we must learn to "Read both behind and between the signs." See further, Foley, *How to Read an Oral Poem*, 139-41.

be a suicide mission to recover his son's remains; Achilles has shown himself to be merciless and crazed, and Hekabe has specifically warned her husband against his mission. Everything points toward the old man's impending death. Even should he somehow reach the Greek hero's tent (and we recall that the successful passage is accomplished only through the divine intervention of the messenger-god and master-of-transit Hermes), what chance does he stand of surviving long enough to state his case, never mind actually to ransom his son's body? Before the two mortal enemies actually meet and share a healing feast, who could have anticipated such an outcome? On logical grounds, Priam's errand seems but a futile and desperate gesture.

It is within that scenario that we encounter the three "boundless ransom" signals, each of them warning once again that the negotiation must indeed founder. When Priam's sons load the gifts onto their father's wagon (24.276), Homer is implying, they are performing a useless exercise that can lead only to death. When Priam urges Achilles to accept the *apereisi' apoina* (24.502), we are led to believe that his demise must be imminent.[32] Instead, and dramatically against all expectation, the ruthless Greek champion is moved to weep in memory of his own father Peleus and of Patroklos, and eventually to secure Priam's ritual participation in a feast that by convention promises reconciliation. By the time Automedon and Alkimos remove the "boundless ransom" from the cart (24.579), the bargain has been struck. All of the idiomatic force of the phrase has been countered, everything it predicts has been short-circuited in this unprecedented reaction to a (usually hopeless) attempt at barter. The "life-or-death" context has here shifted to a father's successful rescue of his child, exactly the result that Chryses could not manage in regard to his living daughter Chryseis and at cross-purposes to so many other characters' fruitless proposals in the *Iliad*. The key phrase *apereisi' apoina*, which cues futil-

---

[32] Despite being followed by Priam's heart-wrenching plea, some of the most memorable lines in Greek literature (I follow Reck's direct and unpretentious translation, 446) –
    Respect the gods, Achilles – pity me
    for your father's sake! I am more piteous
    since I've suffered more than any mortal:
    to kiss the hands of him who killed my son. (24.503-6) –
everything points toward Achilles' quick and mindless dispatching of the old man.

ity and death, here serves as a strategy to amplify the uniqueness of Priam's achievement. He and Achilles proceed by refuting traditional expectation, as does Homer. How remarkable is the ransoming of Hektor's corpse? So remarkable that it denies the force of tradition, explains our informant. It embodies that rarest and most powerful of strategies — the unacceptable because counter-idiomatic outcome.

Homer's answer to the first question we posed — namely, "What does the phrase — and single 'word' — 'boundless ransom' [*apereisi' apoina*] mean?" — illustrates how his specialized way of speaking can support much more than lexical denotation. By collating the eleven instances in the *Iliad* we can see that this unit bears an additional layer of signification. When we encounter the promise or bestowal of "boundless ransom," we learn to expect more than the convenient satisfaction of metrical demands, more than a hackneyed filler, more even a smooth surface of expression wherein "every phrase has its perfection of style."[33] What we expect is futility and death: either the *apereisi' apoina* are unconditionally refused and death comes swiftly or the gifts in some way betoken an eventual demise. Against this background Priam's attempt at buying back Hektor's corpse is marked as doomed to failure, and yet so brazen is his fatherly heroism (and so strong if covert the divine support behind this task impossible of achievement) that the old man overcomes even a highly dependable proverbial signal. In this one aberrant case, unique among all others, "boundless ransom" *does* win the day.

From this first "word" and its idiomatic implications we turn now to a second stage of our interview with Homer and to another recurrent phrase in his traditional vocabulary. Once again we will be posing a question intended to unlock the referentiality of a standard item in his epic way of speaking, and once again we will elicit his response by examining the evidence available in his poems.

II. What does the phrase — and single "word" — "day of return"
 [*nostimon êmar*] mean?
We start as before with a text-ethnographic profile of this vocabulary item. First, it occurs eleven times in the Homeric poems and involves a variety of characters and situations; that is, the phrase does not always refer to Odysseus's own return, but rather to the idea of *nostos* or homecoming in

---

[33] Parry's description, from "Homer and Homeric Style," 306.

general.[34] Second, it always occupies one of two positions in the hexameter: either line-final position in the so-called adonean clausula, a favorite spot for formulas; or as the opening of a consistently realized second-hemistich formula with some form of the verb "to see." Third, "day of return" regularly combines with quite a few different phraseological partners, although their range is more limited than those associated with "boundless ransom." Fourth, *nostimon emar* never turns up in either the *Iliad* or the *Homeric Hymns*; it is exclusively an Odyssean "word."

To gain an idea of the range of applicability of this signal, consider a few examples from various parts of the *Odyssey*. As early as the ninth line of the poem, within his appeal to the Muse, Homer documents Odysseus's companions' loss of their "day of return," a casualty of their having violated the express prohibition against eating the cattle of the sun. Soon afterward at 1.168 Telemachos pronounces Odysseus's *nostimon emar* lost, as all in Ithaca fear may have happened. Near the start of the Phaeacian episode, Nausikaa offers the hero, lately emerged from the sea and Poseidon's wrath, a fail-safe strategy to gain his "day of return" (6.311): he must approach her mother Arete as a suppliant. Much further on and in a very different situation, the menacing goatherd Melanthios threatens Eumaios and wishes someone would strike down Telemachos, so that the son's fate would mirror the father's lost "day of return." As noted above, the cast of characters involved in these and the seven other passages that Homer furnishes us as a response to our query is relatively large and varied — not only the companions, Athena, Nausikaa, and Melanthios are included, but also Penelope, other Trojan heroes, Kalypso, Zeus, and Eurykleia appear in scenes marked by this phrase. Counterbalancing that breadth of reference, however, we also observe from Homer's remarks that in some fashion the central epic protagonist Odysseus figures in every scene.

Typically for the Homeric register — and to a degree for most traditional oral registers — the phraseology surrounding "day of return" varies within limits. Part of its systematic organization can be glimpsed in the seven instances that are located at line-end. As an adonean clausula, it precisely fits one of the two shapes taken by the fourth colon in the hexameter, described by some metrists as the final two feet or metra and schematically of the shape – u u – x. Whether composed of one or more of our

---

[34] For the record, the eleven instances occur at *Odyssey* 1.9, 1.168, 1.354, 3.233, 5.220, 6.311, 8.466, 16.149, 17.253, 17.571, and 19.369.

lexicon-based words, a "word" of this shape regularly seeks this line-ending, colonic position.[35] All signs point toward *nostimon êmar* as constituting an indivisible unit of utterance, a phrase that functions as an amalgam.

However, the unitary identity of "day of return" as an element in its own right hardly exhausts the web of diction in which the phrase is enmeshed. Two of the seven line-ending instances are also part of a half-line or hemistich formula:

> they ate. But their *day of return was lost*.
> êsthion. Autar ho toisin *apheileto nostimon êmar*. (1.9)

> But now I believe your *day of return was* entirely *lost*
> nun de toi oiôi pampan *apheileto nostimon êmar* (19.369)

Interestingly, although the half-line formula recurs exactly, it combines with two very different partner hemistichs, illustrating the flexibility of the specialized epic language at another level. We can see the same mix of recurrency and adaptability in two more of these same seven lines, this time involving a different but semantically related hemistich phrase:

> for not Odysseus alone *lost his day of return*
> ou gar Odysseus oios *apôlese nostimon êmar* (1.354)

> as for Odysseus far away *the day of return was lost*
> hôs Odusêi ge têlou *apôleto nostimon êmar* (17.253)

Metrically, these two lines fill the same half-line increment, but syntactically they show a slight (and serviceable) variation: in the former Odysseus actively loses his "day of return," while in the latter a middle-voice form of the verb makes for a passive, more indirect attribution to the struggling hero. Of the first seven instances examined, then, two follow a hemistich pattern exactly (though with variant combination with other partners), two

---

[35] See Foley, *Traditional Oral Epic*, esp. 144.

follow a half-line pattern that itself is flexible, and the remaining three seem largely unrelated.[36]

How about the last four of Homer's eleven responses to our query, where "day of return" does not occupy final position in the hexameter line? Above we noted that they all feature a second-hemistich phrase that ends with some form of the verb "to see," but a closer look narrows the focus considerably. In short, three of the four recur verbatim (3.233, 5.220, and 8.466):

> and go back home, <u>and see the day of return</u>
> oikade t' elthemenai <u>kai nostimon êmar idesthai</u>

In such cases – as well as with other patterns – we might productively think of the simplex *nostimon êmar* as a "word" that can also be inflected, that is, as a unit that can assume certain permitted metrical-phraseological shapes. The final instance of this group then presents another permissible inflection (6.311):

> throw [around] her [knees], <u>so that you may see your day of return</u>
> ballein hêmeterês, <u>hina nostimon êmar idéai</u>

This last of Homer's responses deserves categorization along with the preceding three on the basis of a shared B1+ second half-line, but once again we note the flexibility within the systemically related diction. Homer thrice uses a whole-line inflection of "day of return," but he also takes advantage of the half-line form to answer a different syntactic challenge. Taken as a whole, these last four responses reveal a competence in the epic register: by inflecting his "word" to meet the exigencies of many different phraseological situations, Homer is showing his ability to speak the specialized poetic language fluently.

With this information in hand, we can turn to the final stage of our interview with Homer. In seeking to discover the traditional referentiality of "day of return" in its various phraseological incarnations, it will prove

---

[36] Note that 1.168 shares a simplex form of *ollumi*: "*phêisin eleusesthai. tou d' ôleto nostimon êmar*" [says that he will come back. But his day of return has been lost]. However, this hemistich pattern is a B1+ sequence that does not share an overall phraseological definition with the patterns discussed, which are all configured as B2+ half-lines.

productive to consider two aspects of his answers at once: namely, what the "word" means idiomatically and why it occurs only in the *Odyssey*.

The first clue is the attribution of *nostimon êmar*. As mentioned earlier, Homer implicates other figures besides Odysseus in his eleven-part response to our question, among them Odysseus's companions (1.9), other Achaean comrades who fought at Troy (1.354), Agamemnon's sorry fate (compared at 3.233ff.), and Telemachos (linked at 17.251-3). This is to say nothing of the wide variety of respondents and situations we encounter over the eleven instances. In short, collation and comparative analysis indicate that what Homer designates by this "word" is not Odysseus's homecoming (or its lack), or for that matter any particular character's *nostos*, but rather the *traditional idea* of "day of return." The phrase *nostimon êmar* stands as a kind of goal to which many aspire, a beacon toward which heroes may struggle either successfully or unsuccessfully. Indeed, the morphology of the "word" — its flexibility as a sign that can take on different nominal shapes according to the situation — is perhaps the most compelling empirical evidence of its importance as a cardinal value in this poem and the tradition from which the poem derives.

A brief review of the instances will confirm this perspective. At 1.9 the poet recounts how the comrades lost their "day of return" and perished on Hyperion's island. In the same book (1.168) Telemachos seems sure that Odysseus's *nostos* has indeed been derailed and then launches into the traditional host's questioning of his guest, Athena disguised as pseudo-Mentes. Two books after Telemachos dismissively tells his mother Penelope that Odysseus was not the only one to lose his "day of return" at Troy (1.354), he is upbraided by pseudo-Mentes, who chides the young man for his weakness and affirms that "he" would prefer a long, woe-filled journey linked with an eventual homecoming to the everlasting ignominy of Agamemnon's deadly reception (3.233). We will have reason to come back to this last instance toward the end of our fieldwork analysis.

In Book 5 Odysseus uses the "day of return" touchstone to help explain to Kalypso why he favors Penelope and homecoming over even her immortal gifts (220), and in the next book the "word" and idea are summoned by Nausikaa as she describes to Odysseus the necessity of petitioning Arete for his conveyance to Ithaca (6.311). Paired with this last instance is Odysseus's farewell to the young girl, whose aid in securing his *nostimon êmar* he promises never to forget (8.466). As with the first few of Homer's responses, these three exemplify the broad range of the "day of return" phraseology: it seems to serve as a reference or focus for a large and complex set of actions and ideas, as the culminating point of a long, convoluted process. The "word" – in its many inflections – is the shorthand sign or *sêma* for a particular story.

It is that same story, capped by a wished-for homecoming, to which Telemachos wistfully refers some eight books later (16.149) as he pities the pathetic Laertes, whose mourning has led to fasting and neglect of his farm. Likewise, Melanthios adverts to the "day of return" and its idiomatically attached tale (portraying it as frustrated striving, though that can't be known yet) when he threatens Eumaios and wishes Telemachos the worst at 17.253. When Odysseus instructs Eumaios to tell Penelope to delay her questions concerning her husband's *nostimon êmar* at 17.571, he is as much as saying that he does not wish to rehearse the story in front of the suitors. Finally, at 19.369 Eurykleia seems to speak both to the disguised, unrecognized stranger and to her long-lost master Odysseus when she bemoans his (their) fate and loss of the "day of return." Her speech draws special significance from the implied story-in-the-making.

Over these eleven instances of the "word" we can appreciate both its broad applicability and its power as an idiom. No matter the situation, the coded meaning of the phrase is a story: an epic tale that commences with a hero going off to war, continues with his battles against terrible foes over a succession of mortally threatening events, and culminates – or, in Agamemnon's and the suitors' cases, leads to death and destruction – in a long-desired homecoming. To put it as analytically as possible, *nostimon êmar* stands for an Odyssean tale, a story of striving toward home. But just as that "day of return" can be won, it can also be lost; the outcome remains in doubt until the end because the hero may succeed or fail. The crucial observation is that the signal stands, *pars pro toto* and very economically, for the entire swath of the story, complete with at least one stock character, a crippling series of obstacles to confront, and a dénouement that is yet to play itself out. In each of his eleven responses Homer has "slotted" a unique narrative moment within a familiar frame of reference, melding the specifics of this or that situation with the traditional referentiality of all that the signal "day of return" conventionally implies.

This powerful sign takes on added significance once we realize what hangs in the traditional balance. As I have discussed elsewhere, by contextualizing Homer's *Odyssey* in the larger Indo-European frame of reference we can glimpse its flexible story-pattern of Return, a tale-type attested across the face of Europe from ancient times to the present.[37] Suffice it to say that our interview with Homer is unfortunately (and inevitably) somewhat misleading on this score, since he has given us only one version of this pliable story-type — the "happy ending" that features the faithful mate testing and then finally welcoming home her long-absent husband or fiancé. Had Homer given us a more complete reflection of the natural morphology of this pattern, wherein wives and fiancées are just as often duplicitous and Clytaemnestra-like as not, we would have a better appreciation of the inherent tension and suspense woven into the story of *nostimon êmar*. Hundreds of South Slavic witnesses, recorded by Parry and Lord as well as by native investigators in various parts of the former Yugoslavia, for example, establish this international morphology. From this perspective — which derives from extending our fieldwork on Homer to interviewing other epic singers of Return Songs — it is in fact Penelope and her sisters (and not the center-stage male heroes) who tip the narrative balance. The women are in charge of how this story concludes.

Although Homer does not explicitly identify this binary pathway resolved only by the wife or fiancée, his nine references to the Agamemnon–Clytaemnestra–Orestes triangle in the *Odyssey* stand as a recurrent reminder that the Return Song can end with either of two climaxes. Indeed, as we mentioned earlier, Homer applies the *nostimon êmar* "word" to describe what Agamemnon didn't achieve as a result of his disastrous homecoming. Mythic mirror-opposites of one another, the two families collectively image how the "day of homecoming" tale can turn out, for good or for ill.

For confirmation of that implicit, lurking tension we can take our fieldwork one last step further by interviewing Agamemnon himself on the meaning and context of the implied story of Return. In the final book of the *Odyssey* Homer allows the beleaguered shade of the son of Atreus to sketch what amounts to a metapoetics of the Return Song in the ancient Greek epic tradition:

> O fortunate son of Laertes, Odysseus of many devices,
> surely you won yourself a wife endowed with great virtue.
> How good was proved the heart that is in blameless Penelope,

---

[37] On the prevalence and dynamics of this story-pattern, see esp. Foley, *Homer's Traditional Art*, 135-67.

> Ikarios' daughter, and how well she remembered Odysseus,
> her wedded husband. Thereby the fame of her virtue shall never
> die away, but the immortals will make for the people
> of earth *a pleasing song* for prudent Penelope.
> No so did the daughter of Tyndareos fashion her evil
> deeds, when she killed her wedded lord, and *a song of loathing*
> will be hers among men, to make evil the reputation
> of womankind, even for one whose acts are virtuous.
> (24.192-202)

Agamemnon's morphology of the "pleasing song" (197-8) [*aoidên ... chariessan*] versus the "song of loathing" (200) [*stugerê ... aoidê*] squares with the double outcomes of the Return Song, which as noted above takes one of two diametrically opposed directions in all Indo-European traditions. Homer says as much when he has Athena (pseudo-Mentes) refer idiomatically to Agamemnon's loss of his "day of return" in Book 3. Even if circumstances have conspired to provide us only one-half of this story's morphology in the partially preserved ancient Greek corpus, our interview with Agamemnon takes up the slack.

Summary

Even if this initial interview with Homer must now come to a close, our long-term fieldwork need not — indeed, should not — end here. By venturing out into the "field" of the Homeric epic texts, by continuing to ask our informant questions like the two posed above, we can start to learn the language and begin to establish a context for reception of his highly structured and deeply resonant idiom. This kind of initiative can profitably examine myriad other phrases, to be sure,[38] but it can also illuminate the

---

[38] For example, Homer's brief phrase "he/she did not disobey" [*oud' apithêse*, etc.] creates, as he testifies via consistent idiomatic usage over 31 occurrences (28 in the *Iliad*, 3 in the *Odyssey*), a specific frame of reference to guide our reception of various narrative moments. The characters who are described in this way as heeding a command could in fact have disobeyed; indeed, it conventionally requires some effort to accede because a change of course is required, a change that will have important, possibly life-or-death, repercussions. The signal *oud' apithêse* and its close relatives thus "slot" the particular situation within a recognizable, generic context. They amount to instances of a reading signal.

larger "words" of recurrent, idiomatic typical scenes and story-patterns.[39] As observed at the outset of this essay, fieldwork has always meant more than collecting, examining, and reporting on items; properly adapted to the task at hand, it can also help us to get beyond the massive silence of the ancient Homeric texts and become a more fluent audience.

---

[39] For examples of analysis involving these larger units, see Foley, *Homer's Traditional Art*, chaps. 5-6.

STEVE REECE

Homer's *Iliad* and *Odyssey*: From Oral Performance to Written Text

Prefatory Remarks
In the very fertile field of Homeric studies there were published in the last *year* of the twentieth century more than a dozen new dissertations, two dozen new scholarly books and monographs, and over 250 new articles and reviews in scholarly journals — a total of almost 10,000 pages of text (and that does not include reprints, translations, popular literature, conference talks, or the ever-growing corpus of electronic text on the World Wide Web).[1] From the last *decade* of the twentieth century I have personally collected more than 2,200 titles of new books, monographs, and journal articles — a total of over 60,000 pages of text (and I must be missing at least a few!). I estimate that in the last *century* around a half-million new pages of scholarly text were printed; this adds up to 460 pages of commentary for each page of Homeric text, including the *"Homeric"* Hymns! And this has gone on year after year for at least the last two centuries, and, though sometimes with somewhat less enthusiasm and prolificacy, for twenty-four centuries before that.

There is a very present danger that we as Homeric scholars will fail to keep up with all the new discoveries and insights in our field as a whole. This is inevitable, and we recognize it. We do well if we can manage the bibliographical searching tools for the material published during the twen-

---

[1] The number of dissertations is derived from *Dissertation Abstracts*; the numbers of books, monographs, articles, and reviews are derived from *L' Année philologique*.

tieth century, if we have a grasp of the general flow of scholarship during the nineteenth, and if we can get access to and comprehend the commentaries on Homer that have survived from earlier centuries (from the Alexandrian *hypomnemata*, vestiges of which are embedded in the Homeric scholia, to Eustathius's *magna opera* on both epics, to Wolf's *Prolegomena ad Homerum*). Some new and even important discoveries in the field will pass many of us by.

But there is another danger, I think, more sinister than this one: that the ever-rising inundation of new material will cause us to drift away from those moorings established by the toilsome research of our predecessors. I propose to offer here not something entirely new and imaginative, not something more to add to the mass of material to be mastered, but simply a reminder of some of those moorings of which we seem to have lost our grasp.

Introduction
It has to do with one of the most fundamental methodological issues in Homeric studies — the centerpiece of all "Homeric Questions": what is the relationship between our inherited texts of Homer's epics — a modern, eclectic, scholarly edition such as the Oxford Classical Text, for example — and the historical, live, oral performance of the epic by a Greek bard on (let's say) the island of Chios in (let's say) the eighth century B.C.E.?[2]

To put it in the language most familiar to Homerists: are our inherited texts more or less reliable records — though passed through countless hands over many generations — of what was once an oral-dictated text, i.e., a scribal transcription of a performance orally delivered by a historical Homer in the eighth century and thereafter for the most part, except for some surface corruption, fixed in its form? Or are our inherited texts the

---

[2] The phrase "our inherited texts of Homer" can, of course, mean many different things. I use the term in a conventional way to designate the text found, for the most part, in modern scholarly editions, such as the Monro-Allen Oxford Classical Text, which is essentially the text of Wolf, which is, in turn, a reservoir of the stable and standardized text of the Roman papyri (ca. 150 B.C.E.-seventh century C.E.) and medieval codices (ca. 900-1550) — i.e., the Roman and Byzantine "vulgate" — which is, in turn, the offspring of the recension of the Hellenistic scholar Aristarchus around 150 B.C.E. The status of the Homeric texts before Aristarchus is much less clear; this will be an object of scrutiny in the examination to follow.

final product of a long evolution of a fluid oral *and* textual transmission, attributable to a mythic figure, a symbol of oral tradition that we can call, for the sake of shorthand, "Homer," but actually shaped by generations of mouths *and* hands, slowly crystallized, and not really fixed until the late classical or even Hellenistic period?

Albert B. Lord's "oral-dictation" model was challenged early on by Geoffrey Kirk's "evolutionary" model, and the debate has continued, with refinements and shifting terminology, most recently, on the one side, by, among others, George Goold, Adam Parry, David Gunn, Richard Janko, Martin West, Barry Powell, Cornelis Ruijgh, Michael Haslam, and Minna Skafte Jensen, and, on the other side, by, among others, Raphael Sealey, John Miles Foley, Gregory Nagy, Richard Seaford, Erwin Cook, Thérèse de Vet, Steven Lowenstam, and Robert Lamberton.

The question is of great importance in establishing a theoretical foundation for the types of aesthetic judgments about which this volume is concerned. Before embarking on a quest to "Unbind Proteus," we must make as clear as possible what "Proteus" we intend to unbind. When we wish to praise "Homer" for an aesthetically pleasing device – a leitmotif that develops over a long stretch of narrative, for example – we must confess openly if we are attributing this to the design of a human poet, to the outcome of a less personal oral tradition, or simply to the inherited text as we have it. Moreover, we must ask – even if we cannot fully answer – what the relationship is among these three. Lack of clarity on this issue can easily lead to misunderstanding: for example, many clever theories about Homeric aesthetics have been based at least partly on verses that entered the Homeric textual tradition long after the traditional date ascribed to Homer, some at the hands of scribes even as late as the Roman and Byzantine periods.[3] This can be a legitimate type of aesthetic criticism (a "reader response" to the "text as we have it"), but only if what is meant by "Homer" is clearly communicated. The present examination of the relative merits of the oral-dictation and evolutionary models, with all its implications for the genesis and transmission of the Homeric texts, is intended to contribute to this clarity.

---

[3] On the post-Aristarchean scribal interpolations generally, see Bolling, *External Evidence*, 3–30, and Apthorp, *Manuscript Evidence*, 35–125; on the particular challenge of these late scribal interpolations to the articulation of aesthetic theories, see Reece, *Stranger's Welcome*, 40–6.

Of the two models under consideration here, it is the evolutionary model that appears to me to be the one currently gaining momentum among classical scholars. One often reads and hears such phrases as "the fluidity and multiformity of the epic tradition," "multiple variants of the *Iliad* and *Odyssey*," and so forth, when referring not only to the archaic period but to the classical and Hellenistic periods as well, long after the date traditionally ascribed to Homeric composition. This model is in many respects very attractive, since it offers an explanation for several curious developments relevant to the transmission of the epics: the relative paucity of depictions of Iliadic and Odyssean scenes in the graphic arts during the archaic period, followed by a surge in popularity of such scenes in the late sixth century; the sometimes remarkable differences between our inherited texts, on the one hand, and, on the other hand, the quotations of Homer by classical authors, the textual versions reported to have existed in the manuscripts available to the Alexandrian editors, the longer and "eccentric" readings of the Ptolemaic papyri, and other readings reported or suggested by the Hellenistic scholars; and the late linguistic forms, especially the "Atticisms," that reside in our inherited texts.

That the Homeric epics reached the form in which we have inherited them through a long evolutionary process is, of course, not a recent idea. Though in many and various incarnations, this notion lay at the foundation of the analytical approach to the genesis of the Homeric epics (e.g., Wolf, Lachmann, Kirchhoff, Wilamowitz, Leaf). Gilbert Murray, in his influential book *The Rise of the Greek Epic*, invoked all the standard evolutionary arguments in his proposal, based on his consideration of variants in ancient quotations of Homer, in the reports of the readings of early manuscripts of Homer, as well as in the later Ptolemaic "wild" papyri, that the Homeric epics continued to remain in a fluid state through at least the end of the Classical period, not only in matters of words and verses but even in large portions of the story, and that they did not take on their final form until the Hellenistic period, during which time the editors of Homer continued to rewrite passages with the freedom of the old bards.[4]

But the form of the evolutionary model has been reshaped with many new angles since the almost universal acceptance of Milman Parry's and Albert B. Lord's theory that the Homeric epics, like the Serbo-Croatian epics that they were recording in their fieldwork, were in origin oral "compo-

---

[4] Murray, *Greek Epic*, esp. 298–325.

sitions-in-performance."[5] Let me trace the development of this newer form of the evolutionary model by briefly summarizing the contributions of three of its most influential advocates.

G. S. Kirk, one of the most widely read Homerists of the twentieth century, articulated, first in his article "Homer and Modern Oral Poetry: Some Confusions," the theories that were to become the underpinnings for his very influential book *The Songs of Homer*:[6] namely, that the "monumental" epics – versions of great length and strong central themes by individual singers – were shaped in the late eighth century but were then transmitted, for the most part orally, via the memorization of rhapsodes, for two hundred years in only a relatively stable form before being committed to writing in the late sixth century. His evolutionary model – unlikely as it seemed to comparatists familiar with the vagaries of truly oral traditions – held the advantage of allowing for a purely oral composition, performance, and early transmission of the epics while still holding out comfortably the possibility that the texts of these epics, though written down much later, were a relatively accurate record of the early performances.

John Miles Foley, currently the single most influential force behind the renaissance in the discipline of comparative oral traditions, sees the genesis of the Homeric texts through the prism of other oral and oral-derived traditions. In a section of his book *Traditional Oral Epic* comparing the documents that have preserved the Homeric, Anglo-Saxon, and Serbo-Croatian traditions, Foley, while paying obeisance to Lord's hypothesis of an oral-dictated Homeric text, prefers to imagine a more fluid and evolu-

---

[5] The Parry-Lord theory is still best observed in its seminal forms in A. Parry, *Making of Homeric Verse*, and Lord, *Singer of Tales*. By "composition-in-performance," a term that I will use often in this essay, I mean what Lord, 99, described in his observations of a Serbo-Croatian singer's technique: "When the singer of tales, equipped with a store of formulas and themes and a technique of composition, takes his place before an audience and tells his story, he follows the plan which he has learned along with the other elements of his profession.... [He] thinks of his song in terms of a flexible plan of themes, some of which are essential and some of which are not.... His idea of stability, to which he is deeply devoted, does not include the wording, which to him has never been fixed, nor the unessential parts of the story."

[6] G. S. Kirk, *Songs of Homer*, esp. 98–101, 301–34; cf. also his reply to A. Parry's criticism, "Homer's *Iliad*."

tionary genesis and transmission.[7] In this more evolutionary model, while at the earliest stages of transmission fixed or semi-fixed texts of Homer may have been memorized (as in G. S. Kirk's reconstruction), at the same time truly oral composition of Homeric type continued to thrive. Parochial versions of Homer were orally composed by bards (*aoidoi*) and then creatively memorized by rhapsodes, who embellished and personalized their own performances, thus proliferating versions that were different not only in phraseology but also in narrative structure. Although a Panhellenic version in polydialectal Greek was eventually written down at the Panathenaic festival in the late sixth century – a monumental fixed text that was passed on to the Alexandrians – disparate and diverse local traditions continued to flourish, since the art of oral verse-making survived for some time.

Thus the Homeric tradition was, if not active and primary oral, at least fluid and responsive possibly as late as the second century B.C.E. It is only to be expected under these circumstances that the Alexandrians, and the Greek world as a whole, were awash in versions of Homer. Noting the many readings attributed in the Homeric scholia to individual scholars (13), to city editions (66), and to the *Koine* (52), Foley concludes that there were no fewer than 131 separate and different editions of Homer deposited in the Alexandrian library. Further, he regards the plus-verses of the Ptolemaic "wild" papyri not as examples of concordance interpolation of verses that occur elsewhere in the texts of Homer, as Stephanie West proposed in her edition of the Ptolemaic papyri,[8] but as evidence of the multiformity of a still fluid Homeric epic tradition, even into the second century B.C.E. Foley proposes that up to the time of Aristarchus the Homeric poems existed not in one exclusive version but rather in many versions of different but equal authority; searching for a textual archetype under such conditions must be as futile an exercise, he concludes, as searching for the archetypal form of a story.

As far as the person of "Homer" is concerned, Foley proposes in his book *Homer's Traditional Art*, again supported by the comparative evidence of interviews with Serbo-Croatian *guslari* about their ancestral and legendary *guslari* who lived just beyond the limits of recorded history, that Homer was not a personal name of a historical singer but an eponym des-

---

[7] Foley, *Traditional Oral Epic*, 20–31.
[8] S. West, *Ptolemaic Papyri*, 11–28.

ignating a tradition of ancient Greek epic.[9] As a legend rather than a historical singer, he serves his various constituencies — e.g., later singers who invoke the mythic Homer as their source and inspiration — through his multiformity and ubiquity. This view is confirmed, claims Foley, by the many variations and inconsistencies in the later Greek biographies of Homer, which offer different genealogies, birthplaces, dates, and repertoires. "Homer," then, is a composite representation of the Greek epic tradition, removed to the origin of the bardic lineage from the matrix of time and place of subsequent singers; he is, in short, an anthropomorphization of the poetic tradition.

Gregory Nagy, one of the most well-known and influential of active Homeric scholars, has recently become the name most closely associated with the evolutionary model. Nagy's version of the evolutionary model is itself the result of a rather long process of evolution: one may observe it already in seminal form in his pathbreaking book *The Best of the Achaeans*, where he prefers to speak of a traditional process rather than an authorial event;[10] more concretely in his short essay "An Evolutionary Model for the Text Fixation of Homeric Epos," where he states simply that because the Homeric epics have a Panhellenic orientation, they cannot be traced back to a local tradition of a specific place and time; all this more exhaustively, with the extension of the model to other forms of Archaic Greek poetry, in a chapter titled "The Poetics of Panhellenism and the Enigma of Authorship in Early Greece" in his book *Pindar's Homer*.[11]

Nagy presented his version of the evolutionary model more systematically and very publicly in his 1991 presidential address to the American Philological Association, later published in expanded form as an article titled "Homeric Questions," where he acclaims the benefits of an evolutionary model over that of oral-dictation, regarding text-fixation as a process rather than an event, and asserting on the basis of comparison with the earliest surviving poetic inscriptions that the very concept of a poetic tran-

---

[9] Foley, *Homer's Traditional Art*, 49–61. Here Foley is influenced by G. Nagy's definition of "Homer" not as a historical poet but as a retrojection of the Panhellenic tradition representing the traditional and idealized functions of epic poetry: a symbol, as it were, of the oral tradition. See G. Nagy, *Pindar's Homer*, 55, 79–80; "Homeric Questions," 29; *Homeric Questions*, 89–90, 111–12; and *Poetry as Performance*, 76.

[10] G. Nagy, *Best of the Achaeans*, esp. 1–11.

[11] G. Nagy, *Pindar's Homer*, 52–81.

scription could not have evolved in Greece until after 550 B.C.E. He provides parallels to his model from other oral and textual traditions of poetry in a chapter titled "An Evolutionary Model for the Making of Homeric Poetry: Comparative Perspectives."

Much of Nagy's earlier work reappears in revised and expanded form in his two longer monographs *Homeric Questions* and *Poetry as Performance: Homer and Beyond*.[12] Here, with a more fully developed methodology, Nagy reasserts that a textualization even in the late sixth century resulted not from a single archetypal written text but from a process of seasonally recurring performances at the Panathenaia – a textualization that, moreover, could have taken place without the intervention of writing (i.e., it had a "near-textual" or "quasi-textual" status). Nagy then extends this condition of fluidity and multiformity even beyond the so-called Pisistratean recension and into the Classical and Hellenistic periods, suggesting that the performance traditions of the third and second centuries, as revealed by the "eccentric" papyri with their plus-verses, were even more fluid than they had been earlier, when the Athenian state regulated such performances. The Hellenistic scholars, Nagy claims, were faced in the larger context with both longer and shorter versions of the Homeric texts, and in the smaller context with a mass of variants in the wording of individual verses, all of which must still have a claim to authenticity in terms of the tradition, none being more original, more correct, or in any way better than another, except insofar as one might be more traditional than another. In such circumstances, Nagy concludes, the search for an archetype is a vain, indeed meaningless, enterprise.

Nagy warns that the extension of the evolutionary model to include the Hellenistic period brings with it some new and fundamental challenges for the modern editor of the Homeric texts. He rejects the conventional editorial practice of attempting to reconstruct *the* authentic reading of the text of Homer and instead wishes to account for the plethora of ancient recorded variants by regarding them all as *potentially* authentic readings inasmuch as they have been generated from the formulaic system of Homeric diction.[13] But how is the modern editor to present the fluidity

---

[12] G. Nagy, *Homeric Questions*, esp. 29-112; *Poetry as Performance*, esp. 107-206.

[13] G. Nagy, "Homeric Scholia," esp. 111-12; "Response," and "Review of M. West."

and multiformity of the epic tradition in the form of an edited text that has conventionally placed readings of a supposed original in the favored position above, while supposed variants are demoted to the ignominy of an apparatus criticus below? A new multitext format that does not so simply privilege one reading over another is needed — one that optimally will relate various readings to different periods in the transmission of the epics (i.e., perhaps something along the line of computer hypertext). Already the seeds of such a project are beginning to germinate in the fertile field of the Center for Hellenic Studies in Washington, DC.[14]

Scholars of Homeric studies and related fields have increasingly begun to abandon the notion of an early fixation of the Homeric texts in favor of a more or less fluid form, at least through the archaic period if not later.[15]

---

[14] A proposal for this project, provisionally titled "The Center for Hellenic Studies Multitext of Homer," can be viewed on the center's webpage at www.chs.harvard.edu.

[15] Specialists in many fields related to Homeric studies — archaeology, political, social and cultural history, ancient art, comparative epic, comparative oral traditions, myth, religion, etc. — have for various reasons been drawn to the evolutionary model. I mention a few recent proponents: Sealey, *Women and Law*, 110-50, embraces an evolutionary model — formulated earlier in his article "From Phemius to Ion" — as the foundation for his view that the Homeric epics, inasmuch as they reflect any actual historic society or any real historic customs (e.g., marriage customs), reflect those not of one particular period but of an amalgam of many ages and places, from the Bronze Age to sixth-century Athens and beyond. Seaford, *Reciprocity and Ritual*, 144-54, accepts G. Nagy's specific version of the evolutionary model as an explanation for his detection in the Homeric epics of the influence of the development of the Greek city-state. Cook, *The Odyssey in Athens*, esp. 128-70, like Seaford, embraces G. Nagy's evolutionary model and associates the textualization of the *Odyssey* in particular with developments of the city-state, regarding it as a performance tradition that became crystallized into a text in Athens simultaneously with the growth of Athenian civic ritual and the process of Athenian state formation. De Vet, "Joint Role of Orality and Literacy," proposes that the continuous interaction between the oral and the written in the evolving Balinese epic tradition provides a better analogue for the situation of the Homeric epics down to the Alexandrian period than the often cited Yugoslavian oral-dictated texts. Lowenstam, "Talking Vases," argues that the disparities between archaic vase paintings of epic scenes and the Homeric narrations as we have inherited them in the *Iliad* and *Odyssey* reveal that the Homeric epics had not become canonical in the seventh, sixth, or even early fifth centuries B.C.E. In his work on the ancient reception of Homer, Lamberton, "Homer in Antiquity,"

Among younger Homeric scholars, at least in the United States, the evolutionary model has almost achieved the status of orthodoxy, while the model of a text generated by the process of oral-dictation, and the concomitant hope of a recoverable archetype of an epic song performed by a real person at a particular time and place, is often dismissed as naive and romantic.

At the risk of sounding naive and romantic, I wish to suggest that oral-dictation is not only still a valid model, but that certain features of our inherited texts point to it as the more plausible of the two models.

The theory of an oral-dictated text of the Homeric epics can be found in a seminal form already in Milman Parry's unfinished work "Ćor Huso: A Study of Southslavic Song," in which he imagines Homer dictating his song while someone else with writing materials writes it down verse by verse, much as the Serbo-Croatian *guslari* whom he was observing dictated their songs to his assistant Nikola Vujnović.[16] But Parry's theory did not receive a clear and thorough articulation until his student Lord published an article, "Homer's Originality: Oral Dictated Texts," which laid out in a

---

33-5, envisions a rather extreme version of the evolutionary model, whereby the texts of the *Iliad* and *Odyssey* were recomposed over a long span of time by inventive rhapsodes, were caused to suffer along the way the literary interpolations of poets, politicians, and ultimately textual critics, and were finally carved down and shaped into the poems we know by nameless editors, who attributed them to an author named Homer, the details of whose biography they invented and embellished in their introduction of the epics to a reading public.

[16] I quote Parry's own words in an excerpt from his unfinished work, "Ćor Huso," 451, written less than a year before his death: "The more I understand the Southslavic poetry and the nature of the unity of the oral poem, the clearer it seems to me that the *Iliad* and the *Odyssey* are very exactly, as we have them, each one of them the rounded and finished work of a single singer; though whether they are both the work of *one* singer I do not yet know. I even figure to myself, just now, the moment when the author of the *Odyssey* sat and dictated his song, while another, with writing materials, wrote it down verse by verse, even in the way that our singers sit in the immobility of their thought, watching the motion of Nikola's hand across the empty page, when it will tell them it is the instant for them to speak the next verse. The reasons I have for such an opinion are many, some of them still very vague, some very exact." Unless otherwise noted, I cite Parry's work from A. Parry's edition.

concise form the theory about the genesis of the epics that he later developed in his very influential book *The Singer of Tales*.[17]

Lord's theory generated some immediate positive responses. George Goold, in his article "Homer and the Alphabet," embraced the oral-dictation model on the basis of his conviction that the original text of the epics was in the Ionic alphabet. Early and energetic objections to Lord's theory by G. S. Kirk were effectively countered by Adam Parry in an important article called "Have We Homer's *Iliad*?" David Gunn, in an article titled "Narrative Inconsistency and the Oral Dictated Text in the Homeric Epic," concluded, on the basis of a comparison of narrative inconsistencies in Homer with those in demonstrably orally dictated Serbo-Croatian epics, that Homer's epics too were orally dictated, without an opportunity for revision thereafter.

The question of dictation overlaps many other of the "Homeric Questions," and there has continued a lively debate on this question among Homeric scholars. Strong and up-to-date arguments in favor of an early dictation, hence in favor of a more or less fixed text from an early period, can be found in Janko's two articles, "The *Iliad* and its Editors: Dictation and Redaction" and "The Homeric Poems as Oral Dictated Texts," Powell's book *Homer and the Origin of the Greek Alphabet*,[18] Ruijgh's chapter titled "D'Homère aux origines proto-mycéniennes de la tradition épique,"[19] and Haslam's chapter titled "Homeric Papyri and Transmission of the Text."[20] M. West has argued forcefully for an early written text, though not necessarily a dictated one, in his two chapters titled "Archaische Heldendichtung: Singen und Schreiben" and "The Textual Criticism and Editing of Homer," as well as in his article "The Date of the *Iliad*"; conversely, Jensen has marshalled in great detail the evidence for a dictated text, though of the sixth century rather than the eighth or seventh, in her published debate "Dividing Homer: When and How Were the *Iliad* and *Odyssey* Divided into Songs?"[21] For much of what I have to say in what follows, I am indebted to these scholars.

---

[17] Lord, *Singer of Tales*, 124-38.
[18] Powell, *Origin of the Greek Alphabet*, 221-37.
[19] Ruijgh, "D'Homère aux origines proto-mycéniennes," 25-6.
[20] Haslam, "Homeric Papyri," 79-84.
[21] Jensen, "Dividing Homer," esp. 25-33.

Four Features of Our Inherited Texts that Point to the Oral-Dictation Model
Obviously, the oral-dictation model will bring us closer than the evolutionary model to a real historical performance, delivered at a particular time, in a particular place, by a real living person whom we may call by the name Homer; and in spite of the fact that the oral-dictation model is increasingly regarded as naive and romantic, I lean in its direction because of four prominent features of the narratives of our epics as we have inherited them: the unity of the narratives; the various levels of inconcinnities that remain embedded in the narratives; the absence of multiple versions of the *Iliad* and *Odyssey*; and the fixation in time of the epic art-language.

I. The Unity of the Narratives of Our Inherited Texts
On the one hand, our epics are unified narratives whose structures are most clearly observed, whose plots are most intelligently followed, and whose nuances are most pleasurably appreciated, whether by ancient listeners or modern readers, when experienced in their entirety and within a limited time frame. Episodes are not simply heaped one upon the other; they are organized in a thoughtful sequence from beginning to end and bound together by a network of interconnected references, by anticipatory and retrospective allusions, by comparative and contrasting parallelisms, and many other similar structuring devices. Further, although the events of the Trojan War are well understood to have consumed ten years, and the adventures of Odysseus's return home an additional ten years, in both the *Iliad* and *Odyssey* the narratives cover only a very narrow time frame – a matter of days rather than years – the rest being conveyed by means of flashback (through stories and allusions) and anticipation (through prophecy and foreshadowing). This unity of plot and time struck Aristotle as a unique feature of Homeric epic as early as the fourth century B.C.E. (*Poetics* 1451a, 1459a), and most critics and commentators since then have continued to be impressed by the architectonic unity of each epic as a whole.[22]

---

[22] For a recent general treatment of architectonic devices – ring compositions, polarities, and other balancing structures – that overarch the entire narrative of the *Iliad*, see Schein, "Structure and Interpretation," who draws upon the seminal works of Sheppard, *Pattern of the Iliad*; Myres, "Last Book of the *Iliad*"; van Otterlo, *De ringkompositie als opbouwprincipe*; Whitman, *Heroic Tradition*; Lohmann, *Die Komposition der Reden*; Taplin, *Homeric Soundings*; and K. Stanley, *Shield of Homer*. See also Heiden, "Three Movements," and "Thematic Reso-

The arousal of Achilles' wrath because Agamemnon deprives him of Briseis at the very beginning of the *Iliad* is framed by the resolution of that wrath at the end of the epic, where we last see Achilles sleeping with the recovered Briseis in the corner of his shelter (24.675-6) — and everything in between this frame is somehow affected by Achilles' condition. If we speak — anachronistically I think — in terms of book units, Book 1, in which Agamemnon rejects the supplication of the priest Chryses and refuses to release his daughter Chryseis in exchange for a ransom, is framed by Book 24, in which Achilles does precisely the opposite, accepting the supplication of king Priam and releasing his son Hector in exchange for a ransom. Further parallels between the first and last books abound: Apollo sets the action in motion in each case; both contain an episode in which Zeus and Thetis discuss Achilles; both describe a divine assembly on Olympus in which Zeus imposes his will on a resistant Hera; and the pattern of the passage of days is almost exactly balanced, both narrating actions over nine-day and twelve-day periods. Likewise Book 2 is framed by Book 23, Book 3 is framed by Book 22, and so on, though in a less structured pattern. Thus the "onion ring" composition of the *Iliad* as a whole can be peeled off, layer by layer, all the way to the core; if any major episode were left out, it would result in damage to the epic's integrity. The *Iliad* is not a random collection of episodes having to do with the Trojan War; it has an architectonic structure, complemented by a unity of plot and time, that points to a performance *in toto* on an occasion that provided considerable leisure, both for the singer and his audience.

The *Odyssey* too is a unified work, designed to be performed as a whole. In its plot it is thoroughly focused on the person of Odysseus (even when he is not present) — his unparalleled suffering followed by his triumphant return home — and for its structure it relies on ring compositions, half, three-part, and six-part divisions of narrative, parallelisms, and

---

nance." For a comparable treatment of ring compositions, half, three-part, and six-part narrative and narratological divisions, and other examples of parallelism in the *Odyssey*, see Tracy, "Structure of the *Odyssey*," who draws upon the seminal works of Bassett, "Structural Similarity"; Myres, "Patterns of the *Odyssey*"; Kitto, *Poiesis*; Gaisser, "Structural Analysis"; Fenik, *Studies in the Odyssey*; and his own *Story of the Odyssey*. See also Louden, *Structure, Narration*. On the use of type-scenes as building blocks for the architectonic structure of the *Odyssey*, see Reece, *Stranger's Welcome*, 189-206; on a specific use of ring composition to tie together a long stretch of Odyssean narrative, see Reece, "Three Circuits."

such, both on a small and large scale. But it is somewhat different from the *Iliad* in that it is a work unified more by its narratology than its plot. Indeed much of the special force of the *Odyssey* lies in Homer's arrangement of his narrative, beginning as he does almost at the end of the tale chronologically, and then filling in the background through the technique of flashback — what Cicero called "hysteron proteron Homericos" (*Ad Atticum* 1.16.1) [Homer's tendency to place "later" in the narrative the events that occurred "earlier" in time]. The arrangement of the epic is artistic and pleasing: the simultaneous experiences of son and father in Books 1–4 and 5–8 as they both travel abroad and with Athena's help encounter various obstacles to their common endeavors; the flashback in Books 9–12, in Odysseus's own tale to his audience of Phaeacians, of the earlier nine years of his return; the returns complete, the vengeance against the suitors by three generations of the family — Telemachus, Odysseus, and Laertes. Indeed, perhaps one of the most psychologically pleasing devices, and one that most clearly demarcates and unifies the epic as a whole, is the tripartite arrangement whereby the son Telemachus is the central figure at the beginning (Books 1–4), the father Odysseus in the middle (Books 5–23), and the grandfather Laertes at the end (Book 24), an arrangement that underscores on a structural level the leitmotif of the relationships between fathers and sons that is so visible throughout the epic.

In short, neither epic is simply a collection of loosely related episodes, which would be the predictable result of a process of compilation by various hands over a long period, or of a process of gradual accretion within an impersonal oral tradition. Each epic is a work carefully arranged by a personal and inspired singer composing in a performance that was experienced *in toto* on some occasion that provided considerable leisure (a festival, perhaps, or a nobleman's funeral or wedding). The length of the two epics was no detriment to performance: if the fifth-century Athenians had the patience to sit through 17,000 verses of tragedy during the three days of the Greater Dionysia (three tragedies, a satyr play, and a comedy on each day), surely the eighth-century Ionians could endure — over the course of perhaps three or six days — a 16,000-verse performance of the *Iliad* or a 12,000-verse performance of the *Odyssey*.

II. The Inconcinnities Embedded in Our Inherited Texts

On the other hand, the *Iliad* and *Odyssey* have survived to our day as texts that, even in the forms that have been copied and recopied for many generations, do not have the appearance of having gone through an extensive editorial process — proofreading, correcting, reworking, tidying up of loose ends, polishing up of rough spots, and so on. On the contrary, they retain many features typical of oral compositions-in-performance that once uttered could not be retracted. The Roman poet Horace unknowingly provides the solution to his own complaint about Homer's lapses in the *Ars Poetica* — "indignor quandoque bonus dormitat Homerus" (359) [I'm displeased whenever good Homer dozes] — when a few verses later in the same treatise he observes that "nescit vox missa reverti" (390) [once a speech is uttered it cannot be brought back]. Indeed inconcinnities remain at every level of our inherited texts as vestiges of their origin in oral performance.

Metrical Blunders: I am not referring here to metrical oddities that have resulted from historical changes in the Greek language: the loss of such sounds as *w* before a vowel (*eeikoston etos estin*) or before *r* (*teikhos te rêxein*); the loss of *h*, from original *s* (*Dii mêtin atalantos*); the loss of *sw* (*pateri hôi*); the loss of *s* before *r* (*peri de roos Ôkeanoio*), before *m* (*panta kata moiran*), or before *n* (*orea niphoenta*); the loss of *y* (*theos hôs*); and the loss of syllabic *r* (*Enualiôi andreiphontêi*). Nor am I referring to so-called "metrical lengthening" of a vowel to allow certain words into the dactylic hexameter that could not otherwise have been accommodated (e.g., *athanatos, ounoma, ein*). I even leave aside what the ancients called *stikhoi akephaloi, lagaroi*, and *meiouroi* (cf. Athenaeus's *Deipnosophist* xiv. 632 c-f), the inexplicable lengthening of short syllables at the beginning, middle, and end of the verse (e.g., "epei dê nêas te kai Hellêsponton hikonto," "tôn auth' hêgeisthên Asklêpiou duo paide," "Trōes d' errigêsan hopôs idon aiolon ophin"). More relevant to our present inquiry are those metrical irregularities that have resulted from the modification or juxtaposition of formulaic phrases, whose abundance in our Homeric texts can be attributed to the pressures of oral composition-in-performance by a singer who did not pause for long during his performance to deliberate over *le mot juste*, and did not go back to his verses after his performance to tidy up the prosodic loose ends.[23] For example:

---

[23] For more examples of metrical irregularities resulting from the modification and juxtaposition of formulaic phrases, all of which Parry attributed to the interplay of formulas by a singer composing in the unhesitating speed of a live performance, see Parry, "Homeric Formulae," and "Homer and Homeric Style."

1) *Il.* 18.288 – "prin men gar Priamoio polin meropes anthrôpoi" [a modification of *meropôn anthrôpôn*]

2) *Od.* 6.294 – "tosson apo ptolios, hosson te gegône boêsas" [the juxtaposition of two formulas].

But I am referring primarily to metrical blunders that do not yield to any explanation, such as:

1) *Od.* 7.89 – "argureoi de stathmoi en khalkeôi hestasan oudôi"

2) *Od.* 13.194 – "tounek' ar' alloeidea phainesketo panta anakti"

These are best regarded simply as metrical blunders that have naturally and understandably resulted from the pressure of oral composition-in-performance; they would surely have been corrected had the poet had the opportunity and leisure to review the passages, or had the text later gone through an extensive editorial process.

Dictional Inconcinnities: In this category I include those oddities that have resulted from stock formulaic phrases being used in contextually inappropriate circumstances. I am not speaking of the so-called "ornamental" epithets that may strike a modern literate audience, more concerned with *le mot juste* than their ancient illiterate counterparts, as contextually inappropriate: e.g., the recently wounded Aphrodite is *philommeidês* [sweetly-smiling], while the rejoicing Odysseus is *polutlas* [much-suffering]; the adulterous villain Aegisthus is *amumôn* [blameless], the shameful suitors are *antitheoi* [godlike], the lowly swineherd is *orkhamos andrôn* [chief of men], and the beggar has a *potnia mêtêr* [queen mother]. Nor do I include the longer formulaic phrases that appear too loosely used – at least to the modern reader – when the context is not so typical, such as the several times in the *Odyssey* when the plural form of the dative pronoun is used to designate even a single addressee of a speech: *tois ara muthôn êrkhe* (*Od.* 5.202) [to them, then, did she begin a speech]; *toisi de muthôn êrkhe* (*Od.* 7.47, 13.374, 17.100, 184, 19.103, 508) [and to them did he/she begin a speech]. I am speaking rather of passages where, on the one hand, the singer seems to have had somewhat more latitude in his selection of phrases, and where, on the other hand, the phrases have been selected with such little consideration of the context that one can scarcely deny that, had the singer had an opportunity to summon back his words and revise them, he would readily have done so.

1) The scene of an omen from Zeus at *Od.* 20.102-19 provides an egregious example. In response to Odysseus's prayer for an omen Zeus thunders formulaically *hupsothen ek nepheôn* (104 = Hesiod *Op.* 449) [from

the clouds on high]. But only a few verses later a servant-girl emerges from the house and expresses her amazement at the peculiar nature of this event: i.e., that she hears thunder when there *oude pothi nephos esti* (114) [is no cloud anywhere].

2) In a scene on the battlefield at *Il.* 13.402-23 Deiphobos hurls a spear that pierces Hypsenor in the liver under the midriff and *eithar d' hupo gounat' eluse* (412) [immediately loosened the knees from beneath him]. Deiphobos vaunts over his victim, boasting that he has sent him to Hades as an escort for his own recently slain friend Asios. The Argives, in great grief, carry Hypsenor back to the ships. By all accounts he is dead, and his companions are understood to be retrieving his corpse from the battlefield. This particular formula *hupo gounat' eluse* is always used in Homer of killing, not simply wounding, and that Hypsenor is actually dead is confirmed shortly when Idomeneus recalls his death in a taunt of Deiphobos (446-7). It comes rather as a surprise, then, when Hypsenor's corpse begins *barea stenakhonta* (423) [groaning heavily], a formula that is used elsewhere in Homer of wounded, weary, and despondent men, but never of a dead one.[24]

3) At the end of *Iliad* 16 Apollo deals Patroclus a blow to the back and shoulders so hard that his eyes spin; his helmet is struck off his head and rolls away under the feet of the horses, his spear splinters in his hands, his shield and baldric fall from his shoulders to the ground, and his corselet is loosened (786-804). Euphorbos then strikes him in the unprotected back with a javelin, and Hector finishes him off with a spear clean through the belly (805-29). Patroclus is easy prey: he is without arms (*gumnos* [815, cf. 17.122]), since the gods have snatched them away (846). It defies expectation, then, when shortly thereafter Hector returns and *Patroklon epei kluta teukhe' apêura* (17.125, cf. 187, 22.323) [strips Patroclus of his glorious arms]. Even more unexpected is Zeus's subsequent comment that Hector has "teukhea d' ou kata kosmon apo kratos te kai ômôn heileu" (17.205-6, cf. 19.412) [snatched the armor indecently from (Patroclus's) head and shoulders]. The poet has apparently reverted here to his customary diction, created for normal circumstances in which armor is stripped

---

[24] Noting the absurdity of this reading, the Hellenistic scholar and editor Aristarchus changed the singular to the dual form (*stenakhonte*), thereby having the two bearers of the corpse do the groaning rather than the corpse itself. It is a testament to the faithfulness of the textual tradition that the vulgate was not led astray by Aristarchus's attractive emendation.

from the corpse of a dead hero, not for these very unusual circumstances in which the armor has been knocked off the body of a living hero.

These three dictional inconcinnities go beyond the tolerable extension of ornamental epithets and stock formulaic phrases to inappropriate contexts; they are blunders, even by the aesthetic standards of oral poetry. For our present purposes, such blunders serve as small but significant clues that point to oral-dictation as the mode of creation for the archetypes of our epics. It appears from such passages as these that each of our epic texts is a record of a composition-in-performance by a singer who had no opportunity and no desire to summon back his words or revise them — and, perhaps more surprising, neither did hundreds of years of later editors. As Janko says of the first passage: "Neither Homer nor his putative editor makes any use of the technology of writing to correct [this contradiction]. How remarkable that it is still in our text!"[25] And of the second passage: "Such blunders decisively support Lord's view that the *Iliad* is an oral-dictated text; had Homer used writing to better his poem, he would surely have erased this error."[26]

Small Factual Errors: It is natural, perhaps even inevitable, that small factual errors should occur over the course of epics the size of the *Iliad* and *Odyssey* (115,477 and 87,765 words respectively), especially since they contain such a great quantity of personal and place names (slightly under 1000 and slightly under 500 respectively). These errors are not serious in the context of the larger narratives, and they probably went unnoticed by Homer's listening audience. But, with regard to our present concern, they still lend support to the model of a one-time oral-dictation of an epic composition-in-performance that was transmitted with remarkable faithfulness thereafter in its textual avatars.

1) The Trojan soldier Melanippos, perhaps the most resilient of all Homeric heroes, is killed three times over a nine-book stretch of narrative: first by Teukros (*Il.* 8.273-7), then by Antilochos (*Il.* 15.572-84), and finally by Patroclus (*Il.* 16.692-7).

---

[25] Janko, "Homeric Poems," 8.

[26] Janko, *Commentary* on 13.419-23. On the implications of such contradictions for the composition and transmission of our texts, see Janko, "Iliad and its Editors," and "Homeric Poems." Of course, where some find in these passages dictional and narrative inconcinnities attributable to the pressures of oral composition-in-performance, others find clever and sophisticated devices attributable to poetic virtuosity and artistic genius; see G. Nagy, "Irreversible Mistakes."

2) Pylaemenes, leader of the Paphlagonians (*Il.* 2.851-5), is killed by Menelaus in Book 5 of the *Iliad* (*Il.* 5.576-9), but eight books later, though tearful and in mourning, he is still vigorous enough to convey his slain son's body off the battlefield (*Il.* 13.643-59).

3) Schedios, one of the leaders of the Phocians, called son of Iphitos in Book 2 (*Il.* 2.517-26), is killed by Hector in Book 15, where he is called the son of Perimedes (*Il.* 15.515-16), and then he is killed again by Hector, in much more graphic detail, two books later (*Il.* 17.304-11).

Larger Narrative Anomalies: Again, it is natural, though perhaps not entirely inevitable, that over the course of oral performances of epics the size of the *Iliad* and *Odyssey*, which, moreover, draw upon many and sometimes disparate traditions, a number of larger narrative anomalies should occur.

1) In his conversation with Penelope at *Od.* 17.150-65 the prophet Theoklymenos assures her that Odysseus has already returned to Ithaca and is plotting destruction for the suitors. He recalls the omen of the bird that he had earlier observed, and his prophetic interpretation to Telemachus, as he sat on the well-timbered ship (160-1). But two books earlier, when the omen actually occurred, the entire crew, including Theoklymenos and Telemachus, were explicitly said to have already disembarked and to have gathered on the shore (15.495-538). It is not surprising to find narrative inconsistencies of this sort in a long orally performed epic; they are a feature of most truly oral traditions. It is a rather pleasant surprise, though, to find that during the textual transmission of the *Iliad* and *Odyssey* the original form was faithfully retained in spite of what were perceived even in antiquity as blemishes. The scholia to this passage report that these verses – in some cases 17.150-65, in other cases just 17.160-1 – were athetized in many of the texts available to the Hellenistic editors (i.e., not omitted, but simply marked with an obelus, a horizontal stroke, to express some doubt about authorship), apparently because of this narrative inconsistency.

2) Having met up with each other in Eumaeus's hut in Ithaca Odysseus and Telemachus plan together the slaughter of their enemies (*Od.* 16.186- 321). In the face of daunting odds, Odysseus devises an elaborate plan to overcome the 108 suitors: after they are both in the palace, he will at the appropriate moment nod to his son, who is then to gather up all the weapons that are lying about the hall and place them in a lofty chamber; if the suitors ask what he is doing, he is to claim that he is removing the

weapons from the smoke of the fire, which is befouling them, and that, moreover, their removal will prevent the suitors, drunk with wine, from using them in the event of a quarrel; further, Telemachus is to leave two swords and two spears and a pair of oxhide shields in the hall for himself and his father (16.281-98). It comes as somewhat of a disappointment that this well-devised and elaborate plan is abandoned with no comment three books later (19.1-46): at Odysseus's initiative both father and son remove the weapons together, with the help of Pallas Athena; there is no surreptitious nod; the false explanation for the removal of the arms is directed at the nurse Eurycleia rather than the suitors; and no mention is made of retaining a pair of arms for father and son — an oversight that challenges them sorely in the initial stages of the combat to follow (22.100-25).[27] It appears that here the singer was steering the narrative in one direction, but then he changed his mind in the course of his performance. For our present purposes it is sufficient to note that the singer did not take the initiative, and probably did not have the opportunity, to go back and correct the anomaly. Nor did the discomfort of later editors with this anomaly, as attested by the athetesis by Zenodotus of 16.281-98 and the asterisks attached by Aristarchus to 19.4-12 (to signal that these verses were wrongly repeated elsewhere), lead to the expulsion of any of these verses from the textual tradition. Again, this is a testament to the model of an oral-dictated text that was subsequently copied and transmitted faithfully in textual form.

3) The notorious duals at *Il.* 9.165-98 should perhaps be included in this category. Nestor nominates the following as envoys to Achilles: first, Phoenix, as leader, and then Ajax and Odysseus, and, finally, of the heralds, Odios and Eurybates. The situation is very clear: three envoys and two heralds. But as soon as they are on their way they are described between verses 182 and 198 with no fewer than ten grammatical forms — finite verbs, participles, and demonstrative pronouns — that are in the dual number. Almost every possible combination of pairs has been suggested to account for these duals: the two separate groups of envoys and heralds; the

---

[27] I still find the most articulate summary of the problems in these passages to be that of Woodhouse, *Composition of Homer's Odyssey*, 158-68, though it is somewhat dated by its lack of awareness of oral theory.

two heralds; Odysseus and Ajax, Phoenix and Ajax.[28] But none of these pairs makes sense in the story as we have it in our inherited text. It is apparent that in a different version of the story known to Homer there really were only two envoys, and that the poet has here simply lost track of what version he was telling. That these clearly inorganic duals occur in our text at all, and that they have, moreover, been retained through generations of textual transmission, is strong support for oral-dictation followed by faithful transmission of the resulting text.

The examples of inconcinnities in Homer marshalled above could be multiplied manyfold in each of the four categories.[29] Further, one may find useful comparanda of all these categories of inconcinnities, from the smallest to the largest, in many other demonstrably orally composed narratives; for they are common, perhaps necessary, features of oral composition-in-performance.

For example, one may compare with great benefit Homer's *Odyssey* and Salij Ugljanin's *Captivity of Đjulić Ibrahim*, a Serbo-Croatian Return Tale that resembles the *Odyssey* in many of its themes and details:[30] a seemingly long-dead hero attempts to return home from a military mission but confronts many obstacles to his return; meanwhile, his wife is on the verge of remarrying; he finally arrives home in disguise and goes about the task of testing his servants, friends, family members, and wife; he is identified by means of a token; the tale ends in a "remarriage," followed by the departure of the hero to fulfill an oath. I would encourage all students of Homer, and of comparative oral traditions in general, to consider, in addition to these thematic similarities, the many vestiges of orality that these two epic texts have in common: namely, the inconcinnities that they share at all the various levels discussed above. In the case of Ugljanin's *Captivity of Đjulić Ibrahim*, the causes of these inconcinnities are demonstrable; they arise from the exigencies of live oral performance: on the one hand, the

---

[28] For a concise synopsis and evaluation of the various possibilities that have been proposed, see Hainsworth, *Commentary* on 9.182.

[29] On formulary illogicalities, see Combellack, "Formulary Illogicalities"; on factual and narrative anomalies, see J. Scott, *Unity of Homer*, 137-71; Bowra, "Composition," 44-60; and G.S. Kirk, *Songs of Homer*, 211-52.

[30] Parry Collection number 674, sung and recorded on 24 November 1934, at Novi Pazar; transcribed in Parry and Lord, *Serbocroatian Heroic Songs*, 2:55-74; translated, with notes, in Parry and Lord, *Serbocroatian Heroic Songs*, 1:90-113, 339-58.

pressure on the singer to extemporize as he, at least at some level, composes during the very act of performance, and, on the other hand, the inability of the singer to retract or correct his song once it has left his mouth. It follows by way of analogy that the same causes are probably responsible for the inconcinnities embedded in our texts of Homer's *Iliad* and *Odyssey*.

Like the Homeric inconcinnities listed above, the ones in this Serbo-Croatian return song span a wide range: unfinished or metrically faulty verses; formulaic phrases that are blatantly inappropriate to the context; factual blunders, especially involving names and characters; and larger narrative anomalies. It is this last category that provides us with a most instructive comparandum to Homer:

On his return home from prison the hero Đulić confronts the warrior Milutin, who refuses to allow him to pass. Đulić promptly cuts off Milutin's head, strips him of his clothes and arms, and puts them on himself; he then continues on his journey (verses 456-508). But 250 verses later (after verse 763) the singer Salih pauses in his performance, realizing that he has made an error: if Đulić is wearing Milutin's clothes and arms, those at his home will not recognize him as a prisoner who has recently escaped. Parry's assistant Nikola Vujnović asks Salih to go back and start his song again from the point of the combat with Milutin; Salih does this, correcting his error by stating emphatically that although Đulić killed Milutin, he did *not* strip him of his clothes and arms (verse 810).[31]

We return now to Homer, who, unlike Salih, was apparently never given the opportunity to go back and tidy up the loose ends of his narrative of Theoklymenos's omen in *Od.* 17, or of Odysseus's elaborate plan to slaughter the suitors in *Od.* 16, or of the embassy to Achilles in *Il.* 9, and so on. Comparative analysis allows us to say with more confidence than ever that, in the case of the Homeric epics, the fact that such inconcinnities were recorded in textual form in the first place points to initial textualizations by means of oral-dictation, and, further, that the fact that these

---

[31] For examples of similar narrative "slips" on the part of extemporaneously composing Serbo-Croatian singers, see Lord, "Homer and Huso II," and *Singer of Tales*, 94-5; Gunn, "Narrative Inconsistency"; Foley, *Traditional Oral Epic*, 47-8, 359-61, 373-7. If left to their own devices, the singers will often begin to set the narrative anomaly straight in as unobtrusive a way as possible as soon as they recognize it. On the other hand, sometimes a singer will not perceive the anomaly and will continue to repeat it in subsequent performances.

inconcinnities were retained in the subsequent copies of these texts through hundreds of years of transmission attests to the faithfulness of the textual tradition to the original archetypes.

To summarize the results of our observations of the first two features: we appear to have in our inherited texts of the *Iliad* and *Odyssey*, on the one hand, unified narratives, intended to be performed as units, and within a limited time frame, and, on the other hand, narratives that have not been thoroughly proofread, reworked, and corrected. The oral-dictation model — i.e., that we have captured in our inherited texts the very words of an epic composition-in-performance — seems to me to account for these features much more convincingly than the evolutionary model, according to which our texts are the result of a process of reconstitution and accretion over many generations by many mouths and hands.

III. The Absence of Multiple Versions of the *Iliad* and *Odyssey*

The evolutionary model, hypothetical in the case of the Homeric epics, has been applied appropriately and productively to the presumed — and in some cases demonstrable — histories of several other oral epic traditions that were eventually fixed in textual forms: the Sumerian and Akkadian versions of the *Epic of Gilgamesh*, the Sanskrit *Mahabharata* and *Ramayana*, the Persian *Shahnama*, the Spanish *Cantar de Mio Cid*, the French *Chanson de Roland*, the German *Nibelungenlied*, the South Slavic Return Song, and the medieval Greek epic *Digenis Akritis*. It will be instructive, then, to compare the features of the surviving texts of these other epic traditions with those of the Homeric tradition in order to determine if the (hypothetically) similar circumstances during the composition and transmission of these documents have produced similar outcomes.

To anticipate, we will find that in these other epic traditions there have survived multiple versions that are substantially different from one another, not only in small matters of diction and detail, but also in their essential poetic forms, their larger themes and narrative patterns, their overarching plot structures, and even their total lengths. These multiple versions all have equal claim to authenticity; hence, the search for an archetype is meaningless. In the case of the *Iliad* and *Odyssey*, however, multiple versions have not developed. We have only one version of the *Iliad* and one of the *Odyssey*, with the same characters, the same story, and even the same sequence of episodes — all of which are, moreover, told in a very uniform meter, dialect, diction, and style throughout. There is no evidence that there ever existed any texts of Homer's *Iliad* without a Patroclus, or of Homer's *Odyssey* without a Telemachus. Nor is there any evidence of texts of the *Iliad* and *Odyssey* that were half the size, or twice the size, of our inherited texts.[32] It seems likely, then, that, unlike these other epic traditions, our *Iliad* and *Odyssey* each go back to a single archetype that was fixed in writing and whose text did not thereafter suffer substantial editorial tampering.[33] This is the essence of my third argument — a comparative one — in favor of the oral-dictation model. Here follows an evaluation of the textual outcome of the Homeric tradition in the light of the textual outcomes of three other epic traditions that had their roots in oral performance.

The South Slavic Return Song *The Captivity of Djulić Ibrahim*: The field work of Parry and Lord among the singers of Yugoslavia, especially the Muslim epic singers, and the resulting corpus of dictated texts and recordings, along with their field notes, have provided a laboratory-like testing ground for comparison with Homer as to the manner of composition and transmission of orally performed and orally disseminated songs.[34]

Parry and Lord concluded, and field work since confirms, that even a single singer, when asked to repeat a song that he has only just heard, will introduce significant changes in his own performance. While the underlying story remains the same, the words and formulaic phrases will be considerably different: there will be details, descriptions, and ornamentation added or omitted, there will be changes in the action, in the order of appearance of characters, in the use and length of themes, and there will sometimes be considerable variation in the length of the whole song. In perhaps the most famous example of epic expansion, the singer Avdo Medjedović, when asked to perform the song about Bećiragić Meho just

---

[32] This is not to deny, of course, that there once existed tales, and even oral epic performances, of the events surrounding the Trojan War that were substantially different from the two versions that we have inherited — ones that may have been much shorter, for example, or ones in which Patroclus played no part, or in which Telemachus played a less important role.

[33] On the contrast between the basic fixity of the Homeric texts and the relative fluidity of some of these other epic traditions, see Merkelbach, "Die pisistratische Redaktion," 34-53; Lord, *Singer of Tales*, 198-221; S. West, *Commentary*, 36; Janko, "*Iliad* and its Editors," 330-1, *Commentary*, 29, and "Homeric Poems," 11-12; and Finkelberg, "Problem of Multiformity."

[34] Parry and Lord, *Serbocroatian Heroic Songs*; Lord, *Singer of Tales*.

performed by Mumin Vlahovljak, expanded it in his performance from 2294 to 6313 verses.[35] This is but one extreme example of what happens regularly in the South Slavic oral traditions.[36]

Even separate performances within a short time frame by the same singer of "the same song," while retaining the general outline of the story, produce large discrepancies at every level: the wording and formulaic phrases are very unstable; details of names and places are variable; there is considerable elaboration, substitution, and change in the sequences of themes; the endings of the tales are often different; the overall length of the songs may vary considerably (a one hundred percent increase, or a fifty percent decrease, is not unusual). One may compare, for example, the three versions of *The Captivity of Djulić Ibrahim*, sung, recited, and dictated, by the same singer, Salih Ugljanin, within a five-day period in November of 1934.[37] The discrepancies at every level mentioned above are substantial, including the overall length: 1811, 689, and 1480 verses respectively. And all these changes are generated by a single singer performing "the same song" within a narrow time frame.

When the time period is extended to months and years the discrepancies are greater; and when the song is passed from singer to singer through the generations, with the attendant modernization of diction, details, characters, and events, the discrepancies are greater still. When the song travels throughout a district, or even the entire country, over space and time, when it is performed to various audiences under various circumstances, when it is written down, whether in the form of a dictated text carefully recorded by a professional scholar or in an inexpensive song book or pamphlet that is later used by illiterate, semi-literate, and fully literate singers to learn new songs, when these written versions suffer editorial activity, or at least some "polishing up" and "correcting," and when the oral and written versions survive side by side, interacting with one another in a

---

[35] Texts 12468 and 12471 in the Parry Collection; cf. Lord, *Singer of Tales*, 102-5, 223-34.

[36] Parry's and Lord's predecessor, Matija Murko, "Singers and their Epic Songs," 117, cites the example of a singer from Croatia who, in singing "the same songs" that he had been taught by a singer in Bosnia, expanded them from 1,200 to 2,500 and from 1,500 to 4,400 verses.

[37] Numbers 4, 5, and 6 in *Serbocroatian Heroic Songs* (674, 659, and 667 in the Parry Collection); cf. Parry and Lord, *Serbocroatian Heroic Songs*, 1:55-98, 342-52, and 2:90-113, 339-58.

complex web of influence – in short, when an epic tradition experiences precisely that scenario painted by proponents of the evolutionary model – are we surprised to find the types of discrepancies listed above magnified exponentially?[38]

As a witness to this evolution, one need only compare the multiple versions of the South Slavic Return Song – the same song as *The Captivity of Đjulić Ibrahim* mentioned above – that were recorded by Parry and Lord and catalogued in *Serbocroatian Heroic Songs*: nineteen different Moslem versions, sung, recited, or dictated between 1934 and 1951 by fifteen different singers from all over Yugoslavia.[39] The complex evolutionary process of composition and transmission has resulted in so many multiforms, with so many and substantial discrepancies (even in the name of the central hero!), that it is utterly futile to attempt to reconstruct an original version. In this protean nebula there exists no archetype.

In sum, in a process of composition and transmission not unlike the one hypothesized for Homer by proponents of the evolutionary model, the outcome is not unexpected: substantially different multiforms, none of which can be regarded as the original, but which are rather all equally authentic with regard to the tradition. How utterly different from the outcome of the Homeric epic tradition, as attested by our surviving manuscripts – manuscripts whose slight verbal discrepancies are dwarfed by comparison with what we witness in the South Slavic songs.

Digenis Akritis: The Greek epic of the tenth-century Byzantine hero Digenis Akritis retains even in its relatively late manuscripts many of the vestiges of orality, and there is little doubt but that the main story upon which the epic is based was in its earlier forms orally composed and per-

---

[38] For first-person accounts of the process of transmission of South Slavic epic songs, see Murko, "Singers and their Epic Songs," 115-19, 124-5; Parry and Lord, *Serbocroatian Heroic Songs* 1, esp. 11-15; Lord, *Singer of Tales*, 105-23, 235-65.

[39] Numbers 674, 659, 667, 277b, 281, 683, and 665 in the Parry Collection appear in Parry and Lord, *Serbocroatian Heroic Songs*, vols. 2 and 1 as numbers 4, 5, 6, 20, 21, 28, and 32; the other twelve versions in the Parry Collection are 275a, 291b, 6597, 6618, 6633, 6580, 1280a, 2099, 1905, 1920, L 11, and L 198. In addition, one may usefully compare the ten Christian versions of the song, in which Janković Stojan substitutes as the hero (numbers 2, 199b, 226, 274, 430, 1950, 4272, 6784, L 51, and L 102 in the Parry Collection). More avatars of the Return Song can be found in Lord, *Singer of Tales*, 242-65.

formed.[40] Over the course of several generations various episodes, both oral and written, were added to the main story; these versions with various accretions were then altered, refined, and corrected by scribes who copied the earliest written versions. The result of this evolutionary process is that the *Digenis Akritis* has survived in five Greek poetic versions (and one Greek prose version, as well as two Slavonic versions), dating from the thirteenth to the seventeenth century, that are of various lengths, in various poetic forms, in various dialects, and in which, while the core of the story remains essentially the same, there are considerable differences in the telling of the tale: in language and style, in the details of names and places, and even in the selection and arrangement of episodes. These five versions are textually fossilized in the following manuscripts: Grottaferrata, consisting of 3749 metrical verses, and divided into eight books; Athens, consisting of 4778 metrical and some rhymed verses, and divided into ten books; Trebizond, consisting of 3182 metrical verses, and divided into ten books; Escorial, consisting of 1867 verses, some shorter than normal, and some reduced to prose, with no book divisions; and Oxford, consisting of 3094 rhymed verses, and divided into eight books.[41]

Given the circumstances of this manuscript tradition it is of course impossible to reconstruct an archetype; and it would be fruitless to attempt such a reconstruction, since what we have in our manuscripts are the remnants of various versions first performed by various singers, then written down much later by various hands, and finally copied and edited by various scribes. There never existed a single archetype of *Digenis Akritis* – only a commonly shared tale of the life and exploits of Digenis Akritis that was orally performed and disseminated over the course of several generations. Again, this describes in essence the scenario that has been visualized for the *Iliad* and *Odyssey* by proponents of the evolutionary model. But while the outcome in the manuscript tradition of *Digenis Akritis* is quite predictable, it is utterly different from what we find in the case of the Homeric manuscripts.

---

[40] On the vestiges of orality to be found in the manuscripts of the *Digenis Akritis*, see Lord, *Singer of Tales*, 207-20; on the oral roots of the tradition as a whole, see Beaton, "Was *Digenes Akrites* an Oral Poem?"

[41] For an edition that includes all the manuscripts, see Kalonaros, *Basileios Digenes Akritas*. For details of the relationship among the various manuscripts, see Grégoire, *Digenis Akritas*, esp. the stemma on 301. For the different presentations of the story, see Mavrogordato, *Digenes Akrites*, xi-lxxxiv, 258-9.

Chanson de Roland: The French epic of the eighth-century hero Roland, Lord of the Breton Marches, also has its roots in oral tradition – the public performance of a *chanson de geste* by a *jongleur* to the musical accompaniment of a stringed instrument called a *vielle*. But several hundred years of evolution in language and poetic form, and in the content and larger structure of the narrative, as the epic developed through a rich cross-fertilization of both oral and written forms, has resulted in a group of written versions that are substantially different from one another. The twelfth-century Oxford manuscript, of 3998 largely decasyllabic assonanced verses, includes linguistic features from the Anglo-Norman dialect of French spoken in England after the Norman Conquest. The fourteenth-century Venice IV manuscript is the closest in form to the Oxford, being the only other version with assonanced verses, but it is much longer – 6012 verses – and it is in a Franco-Italian hybrid dialect. The Venice VII and Châteauroux manuscripts, both from the late thirteenth century, appear to have a close relationship to each other; they are even longer than Venice IV (8880 and 8330 verses respectively), and they are in rhymed rather than assonanced verses. The fragmentary Paris (late thirteenth century), Lyon (fourteenth century), and Cambridge (fifteenth century) manuscripts, along with the 347 verses of the Lorraine fragments and 108 verses of miscellaneous fragments, appear to have a close relationship to one another; they too are in rhymed verses. There also survive early versions of the *Chanson de Roland* translated into Middle High German, Old Norse, Welsh, Dutch, and Middle English.[42]

Although all these manuscripts share the same basic narrative content, there are substantial differences in dialect (both between those that are earlier and later – reflecting an evolution in the poetic language that mirrors the evolution in the vernacular – and between those from different regions), wording, formulaic phrases, poetic style and form (assonance versus rhyme), use of themes, degree of ornamentation, inclusion or omission of verses, scenes, and even entire episodes, and, consequently, in overall length. These are not simply variant manuscripts of a common textual ar-

---

[42] For an edition that includes all the manuscripts, with an attempt to draw concordances in the verses, see Mortier, *Textes de la Chanson de Roland*; for a concise description of each manuscript, with a sample passage for comparison from each, see Bédier, *La Chanson de Roland*, 65-81. On the vestiges of orality to be found in the manuscripts, see Lord, *Singer of Tales*, 202-6. For a comprehensive treatment of the poem's orality, see Duggan, *Song of Roland*.

chetype; they are, rather, substantially different versions of a common epic narrative.

Once again we observe how slight are the discrepancies in our Homeric texts in contrast to those in the manuscripts of a tradition that has undergone a process of composition and transmission not unlike the one articulated by proponents of the evolutionary model. And once again I repeat that the unique outcome that we observe in the Homeric manuscript tradition points to an explanation other than that offered by the evolutionary model.

The evidence of many other epic traditions — e.g., the *Epic of Gilgamesh*, the *Mahabharata* and *Ramayana*, the *Shahnama*, the *Cantar de Mio Cid*, the *Nibelungenlied* — could be marshaled to demonstrate the same connection: that the evolutionary model of composition and transmission leads necessarily to multiple versions, i.e., multiforms, in the manuscript tradition. But I limit my extended comments to these three and turn our attention now back to the Homeric texts with a view to considering the outcome of its manuscript tradition in the light of these comparanda.

The *Iliad* and *Odyssey*: When compared with these other epic traditions, the textual situation of the Homeric epics distinguishes itself as something unique. To repeat: we have only one version of the *Iliad* and one of the *Odyssey*, with the same characters, the same story, and even the same sequence of episodes — all of which are, moreover, told in a very uniform meter, dialect, diction, and style throughout. Multiple versions, i.e., multiforms, have not developed. It follows, therefore, that, unlike these other epic traditions, our *Iliad* and *Odyssey* each go back to a single archetype that was fixed in writing and whose text did not thereafter suffer substantial editorial revision.

The proponents of the evolutionary model, in their attempt to subsume the Homeric epics under the same rubric as these other epic traditions, have marshaled as evidence the many variants that have occurred, or are reported to have occurred, in the Homeric texts during the long history of their transmission. Because these variants in the Homeric manuscripts, and in the reports of the readings of no longer extant manuscripts, are the strongest and most central evidence in support of the evolutionary model, we will need to consider them in some detail.

It is true that variants occur in quotations of "Homer" by later classical authors of the fifth and (mostly) fourth centuries, in the reports of the third- and second-century Alexandrian scholars about what they read in earlier editions of Homer, in the readings of the forty or so surviving remnants of Homeric texts on papyri from the early Ptolemaic period (third–second century B.C.E.), and, though to a much lesser degree, in the nine hundred or so surviving manuscripts of the post-Aristarchean "vulgate" (i.e., after ca. 150 B.C.E.). But from the perspective of the monumental epics as a whole these variants are comparatively trivial and do not provide the evidence for substantially different versions of the Homeric texts that the evolutionary model expects and indeed requires.

Quotations of Homer: First-hand quotations of "Homeric" verses by later classical authors include: from the fifth century, Herodotus (11 verses), Thucydides (1), Aristophanes (7?), and Hippocrates (1); and from the fourth century, Xenophon (14), Plato (209), Aeschines (32), Aristotle (98), and Lycurgus (6).[43] Our first inclination may be to focus attention on the variations between these quotations and our inherited texts, but we do so at the expense of losing sight of the overwhelming similarities. In contrast to the substantial differences in diction, dialect, poetic form, style, and so on that we have observed in the manuscripts of other epic traditions, it is remarkable, for example, that all eleven verses of Homer quoted by Herodotus, our earliest author to quote explicitly a full verse of Homer, agree with the vulgate Homeric text that we have inherited, line for line, word for word, particle for particle (with the exception of Herodotus's quotation of *Od.* 4.85, where, in agreement with the minority over the majority of Homeric manuscripts, he writes the adverb *hothi* instead of *hina*). The same can be said of the verse quoted by Thucydides (although he omits a prosodically necessary movable-nu), the four full verses quoted by Aristophanes that are found in our Homeric texts, and all twelve full verses quoted by Xenophon (except that *deur' age dē* replaces *deur' ag' iōn* of our inherited text). Even of the quotations of Homer by Aeschines, which are often presented as the strongest evidence for multiple versions, two-thirds are verbatim in every detail, and a few more show only slight variations. (I will consider the more substantial variations below.) Likewise, the vast majority of Plato's and Aristotle's many quotations of Homer are identical in every detail to the readings of our inherited texts. In short,

---

[43] Ludwich, *Die Homervulgata*, 71–132, who collects the Homeric quotations down to 300 B.C.E., counts a total of 480 quoted verses. Many of the quotations that contain variants are conveniently presented by T. Allen, *Origins and the Transmission*, 249–70, and much more exhaustively by van der Valk, *Textual Criticism*, 278–85, and *Text and Scholia*, 264–369.

Homer's Iliad *and* Odyssey

there is an astonishing amount of verbatim coincidence between the ancient quotations of Homer and our inherited texts of Homer. This evidence points to the likelihood that these ancient authors had at their disposal texts of the *Iliad* and *Odyssey* that were very much like our own.

Nonetheless, we must also give full consideration to those ancient quotations of Homer that do not coincide so closely with our inherited texts.

Most of these discrepancies are quite trivial: the omission or addition of a movable-nu (Thucydides' *polléisi* for *polléisin*; Plato's *ken* for *ke*); spelling differences (Aeschines' *geinomenon* for *gignomenon*); slight differences in verbal forms (Lycurgus's *hikôntai* for *oikhôntai*; Plato's *helkein* for *helkemen*; Aristotle's *anôgen* for *anôgei*); slight differences in nominal forms (Plato's *ep' oudeos* for *ep' oudei*; *andrôn* for *aneros*); the substitution of a metrically equivalent word (Herodotus's *hothi* for *hina*, and conversely, Aristotle's *hina* for *hothi*; Aeschines' *all'* for *nun*; Plato's *astu* for *teikhos*); the inversion of a pair of words (Lycurgus's *klêros kai oikos* for *oikos kai klêros*); the substitution of a metrically equivalent phrase (Xenophon's *deur' age dê* for *deur' ag' iôn*; Lycurgus's *nêpia tekna* for *paides opissô*; Plato's *ai ai egôn* for *ô moi egôn*; *hôs teleesthai oïô* for *hôs tetelesmenon estai*; Aristotle's *autar epei* for *all' hote dê*); the substitution of a metrically equivalent formulaic verse (Aeschines' *tên d' aute proseeipe podarkês dios Akhilleus* for *tên de meg' okhthêsas prosephê podas ôkus Akhilleus*).

But some discrepancies are more substantial: sometimes verses are attributed by the ancients to "Homer" that are completely lacking anywhere in our inherited texts of the *Iliad* and *Odyssey*; sometimes a quotation of a long passage will lack a verse, or verses, that are present in our texts of the *Iliad* and *Odyssey*; on the other hand sometimes a quotation of a long passage will contain a verse, or verses, that are absent from that passage in our texts of the *Iliad* and *Odyssey*; sometimes a verse attributed to Homer will be a combination of two half-verses in our texts of the *Iliad* and *Odyssey*; sometimes verses in a quotation of a long passage will be displaced; and sometimes verses will in some other way be distorted. I offer the following two observations:

1) Many, perhaps most, of these more substantial discrepancies can be explained in other ways than by assuming an evolutionary model whereby many different versions of the *Iliad* and *Odyssey* were circulating among these ancient authors. Quotations attributed by these ancient authors to "Homer" that are not found in our inherited versions of the *Iliad* and *Od-*

yssey may have been drawn from the hoard of other epic verse known to them at the time but no longer available to us. "Homer" meant much more to the ancients than the *Iliad* and *Odyssey*; for example, the *Thebaid* and *Epigonoi*, some of the epics of the Cycle (*Cypria, Little Iliad, Returns*), the *Certamen*, the *Margites*, and the "*Homeric*" *Hymns*, were all at one time attributed to "Homer." Moreover, we must keep in mind that since the ancients usually quoted from memory rather than from a written text, and since the *ipsissima verba* were not their primary concern, they are prone to loose rendering, embellishment, and, especially, to adaptation to their immediate poetic, rhetorical, philosophical, or scientific purposes. The omission of verses within a long passage could be unintentional, i.e., due to faulty memory, or it could be intentional, i.e., simply the result of the author's decision to pick out the most pertinent verses in order to make a point. The verses that are omitted tend to be ornamental and inorganic, and are therefore dispensed with, whether deliberately or not, without any perceptible damage to the integrity of the passage. The same holds true for verses that are added in a quotation of a long passage. Since these verses are mostly ornamental and highly formulaic, they could easily have been assembled from other Homeric passages, or, more rarely, from other epic verse. Likewise, the combination, displacement, and distortion of verses in quotations of Homer may sometimes be due to a faulty memory, and sometimes to the intent of the author, as when Aristophanes weaves a tapestry of Homeric phrases, when Plato transforms a Homeric speech into indirect discourse, or when Aristotle molds Homeric verse into a prose paraphrase.

2) Even if we were to assume that all the discrepancies in the ancient quotations stemmed from real differences in the manuscripts (and performances) of the Homeric texts that were available to these authors, the sum total of these discrepancies does not approach the degree of difference we have just observed in the manuscripts of other epic traditions. In the case of Homer we may speak of variants of a text, but we should not speak of multiple versions and multiforms. Even as early as the Classical period the Homeric tradition appears much more homogeneous than the proponents of the evolutionary model would have us believe.

Early Editions of Homer: We turn now to the early editions of Homer, none of which has survived, of course, but about some of whose readings we have the testimony, as reported in the Homeric scholia, of the third- and second-century B.C.E. Alexandrian scholars. The Alexandrians

Homer's Iliad *and* Odyssey

differentiated among scholarly editions, city editions, and *Koine* editions, a multiplicity that is marshaled by proponents of the evolutionary model as strong evidence for the continued multiformity, even fluidity, of the Homeric epic tradition into the Hellenistic period. Foley, as noted above, buttresses his case for multiformity by calculating that there were at least 131 separate editions of Homer available to the Alexandrians, and by implying that there were great variations among these editions. This calculation is overstated, however, being derived by equating the total of variant *readings* reported by the Homeric scholia with the total of variant *editions*. There are in fact cited in the scholia only a handful of individual scholarly editions: in addition to those of the great Alexandrian scholars Zenodotus, Aristophanes, and Aristarchus, there are references to editions of Antimachus, the younger Euripides, Rhianus, Sosigenes, and Philemon; Aristotle and Aratus are elsewhere reported to have produced their own editions, but no mention is made of them in the Homeric scholia. There are references to only seven city editions: Marseilles, Chios, the Argolid, the Aeolid, Crete, Sinope, and Cyprus. And, finally, there are references to a *Koine* edition — or perhaps we should say *editions* — since a plural form is often used: *koinai, koinoterai, dêmôdeis, eikaioterai, phaulotera*.[44]

More important than the number, however, is the content of these editions. The individual scholarly editions may have simply comprised critical notes in the margins of a pre-existing (probably *Koine*) text, and so they should not be counted as different textual editions, much less considered multiforms, of the Homeric epics.

The city editions were probably manuscripts obtained from the places after which they were titled; but although they had different names, they do not seem to have varied greatly from one another: they often agree with one another against the vulgate, and they are often cited as a group — e.g., *hai apo tôn poleôn* — rather than individually. Moreover, their variations from the other manuscripts available to the Alexandrians are trivial: a few spelling differences, differently contracted vowel combinations, and other such slight dialectal peculiarities; variation in the choice of particles and prepositions; variation in the case of a noun, or in the tense or number of a verb; the substitution of metrically equivalent synonyms or formulaic

---

[44] The variants recorded in these early editions are clearly organized and presented in T. Allen, *Origins and the Transmission*, 271-99. A more detailed survey of the city editions may be found in Citti, "Le edizioni omeriche."

phrases; the addition of a sum total of two highly formulaic verses, one in the *Iliad* and one in the *Odyssey*, and the omission of a sum total of twenty-three verses — enough to raise one's eyebrows, to be sure, but not enough to justify regarding these as separate and different versions, especially when the ornamental (hence readily dispensable) nature of the omitted verses is considered (a three-verse lion simile; an eleven-verse catalogue of Nereids; a six-verse messenger type-scene; plus three more verses).[45]

As for the *Koine* edition(s), it may simply have been the edition current in Athens; how else can we account for the absence of any mention of an Athenian edition in the Homeric scholia, given that they regularly cite editions from places such as Marseilles, Crete, and Cyprus that played much less significant roles than Athens in the transmission of the Homeric texts? The *Koine* edition(s), once again, differs from the other manuscripts available to the Alexandrians in only trivial matters: spelling, choice of particles, neglect or observation of digamma, case of a single noun, number of a single verb, comparative instead of superlative adjectival form, transposition of two words, substitution of a metrically equivalent synonym, and so forth.

In sum, the editions of Homer available during the Alexandrian period reveal a textual tradition that is much more homogeneous than the evolutionary model will comfortably allow.

Early Papyri: Finally, we turn to the evidence of actual surviving Homeric texts, fragmentary though they be, on scraps of papyri.[46] The variants in the forty or so remnants of Homeric texts on papyri surviving from the early Ptolemaic period (third–second century B.C.E.) — the so-called "wild" or "eccentric" papyri — are for the most part quite trivial: variations in the treatment of iota adscript and movable-nu, spelling, choice of particles and prepositions; (dis)regard for hiatus; slight differences in verbal or nominal inflectional forms; some dialectal variations; some transposition

---

[45] To the two additional verses of the city editions we may now perhaps add four more: a recently edited fragment of a second-century C.E. commentary on *Iliad* 19 includes a lacunose block of five verses (at *Il.* 19.351) — four of which are not transmitted by the vulgate — that are apparently attributed by this commentary to the city edition from Marseilles; see Haslam, "Papyrus #4452," esp. 39-40. But these verses too are highly formulaic and ornamental.

[46] The Ptolemaic papyri are usefully surveyed in S. West, *Ptolemaic Papyri*. Since this publication appeared, a few more papyri have surfaced, though they are not very extensive.

of words and phrases; occasional substitutions of metrically equivalent formulaic phrases; and sometimes missing or, more often, additional verses. These additional verses — the feature that causes Homerists the most consternation — are usually flaccid and inorganic; they are almost always imitative rather than innovative, being simply verses and combinations of half-verses that recur elsewhere in Homer, or in Hesiod or the *Hymns*, rather than new inventions — i.e., they appear to be what textual critics call "concordance interpolations." They do not introduce new characters, they do not change the plot, and they do not alter the sequence of episodes; in short, they do not significantly affect the narrative.

The sum total of the textual variants in the Ptolemaic papyri does not by any measure offer sufficient evidence to support an evolutionary model whereby a multiplicity of versions of the *Iliad* and *Odyssey* continued to retain their fluidity as living, changing, performative traditions well into the Classical and Hellenistic periods. In fact they are not so dissimilar in quality (though perhaps more numerous in quantity) from the types of textual variants found in the later Roman and medieval manuscripts of Homer, or even in the manuscript traditions of other ancient authors such as Euripides. A particularly useful analogue may be found in the textual variants — including concordance interpolations — of the manuscripts of the New Testament, which is the only ancient work to have generated more extant manuscripts than Homer.

Later Papyri: The variants found in the nine hundred or so papyrus manuscripts that have survived from the period between ca. 150 B.C.E. and the seventh century C.E. need not be considered here, since they are variants, strictly textual in nature, of an Aristarchean "vulgate," which had attained a relatively stable form, and thereby a status that ushered in the demise of competing texts.[47] Even though this "vulgate" is based on an extremely large number of manuscripts, the text is remarkably uniform. There are several dozen concordance interpolations that have crept into the "vulgate" and still reside in many modern scholarly editions, but these

---

[47] A list of the entire corpus of Homeric papyri is accessible in electronic form on Sutton's World Wide Web page, "Homer and the Papyri." This list, which is periodically updated to accommodate the influx of new papyri, is complemented by a hypertextually linked repertoire of the textual variants presented by this body of material. There is also the electronic Leuven Database of Ancient Books. For late antiquity, an illuminating study is Fournet, "L''homérisme' à l'epoque proto-byzantine."

are easily identifiable, and, in any case, they have no relevance to the condition of the pre-Aristarchean text and its implications for a hypothetical oral-dictated or evolutionary model of composition and early transmission.[48]

In sum, the documentary evidence from the Classical and Hellenistic periods presents a picture of a Homeric text much more homogeneous than the proponents of the evolutionary model have envisioned. In any event, we can speak with some confidence about a single *Iliad* and a single *Odyssey* of Homer that enjoyed a uniformity and integrity on a scale so different from the texts of traditions like *The Captivity of Đjulić Ibrahim*, the epic of *Digenis Akritis*, the *Chanson de Roland*, etc., that we cannot but surmise that something unusual occurred in the history of the composition and transmission of these Homeric texts. I propose that this "unusual something" was oral-dictation of a composition-in-performance, followed by a remarkably faithful transmission of that oral-dictated text.

IV. The Fixation of the Homeric Epic Art-Language

And, finally, the fourth feature of the Homeric text that causes me to favor the oral-dictation model over the evolutionary model is the language: our inherited texts of the *Iliad* and *Odyssey* reveal a language that was frozen in time, a language that had previously been evolving hand in hand with the vernacular but that had in its eighth-century Ionic form become fixed. There had once existed a vibrant Mycenaean epic tradition, but our inherited texts are not Mycenaean (though there are Mycenaean words and phrases, even poetic formulaic phrases, embedded in them – e.g., *phasganon arguroêlon, depas amphikupellon, lipous' androtêta kai hêbên*); and thereafter there had existed a vibrant Aeolic epic tradition, but our inherited texts are not Aeolic (though Aeolic words and phrases abound, especially ones that provide metrically useful alternatives to the corresponding Ionic forms – e.g., *ammes* for Ionic *hêmeis* before vowels, *emmen/emmenai* for Ionic *einai, pisures* for Ionic *tessares*); and thereafter there arose a vibrant Ionic epic tradition, and this is when the linguistic evolution that had so characterized the epic tradition previously was arrested.[49] Though the ep-

---

[48] For a list of post-Aristarchean concordance interpolations, see Bolling, *External Evidence*, 3-30 and Apthorp, *Manuscript Evidence*, xvii–xix.

[49] For an engaging presentation by Parry of this theory of three dialectal phases from the viewpoint of oral poetics, see "Studies in the Epic Technique of

ics continued to be performed and enjoyed — recited orally and received aurally — the epic *Kunstsprache*, the "art-language," in which they had been for so many generations composed had become a "dead" language. The language of both the *Iliad* and *Odyssey* attained a high degree of fixation precisely at this period, substantially in the Ionic dialect, and they continued in their later transmission to retain their Ionic forms. Why this fixation? Textualization. Whether the writing down of these epics enabled them to gain an exceptional status, or whether an exceptional status caused them to be written down, it was textualization, the result of oral-dictation and transcription at a specific time and place (in the case of the *Iliad* and *Odyssey* during the eighth century in Ionia), that assured linguistic fixation.

As Janko has demonstrated in his statistical analysis of the relative frequency of the occurrences of linguistic innovations in our inherited texts of Homer, Hesiod, and the "Homeric" Hymns (neglect of initial digamma, metathesis of quantity and contraction of masculine a-stem genitive singulars and a-stem genitive plurals, contraction of o-stem genitive singulars, short o- and a-stem dative plurals, short o- and a-stem accusative plurals, oblique forms of the name *Zeus* beginning with *Z-* rather than *D-*, and the use of n-mobile to make position), all these texts were at a specific moment (though different moments in each case) frozen in time linguistically and can therefore be dated, if not absolutely, at least relatively to one another.[50] The conclusions of his study — that the *Iliad* emerges consistently as the most archaic text, followed closely by the *Odyssey*, then after a considerable gap by Hesiod's *Theogony* and *Works and Days*, and finally by the various "Homeric" Hymns — are of secondary importance here. What is of primary importance is that the texts of the *Iliad* and *Odyssey* were fixed at a specific point in time and did not continue to evolve linguistically — to create innovative forms and formulas — through the seventh, sixth, and

---

Oral Verse Making. II." From the viewpoint of legend and language, see M. West, "Rise of Greek Epic"; from the viewpoint of specific linguistic features, see Ruijgh, *L'élément achéen*, "Le mycénien et Homère," and "D'Homère aux origines proto-mycéniennes"; from the viewpoint of history and archaeology, see Sherratt, "Reading the Texts."

[50] Janko, *Homer, Hesiod*; for a synopsis of the results of his study, and a statement of its implications for the genesis of the *Iliad* and *Odyssey*, see Janko, "Iliad and its Editors," 329-30, and *Commentary*, 12-19.

fifth centuries, and thereafter, as they had in their more fluid oral forms before the eighth century.

Janko's tentative proposals about the absolute dates of composition of Homer, Hesiod, and the "Homeric" Hymns have been challenged from time to time. The rate of linguistic change in a language, after all, is not constant, and many external factors could have influenced a particular tradition's tendency toward archaism or innovation. Janko's proposals for the relative dates of Homer, Hesiod, and the "Homeric" Hymns, however, have never been seriously challenged. The implication for our present study is this: it would appear that the archetypes of our inherited texts of the Homeric epics were stabilized at a particular time, and that, further, this stabilization occurred earlier than the stabilization of Hesiod and the "Homeric" Hymns. If the Homeric epics had continued to exist as a living, changing, fluid oral tradition that was performed and reperformed throughout the Classical and even Hellenistic period, as the proponents of the evolutionary model would have us believe, then Hesiod's poems and the "Homeric" Hymns, which are linguistically more advanced, must be dated even later — and this is of course incredible.

Our present concerns require us to follow the linguistic evidence a step further chronologically. All the linguistic innovations that Janko examines had already entered the epic *Kunstsprache* by the time of the traditional date of Homer in the late eighth century; their increase in frequency thereafter allows them to be used as a mechanism to place in sequence the relative dates of Homer, Hesiod, and the "Homeric" Hymns. But in view of the claims by proponents of the evolutionary model that the Homeric epics continued to change and develop through the Classical and Hellenistic periods, it is imperative that we consider what influence the vernacular of these later periods may have had on the language of the epics. Since Athens played the central role in the performance and transmission of the Homeric epics from at least as early as the late sixth century, our examination will entail, for the most part, a search for influence from the Athenian vernacular.

And on the surface, at least, our inherited Homeric texts appear to be rife with Attic forms, thereby apparently supporting the evolutionary model. Indeed it is generally acknowledged — and quickly apparent to all Greek readers — that our inherited texts of Homer's epics contain many linguistic forms from the Attic dialect:[51] some Attic aspiration in such forms as *hadên, aphikanô, aph' hekastês* instead of the East Ionic psilotic forms *adên, apikanô,* and *ap' ekastês*;[52] rarely, an Attic *a* instead of Ionic *ê* after *e, i, r,* as in *agxêranêi* for *agxêrênêi*;[53] an Attic optative formation in contract verbs such as *philoiê* and *phoroiê* instead of the hypothetical Aeolic forms *phileiê* and *phoreiê*; the Attic forms *meizôn* and *kreissôn* for the comparative adjectives instead of Ionic *mezôn* and *kressôn*;[54] an Attic preposition in the phrase *ôs ton homoion* instead of the usual epic *es* plus accusative; Attic *entautha* and *enteuthen* for Ionic *enthauta* and *entheuten;* Attic *dekhomai* for Ionic *dekomai, oun* for *ôn, khilia* for *kheilia,* sometimes *gignomai* and *gignôskô* for *ginomai* and *ginôskô,* and, though very infrequently, *temnô* for *tamnô,* and *hêkô* for *hikô.*

The Atticisms listed thus far are not negligible; they are a very visible feature of our inherited texts. But it is illuminating to highlight one obvious but very important feature that is shared by all of them: they are all without exception metrically equivalent to their corresponding Ionic/Aeolic (i.e., "epic") forms. Hence they function in our texts simply as a veneer. They play no part in the creation of innovative formulaic constructions and, therefore, provide no evidence of a creative performance tradition in the Attic vernacular during the Classical and Hellenistic periods. On the contrary, their superficial nature shows that they are simply metrically equivalent substitutions by scribes who were modernizing the epic diction during the course of textual transmission in accordance with

---

[51] The seminal – though now much dated – treatment of Atticisms in Homer is Wackernagel, *Sprachliche Untersuchungen zu Homer,* 1–159. A more current and cautionary approach can be found in Chantraine, *Grammaire homérique,* esp. 15–16. Cf. Shipp, *Language of Homer,* esp. 10–15.

[52] But these need not necessarily be the result of Attic influence, for the West Ionic dialect of Euboea shared this feature with Attic (the same applies to *entautha* and *enteuthen* and to *dekhomai*). See Ruijgh, "D'Homère aux origines proto-mycéniennes," 49–50.

[53] Cf. *lampran* in Hesiod's *Th.* 19, 371, and *emarane* at *H.Herm* 140. It is in fact a testimony to the conservative nature of the textual tradition that there is not a lot more of this type of Atticism on the surface of our inherited texts of Homer.

[54] These are probably merely graphic Atticisms, as scribes interpreted MEZÔN and KRESSÔN written in their texts in accordance with their own vernacular.

their own Attic vernacular. This feature holds true for the Atticisms found more deeply ingrained in the epic diction as well.

For example, following the loss of intervocalic *y and *h (from *s), which resulted in many varieties of vowel juxtaposition, Attic Greek readily contracted eo > ou, ea > ê, and eô > ô, whereas Ionic retained the uncontracted forms. This produced major differences in the paradigms of third declension s-stem neuter nouns, Attic *genous*, *genê*, and *genôn* corresponding to Ionic *geneos*, *genea*, and *geneôn*. Considering the abundance of Homeric vocabulary in this single paradigm (*teikhos*, *xiphos*, *egkhos*, etc.), and the metrically useful alternatives that the Attic dialect offered, there was potential for great change to the Homeric *Kunstsprache* through the performance and transmission of epic during a productive Attic stage. But what do we find in our inherited texts? The many hundreds of incidences of these nouns appear almost exclusively in their uncontracted Ionic forms.

Of the very rare contracted genitive singular forms – *tharseus* (*Il.* 17.573), *thereus* (*Od.* 7.118), *oreus* (in some early manuscripts of *Il.* 3.10), *geneus* (in most manuscripts of *Od.* 15.533), *thambeus* (in most manuscripts of *Od.* 24.394), *Erebeus* (*Il.* 8.368; *Od.* 11.37) – all appear in almost all manuscripts as late Ionic contracted forms in *-eus* rather than as their Attic contracted counterparts *tharsous*, *therous*, *orous*, *genous*, *thambous*, *Erebous*. In any case, the uncontracted forms in *-eos*, to be pronounced with synizesis, should be restored to our modern editions.

When the meter requires the genitive plurals to be pronounced as monosyllables they are nonetheless written in our inherited texts as uncontracted Ionic forms (*stêtheôn* [*Il.* 10.95], *kerdeôn* [*Od.* 8.164], *alseôn* [*Od.* 10.350], *teukheôn* [*Od.* 11.554]), to be pronounced with synizesis, rather than as contracted Attic forms (*stêthôn*, *kerdôn*, *alsôn*, *teukhôn*).

As for the nominative/accusative plural forms, the two instances of contracted *teukhê* at verse end in the vulgate manuscripts (*Il.* 7.207, 22.322), the one instance of *algê* at verse end in a few manuscripts (*Il.* 24.7), the one instance of *belê* at mid-verse in a few manuscripts (*Il.* 15.444), and the one instance of *temenê* at mid-verse in the vulgate manuscripts (*Od.* 11.185) are simply Attic spellings of the Ionic forms *teukhea*, *algea*, *belea*, *temenea* with synizesis (cf. *sakea* and *stêthea* at mid-verse at *Il.* 4.113, 11.282, *teukhea* at verse-end at *Od.* 24.534), which should be restored to our modern editions. In short, even these few apparently Attic

Homer's Iliad *and* Odyssey

forms in our texts reflect scribal textual decisions, not bardic oral formulations.[55]

Other kinds of vowel contractions, which are admittedly quite prevalent in our inherited texts, have sometimes been attributed to Attic influence. But many of these contractions were a feature also in the late Ionic dialect (e.g., *klisiôn* beside *klisiaôn*), and the rest can easily be reduced to their metrically equivalent uncontracted Ionic forms with synizesis (e.g., *Od.* 16.372 *mêd' hêmas hupekphugoi* [only here in Homer] > Ionic *hêmeas*), or to their metrically equivalent but differently contracted Ionic forms (e.g., contracted *eporthoun* in the vulgate of *Il.* 4.308, which appears in some manuscripts as uncontracted *eportheon*, with synizesis, and in one manuscript with the late Ionic contraction *eportheun*; cf. Ionic *emeu, erkheu, phileuntas*).

Similarly, the shorter forms of *eimi* (e.g., *ôn* beside *eôn*, *êisin* beside *eêisin*, etc.) that appear infrequently in our inherited texts may at first glance seem to offer evidence of some Athenian influence on the epic diction. But a closer look reveals that all of them are easily reducible to their earlier Ionic forms by means of elision or synizesis: *Od.* 7.94 (*ontas* > *eontas* with synizesis); 8.147 *ophra ken êisin* > *ophra k' eêisin* with elision); 8.163 *êisin* > *eêisin* with synizesis); 8.580 *hina êisi* > *hin' eêisi* with elision); 19.230 (*hôs hoi khruseoi ontes* [as in most manuscripts] > *hôs hoi khruseoi eontes* with synizesis [as in some manuscripts]); 19.489 (*ousês* > *eousês* with synizesis); 24.491 (*ôsi* > *eôsi* with synizesis); *Il.* 14.274 (*marturoi ôs'* > *marturoi eôs'* with synizesis [but there are several other textual variants for this verse that eliminate the Atticism]); 19.202 (*êisin* > *eêisin* with synizesis).[56]

I conclude this section with an example of some Attic variants that have been passed down not in an actual manuscript of the Homeric text but in a quotation of Homer by Plato. These variants provide an interesting glimpse of the outer limits of Atticization of Homeric verse:

---

[55] The contracted Attic forms become more common in the later "*Homeric*" *Hymns* (*temenê* [*H.Aphr.* 267]; *ikhnê* [*H.Herm.* 76]; *orê* [*H.Herm.* 95, *Hymn* 27.4]; *pisê* [*Hymn* 19.2]; *belê* [*Hymn* 27.6]; *teukhê* [*Hymn* 28.15]).

[56] See Wackernagel, *Sprachliche Untersuchungen zu Homer*, 110-11; Schwyzer, *Griechische Grammatik*, 677; Page, *Homeric Odyssey*, 110; Chantraine, *Grammaire homérique*, 286-7; Erbse, *Beiträge zum Verständnis*, 224; and Shipp, *Language of Homer*, 13. The Attic forms become more common in post-Homeric epic verse (*parthenon ousan* [Hesiod fr. 204.91]; *têlothen ousa* [*H.Ap.* 330]; *athroas ousas* [*H.Herm.* 106]; *theos ôn* [*Hymn* 19.32]; *hilaos ôn* [*Hymn* 29.10]).

Iliad 9.499:   kai men tous thueessi kai eukhôlêis aganêisi
Republic 2. 364d7: kai tous men thusiaisi kai eukhôlais aganaisin.

Quoting Homer, no doubt from memory, Plato slightly inverts the word order and converts the epic nominal and adjectival endings into the forms more familiar to him from his own vernacular. Alternatively, Plato may simply be quoting verbatim an already Atticized version of the verse. In either case, this verse illustrates in a synoptic form the limitations in practice of the influence of the Attic dialect on the Homeric *Kunstsprache*. The very fact that there are not many more Atticisms of these sorts in our inherited texts is a testimony to the conservativeness of the textual transmission. And even those Atticisms that do crop up on occasion are easily reducible, as here, to their earlier epic counterparts. In short, the Attic dialect contributed almost nothing of a creative nature to the epic *Kunstsprache*.

I offer an observation and a question, then, to the proponents of the evolutionary model. A fundamental feature in the evolution of the Greek epic *Kunstsprache*, and of any living oral tradition, is its readiness to weave new forms from the vernacular into the fabric of its traditional archaic diction. These innovations from the vernacular are introduced first into the less formulaic diction, then as a way to modify formulaic phrases that have lost their original metrical shape, and finally in the creation of new formulaic phrases.[57] If the Homeric epics had continued to be performed and transmitted as a living, fluid, oral tradition through the Classical period, and even later, as the proponents of the evolutionary model would have us believe, then we should see Atticisms in our inherited texts not only as a veneer of easily reducible forms, not only in a few words and forms in the less formulaic diction, not only in modified formulaic phrases, but also in innovative formulaic constructions. Where are these irreducible Atticisms in our inherited texts? Where are these words and forms that were con-

---

[57] Parry articulated well this concept of linguistic evolution in oral traditions in "Epic Technique of Oral Verse-Making. II," 333: "The language of oral poetry changes as a whole neither faster nor slower than the spoken language, but in its parts it changes readily where no loss of formulas is called for, belatedly when there must be such a loss, so that the traditional diction has in it words and forms of everyday use side by side with others that belong to earlier stages of the language." For specific examples of the dropping of old and absorbing of new linguistic elements in Greek formulaic verse, see Hoekstra, *Sub-Epic Stage*.

tributed by the Athenian vernacular? Where are these innovative and organic Attic formulaic constructions?[58]

It is not the case that the Attic vernacular was incapable of contributing to the epic *Kunstsprache*. On the contrary, because of the many differ-

---

[58] I have been able to identify very few candidates, and I offer even these with serious reservations: 1) The formula *dendreôi ephezomenoi* at *Il.* 3.152 (= Hesiod's *Op.* 583; cf. *dendreôn* at *Od.* 19.520) may be an Atticism, since here alone does the word seem to depend on Attic *dendron* rather than Ionic *dendre(w)on*. Yet *dendron* may have already been in place in the Ionic vernacular in Homer's time (as it certainly was in Herodotus's Ionic prose). And even if there is to be a dialectal distinction observed here, the passage can be reduced to its Ionic form by assuming that synizesis occurred over the lost digamma, followed by correption of the resulting long syllable (as also in the Hesiodic passage). And, finally, one should observe that the manuscript variations of this passage (*dendreôi, dendrei, dendrôi*) attest to some uncertainty about the original reading; the variant *dendreôi hezomenoi*, found in some manuscripts, restores an unproblematic Ionic collocation. In sum, there are many cautions against taking the formula at *Il.* 3.152 as an Attic formulaic construction. 2) The *heôsphoros* [morning star] at *Il.* 23.226 has long been thought to be an Atticism, since only Attic has *heôs* for "dawn," beside Ionic *êôs* and Aeolic *auôs*. Yet Ionic has retained in other compounds short forms that have resisted quantitative metathesis: e.g., *heôthinos, leôspheteros* (both in Herodotus). It would appear that the largely Ionic *Kunstsprache* could accommodate *heôsphoros*, pronounced with synizesis, beside *êôs* (cf. Hesiod's *Theogony* 381). 3) The metrically useful alternative Attic -*nto* for Ionic -*ato* in some secondary, third-person, plural verb forms may have stimulated one or two Attic formulas. The formula *thurai d' epekeinto phaeinai* — for *epekeiato* — (*Od.* 6.19) is difficult to reduce to its Ionic form. Perhaps it is a real Attic formulation; but if so it is nonetheless clearly derivative, as it is modeled on *thuras epethêke phaeinas* (2x in Homer) or *thuras ôixe phaeinas* (3x in Homer), or perhaps on a singular form — *thurê d' epekeito phaeinê* — that did not chance to survive in our inherited epic corpus. Its simplex form *keinto epi khthoni* (*Il.* 21.426) appears in no less than four variations in the surviving manuscripts of this verse, indicating considerable uncertainty as to the correct reading. In any case it is easily reducible to its Ionic form with elision — *keiat' epi khthoni* — which has the added advantage of getting rid of the hiatus. The phrase *hênt' epi purgōi'* (*Il.* 3.153), for Ionic *hêato* or *heiato*, is possibly an Attic formulation. Yet it is reducible to the shorter Ionic form *heat'*, with synizesis, a form seen elsewhere in Homer — *oi d' heat' ein agorêi* (*Il.* 7.414) — though without synizesis. Finally, *makheointo Akhaioi* (*Il.* 1.344) can easily be reduced, with elision, to its metrically equivalent Ionic form *makheoiat' Akhaioi* — which change has the added advantage of getting rid of the hiatus.

ences in word shapes between the archaic epic diction and the Attic vernacular, which by virtue of their very differences presented many metrically useful alternative forms, there was great potential for the Attic vernacular to contribute productively to the epic *Kunstsprache*. The fact that this potential was never realized in our *Iliad* and *Odyssey* — i.e., that we see only a superficial veneer of Atticisms in our inherited texts — suggests that a living, fluid, oral Attic stage of epic production never existed.[59]

---

[59] An analogue to the linguistic argument for an early fixed form of the Homeric epics — i.e., that the absence of organic late linguistic forms provides a *terminus ante quem* for the date of textual fixation — is the historical and archaeological argument, in which the evidence of cultural institutions and physical artifacts mentioned in the Homeric texts substitutes for the evidence of linguistic forms. But the dating of institutions and artifacts during this historic period is a difficult task for many reasons. The period itself is still little known because of the paucity of archaeological material. The recent discovery of a free-standing temple that dates back to the tenth century, for example, has cast doubt on what was once considered to be a "late" element in Homer. The same can be said of many other so-called "late" elements: e.g., seated statues of divinities, oil lamps, and depictions of Gorgons. The problem is compounded when one relies for evidence primarily on the Homeric texts themselves, for traditional epic drew its cultural institutions and physical artifacts from many periods, from early Mycenaean (and earlier?) to Dark Age to Archaic (and later?). Is Homer's knowledge of Egyptian Thebes or of Phoenician sailors, for example, a memory from the Mycenaean period or a reference to renewed contact in the eighth or seventh century? Moreover, among the goals of epic narrative, the accurate description of cultural institutions and physical artifacts does not hold a high priority. It remains an open question, for example, whether or not what Homer is describing on the battlefield reflects knowledge of seventh-century hoplite fighting tactics, or whether the Homeric reference to sending home the ashes of dead warriors assumes knowledge of a particular historical custom. One must leave room for the poetic imagination. The overall result is that often the same evidence is used to argue both for early and for late composition of the Homeric epics. I am still unpersuaded that any cultural institution or physical artifact mentioned in Homer points to a date of composition much later than the end of the eighth century. On the contrary, the absence of references to writing and literacy seems to point in the opposite direction — to an earlier date of composition. Other than the mention of the mysterious *sêmata lugra* [baleful signs] in the story of Bellerophon (*Il.* 6.168-70) — a tale drawn wholesale (including the motif of the fatal letter) from the Near East, where writing had been known for millennia — Homer seems to be utterly ignorant of lexigraphic writing. (Cf. Steiner, *Tyrant's Writ*, 10-16.) This suggests a *ter-*

Some Conclusions

We can say very few things about the Homeric epics with utmost confidence, but among these few things is that at some moment in time the fluid words of an orally composed and performed epic song were recorded as written text and were thereby fixed as physical objects in space and time; for if this event had not occurred, we would have today no texts of the *Iliad* and *Odyssey* of Homer. The circumstances surrounding this event, however, are shrouded in the mists of antiquity.

We do not know, for example, when, or where, or by whom this textualization was initiated. Nor do we know whether it was a single event or a series of events, whether there was just one or many scribes present to record the words of the singer, whether the singer was literate or illiterate, and, if literate, whether or not this enabled him to assist in some way in the recording. We do not know how long the singer performed in one sitting, whether or not he tolerated interruptions and questions by the scribe(s), whether or not he repeated for the convenience of the scribe(s) material already recited, how accurately the scribe(s) recorded the very words of the singer, or even what specific tools and materials were used.

It is likely that the occasion of recording was in many ways unusual for the singer: it was not a typical epic song performed under typical circumstances in the presence of a typical audience. The singer may have recited rather than sung to the accompaniment of his lyre; his tempo may have been slower than usual, since the pace of normal live performance would probably have been too rapid for a scribe to keep up; and the unusually attentive and cooperative demeanor of his audience (i.e., the person[s] recording the song) may have allowed him the leisure to be more careful about details than usual, to consider where the song was leading more de-

---

minus ante quem for the date of composition in the mid-eighth century; it is certainly not as late as the sixth, not to speak of the Classical and Hellenistic periods, when literacy was thoroughly embedded in the Greek culture. For historical and archaeological support for an early fixation of the Homeric texts (i.e., early eighth-early seventh century), see G. S. Kirk, "Objective Dating Criteria," 191-6, *Songs of Homer*, 179-92, 282-7, "Homeric Poems as History," and *Commentary*, 7-10; Morris, "Use and Abuse," esp. 93, 104; Powell, *Origin of the Greek Alphabet*, 190-206; Crielaard, "History and Archaeology"; and Raaflaub, "Homeric Society."

liberately than usual, and to produce in the end a somewhat longer song than usual.[60]

We will probably never know who had the idea of writing down the song or why. Lord quite reasonably concluded that it would never have occurred to an orally composing singer to have the songs written down. Why should he? Preservation was not a goal, since he could perform the song again at any time. Nor would he have considered it desirable to record the exact words of his song, since he knew nothing of fixed texts. A written text served him no purpose in performance; on the contrary, he probably performed most freely and comfortably when allowed to sing at his own pace to the accompaniment of his instrument, not at the artificially slow pace of dictation, and certainly not with an unwieldy text to encumber him. No, it was someone other than the singer who initiated the dictation of the song. Of all else we are ignorant.[61]

But though we may in the end have to confess ignorance, we can still venture some guesses. Since there existed in antiquity no other technological method for recording an epic song, we must assume that it was written down as a text; and since the texts that we have inherited retain many of the vestiges that would result naturally from an oral song being textualized at a particular moment in time, we may assume that this moment occurred on an occasion when a live oral performance *and* the recording of that performance into text were one and the same event. If the idea of textualizing the song did not come from the singer, it must have come from someone else — a patron, a sponsor, or a simple admirer — who was familiar with the only mechanism capable of accomplishing this task: oral-dictation. And just as the alphabet with which the song was first textualized originated in Phoenicia, and just as the papyrus upon which the text was first transcribed originated in Egypt, and just as many components of the song itself — the tale-types, themes, and poetic forms — originated in the Levant and Mesopotamia, so it does not require too great a leap of faith to suppose that the very idea of writing down the song originated from someone acquainted with the civilizations of the Near East,

---

[60] On the mechanics and challenges of oral-dictation in general, both for the singer and the scribe, see Lord, *Singer of Tales*, 124-38, Parry and Lord, *Serbocroatian Heroic Songs*, 2:7-11; on the hypothetical oral-dictation of the Homeric texts, see Lord, *Singer of Tales*, 141-57.

[61] Lord, *Singer of Tales*, 150-7, and "Other Epic Poetry," 193-7.

where the writing down of epic songs, some even through the process of dictation, and their transmission by means of written text, had been practiced for more than a millennium.

We can conjecture all we wish. What is most important for the present study is that the act of dictation resulted in a written text that could now be regarded as *the* song rather than *a* song — the archetype of all the texts that are directly or indirectly descended from it. This archetype was transmitted with such remarkable care and conservatism that it has retained in its textual form even to this day, more than 2700 years after its first recording, many clear vestiges of that historic event of oral-dictation.

DANIEL F. MELIA

Orality and Aristotle's Aesthetics

Little that I have to say here, taken as an individual piece of information, is going to be news. What I hope to do, rather, is to try to offer some suggestions for interpreting a few sections of Aristotle's *Art of Rhetoric* and *Poetics* in light of what we know about the nature of aesthetics in primarily oral cultures.[1] I use the term "oral" in this essay in two technical senses. First, I use it to designate works of art, such as the Homeric poems, that originate and take their shape in a culture without writing and which show the characteristics of oral composition in the Parry-Lord sense.[2] Included in this definition would be traditional forms which have become frozen by memorialization and/or writing. Second, I use the term "oral" in the still technical, but broader, sense of the wide variety of traditional popular forms of linguistic artifact which circulate in relatively stable form

---

An earlier version of this essay was delivered at the Epea and Grammata Conference, University of Missouri, Columbia, 6 June 2000.

[1] Unless otherwise noted, I cite Roberts's translation of the *Rhetoric* and Golden's translation of the *Poetics* because they are readable in English and accessible. My own translations are noted as [DFM]. Citations for both works are to Book and Chapter numbers (Chapter only for the *Poetics*) with the standard page, column, and line numbers (e.g., 340b26) from the Bekker edition appended for those who wish to consult the original Greek or other translations. As my arguments seldom involve the actual wording of the Greek, I generally give only the English translations.

[2] For the seminal studies of oral performance see Lord, *Singer of Tales* and *Singer Resumes the Tale*; Parry, *Making of Homeric Verse*; and Foley, *Theory of Oral Composition*.

amongst the general populace, or significant sub-groups, in a given culture. Examples of the latter would be proverbs, memorates, jokes, anecdotes, onomastic and genealogical lore, children's rhymes, and the like. I specifically do not include in either sense of "oral" here everyday verbal behavior of a less formal kind, including common fixed expressions such as "horse of a different color" and "Great Caesar's ghost" which may exhibit some level of complexity, but are essentially lexicalized.

This project arose largely out of pedagogical concerns. Over the last thirty years of teaching undergraduate courses on Aristotle, I have repeatedly had to answer questions from the brighter students about the following issues: 1) Why did the Greeks have no name for "The art that imitates by words alone, in prose or in verse"?[3] 2) Why does Aristotle say that "Similes are useful in prose as well as in verse; but not often, since they are of the nature of poetry"?[4] 3) Why does Aristotle lay out the interdependence of the six parts of tragedy (plot, character, diction, thought, spectacle, and melody)[5] but then claim that "The poet should construct the plot so that *even if the action is not performed before spectators*, one who *merely hears the incidents* that have occurred both shudders and feels pity from the way they turn out"?[6] and 4) Why is there no explicit discussion of memory in Aristotle's *Art of Rhetoric* when he discusses the other traditional parts of the art (invention, arrangement, style, delivery) in their traditional order?

There is, of course, a set of glib, ten-second, answers to these questions: 1) [With respect to the "nameless art,"] The Greeks didn't have a word for *Fachprosa* because they didn't need one until non-traditional material (legal arguments, Platonic dialogues) started to be written down. 2) [On simile vs. metaphor,] Aristotle was thinking here only of Homeric epic, the extended similes of which are highly characteristic of the genre. 3) [On the independent power of plot,] In addition to being deeply concerned with origins, as illustrated by his sketch of the beginnings of tragedy and comedy,[7] Aristotle was fascinated by plot. Because tragedy is about reversal of fortune, you need a plot which illustrates such a reversal. 4) [Lack of explicit discussion of memory in the *Rhetoric*,] Aristotle wrote a

---

[3] *Poetics*, I, i, 1447b1.
[4] *Rhetoric*, III, iiii, 1406b24.
[5] *Poetics*, VI, 1450a40.
[6] *Poetics*, XIV, 1453b5; my emphasis.
[7] *Poetics*, I, 1449a10.

separate treatise (surviving as *De Memoria*) on memory.[8] Now, while none of these brief answers is absolutely wrong, some of them, I want to argue here, are seriously misleading. Perhaps the most misleading thing about these short answers is that they treat these textual anomalies as if they were independent of one another. I think they are not. I think that each of these textual peculiarities derives from an underlying aesthetic of orality — an aesthetic which, of its own historical necessity, values certain compositional techniques and assumes certain audience responses. I do not mean to offer here a grand general description of the respective cultures of orality and literacy in the manner of Eric Havelock or Walter J. Ong,[9] but, rather, to try to contrast some specific practices that can be associated with the reception and explicit understanding of texts in cultures with and without prestige written materials.

Aristotle doesn't come up much when examples of orality or oral technique are offered. In fact, at least since Havelock's *Preface to Plato*, Aristotle has been the poster boy for Greek literacy. (After all, Havelock didn't call his book "Preface to Aristotle"!) In his recent book *Literacy and Paideia in Ancient Greece*, Kevin Robb opines that "Higher education inextricably bound to the study of the content of texts became ... a distinguishing feature of the type of education found in Aristotle's Lyceum."[10] In *The Muse Learns to Write*, in arguing that Callimachus's *Hymn to Zeus* is a literarily composed poem, Havelock says, "The verb 'to be,' linking a subject and its property in a timeless connection, intrudes as it never could in oralist language.... The Muse has learnt to put her song into writing and in doing so tries to sing in *the language of Aristotle*."[11] Aristotle's own diction is, of course, notoriously knotty and intractable, and his entire method of inquiry and explanation with its incessant categorization, subordination, and deductive argument is clearly both the product and producer of the kind of analytic attention to the "surface of abstraction" which differentiates the mental culture of writing from the mental culture of orality. In inventing the term "surface of abstraction" I am not trying to be cleverly obscurantist. I mean by the phrase to describe phenomena connected with

---

[8] For translation and commentary, see Sorabji, *Aristotle on Memory*.

[9] See Havelock, *Preface to Plato* and *The Muse Learns to Write*; and Ong, *Orality and Literacy*.

[10] Robb, *Literacy and Paideia*, 221.

[11] Havelock, *The Muse Learns to Write*, 109; my emphasis.

writing such as 1) grammatical description, 2) openly deductive reasoning, or 3) subordinating classification – the marks of the existence of the notion and reality of fixed texts and of the external storage of information – in contrast to their embodied equivalents in oral traditions: 1) dialectal code-switching in formal texts, 2) exemplary depiction of individual action, and 3) associative references, which accomplish the equivalent tasks in the absence of the notion of the fixed text. For the contrast proposed under the first point compare Aristotle's advice for adding impressiveness to a speech, "Use plural for singular, as in poetry, where one finds, 'Unto havens Achaean,' though only one haven is meant,"[12] with the Serbo-Croatian oral singer's ability to "speak" in verse, in a special sub-dialect of his own language in which all utterances scan properly, while he composes during performance, although he himself is unlikely to have a concept such as "word" as an abstract entity. As Albert B. Lord puts it, "When asked what a word is, he [the singer] will reply that he does not know, or he will give a sound group which may vary in length from what we call a word to an entire line of poetry, or even an entire song."[13] For the second point, contrast Aristotle's small enthymeme, "And since the signs of virtue, and such acts as it is the mark of a virtuous man to do or have done to him, are noble, it follows that all deeds or signs of courage, and everything done courageously, must be noble things,"[14] with Homer's depiction of the naively noble behavior of Patroklos in Book 16 of the *Iliad* when he cries out to the stubbornly withdrawn Achilles, "then send me out at least, let the rest of the Myrmidon people / follow me, and I may be a light given to the Danaans."[15] As to point number three, observe the contrast between Chapter six of the *Poetics*, "There are six parts consequently of every tragedy, as a whole (that is) of such or such quality viz. a Fable or Plot, Characters, Diction, Thought, Spectacle and Melody; two of them arising from the means, one from the manner, and three from the objects of the dramatic imitation,"[16] and Homer's "accompaniment motif" by which important women descend from their quarters to the main hall accompanied by two or more maidservants. Michael Nagler schematizes the

---

[12] *Rhetoric*, III, vi, 1407b32ff.

[13] Lord, *Singer of Tales*, 25.

[14] *Rhetoric* I, ix, 1366b27ff.

[15] *Iliad* 16.331. I cite the poem from Lattimore's translation.

[16] *Poetics*, VI, 1450a6ff.

formula as: "not alone, for with her two/others maidervants followed/went."[17] The formula is used three times of Penelope (1.331, 18.207, 19.601) and once of Nausicaa (6.84) in the *Odyssey* and once of Helen in the *Iliad* (3.143). The importance of the women and of the occasion are guaranteed by the use of this formula, but the concatenation of the maidservants and an important female figure is embedded in the formula itself, forming an obligatory cluster of associational reference, recognizable by the experienced audience of an oral culture.[18] At the larger compositional level of the "theme" John Miles Foley has described another such associational cluster in the *Odyssey* at 23.153-64:

> these grouped actions of bathing, anointing with olive oil, and donning new clothes constitute a typical scene that appears seven times in the *Odyssey*, taking a similar shape with certain regular features in each occurrence. More to the point ... however, this modest-seeming 'stock' description is also rife with traditional implications. Without fail, in Books 3, 4, 8, 10, 17 and 24 the Bath-Anointment theme forecasts a consequent feast.[19]

The first chapter of the *Poetics* fully illustrates the literate aspects of these generalizations. It begins with *poietike*, "making," then divides that genus into its various species: "applied art" and "imitative art," the latter of which is then differentiated by the usual Aristotelian distinctions of means and manner into painting, dance, flute and lyre music, drama, and the "nameless art." Drama is further divided into mixed dithyramb and Comedy/Tragedy, and the "nameless art" into prose (such as the Socratic dialogues) and unaccompanied (= fixed text?) verse (such as Chaeremon's *Centaur*). But, if Aristotle represents an individual immersed in writing, he was not living in a world similarly immersed. Even if one does not subscribe to the rather severely restrictive views of literacy put forward in William V. Harris's *Ancient Literacy*, it is clear that Athenians (and, presumably even more so, Stagirites) of the middle of the fourth century were not living in a thoroughly "literized" world. The repeated insistence on the ex-

---

[17] Nagler, *Spontaneity and Tradition*, 65.
[18] For an extended discussion see Nagler, *Spontaneity and Tradition*, chap. 3.
[19] Foley, *Homer's Traditional Art*, 244-5.

clusive use of the written statutes in Athenian court proceedings after 399 B.C.E. suggests that reliance on written witness and written authority even in the law courts was not yet natural in the early fourth century. To quote Robb again,

> We can say only that [writing and documents ... becoming a presumption of the daily functioning of the courts] could hardly have sprung, like Athena from the head of Zeus [*recte*], full grown and mature, on that day in 399 B.C. when Nichomachus and his committee halted the laborious cutting of the mason's chisels and declared their great work [the inscribing of the "laws of Solon"] done.[20]

To put it another way, the Lyceum existed because Aristotle had had to go to Athens to study at the Academy. There was no equivalent to the Academy available to the younger Aristotle, and, for the older Aristotle, there was apparently a larger market for two such establishments in Athens than for one such establishment elsewhere. Now, one need not be as skeptical as Harris to accept the notion that the world of Aristotle's upbringing, if not, indeed, of his adulthood, was one in which the production, use and, most particularly, *editing*, of long written texts was an everyday activity only for a tiny minority, and a no-day activity for the vast majority even of those with relatively sophisticated reading and writing skills (as is, in fact, the case even in our own society). Robb notes that "A similar distrust of writing ... was still a characteristic of fourth-century Athenian juries."[21]

Paradigms are hard to shift. Early television shows resemble nothing so much as filmed radio or theatrical shows: the Stu Erwin show was so static that it might as well have been on the radio, the Ed Sullivan Show (which ran well into the 1960s) was vaudeville, filmed on a proscenium stage, and even *Father Knows Best* was, as one thinks back on it, curiously focused on one corner of the Anderson living room. These features of early television were not so much the result of technical constraints as of a failure of imagination. It took a full generation of producers, directors, and executives to understand the freedom afforded by the new medium. And it is not just the surface features of the "old" genres that are retained

---

[20] Robb, *Literacy and Paideia*, 140.
[21] Robb, *Literacy and Paideia*, 101.

so powerfully, though some may be, from the old ways of imagining; it is the deeper assumptions of structure and association that are so hard to shake off, because they are inherently so hard to spot, particularly in oneself. I want to propose here that we can find something of the same state of "intellectual hangover" in the Aristotelian difficulties I enumerated above. While Aristotle's surviving works never, or almost never, betray a residual oral *style* (formulaic verse), his ready and frequent quotation from a wide variety of texts (often in a form at some variance from what survives to us) indicates a mind well furnished with remembered texts. The ease of such remembrance to a trained mind has been demonstrated recently and notably by David C. Rubin and Mary Carruthers.[22] Aristotle's early training in *mousike* undoubtedly provided the basis for his ability to quote thus from memory, and his ability to do so with ease may be part of the explanation for the lack of a "memory" component in his treatment of Rhetoric as an art. These obvious aspects of his written practice betray his continuing interaction with the world of, at least, "secondary orality," to use Ong's terminology.

It is worth calling to mind the fact that most knowledge that each of us has, now as well as then, is "unofficial" knowledge, for instance, that George Washington and Abraham Lincoln were exceptionally honest, or that one pushes the elevator button for the direction one wishes to travel regardless of the position of the elevator when the button is pushed. Aristotle is no exception. We find bits of such unofficial lore cropping up from time to time in his formal writings. In Bk. III, Ch. 2 of the *Rhetoric* (1405b1) he cites the "celebrated riddle" "I marked how a man glued bronze with fire to another man's body," a somewhat alarming metaphor for the medical practice of "cupping" to draw blood to the surface of the skin, a practice Aristotle had no doubt seen first in his youth since his father was a physician. This vivid metaphor serves as a useful example for my general argument; it represents the casual use by Aristotle of "popular" lore in a formal argument about a formal art. And it shows that he was able to integrate, with no more difficulty than we experience, official and unofficial kinds of knowledge in his own head.

But Aristotle's entanglement with what I will call "oral aesthetic assumptions" shows itself on a deeper level if we examine more carefully the four student questions I raised above. A less dismissive answer to the ques-

---

[22] See Rubin, *Memory in Oral Traditions* and Carruthers, *Book of Memory*.

tion about the reason that the "nameless art" has no name is not just that the Greeks didn't need one until they started writing prose, but that even after Aristotle "discovered" this nameless art, they *still* didn't need a name for it because such a name would not have described any discrete concrete thing in their real world, *including Aristotle's*. It is, I think, notable that Aristotle, having identified this genre, "the art that imitates by words alone in prose or in verse," feels no need to assign it a name. Furthermore, having identified this notional genre solely by his method of division and redivision according to attributes and causes, he spends the next few sentences complaining that the term "poet" is attached by the general public to the act of versifying ("epic poet" or "elegiac poet") rather than to the act of creating artistic works of various kinds. It interests me that although Aristotle seems acutely interested in pushing his point that a proper understanding of various genres (notably, of course, drama) must depend, as he has just shown, on a recognition that mimesis (by various means) lies at the definitional core of all kinds of art, he seemingly has no interest at all, despite his evident irritation with the erroneous terminology of the *polloi*, in providing a proper name (evidence of its existence in the real world) to his newly-designated genre. This lack of interest, I believe, particularly in light of the other cases I discuss below, is a small piece of evidence that Aristotle is allowing the assumptions of orality (in this case, that genre-designations are not analytic, but designative, like personal names) to dictate his own written practice.

Regarding simile versus metaphor and their relative appropriateness to verse and prose, Aristotle's statement really goes beyond the simple identification of Homeric extended simile as determining what is appropriate for verse, since he explicitly gives as an example "rushed as a lion" vs. "a lion rushed" and asserts that there is little theoretical difference between the two figures. What then makes simile poetic by nature? The answer I offer here is one that might be conclusively demonstrated statistically, though I haven't done the actual counts: Homeric (long) similes are "themes" in the Parry-Lord sense, and thus *of the very nature* of oral-traditional poetry;[23] short similes ("leapt on the foe as a lion," "ran like a hare," "light as a feather") by their relatively anchored syntax lend them-

---

[23] I take the position here that story-patterns consist entirely and only of "themes." The classic discussion of Serbo-Croatian traditional themes is in Lord, *Singer of Tales*, chap. 4.

selves readily to forming easily substitutable formulaic systems composed of any verb in a given tense and any singular noun, and, furthermore, are often sententious as well — clearly *of the very nature* of oral-traditional poetry, too. Metaphor is far less often sententious and far more open to syntactic variety than simile, not unusable in traditional oral forms, but less likely to be found there or to "feel" characteristic of them. Aristotle here not only fails to offer justification for his statement that simile is more "poetic" than metaphor, but actually offers arguments to the effect that there is little difference between the two figures in import or intent. I would contend that in this case in asserting without demonstration or argument that simile is proper to poetry and metaphor to prose, he unconsciously reveals an unexamined bias toward the norms of oral-traditional aesthetics rather than a recognition of potentially new standards of fixed texts.

In discussing the importance of plot in the *Poetics*, Aristotle notably insists on plot as the crucial element of mimesis:

> The most important of these parts is the arrangement of the incidents; for tragedy is not an imitation of men *per se*, but of human action.... Poets do not, therefore, create action in order to imitate character; but character is included on account of the action.... Furthermore, without action tragedy would be impossible, but without character it would still be possible.[24]

For him, "The first principle, then, and to speak figuratively, the soul of tragedy is the plot."[25] Aristotle notes that not all playwrights adhere to these strictures, but ties them directly to the unities to which he claims tragedy must adhere. The fact that in the *Poetics* Aristotle attributes the necessity for the primacy of plot to the necessity for plausibility of the causation of the action depicted ought not to blind us to the similarity his aesthetic judgment here shows to that of the Serbo-Croatian singers interviewed by Parry and Lord, for whom a question like, "what would you do if you had only one hour to sing a song which would ordinarily take you two hours?" literally makes no sense. Under questioning from Milman

---

[24] *Poetics*, VI, 1450a15ff.
[25] *Poetics*, VI, 1450a37.

Parry (through his capable assistant Nikola Vujnović) in 1934, the singer Đemail Zogić responded first to that very question that if a singer could not finish he should take a break and then continue. When pressed further he said of a truncated song, "That's no good. I have a liking to listen to the songs of the Border. And I would think afterwards what happened in the song ... and I would not be satisfied."[26] For the Serbo-Croatian singers, the story-pattern (= Aristotle's plot) consists of the correct sequence of obligatory themes in the correct order. If you need to sing a "border song" in twenty minutes, you strip out the optional ornamentation within each theme and any optional or repeated themes and sing only the themes essential to that story-pattern. The eternal present of the tradition certifies the validity of the story itself.

Aristotle here seems to recognize the analogy, at least, with oral-traditional modes. In criticizing those who produced simple biographies, "All those poets seem to have erred who have written a *Heracleid* or a *Theseid* and other poems of this type; for they think that since Heracles was one person it is appropriate for his story to be one story,"[27] he also points out that "Homer, just as he was superior in other respects, also seems to have seen this point well, whether through technical skill or his native talent, since in making the *Odyssey* he did not include all the things that ever happened to Odysseus."[28] In this same passage, Aristotle goes on to insist that the "parts of the action be put together in such a way that if any one part is transposed or removed, the whole will be disordered and disunified." In taking such a position, he anticipates and validates the Serbo-Croatian singer Salih Ugljanin who, having discovered toward the climax of one of his songs that he is in the "wrong" recognition theme, has to return to the point earlier in his song (*The Captivity of Đulić Ibrahim*) at which he has erroneously had his hero put on the clothes of a slain border-guard and has to re-sing the entire song again back to the "correct" recognition scene.[29] Such is the power of story-pattern in an oral tradition. To be sure, one can extract from the explicit argument of the *Poetics* reasons for making plot important, but none of the reasons offered ade-

---

[26] Parry and Lord, *Serbocroatian Heroic Songs*, 1:240.

[27] *Poetics*, VIII, 1451a20ff.

[28] *Poetics*, VIII, 1451a23ff.

[29] Parry and Lord, *Serbocroatian Heroic Songs*, 1:60 and notes. Interestingly, this song has the same rescue-return story-pattern as the *Odyssey*.

quately explains the insistence on the efficacy of *plot alone* to elicit pity and fear. Again, I think, we are seeing an aesthetic judgment on Aristotle's part that he does not clearly recognize for what it is. He sees, he feels the innate power of traditional plots and, since he wishes to make catharsis (whatever it may be) via pity and fear the touchstone of effective tragedy, he judges that only drama following the aesthetics of oral tradition (as does Homer) can be truly effective. The extreme bias toward plot (story-pattern) looks natural (and is, indeed, unavoidable) in an oral-traditional setting, but obviously was not a compelling interest for playwrights and poets roughly contemporary with Aristotle, as many of them, by Aristotle's own account, do not share it: "This is shown by the fact that all who have dramatized the fall of Ilium in its entirety ... either fail utterly or have but ill success on the stage."[30]

There is another feature of plots/story-patterns that is of interest in this discussion. Story-patterns are indexical. They constitute classes of knowledge carried by narrative. It is this feature of oral tradition which allows for the creation of tale-type indices in folklore, designations such as "rescue-and-return song" by Parry and Lord, and even the lists found in eleventh-century Ireland listing "prime-tales" arranged by plot-structure ("tragic deaths," "wooings," "heroic births," etc.).[31] The story patterns themselves, however, are composed of formulas and themes that are shared throughout the tradition. Themes and formulas, on the other hand, are not indexical, but associative, carrying with them not only the designation of their immediate use, but the connotations of their other possible uses.[32] A striking example of such associative links is the homeric pun on *pioni demo* (πίονι δημῷ [rich fat] vs. πίονι δήμῳ [flourishing populace]) in which the notion of sacrifice insinuates itself into the description of a rich city.[33] "Horizontally" (across the tradition) formulas and themes suggest their other uses; "vertically" (within a given story) each suggests its own immediate context, the next item in the story, for instance.[34] It is such an *oral* notion of what can or should constitute a "good" (aestheti-

---

[30] *Poetics*, XVIII, 1456a16ff.

[31] For a discussion, see MacCana, *Learned Tales of Medieval Ireland*.

[32] For an extended discussion, see Foley, *Homer's Traditional Art*, esp. 115-240.

[33] See Nagler, *Spontaneity and Tradition*, 5-7.

[34] See Foley, *Homer's Traditional Art*, 244-5, cited above, 95 n. 19.

cally effective) story that characterizes the kind of bias we see in Aristotle's account.

I emphasize here the strongly associational nature of oral-traditional transmission because it forms the foundation for my final assertion about Aristotle: that the omission of "memory" as an explicit part of his discussion of rhetoric is tied to an underlying orally-determined notion of how to retrieve things from one's memory. The indexical nature of story-patterns is responsible for the fact that they are consciously "learnable" by mature oral performers in a way that themes are less likely to be, and formulas cannot be, so firmly are the latter tied to language itself.

The most misleading of the proposed "short answers" to my students' questions about Aristotle is the one concerning memory. While it is technically true that Aristotle wrote a treatise on "memory," *De Memoria* does not constitute the kind of discussion of "memory" as an element of rhetorical training that one might call "missing" from the *Art of Rhetoric*. *De Memoria* is, in fact, more a physiological treatise than a psychological or rhetorical one, concentrating as it does on perception and mental function (comparing, for instance, human and animal memory [450a15]) rather than on techniques of memorization or recall. So, that's not the answer. I should say here that for the purposes of this discussion I am not going to take up the vexing problems of the state of our text of the *Rhetoric*. It is, of course, remotely possible that there once was a section on memory, but my argument here does not depend on the state of the manuscript tradition or on whether Aristotle is entirely responsible for the shape of the text as we have it.[35] The better short answer is that, for Aristotle, Invention and Arrangement covered the serious issues of memory with respect to rhetoric, and thus a separate section with the title "memory" would have been superfluous.

Part of the problem here, of course, is our expectation that "memory" is a matter of putting stuff into our heads, while for the ancient world this was a matter so childish, so ordinary, that it required hardly any comment, and most Greek and Roman rhetorical handbooks pay that aspect of memory little or no attention. Most of them do, however, discuss mnemonics of various kinds, most famously spatial tricks for recalling various subjects in a prepared oration. (For example, imagine that you are in a

---

[35] For a specific discussion of the history of the text and manuscripts, see Kennedy, *On Rhetoric*, 299-309.

house you know well. Go into the first room on the right. In that room imagine a vivid scene connected with your first topic. For instance, if you wish to impugn the character of someone, imagine him committing the crime you impute to him in that room, etc.).[36] Even this sort of discussion of mnemonics is insufficiently grounded in human mental activity to serve as a basis for Aristotle's notion of rhetoric as the "faculty of discovering (*theoresai* [lit. seeing]) in any given case the available means of persuasion" [DFM], though.[37] Aristotle's system of invention interestingly derives the sources of invention itself from the nature of the speaker's intentions with respect to the audience.

In deriving the three kinds of rhetoric (deliberative, forensic, and epideictic) from the kinds of mental judgments made in each case by the audience (what should be done in the future, what likely happened in the past, and how appropriate a verbal artifact one can offer in the present, respectively) Aristotle creates a "natural" system of finding the appropriate enthymemes (which I will take here to mean "inferential lines of argument") by which the subjects under discussion themselves lead to the appropriate branches of already-stored enthymemes and examples.[38] Thus epideictic rhetoric's concern with praise and blame (as in a funeral oration) leads the rhetor naturally to an entire set of enthymemes and examples connected with those headings, which, in their own turn, lead to other related topoi and so on and so on:

> Things that deserve to be remembered are noble, and the more they deserve this, the nobler they are. So are the things that continue even after death; those which are always attended by honor; those which are exceptional, and those that are possessed by one person alone — these last are more readily remembered than others.[39]

This passage describes (and illustrates) an associational chain such as those described by Parry and Lord in explaining the techniques of Serbo-

---

[36] See, for example, the discussion of memory technique in pseudo-Cicero, *Ad Herennium*, Bk. III, Ch. XVI. I cite Caplan's edition and translation here.
[37] *Rhetoric* I, 2, 1355b26.
[38] *Rhetoric* I, iii, 1358b21ff.
[39] *Rhetoric*, I, ix, 1367a23ff.

Croatian heroic singers. Likewise with the concern of forensic rhetoric with the just and the unjust, each a treasure chest of topoi and, like the topics connected with praise and blame, one need remember only either the positive or negative set since each item of praise/justice has contradictory and contrary statements which are easily derivable. Aristotle has here explicated a theory of mental associations that gives names to activities and items that remain unnamed in oral-traditional performance. Rubin has described this situation aptly in *Memory in Oral Traditions*:

> The distinction between explicit and implicit memory can also be used to clarify one use of oral traditions. Implicit memory is *knowing how*. It shows the effects of past experience, but not in an intentional, declarative way. It is demonstrated by doing, and therefore requires a situation in which the known behavior can be executed. In contrast, explicit memory is *knowing that*. It is a conscious, declarative recitation, explanation, or communication. It can occur in a situation where the behavior can be talked about, but not executed.[40]

In the *Rhetoric*, Aristotle proposes a system of invention which allows conscious access to and conscious use of a set of mental activities which are produced unconsciously by oral-traditional performers during performance. The rhetor can compose an effective speech, either in advance or extemporaneously, by learning how to obtain access from his own mind to all and only the topoi appropriate to his subject. The associational process by which he does this is essentially identical in its mental operations to that used by the oral-traditional poet during composition.

Aristotle's system, because it derives the essential elements of the art of rhetoric from the mental activity of the audience and explicates the mental activity of the speaker, differs radically from the "cookbook" handbooks of rhetoric which were its "competition," and it had surprisingly little direct influence on ancient rhetorical practice. It does something, though, that is worthy of our attention beyond the question of ancient rhetorical theory: it provides, quite unconsciously, I think, the first systematic description of the mental structure of oral tradition. Just as the

---

[40] Rubin, *Memory in Oral Traditions*, 191; his emphasis.

traditional singer's choice of story-pattern is determined by what he wants to instruct the audience (however obliquely) about, the aim of the rhetorical speech is to persuade the audience of something the speaker wants. More interestingly, just as the story-pattern is composed all and only of traditional themes, so is the speech composed all and only of topoi. Just as the themes are common to the tradition, but arranged in story-appropriate "vertical" arrays, so topoi exist as a common property (hence their power to persuade) but also constitute the very matter of the speech itself. The associative retrieval of topoi in Aristotle's rhetoric seems to operate exactly as the retrieval of themes operates in oral tradition and to have the same kind of impact on the audience.[41] Thus, for Aristotle, the most effective speech by a trained speaker would be constructed in a manner exactly analogous in its mental activity to the construction of the best epic or drama. The seeming naturalness and inevitability of Aristotle's system of rhetorical invention is owing to its congruence with the "natural" construction of oral epic tradition. I would thus argue that these four examples of odd aesthetic choice in Aristotle's *Art of Rhetoric* and *Poetics* are not independent of one another, but are, rather, individual expressions of an underlying sense of aesthetic congruity which derives from Aristotle's conscious or (more likely) unconscious assumption of a system of aesthetics originating in the emotionally powerful products of the mature oral tradition to which he was exposed in his youth, if not throughout his life. If we look at Aristotle as an individual living at a specific time and place, rather than as the embodiment of a set of formal texts, it is, of course, not at all surprising that his mental apparatus should contain the richness and confusion of that time and place. What interests me about the questions raised above, however, is what seems to me to be a curiously coherent set of aesthetic biases in some of Aristotle's work which are both interconnected and characteristic of the art of cultures without writing. If I'm at all right about this, Aristotle becomes an interestingly transitional figure, committed consciously to the new science of production and analysis of fixed texts, while tied subconsciously to the standards of the expiring oral tradition.

---

[41] See Rubin, *Memory in Oral Traditions*, 41, for associative memory.

ALEXANDRA HENNESSEY OLSEN

Proteus in Latin: Vernacular Tradition and the Boniface Collection

"Imagine trying to catch the Greek god Proteus, who shifts his form in myriad ways, from bird to horse to crashing ocean waves," says Elizabeth C. Fine. She continues, "It is no less difficult to capture oral tradition."[1] During the Middle Ages, however, authors captured oral tradition by composing works in writing, characterized by what Mark C. Amodio calls "the persistence of oral habits of mind."[2] "It was a period," says Albert B. Lord, "when the prestigious Latin language and its written literature and culture were introduced into the non-Romance cultures that already possessed their own traditional native literatures."[3]

When we study the Latin literature of the Middle Ages, we are confronted with an important question: how did the vernacular cultures (which were primarily oral) influence the Latin (which was primarily literate although it was taught orally as a second language in academic settings)? Although the Latin Middle Ages are both chronologically and geographically diverse, the early Middle Ages in the areas speaking Germanic languages were an age which has been called "Germania Latina" [Latin Germany].[4] There was considerable exchange between the late Roman and Germanic cultures, and we can therefore trace the influence of the oral vernacular cultures on the literate Latin culture. Walter J. Ong, S.J., has

---

[1] Fine, "Leading Proteus Captive," 59.
[2] Amodio, "Tradition, Performance," 192.
[3] Lord, "Oral Composition and 'Oral Residue,'" 7.
[4] North and Hofstra, *Latin Culture*, ii.

called the age one of "cultural diglossia"[5] (when educated people both spoke their vernacular cradle tongues and spoke and wrote Latin). Latin influenced the Germanic vernaculars, providing new ideas and images. What has been little discussed is the fact that the vernacular languages influenced the Latin works written in the Germanic-speaking countries. Specifically, the Latin texts show signs of vernacular influence, unsurprising in this time of close contact.

One area particularly rich in texts that show the interaction between Latin and the vernacular is Anglo-Saxon England. There is a group of eighth-century epistles known collectively as the Boniface Collection.[6] They are 150 letters by St. Boniface (c. 675-754), Archbishop of Mainz, his successor St. Lull, male and female members of his mission in Germany like Leoba, Abbess of Bischofsheim, friends who remained in England like Ælflæd, Abbess of Whitby, and continental Bishops and Popes. The Boniface mission is especially connected with Hesse and Thuringia. For example, Otloh's *Vita Bonifatii* says that "Chunihilt et filia eius Berhtgit ... in Turingorum regione constitiebantur magistrae" (138) [Cynehild and her daughter ... were appointed as teachers in the region of Thuringia].

Christine E. Fell calls the Boniface Collection "one of the more neglected areas of Anglo-Saxon studies."[7] Boniface and his friends are keenly aware of the literate Latin tradition, and many of the letters request books or thank people for the gift of books. In Tangl 91, Boniface speaks of Bede as "spiritalis presbiter et investigator sanctarum scripturarum" (207) [inspired priest and student of the holy scriptures], and he says that the manuscripts copied by Abbess Eadburga (Tangl 35) "aureis litteris fulgeant" (60) [shine with golden letters]. Boniface and his circle are reminis-

---

[5] See Ong, "Orality, Literacy," 1-12.

[6] Although the Boniface Collection is preserved in manuscripts found in Germany and was edited in MGH, it consists of letters between Anglo-Saxon monks and nuns, both in England and on the Continent. Throughout this study, I follow the convention of identifying the epistles by their numbers in the edition of Tangl. Quotations from the epistles are cited from Tangl's edition by page number. I have not used the 1968 edition of Rau because it primarily includes only letters to and from Boniface. The exceptions are letters of condolence to Lull on the martyrdom of Boniface from Archbishop Cuthberht of Canterbury (Tangl 111) and Bishop Milret of Worcester (Tangl 112).

[7] Fell, "Boniface Correspondence," 41.

cent of St. Wilfrid of York, who, according to Eddius Stephanus, owned "quattuor evangelia de auro purissimo in membranis depurpuratis, coloratis" [the four Gospels written in the purest gold on purple parchment and illuminated].[8]

Studying the vernacular influence on the letters provides insights into their debt to more than the literate Latin tradition, even though epistles are a non-narrative genre that did not exist in the pre-literate society of the Anglo-Saxons. Fell speaks of Old English lexical items, vocabulary, and concepts underlying the Latin. Fell and Peter Dronke have each identified influence from vernacular poetry on some of the letters,[9] and Nicholas Howe compares Boniface to "the wandering scop of *Widsith*."[10] Michael Lapidge has argued that Aldhelm, to whose works the writers of the Boniface Collection owe a substantial debt, "in ignorance of classical techniques of verse composition ... resorted to techniques familiar to him from native English poetry,"[11] primarily alliteration and the use of phrases that recall vernacular formulas. Even Patrick Sims-Williams, whose main concern is to identify the debt of various letters to the Latin tradition, suggests that Ecgburg's "predilection for sea-imagery ... probably corresponds to a real element in the Anglo-Saxon poetic sensibility."[12] Echoes of vernacular poetry are frequently found in the letters. I would, for example, interpret Boniface's letter to Bugga (Tangl 94) and his letter to Abbot Aldhere (Tangl 38) as reminiscent of *The Seafarer*. He speaks to Bugga of "amor peregrinationis" (214) [the love of traveling abroad] and to Aldhere of God as the "causa ... peregrinationis nostrae" (63) [cause of our traveling abroad]. Boniface's words recall the Seafarer's "ealle þa gemoniað modes fus, / sefan to siþe" (50-1a) [all then admonishes the mind of the one eager of spirit to the journey].[13]

Despite observations such as those of Fell and Dronke, the conventional wisdom is that Anglo-Latin epistles like the Boniface Collection are fully in the classical tradition. According to Ephraim Emerton, one of the modern translators of the letters, they "follow the usual fourfold pattern of

---

[8] Colgrave, *Life of Bishop Wilfrid*, 36.

[9] See Fell, "Boniface Correspondence," 41; and Dronke, *Women Writers*.

[10] Howe, *Migration and Mythmaking*, 137.

[11] Lapidge, "Aldhelm's Latin Poetry," 228.

[12] Sims-Williams, *Religion and Literature*, 221.

[13] I cite Krapp's edition of the *Seafarer* in the *Exeter Book*.

greeting, preamble, main business, and conclusion."[14] Sims-Williams argues that the "Anglo-Saxons played a full part in continuing the *ancient literary tradition* of letter-writing and letter-collecting,"[15] and he identifies many specific classical borrowings in the letters. In addition, Sims-Williams shows the debt that the letter-writers owe to "earlier hexameter verse,"[16] both that of Virgil and that of Christian Latin poets like Arator. It is, however, possible to overstate the Latin influence, even while acknowledging the presence of vernacular influence.

When writing to each other, St. Boniface, St. Lull, and their intimate friends were writing to other Old English speakers attuned to vernacular poetics. They therefore use an idiom that merges Latin and Anglo-Saxon. In addition to using alliteration and formulaic language, these epistles show the influence of themes from formulaic vernacular poetry, including such frequently occurring ones as Journey to Trial,[17] the Sea Voyage,[18]

---

[14] Emerton, *Letters of Saint Boniface*, 19.

[15] Sims-Williams, *Religion and Literature*, 211 (emphasis added).

[16] Sims-Williams, *Religion and Literature*, 216.

[17] In *Key to Old Poems*, 93, Renoir describes a thematic pattern that he calls Journey to Trial: "a hero or heroine (a) makes a journey or at least moves from one location to another, (b) is in serious danger, (c) experiences one or more confrontations, usually in the form of some kind of physical or spiritual trial, and (d) emerges physically or spiritually victorious."

[18] Ramsey, in "Sea Voyages in *Beowulf*," 55, describes the paradigmatic shape of the theme in *Beowulf* as follows: "Beowulf gives an order to his men ... and explains the purpose of his voyage.... He leads the way to the ship ..., which waits at the shore laden with treasures.... The men depart in the ship and sail until they can observe the opposite shore.... They moor the ship and proceed to the hall." A clear example of the theme is found in *Andreas*, 235-9a, in the passage in which Andreas meets the Steersman who is Christ:

> Gewat him þa on uhtan   mid ærdæge
> ofer sandhleoðu   to sæs faruðe,
> þriste on geþance,   ond his þegnas mid,
> gangan on greote;   garsecg hlynede,
> beoton brimstreamas.
>
> [Then he departed in the early morning at daybreak over the sand-hills to the shore of the sea, bold in thought, and his thanes with him, to walk on the earth; the sea roared, the sea-streams beat.]

I cite Krapp's edition of the poem in the *Vercelli Book* here and elsewhere.

and Exile.[19] For example, the passage in Ecgburg's letter (Tangl 13) depicting a sea voyage evokes the Sea Voyage theme, which, as Lee C. Ramsey has shown, occurs at pivotal positions of both heroic and hagiographic Old English poems. In Ecgburg's letter, the references to the sailor who "portum ... desiderat" [longs for the harbor] and to the "litore" [shore] on which the mother awaits her son, reminiscent of "on greote" (238a) [on the shore of the sea] in *Andreas*, are reminiscent of the theme.[20] In addition to containing echoes of the Sea Voyage, Ecgburg's letter, like many others of the collection,[21] expresses the writer's loneliness and sense of isolation. Fell finds Berhtgyth's letters to her brother evocative of the theme of Exile in *The Wanderer*, and the theme of Exile runs through the letters. Ursula Schaefer has argued that Eangyth's letter to Boniface is similar to *The Wife's Lament*, especially in the women's complaints about "the lack or loss of friends."[22] These letters show pervasive influence of the vernacular on Anglo-Latin because the expressive economy of Anglo-Saxon poetics was open to the authors. In contrast, the letters by continental writers like Pope Zacharias and the letters of Boniface to recipients other than his close associates show that the letters between members of the Boniface mission are unique in their use of the English poetic tradition.[23]

In his letter asking Grifo to protect his mission (Tangl 48), Boniface speaks formally of "servos Dei ... qui sunt in Thuringia" (77) [the servants of God ... who are in Thuringia] and gives no indication of the sense of ex-

---

[19] Greenfield, in *Critical History*, 201, has shown that there are "four aspects or concomitants of the exile state: 1. status ..., 2. deprivation ..., 3. state of mind ... [and] 4. movement in or into exile."

[20] See below, 114–15.

[21] See below, 116–17.

[22] Schaefer, "Two Women," 493.

[23] Numerous letters from Pope Gregory II, Pope Gregory III, and Pope Zacharias give instruction to Boniface or answer his inquiries, and others commend him to Frankish noblemen and churchmen. There are also letters from Charles Martel, Cardinal-Deacon Gemmulus, Palace Mayor Karlmann, Archdeacon Theophylactus, Cardinal-Bishop Benedict, King Aelbwald of East Anglia, and King Ethelbert of Kent, as well as accounts of synods, Boniface's oath on the assumption of his episcopate, and the charter of the monastery of Fulda. Although these letters help a historian gain a full picture of the Boniface mission, they are of no interest to the present study because they show no influence from the English poetic tradition.

ile that imbues his letters to his English friends. He speaks to King Pippin (Tangl 107) and to Bishop Daniel of Winchester (Tangl 63) of his "senectutem" (233; 131) [old age]. Although he says to Daniel that he has difficulty "caligantibus occulis minutas litteras ac connexas clare discere" (131) [distinguishing clearly small, connected letters because (his) eyes are growing dim], alluding to Genesis 27:1 and Lamentations 1:15, Boniface gives no indication of his emotional plight in such letters: the description is purely physical. He asks Bishop Daniel only for help to overcome a physical impediment.

The moderation contrasts to Boniface's laments to Abbot Duddo (Tangl 34), not only that he is "in senectutute" [in old age], but also that he is "decrepiti et membris omnibus ad viam universe terre vergentibus" (58) [decrepit and approaching in all limbs the way of all earthly things]. He reiterates that he is "senis" (58) [an old man] and "decrepeti" (59) [decrepit]. The reiteration of the point in a brief letter (it occupies only twenty-one lines in Tangl's edition) shows Boniface's emphasis on his plight. He places the same emphasis on his emotional state when he writes to Bugga (Tangl 27), "multis tribulationibus fatigor et multo maiore mentis tribulatione et sollicitudine quam corporis labore conturbor" (49) [I am wearied by many tribulations and disturbed much more by mental tribulations and anxiety than by bodily labor] and to Eadburga (Tangl 65) speaking of "peregrinationis nostrae variis tempestatibus inliditur. Undique labor, undique meror" (137) [our journey abroad is beaten by many storms. Everywhere toil, everywhere sorrow].

His repetition of "multis tribulationibus" and "multo ... tribulatione" emphasize the fact of great tribulation rhetorically. We also know that Bugga has sent similar laments to him, because he consoles her for "tempestates tribulationum, que tibi in senectute Deo permittente supervenerunt" (214) [the storms of tribulations, which by the permission of God have come upon you in your old age]. The alliteration of "tempestates tribulationum" and "senectute ... supervenerunt" calls attention to her tribulations and old age. In another letter (Tangl 15), Bugga indicates that she has received consolation from Boniface, because his prayers have brought her "ad portum alicuius quietis" (27) [to a harbor of a certain peace]. This brief statement uses the sea imagery that runs throughout the letters of the Boniface circle. It is intriguing that the laments are such a motif in the letters between English friends that Ingalice, writing to Lull

(Tangl 72), speaks of Lull's "diversas molestias et tribulationes" (145) [diverse troubles and tribulations], using the evocative word "tribulationes."

One letter of the Boniface Collection, a description of a vision seen by a monk of Wenlock (Tangl 10), uses the theme of Journey to Trial to depict the liminal situation in which the human world comes in contact with the angelic and diabolic worlds. The monk does not make an actual journey, but he makes a visionary one and feels that he has "egressum de corpore" (8) [passed out of the body], carried by angels. He relates what he saw when he was "extra corpus" (9) [out of the body]: he saw "cunctas terrarum partes et populos et maria sub uno aspectu" (8) [all parts of the earth and the peoples and seas under one range of vision]. The vision is initiated by serious danger, "per violentis egritudinis dolorem" (8) [pain from a violent illness]. He faces a confrontation that is both physical and spiritual, because he sees "flammam immensae magnitudinis anhelantem et terribiliter ad superiora ascendentem" [a blasting flame of immense magnitude, terribly ascending on high], and he suffers "ardore" (9) [from the heat].

He also perceives other souls, and like them he is accused by the devils and excused by the angels. This episode provides the greatest trial, because his sins seem to outweigh his virtues and he seems in danger of being sent to "igneum piceumque flumen bulliens et ardens" (11) [the river, fiery and bubbling and glowing with pitch]. He emerges victorious because of angelic protection: "Tum demum beati angeli precipiebant ei, qui haec omnia extra corpus suum raptus spiritali contemplatione vidit et audivit, ut sine mora at proprium rediret corpus" (14) [Then at last the blessed angels taught him who had seen and heard all these things in spiritual contemplation while he was set free from his body]. By evoking the theme of Journey to Trial, the letter depicts the monk explicitly and affectively as heroic and a worthy recipient of visions, like St. Paul and also like other visionaries of the Other World. It also connects this instance of the theme with every other instance of it. The echoic connections among the various occurrences of the theme run through this one as well.

Ecgburg's letter to Boniface (Tangl 13) shows the syncretic nature of the letters, their debt to the Latin epistolary and the Latin and vernacular poetic traditions. Sims-Williams shows that this epistle was influenced by early Christian epistles (it includes, for example, direct borrowings from Jerome). It also has Virgilian echoes *and*, I would emphasize, includes echoes from Old English poetry. In his edition, Tangl notes the probable sources of Ecgburg's borrowings from classical tradition. For example, she refers to God as "superi rector Olimpi" (20) [the ruler of high Olympus], paralleling "superi regnator Olympi" [the ruler of high Olympus] in *Aeneid* 2.779,[24] and in Aldhelm's *De Virginitate* which merges classical and vernacular tradition.

The same use of alliteration and formulas characterizes the poems included in the epistles. The passage in Ecgburg's letter that Sims-Williams considers reminiscent of Old English poetry runs as follows:

> Quapropter, crede mihi, non sic tempestate iactatus portum nauta desiderat, non sic sitientia imbres arva desiderant, non sic curvo litore anxia filium mater expectat, quam ut ego visibus vestris frui cupio.
> (20)

> [Therefore, believe me, I long for the sight of you more than a storm-tossed sailor longs for the harbor, or thirsty fields desire rain,[25] or an anxious mother watches by the shore for her son.]

Although brief, this passage indeed evokes the mood of Old English poetry: Sims-Williams compares it to the Frisian-wife passage in *Maxims I*. Even more, it evokes the Sea Voyage theme. In Ecgburg's letter, the references to the sailor who "portum ... desiderat" [longs for the harbor] and to the "litore" [shore] on which the mother awaits her son, reminiscent of "on greote" [on the shore of the sea] in *Andreas*, evoke the theme. The sailor is the hero, approaching the "litore" where his mother waits. Because he is a "nauta" [sailor], his ship and companions are suggested but not described. She evokes the theme later in the letter by speaking of "meroris undam" (21) [the wave of grief]. As Alain Renoir says, once the pattern of a theme has been established, only a few details are necessary to recall it to the audience, and the audience is "able to supply the missing elements."[26]

---

[24] I cite the edition of the *Aeneid* by Greenough and Kittredge.
[25] Cf. Psalm 143:6.
[26] Renoir, *Key to Old Poems*, 119.

One of the letters that contains the clearest representation of the Sea Voyage is that which Lull wrote as a young man to an unnamed abbess (Tangl 98).[27] It is unusually full of biographical details, leading Fell to observe that she would be tempted to believe that the letter was addressed to kinswomen except for "the extent to which he provides information in that letter about his own background."[28] Regardless of the recipients of the letter, it is noteworthy that Lull provides biographical information that makes the theme of the Sea Voyage evident.

Lull says that he left Britain "cum totius propinquitatis meae propemodum caterva" (219) [with a crowd of almost all my near kinsmen], a statement that recalls the fact that the hero goes on his Sea Voyage with a troop of retainers. The purpose, missionary work, is clear. The emphasis on the sea is also clear when Lull speaks longingly of "gauca spumantis maris ... undi" (219) [the gray-green waves of the foaming sea] that separate him from his homeland. The group of kinsmen makes a sea voyage, crossing "ferventis ingruentibus pelagi molibus" (219) [the attacking hills of the raging sea] and reaching "regionis marginem" [the shore of these regions]. The word "marginem" calls attention to the shore opposite England that is the goal of the journey. In addition to the letters of Ecgburg and Lull, another letter that recalls the theme is Boniface's letter to Abbot Duddo (Tangl 34). Boniface describes himself as "Germanici maris tempestatibus undique quassantibus fatigati" (58-9) [worn out by the storms and waves of the German sea]. This brief passage recalls the actual crossing of the North Sea and therefore the theme of the Sea Voyage. It represents what Renoir has called "semantic gapping," where even "one single component" can serve "to keep the momentum of the original impact alive" for an audience who has been trained to appreciate the elements.[29]

The echoes of the Sea Voyage in the letters of Ecgburg are the more striking because not all references to the sea, ships, and voyages in the letters of the Boniface Collection are reminiscent of vernacular poetry, since the authors' compositional practices are the result of their engaging in several different traditions. Boniface himself speaks to Abbot Aldhere (Tangl 38) of "navem fragilitatis nostra" (63) [the ship of our weakness], and Lull

---

[27] The writer of the letter is not identified, but the description of the writer's pilgrimage to Rome, exiled state, and illness leads scholars to believe he was Lull.

[28] Fell, "Boniface Correspondence," 39.

[29] Renoir, *Key to Old Poems*, 119.

speaks to Eadburga (Tangl 70) of "meae fragilitatis navem, quae cotidie presentis mundi procellarum turbinibus quatiatur" (143) [the ship of my weakness, which is shaken daily by the violence of the storms of this present world]. The metaphor is clear and easily understood, and since it is used in two letters it must have been meaningful to members of the mission. However, it in no way evokes the English tradition.

In addition to containing echoes of the Sea Voyage, Ecgburg's letter, like many others of the collection, especially those of Boniface and Berhtgyth, expresses the writer's loneliness and sense of isolation. Fell suggests that the letters of Berhtgyth were not preserved "solely for the note of personal anguish" found therein but because of "their formalization of that emotion."[30] The "formalization of ... emotion" that typifies the letters is also found in Old English poetry and helps us understand both the letters and the poetry. Indeed, one reason for the preservation of the letters was undoubtedly that they were imbued with the vernacular tradition inherited by both the Anglo-Saxons and the continental Germans that Karen Cherewatuk has detected in the verse epistles of St. Radegund.[31]

The theme of Exile, which occupies a demonstrably central position in Old English poetics, is important in the collection. Boniface describes himself in a letter to Abbess Eadburga (Tangl 30) as an "exulem Germanicum" [exile among the Germans] who "tenebrosos angulos Germanicarum gentium lustrare debet" (54) [must traverse dark retired corners of the German nation]. The theme of Exile and the sense of deprivation run through the letters. In Tangl 98, Lull says "adfinitatis meae propinquis propemodum longo quietis somno sopitis solus in huius exilii calamitate et orbatus merui" (219) [almost all my near relatives had fallen into the long sleep of peace; I was left alone and orphaned in this misfortune of exile]. In Leoba's letter to Boniface (Tangl 29), the aspect of the state of deprivation is emphasized to the extent that the mention of it alone is enough to evoke the theme of Exile powerfully. Leoba says that her father Dynne "ante VIII annorum curriculum ab hac luce subtractus est" (51) [was taken from this light eight years ago] and her mother Aebbe "ab infirmitate ob-

---

[30] Fell, "Boniface Correspondence," 41.

[31] Cherewatuk, "Germanic Echoes," 3-4, believes that the "Germanic echoes" in the verse epistles of St. Radegund "embody the saint's native Germanic tradition, particularly in their depiction of the lamenting woman," perceiving vernacular influence where many scholars have seen only classical.

pressa est" (53) [is oppressed by infirmities]. Since she was their "unica filia" [only daughter], she asks to have Boniface "in fratris locum" (53) [in place of brothers] and restore her kin-group in that way. It should be noted that Leoba's letter was written before she joined the Boniface mission and journeyed into exile.

All four of the aspects which Greenfield says identify the theme of Exile are present in Ecgburg's letter to Boniface (Tangl 13),[32] and Ecgburg's expression of her concern with exile is typical of the letters of the Boniface Collection. As Fell observes, the letters from both men and women "reveal mental, emotional, and physical suffering and stress."[33] Ecgburg's greeting to Boniface identifies one aspect of her status: she speaks of herself as "ultima discipulorum seu discipularum tuarum" (18) [the least of his male and female disciples]. The other aspect of her status is found in her mention of "germanum meum Osherem" [my brother Oshere] and "carissima soror Uuethburg" (19) [most beloved sister Wethburg]. Although modern scholars are uncertain about the identity of Ecgburg, the names of her sister and brother have led many to hypothesize that she was "a member of the royal house of the Hwicce"[34] and possibly the abbess of Gloucester.[35] Like the speakers in the Old English elegies who allude to their former membership in a *comitatus* (see *The Wanderer*) or a marriage of high status (see *The Wife's Lament*), Ecgburg is a woman of high status, and her state of exile is the more poignant because of the loss of that status.

Ecgburg makes her state of deprivation clear: "amara mors et crudelis" [bitter and cruel death] has separated her from Oshere, Wethburg "ab oculis evanuit" [has vanished from (her) sight], and she has been "defraudata" [deprived] of the "aspectu corporali" (19) [bodily presence] of Boniface. Her use of "defraudata" is significant because it signals the presence of the formulaic theme. She also says that she experiences "ubique dolor, ubique pavor, ubique mortis imago" (19) [everywhere sorrow, everywhere fear, everywhere the image of death] because of her loss of her sister Weth-

---

[32] Schaefer, "Two Women," discusses Greenfield's article, but she prefers (495) to interpret the theme as "the syntagmatic theme" of "loneliness and friendlessness" in both Old English poetry and the Anglo-Latin epistles. In contrast to Schaefer, I am arguing that the vernacular theme influenced the epistles.

[33] Fell, "Boniface Correspondence," 41.

[34] Sims-Williams, *Religion and Literature*, 220.

[35] Sims-Williams, *Religion and Literature*, 229.

burga. The incremental repetition of these images recalls the use of variation in Old English poetry. A similar state of deprivation is also expressed by Lull, who uses the strong image of orphanhood to express it. Only once in the Boniface Collection, in Lull's letter to Leoba (Tangl 100), is the metaphor of the new kin-group of Christians used, when Lull speaks of "sinceram in Domino germanitatem" (223) [our true brother- and sisterhood in the Lord]. Fell suspects that the letter is "a magnificent piece of thinly disguised irritation" in response to a "*cri de coeur* from Leoba,"[36] and it is noteworthy that in this letter Lull speaks of the Christian rather than the literal kin-group so that Leoba does not seem to be in exile from her kin. By practicing an eighth-century version of cognitive psychology, she should be able to find consolation in the new community.

Ecgburg describes her state of mind as clearly as the speakers of the Old English elegies do. The speaker of *The Wife's Lament*, for example, says "Ic þis giedd wrece bi me ful geomorre, / minre sylfre sið" (1–2a) [I recite this tale about myself who is very sad, my own journey].[37] Ecgburg speaks of the "inmensi doloris" (21) [unmeasurable sorrow], the "meroris ... nebula atra" [dark cloud of sorrow] which afflicted her after the death of Oshere, and the "lucra iniuriarum" (19) [sum of her wrongs], phrases which recall the sorrow of the speaker of *The Wife's Lament*. Likewise, Ecgburg's laments for her lost brother, sister, and friend recall the Wife's lament about her loss of her "felaleofan" (26a) [much beloved one].

Ecgburg expresses her concern with her exile "in valle lacrimarum" (20) [in the vale of tears],[38] and her discussion of her exiled state provides the fourth point of Greenfield's paradigm, "movement into ... exile." Oshere has died and presumably is in heaven, and Wethburg "Romana carcer includit" [is enclosed as a recluse in a Roman cell], but Ecgburg must continue "huic seculo servire" (20) [to serve in this world], as an abbess if Sims-Williams is correct. She worries about the sins she has committed. Pilgrimage, especially to Rome ("movement into exile"), was a common solution to such problems because it brought the pilgrim what Boniface calls in a letter to Bugga (Tangl 27) "libertatem quietem mentis" (48) [freedom, quiet of mind], a solution to the problems the letter-writers describe.

---

[36] Fell, "Boniface Correspondence," 35.
[37] I cite the poem from Krapp, *Exeter Book*.
[38] Cf. Psalm 83:7.

Another letter which evokes the formulaic theme of Exile is that of Eangyth and Bugga to Boniface (Tangl 14). Eangyth identifies their status: she is an abbess, "indigna ancilla ancillarum Dei" [unworthy handmaid of the handmaids of God], and Bugga is "unica filia" (21) [her only daughter]. Their deprivation is made manifest by the fact that they are oppressed physically by "paupertas et penuria rerum temporalium" [poverty and lack of temporal goods] and spiritually by "amissio amicorum et contribulium, caterva propinquorum et consanguineorum turba" (23) [the loss of friends and countrymen, the crowd of relatives and the throng of those related by blood]. Like Ecgburg, Eangyth and Bugga make their state of mind clear: "tedebit nos vitae nostrae et pene nobis pertesum est vivere" (24) [our life wearies us and it is almost a burden to us to live]. They compare their misery to a dangerous sea voyage:

> Tamquam spumosi maria vortices verrunt et vellunt undarum cumulos conlisos saxis, quando ventorum violentia et procellarum tempestates sevissime inormem curipum inpellunt et cymbarum carine sursum inmutate et malus navis deorsum duratur.
>
> (22)

> [As when the whirling of the foaming sea sweeps and pulls the mountainous waves broken on the rocks, when the violence of the winds and the fury of the tempests drive wrathfully against the long channel and the keels of the boats are turned up, and the unfortunate ship is turned upside down.]

In this passage, which combines an epic, Virgilian simile with the account of St. Paul's shipwreck in Acts, the heavy alliteration ("*vortices verrunt et vellunt*" and "*ventorum violentia*") and the description of the storms at sea heighten the sense of exile in the letter by recalling vernacular tradition. However, after the lengthy passage on the sea, they use the metaphor of the ship of the soul that Boniface used in Tangl 9, and speak of "animarum nostrarum naviculae" (22) [the little ship of our souls]. The purpose of the letter is to ask Boniface to permit them to move into literal exile from their metaphorical one: they wish to travel "equoreis campis" (24) [the pathways of the sea] and make a pilgrimage to the "orbis Romam" (25) [city of Rome] as other English men and women have done. In Tangl 27, Boniface acknowledges that the "vitam quietem" (48) [quiet life] they seek can be found in exile in Rome.

A letter in which men express their sense of exile in a way that evokes the formulaic theme is that of Denehard, Lull, and Burchard to Abbess Cyniburg (Tangl 49). They describe their status as Cyniburg's "fili ... ac vernaculi" [sons and fellow countrymen] and their deprivation because of "genitoris et genetricis et aliorum propinquorum ... obitum" (78) [the death of their fathers, mothers, and other relatives]. Their state of mind is also clear because their "lintrem procellosis fluctibus huius mundi fatigatam" [boat worn out by the stormy waves of this world] seeks to go "ad portum salutis" (79) [to a safe harbor] under Cyniburg's protection. They also speak of their movement into exile: "ad Germanicas gentes transivimus" (78) [we went over to the German peoples].

In a letter of which he is the sole author (Tangl 98), Lull depicts the movement into exile in a moving way. He speaks of his status, describing himself as one who exercises "spiritalis officii" (219) [spiritual office]. His state of deprivation is expressed in his lament that he is "solus ... et orbatus" (219) [alone and orphaned] and is emphasized by the word "calamitate" [loss, misfortune, or calamity]. The letter emphasizes his state of mind, the fact that he is "tristis" [sorrowful] and "fatigatus" [fatigued], a word with both literal and metaphorical meaning. His movement into exile is stated when he says that he left "Brittanice ... fecundissima natalis patrie" (219) [Britain, the most fruitful country of my origin].

From an affective point of view, the letters which express the sense of exile most fully are those of Berhtgyth to her brother (Tangl 147, 148, and, perhaps, 143). Dronke notes that these "passionate and sensitive letters" have no link with Boniface and have therefore "not appeared in modern selections of the Boniface collection."[39] Part of the reason for their preservation is their use of the vernacular tradition: as Dronke notes, Berhtgyth uses a "vernacular motif" in Tangl 147, that of "the sea that

---

[39] Dronke, *Women Writers*, 30. Because of recent interest in women writers, and because of the important studies of Dronke and Fell, these letters have been brought to the notice of scholars, both Anglo-Saxonists and others. Tangl 143 appears in the manuscript without the names of sender and recipient, but, as Fell argues, "Boniface Correspondence," 38, "stylistic detail, similarity of content, and positioning in the manuscript suggest single authorship" of the three.

sunders those who love each other."⁴⁰ Berhtgyth speaks of the "multae congregationes aquarum" (284) [many congregations of the waters] that separate her and Baldhard. Despite the echo therein of Genesis, like Ecgburg, Berhtgyth recalls the formulaic theme of the Sea Voyage, because the sea for an Anglo-Saxon audience alludes to more than Genesis alone.

One reason for the emotional effect of the three letters is their use of the theme of Exile, which Berhtgyth expresses more fully even than Ecgburg. In Tangl 143, she expresses her status: she is "ultima ancillarum Dei" (282) [the least of the handmaidens of God]. In addition, she addresses Tangl 148 to "fratri unico Baldhardo" (285) [her only brother Baldhard], which indicates her status. Otloh's *Vita Bonifatii* describes the "feminae vero religiosae" [truly religious women] of the Boniface mission, including "materata ... sancti Lulli nomine Chunihilt et filia eius Berhtgit" [the maternal aunt of St. Lull, named Cynehild, and her daughter Berhtgyth].⁴¹

Likewise, all three letters make clear her state of deprivation. According to Tangl 143, she is "sola in hac terra" (282) [alone in this country]; according to Tangl 147, she is "sola derelicta et destituta auxilio propinquorum" (284) [alone, forsaken, and deprived of the support of kin]; and according to Tangl 148, she is "derelicta ... et sola" (286) [bereft and alone]. The alliteration of *d* in "*derelicta et destituta*" calls attention to her state of being forsaken. This emphasis on lack of kin recalls both the Old English elegies and other letters of the Boniface Collection, like those of Lull. She expresses her state of mind with great clarity, her great grief because Baldhard will not visit her: in Tangl 147, she speaks of her "fontem lacrimarum" (286) [fountain of tears]. She begs, "auferas tristitiam ab anima mea" [take away the sorrow from my soul] and asks that he remove "tristitia ab anima mea et dolor de corde meo" (286) [the sadness from my soul and the sorrow from my heart]. At the end of Tangl 148, Berhtgyth expresses her longing to move within exile to the place "ubi requiescunt corpora parentum nostrorum" [where rest the bodies of our parents] and "temporalem vitam ibi finire" (286) [end this transitory life there]. Fell suggests that the letters were not written while Berhtgyth's first cousin Lull

---

⁴⁰ Dronke, *Women Writers*, 31.

⁴¹ Levison, *Vitae Sancti Bonifatii*, 138. Baldhard is not named, presumably because Otloh is naming the *women* of the Boniface mission.

was alive,[42] a likely state because the letters lament most poignantly the absence of kinsmen. This fact would suggest that the sense of exile expressed in them is more than merely conventional because the power of Anglo-Saxon poetics is employed by an author as a way of articulating the real-world situation. In this instance, the traditional expression functions powerfully and dynamically on both the usual global level *and* the local individual level as well.

The world of the Boniface Collection is a world still close to its Anglo-Saxon roots rather than exclusively in the Continental Christian Latin tradition. Boniface addresses Tangl 41 "dilectissimis filiis Geppan et Eoban, Tatuuino et Uuyigberto et omnibus fratribus ac sororibus" (66) [to my most beloved sons Gepps and Eoban, Tatwin and Wigbert, and all my brothers and sisters], reminding us that one thing that Boniface carried from England to Frisia was the Anglo-Saxon tradition of the double monastery. This fact is also recalled in Tangl 49. As Fell points out, Cyniburg seems to be "regarded by ... [the] young men as their spiritual mentor and secular lord,"[43] and she shows that the letter evokes the lord/thane relationship found in *The Wanderer*.

The Boniface Collection is also famous for its inclusion of poetry in the letters, just as Aldhelm merges the techniques of classical quantitative verse with those techniques — alliteration, formulas, and themes — "familiar to him from his native English."[44] Fell points out that in Tangl 140, Lull imitates Aldhelm's *Carmen Rhythmicum* and in Tangl 29, Leoba includes four lines that are "heavily Aldhelm-dependent."[45]

Tangl 9 is from Wynfrith (before he was renamed Boniface) to a young man named Nithard. Tangl dates the letter to 716 or 717. Its debt to earlier Christian Latin poetry is clear; for example it says "Prophietae apostolicis / Consonabunt et laudibus" (7) [Prophets too will harmonize in apostolic praises]. Even a letter that Boniface writes to Pope Zacharias (Tangl 50) contains some alliteration, as "Deo dignum" [worthy to God] and "*domus domini*" (86) [house of the Lord]. Although the letter does not demonstrate the use of Aldhelmian formulaic language, it has striking use of alliteration, as in the first line of "Nitharde, nunc nigerrima / Imi

---

[42] See Fell, "Boniface Correspondence," 40.
[43] Fell, "Boniface Correspondence," 32.
[44] Lapidge, "Aldhelm's Latin Poetry," 217.
[45] Fell, "Boniface Correspondence," 38.

cosmi contagia" (7) [Nithard, now avoid the dark contagion of this world below]. Likewise, Leoba's brief letter (Tangl 29) includes alliteration, speaking of the One "qui cuncta creavit" [who created all things] and "servet semper" (53) [may preserve you forever]. One letter to Lull by Bishop Koaena of York (Tangl 124) and one by Lull also include alliterative poetry. Koaena uses the line "Vita tuis saeclo specimen, carissime caelo" (262) [Your life is a model for the age, most beloved of Heaven]. In Tangl 140, Lull tells an unnamed nun, "Vale Christo virguncula" [Farewell in Christ, young virgin] and bids her "vota redde cum fervore / Altissimo in aethere" (280) [render vows with fervor to the Most High in Heaven]. The poem is heavily alliterative (ten lines of eighteen include alliteration).

Most heavily alliterative in the collection is Berhtgyth's second letter (Tangl 147):

> Vale vivens feliciter, ut sis sanctus simpliciter,
> Tibi salus per saecula tributatur per culmina.
> Vivamus soli Domino vitam semper in seculo.
> Profecto ipsum precibus peto profusis fletibus
> Solo tenus ipissima subrogare auxilia:
> Ut simus digni gloria, ubi resonant carmina
> Angelorum laetissima aethralea laetitia
> Clara Christi clementia celse laudis in secula.
> Valeamus angelicis victrices iungi milibus,
> Paradisi perpetuis perdurrantes in gaudiis.
> Elonqueel et Michael, Acaddai, Adonai, Alleuatia Alleluia.
> (285)

[Farewell, one living happily, that you may be plainly holy. Salvation through the ages will be allotted to you in the heights. Let us always live a life for God alone in the world. Indeed I, alone, most often beseech Him with entreaties, with profuse weepings, to furnish a true source of help: so that we may be worthy of glory, where the joyful songs of the angels resound with joy through the upper air by the famous mercy of Christ, (songs) of high praise forever. Let us be strong, to be united with angelic soldiers as victorious ones everlasting in the perpetual joy of

Paradise. Elonqueel and Michael, Acaddai, Adonai, Alleuatia, alleluia.]

Only two lines of the ten do not include alliteration, and the half-lines usually alliterate as Old English lines do. One line links together the half-lines by double alliteration: "Angelorum laetissima aethralea laetitia." Even the puzzling last line, which Dronke suggests may be a "magic spell" and Fell "a perfect alleluia trope" is alliterative, remembering that all vowels alliterate in Old English.[46] Fell remarks that "a single surviving letter implies the loss of others,"[47] and we therefore have pragmatic reason for assuming that numerous letters contained verse, not just those which were preserved. Because they often composed verse which contained alliteration, the writers of Boniface's circle were presumably cognizant of the techniques of Old English poetry.

As a result of the emphasis on the importance of the English tradition, it is not surprising that the letters use language reminiscent of vernacular poetry. Whether they are in England or in Germany, the monks and nuns associated with the Boniface mission experience a spiritual crisis analogous to what later writers call the Dark Night of the Soul. Without the developed mystical language available to St. John of the Cross, they fall back on the themes of their English poetic tradition (Exile, the Sea Voyage, and Journey to Trial) to express their crises.

Renoir says that "a well-trained craftsman working within a firm tradition will often implement certain requirements of that tradition without questioning their significance."[48] The same is true of people trained to respond to literary works in that tradition. The process by which the tradition is used in an allusive manner "forces us to participate actively in the composition of the very poem we are reading or to which we are listening."[49] I would argue that it was that tradition of participation in the composition of poems that enabled the members of the Boniface mission to engage the poetic tradition although writing in a different language and to speak of their own Dark Night of the Soul. In this way, they unbound Proteus from vernacular poetry alone.

---

[46] Dronke, *Women Writers*, 32; Fell, "Boniface Correspondence," 43.
[47] Fell, "Boniface Correspondence," 31.
[48] Renoir, *Key to Old Poems*, 119.
[49] Renoir, *Key to Old Poems*, 119.

JAN M. ZIOLKOWSKI

Oral-Formulaic Tradition and the Composition of Latin Poetry from Antiquity through the Twelfth Century

The title of this essay may make many a reader raise an eyebrow or two. After all, the creative process in the vast majority of Latin poems can be related far less easily to the fascinating "otherness" of oral-formulaic traditional composition than to the intense literariness of *imitatio* and *aemulatio*.[1] That is to say, the virtues of Latin poetry have been rightly seen to lie rather in the brilliance with which its practitioners have crafted new poetry in response to the literary traditions, mainly Greek and Latin, that preceded them. In the classical and especially the Hellenistic period Latin poetry is associated with elaborate allusivity, which helps to explain why in recent decades Latinists have adopted with speed and success concepts such as intertextuality.[2] Because of the complex and sometimes conflicted relationship of Roman literature to its models (first Greek and later also Latin), the "anxiety of influence" – of textual influence – comes to the fore in almost every major genre, such as lyric, tragedy, comedy, and, of course, epic.

---

[1] In classical rhetoric the fundamental discussion of the relationship between these two concepts is Quintilian, *Institutio oratoria*, 10.2.1-28 (ed. and trans. Russell, 4:322-37). For an examination of the two by a twentieth-century scholar, see Reiff, *Interpretatio, imitatio, aemulatio*. For an exploration of the role of *imitatio* in later Latin culture, see Ziolkowski, "Highest Form of Compliment."

[2] For example, see Thomas, *Reading Virgil and His Texts*.

It is hardly an accident that those active in the study of oral-formulaic poetry have gravitated toward Greek — or, to view the phenomenon from the other end of the telescope, that Hellenists have been drawn to oral-literary theory — while those seeking to contextualize Latin literature have gone to libraries rather than to the former Yugoslavia and to recordings of *guslari* made in the decades around the Second World War. If Homer (by no means without lively debate) has been presented at times as the foundational example of what has been termed "primary," oral, or folk epic, emanating from oral-formulaic tradition, then Virgil (70-19 B.C.E.) has been the avatar of "secondary," literary, or art epic, reflecting a command of preceding literary texts in both Greek and Latin in a way far removed from the tastes and techniques of bards.[3] In late antiquity and the early Middle Ages Latin poets continued to operate within a literary framework that esteemed quotation, allusion, and reference, and they edged ever further from oral-formulaic traditional composition as Latin itself shifted from being a mother tongue to being a father tongue. Medieval education, rarely accused of having fostered spontaneity, was built upon written texts and authorities: *textus* and *auctoritas* were key concepts for the entire millennium.[4] Accordingly, the schoolroom of the Middle Ages conjures up pictures of dreary rote learning from manuscripts and brutal beatings, seemingly anything but a hospitable locus for budding bards or aspiring minstrels.

Although all of the statements in the preceding paragraph have truth to them, there are good grounds for reevaluating such apparently stark and clear-cut dichotomies as those between primary and secondary epic, oral-formulaic tradition and literature, spontaneity and rote learning, or even play and beatings, and for refraining from pinning down Latin exclusively at one extreme of all these categories. The last few decades of scholarship in medieval studies have called into question a number of formerly pat oppositions between on the one hand oral, illiterate, low, vernacular, women, laity, and heretical and on the other written, literate, high, Latin,

---

[3] For the terms "art epic" and "folk epic," see Holman, *Handbook to Literature*, 43-4, 194-5, 227.

[4] On text, see Ziolkowski, "Text and Textuality."

men, clergy, and orthodox.[5] Indeed, the dividing lines between some of these poles have been shown to be so porous as to render arbitrary efforts to set them up in opposition to each other. If there was ever a time when medieval texts could be pinpointed on one of two perpendicular lines — call the one oral and the other written — it has passed. For better or for worse (in my opinion, for better), the texts now are to be located not just on the lines themselves but also in the spaces between them: the lines have metamorphosed into x- and y-axes, sometimes to be supplemented with a z-axis to achieve full three-dimensionality.

What follows cannot claim to be a thorough enumeration or documentation of oral composition in Latin. Instead, it offers a preliminary probing, arranged chronologically, of a few instances from antiquity through the twelfth century in which Latin poets appear to have composed poetry either extemporaneously or in other ways related to oral-formulaic composition. In "Cultural Diglossia and the Nature of Medieval Latin Literature," I turned around the old chestnut of "What did Latin contribute to vernacular literatures?" to consider instead what oral vernacular cultures contributed to Medieval Latin literature.[6] In passing I attended to instances in which Latin writers sought to replicate stylistic features (such as alliteration) of the vernacular traditions with which they were acquainted. Here I would like to consider how the composition of Latin poetry from antiquity through the twelfth century relates to oral-formulaic tradition. Oral performance and delivery in such medieval vernacular languages as Old Norse, Old English, and Old French have been studied for decades.[7] Now the time has come to look further at the other side of the diglossic equation.

Cultural diglossia describes a common situation where a spoken language in which much of daily life is transacted by common people coexists alongside an ancient or at least older scriptural language that plays a central role in religion, education, and various sorts of formal communication. In the Latin Middle Ages the scriptural language was Latin, as repre-

---

[5] For a debate over where to situate Medieval Latin with regard to such categories, contrast Sheerin, "Medieval Latin," and Hexter, "*Latinitas* in the Middle Ages."

[6] See Ziolkowski, "Cultural Diglossia."

[7] Among the key studies would be Crosby, "Oral Delivery in the Middle Ages" and "Chaucer and the Custom of Oral Delivery"; J. Harris, "Eddic Poetry as Oral Poetry"; and Lönnroth, "Hjalmar's Death-Song."

sented in the Vulgate Bible and liturgy; in the texts from antiquity, late antiquity, and the Middle Ages that were staples in Latin grammar school education; and in the texts and conversations that were formulated in the practical, everyday forms of the language.[8] The exact natures of this Latinity varied from region to region and from time to time. Whatever the final consensus may turn out to be, the intense debate of recent decades over the relationship between, on the one hand, the proto-Romance languages spoken on the Iberian peninsula and in France and, on the other, the spoken and written forms of Latin employed there has demonstrated that a term such as "cultural diglossia" can cover a vast range of complex and varied relations between languages.[9]

In this case, the recognition of variation in interlinguistic relations should heighten sensitivity to interliterary relations. Simply stated, the relationship of Latin to the techniques of oral-formulaic composition was not an unaltering constant of rejection or antagonism. John Miles Foley has accepted categories such as "oral-derived" and "oral-connected" as belonging to a spectrum that runs between two extremes, with the purely oral at one end and the purely literate at the other. Although in offering these intermediate terms Foley was concerned with developing a taxonomy to describe literary manifestations in the medieval vernaculars, it would be worth coopting them or devising new ones to extend the range of vocabulary for describing the relationships between Latin and vernacular in the Middle Ages.[10] But before entering the Middle Ages, let us look where so much of the Medieval Latin tradition was rooted: in the literary practices and preconceptions of ancient Rome.

---

[8] See Sharpe, "Latin in Everyday Life."

[9] The term "diglossia," first used in English by Ferguson, "Diglossia," in 1959, received wide exposure among medievalists through its use in Stock, *Implications of Literacy*, 24, and Ong, "Orality, Literacy, and Medieval Textualization," and *Orality and Literacy*.

The controversy over Latin and Romance has been fomented in English most notably by R. Wright, first in *Late Latin and Early Romance in Spain and Carolingian France* (the word "diglossia" appears on page 2, with reference to its application by Helmut Lüdtke in 1968), and then in a volume of essays he edited, *Latin and the Romance Languages in the Early Middle Ages*, where the word appears dozens of times.

[10] Foley, "Implications of Oral Tradition."

Oral-Formulaic Tradition and the Composition of Latin Poetry 129

The stock images of Roman poets could not be further removed from orality. The poster boy for oral-formulaic traditional composition would be, notwithstanding centuries of doubts about his very existence (sighted or unsighted), the blind Homer. In contrast, Roman poets are implicated emphatically in the visual acts of reading and writing: author portraits of Virgil in the surviving manuscripts of late antiquity depict him with codex or scrolls at the ready. Whereas Homer's medium demanded mouth and ears, Roman poets applied their eyes to the trade of literacy as they burned the midnight oil [*lucubratio*]. What they produced were not winged words, but words on wax or papyrus — although if they were unhappy with the results, they could direct their literary executors to consign their writings to the flame (as Virgil instructed Tucca and Varius to do with the *Aeneid*) and to leave nothing but singed words. Yet even as the notion of the bard was displaced by the idea of the poet who writes and rewrites until finally being satisfied, murmurings of different approaches to composition could be faintly heard in Latin literature. These are not direct echoes of oral-formulaic traditional composition and of primary orality ("the pristine orality of cultures with no knowledge of writing"), but rather of phenomena connected loosely with what in later periods has been termed "academic orality."[11] One insight about the Middle Ages that has been emphasized over the past decade is an extension of old debates over the nature of what Albert B. Lord labeled "transitional texts" — texts that inhabit a twilight zone between authorial texts and verbatim transcriptions of oral traditional performances.[12] The insight — advanced among others by Foley — is that the heterogeneity of medieval literary culture cannot be rightly confined to stark divisions between pure orality and pure literacy.[13]

If a historian of literary and intellectual culture had to single out one work of Roman literature that survives in more manuscripts than any other, that was the subject of more glosses and commentaries than any other, that became more closely equated with the curriculum that led to a

---

[11] Ong, *Orality and Literacy*, 1, for definition of "primary orality" and 3, on "academic orality."

[12] In *Singer of Tales*, 128-9, Lord argued against the existence of transitional texts, but later he allowed for it: see "Perspectives on Recent Work in Oral Literature" and "Perspectives on Recent Work on the Oral Traditional Formula." See also Doane, "Introduction."

[13] Foley, "Oral Tradition into Textuality," and "Orality, Textuality, and Interpretation."

grasp of literary Latin, that one work would be Virgil's *Aeneid*. Down to the present day, much of basic training in Latin grammar has been ultimately Virgiliocentric, designed to impart to students the capacity to read and appreciate this epic and to express themselves in manners consonant with it. For this reason it is highly significant that in the *vita* which was the ultimate source of most subsequent biographies of Virgil, the poet is presented as having had the ability to compose extemporaneously. The biographer, after describing Virgil's proficiencies in reciting, relates:

> Erotem librarium et libertum eius exactae iam senectutis tradunt referre solitum, quondam eum in recitando duos dimidiatos uersus complesse ex tempore. Nam cum hactenus haberet: "Misenum Aeoliden," adiecisse: "quo non praestantior alter," item huic "Aere ciere uiros," simili calore iactatum subiunxisse: "Martemque accendere cantu," statimque sibi imperasse ut utrumque uolumini adscriberet.

> [We are told that Eros his freedman and secretary used in his old age to tell how Virgil once in the course of a recitation completed impromptu two unfinished lines. For having in his text "Misenum Aeoliden," he added "quo non praestantior alter," and again after "Aere ciere viros" in a similar fit of inspiration he added "Martemque accendere cantu"; and immediately thereupon told Eros to write both these additions into his text.][14]

The passage makes explicit that the improvisation – if it is legitimate to call it so – occurs during recitation and that it is recorded only afterward by the amanuensis who heard the recitation (which at least in these two instances could properly be called a performance as well as a recitation). Another incident in which a Latin poet is described as engaging in extemporaneous composition appears in Vacca's *Vita Lucani*, where Lucan (39-65 C.E.) is credited with having extemporized an *Orpheus* in hexameters, but the relevance of this extemporization to oral composition is un-

---

[14] Brugnoli and Stok, *Vitae Vergilianae antiquae*, 32.8-33.4; trans. in Camps, *Introduction to Virgil's Aeneid*, 119.

dermined seriously when Vacca specifies that it took place in writing: "ex tempore Orphea scriptum in experimentum adversum complures ediderat poetas" [he produced an *Orpheus* extemporaneously, written in a contest against many poets].[15]

Only the biographical anecdote about Virgil differs from the episode described in a poem (no. 50) by Catullus (born ca. 84-54 B.C.E.), in which he and Licinius Calvus (82-47 B.C.E.) exchanged tablets on which they wrote poems back and forth. One commentator on Catullus referred to the reciprocation as "a contest of improvisation" and envisaged the two as "probably each improvising on a theme suggested by the other's verses"; obviously the improvisation takes place in writing rather than orally.[16] Another commentator on the same poem wrote, with an unforeseen double entendre, of Catullus as having "spent an evening in gay improvisation with the lively little Calvus."[17]

The situations in the *vita* of Virgil and in the episode of Catullus and Calvus differ so greatly, most notably with the one taking place *viva voce* and the other in writing, that it seems risky to subsume them both under the same heading of "improvisation." Indeed, improvisation carries connotations mainly of music, acting (especially comedy), and art, not of literature.[18] If we consider how prominent rhetoric was in Roman education and culture, we would do better to enlist not improvisation but rather extemporization as the preferred term to denote spontaneous literary composition. The phrase Latin writers tended to use themselves was *ex tempore* and the expression "extemporaneous speaking" keeps alive the connection

---

[15] Vacca, *Vita Lucani*, 41-2 (ed. Rostagni, 183). My translation. See *M. Annaei Lucani Belli Civilis libri decem*, ed. Hosius, 335, lines 23-5. For an overview of improvisation in Latin literature, see Kindermann, *Theatergeschichte Europas*, 1:138-44.

[16] Merrill, *Catullus*, 83.

[17] Fordyce, *Catullus*, 215.

[18] Tellingly, the *Encyclopedia of Aesthetics*, edited by M. Kelly, has two essays in its entry on "Improvisation": the first, by Philip A. Alperson, 2:478-9, is devoted to the aesthetic implications of improvisation, most of it being concerned with music, while the second, by Garry Hagberg, 2:479-82, is devoted explicitly to jazz improvisation.

with formal rhetoric that was such an important constituent of extemporaneity in Latinity.[19]

Latin writers on rhetoric, although concerned above all with extemporaneous speaking, had occasion to cite instances of extemporaneous versification as a way of encouraging prospective orators. Thus Cicero (106-43 B.C.E.) cites two examples of poets (alas, both of them Greek poets — but at least they are invoked in Latin before Roman audiences) who had the capacity to compose orally. One is an example from the then-recent past, when in *De oratore* Cicero describes (on the strength of Q. Lutatius Catulus's memory) the aptitude of Antipater of Sidon, author of roughly ninety poems in the *Greek Anthology*, for extemporizing in verse, not only in hexameters:

> Quod si Antipater ille Sidonius quem tu probe, Catule, meministi solitus est versus hexametros aliosque variis modis atque numeris fundere ex tempore, tantumque hominis ingeniosi ac memoris valuit exercitatio ut cum se mente ac voluntate coniecisset in versum verba sequerentur, quanto id facilius in oratione exercitatione et consuetudine adhibita consequemur!

> [But if the great Antipater of Sidon, whom you, Catulus, can remember well, had a habit of pouring out hexameters and other verses of various forms and metres *impromptu*, and as he had a quick wit and a good memory, made himself such an adept by practice, that when he deliberately decided to throw his ideas into verse, words followed automatically, how much more easily shall we achieve this in prose, given practice and training!][20]

The other is from among Cicero's contemporaries. Specifically, Cicero singles out his protégé Archias (Aulus Licinius Archias), a Greek poet

---

[19] The phrase in Quintilian, *Institutio oratoria*, 10.7.1, is "ex tempore dicendi facultas" [<as it were,> is the power of improvisation] (ed. and trans. Russell, 4: 372/373). The word *improvisation* is French in origin.

[20] Cicero, *De oratore*, 3.50.194 (ed. and trans. Rackham, 154-5).

from Antioch who had arrived in Rome ca. 102 B.C.E., for being able to improvise verses on what were then current events:

> quotiens ego hunc vidi, cum litteram scripsisset nullam, magnum numerum optimorum versuum de iis ipsis rebus, quae tum agerentur, dicere ex tempore! quotiens revocatum eamdem rem dicere commutatis verbis atque sententiis!
>
> [how often, I say, have I seen him, without writing a single letter, extemporizing quantities of excellent verse dealing with current topics! How often have I seen him, when recalled, repeat his original matter with an entire change of word and phrase!][21]

It would be a misrepresentation to infer that Archias composed according to the principles of oral-formulaic traditional composition. At the same time it would be anachronistic to assimilate his activity to the improvisation of a twentieth- or twenty-first-century jazz musician. In any case, the sorts of extemporization that Cicero identifies caught the attention of later writers on rhetoric, whose statements on such composition may have given the seal of official approval from within the rhetorical establishment — if any seal was needed — for the valuing of spontaneous composition.[22]

In late antiquity the rhetorical tradition embodied in Cicero pervaded education at both the basic and advanced levels. Simultaneously, in many circles respect for the poet of the *Aeneid* bordered on hero-worship, what could be designated Virgiliolatry. Although this kind of devotion to the verse of a written poet — the *auctor* of all *auctores* — would seem a world apart from immersion in an oral tradition, the two worlds sometimes at least parallel each other in the degree of recollection they required or engendered. Augustine describes in one of his treatises a lifelong friend of his who apparently not only knew by heart the whole of the *Aeneid* and all

---

[21] Cicero, *Pro Archia* 8.18 (ed. and trans. Watts, 26-7).

[22] Quintilian, *Institutio oratoria*, 10.7.19: "non utique melior sit ea sed tutior cum hanc facilitatem non prose modo multi sint consecuti, sed etiam carmine, ut Antipater Sidonius et Licinius Archias" [it will not necessarily be better. Many in fact have acquired this facility not only in prose but even in verse, like Antipater of Sidon and Licinius Archias] (Russell, 4:380/381).

of Cicero's orations but who was even able to recall the text of both backwards.[23] Another manifestation of the same reverence was the cento, a form in which poets expressed new thoughts entirely or almost entirely in lines, half-lines, and phrases woven together out of previous poetry.[24]

The cento is paradoxical in many ways. Although it may have humorous effects, it is often not really parodic.[25] Although the cento is appropriative, the kind of cobbling together that is its very essence does not represent plagiarism. For the present purposes, one of the greatest paradoxes is that although in one regard it is the most definitively textualist of manifestations, in another sense centonization offers the closest parallel to oral-formulaic composition in the Latin literature of late antiquity. We have no external evidence of how the centoists composed – but it seems exceedingly unlikely that centoists in search of material flipped back and forth through codices or scrolled up and down in papyrus rolls. Far likelier is that they carried the texts in their minds, maybe more like the preservers of literary culture in Ray Bradbury's *Fahrenheit 451* than bearers of tradition in a conventional folkloric sense, but more deserving of respect than the disparagement that Domenico Comparetti heaped upon them when he conjectured that Virgilian centos "could only have arisen among people who had learnt Virgil mechanically and did not know of any better use to which to put all these verses with which they had loaded their brains."[26]

The transition from late antiquity to the early Middle Ages in western Europe entailed – among many other things – the arrival and gradual integration of Germanic cultures with the oral poetry that had sharply distressed the aristocrats of the senatorial class when they contrasted it with the Roman poetic tradition that they knew and esteemed so much better. Undoubtedly this Germanic poetry came closer to oral-formulaic traditional poetry than the Latin poetry of the day, but that fact does not mean

---

[23] Augustine, *De natura et origine animae* 4.7.9 (ed. Urba and Zycha, 389, lines 7-18); trans. Schaff, *Nicene and Post-Nicene Fathers*, 5.358, and Carruthers, *Book of Memory*, 19. This example is discussed by Ziolkowski, "Mnemotechnics and the Reception of the *Aeneid*."

[24] For basic information, see Schelkle, "Cento"; also for more recent work see Green, "Proba's Cento."

[25] Lehmann differentiates between the two forms (with a harsh assessment of cento) at the outset of his *Die Parodie im Mittelalter*, 2. The word *cento* is absent from the indices of Bayless, *Parody in the Middle Ages*.

[26] Comparetti, *Vergil in the Middle Ages*, 53.

automatically that all Germanic poetry was somehow spontaneous. Indeed, not all orally delivered poetry, even the earliest poetry in vernaculars that have been regarded as having strong oral-formulaic traditions, was necessarily composed extempore. Take for example the famous scene in Bede's *Ecclesiastical History of the English People* (4.24) in which Cædmon, who is presented as being the first English Christian poet, first demonstrates a knack for composing poetry.[27] Because of his inhibitions about singing, Cædmon leaves a feast to avoid participating. After settling down for a night's sleep nearby, he has a dream in which he is inspired to sing a song of praise to God the Creator. Bede's characterization of this scene is too laconic to allow the reader to determine whether Cædmon's sudden access of poetic ability reenacts classical references to late-night composition [*lucubratio*], whether it is an instance of monastic-style religious meditation [*ruminatio*] imposed upon a layman, or whether it is simply — or not so simply — a miracle (as Bede indicates). Regardless of the causes that explain why the hitherto tongue-tied and stage-frightened Cædmon is suddenly able to produce poetry, we can be sure that at least on this one instance Cædmon does not come forth with a poem that is altogether unrehearsed. Thanks to his dream, he has had a chance to rehearse what he will sing — although obviously we cannot determine if what he sang in his dream was identical with what he sang in reality.[28]

As far as the Latin tradition is concerned, I suspect that many descriptions of medieval Latin poets in the act of composing await identification and discussion. By chance, John of Salerno left us what may be one such depiction in his *vita* of Odo of Cluny, the second abbot of Cluny (926-944).[29] John tells that in his early manhood Odo would go at night to pray at the tomb of St. Martin. One night he was attacked by foxes,

---

[27] I examine this scene *en passant* in "Classical Influences on Medieval Latin Views," 20.

[28] The scholarship on Cædmon continues to grow. Two studies that are most concerned with placing the episode in the context of oral-traditional formulaic composition are Fry, "Cædmon as a Formulaic Poet," and "Memory of Cædmon." For a very different approach to Caedmon's orality, see O'Brien O'Keeffe, *Visible Song*, chap. 2, "Orality and the Developing Text of Caedmon's Hymn," 23-46.

[29] I analyze the meditative nature and composition of this poem in "The *Occupatio* by Odo of Cluny."

which were miraculously dispersed by a wolf. In relating how defenseless Odo was, John reports:

> Non collegæ fultus latere, non bacilli corroboratus munimine, sed duas solum tabellas manu bajulans, scribendi officio aptissimas, fabrili opere ita connexas, ut possent patefieri, non tamen disjungi, quibus scholastici dextro femore solent uti.
>
> [Not relying on a colleague at his side and without the protection of a staff, he carried in his hands only two writing tablets joined by a frail band so that they could be opened but not taken apart, such as scholars are accustomed to carry at their right side.][30]

Since Odo was unlikely to read while praying in the deep of the night, and since John emphasizes that these tablets were suited for writing (not reading), I infer that the tablets were probably at the ready for Odo to record his thoughts after praying. Odo's poem, the *Occupatio*, has been characterized as being "meditations."[31] If my inference is correct, the *meditatio* discussed within the poem and the *occupatio* heralded in the title are one and the same: an engrossment of the mind and soul, both of the poet during composition and of the reader during ruminative reading. If this intuition is right, then Odo's method of composition bears comparison with Cædmon's, except that the Latin poet's is in Latin rather than his mother tongue. Neither Cædmon nor Odo would use writing materials during composition itself — but at the same time neither was genuinely improvising. Yet there *were* individuals who composed extempore, even in Latin.

In January 965 the Italian scholar Gunzo, traveling with Emperor Otto the Great, reached the monastery of St. Gall in what is today Switzerland. While speaking with the monks, the Italian let slip an accusative where an ablative was required. This grammatical failure prompted the monks to ridicule Gunzo. One of them went so far as to lampoon the mistake in verse:

---

[30] *Vita Odonis*, 1.14 (Migne, PL, 133.49D); trans. Sitwell, *St. Odo of Cluny*, 16.

[31] Swoboda, *Occupatio*, xvii; Leclercq, "L'Idéal monastique de saint Odon," 228; Morghen, "Monastic Reform and Cluniac Spirituality," 21.

Nox erat et somnus curas marcore premebat.
Iusque sibi in saturo poscebat ventre Lyęus,
cum fortuna fuit, ut in sermonibus frivolis unius casus mutatione offenderim ponendo videlicet accusativum pro ablativo. Tunc denique palam factum est, quid per totum diem magister improbabilis eruditionis docuerit discipulum illaudabilis obsecutionis. Adfuit tamen quem supra pusionem dixi, culpans tam grave facinus mutationis unius casus, asserens me senem scolaribus dignum flagellis, et hoc lascivulis versibus, quasi in hoc sapiens mihi cucullatio videretur. Verumtamen quis ignorat versus lascivientis monachi? Otio vacans os aperit et poema emittit, ignorans oeconomiam carminis, purpureum pannum qui bene splendeat unum et alterum inserere, mores aetates personarumque observare dignitates in poesi nescit. Porrigit tantum labra et eiectat poema....

[It was night, sleep covered cares in languor,
and Bacchus demanded his due in a full stomach,
when luck had it that in trifling words I committed an offense by switching one case, that is to say, by putting an accusative instead of an ablative. Then at last it happened publicly, what for the entire day the schoolmaster of unapproved learning taught his pupil of unpraiseworthy devotion. Yet he whom above I called a boy was present, faulting so grievous a crime of mixing up one case, asserting that although an old man I deserved to be whipped like a schoolboy, and he did this in insolent verse, as if he would seem wise to me in this assembly of cowled monks. And yet who does not know the verse of a monk who is running amok? Having leisure for idleness, he opens his mouth and lets fly a poem; not knowing how to arrange a poem, he is unable to incorporate one and another purple patch that shines forth and to maintain in poetry the

morals, ages, and status of individuals. He just stretches out his lips and lets loose a poem....][32]

This passage is central in Gunzo's polemical epistle, not by virtue of its position in the text (for it is not in the middle) but because it relates the humiliation that has provoked him to write. From earlier periods we know of monks and pupils who took vows to communicate solely in Latin and who subjected outsiders to what amounted to verbal hazing.[33] Likewise we have evidence of poems being delivered before Carolingian courts, against a backdrop of inter-ethnic rivalries. Here we are given a glimpse of a microcosm in which an isolated error in Latin accidence could bring down upon an outsider an avalanche of ridicule – and in which at least one of the pupils has a mastery of Latin sufficient to extemporize and deliver a poem in Latin.

What else can be gleaned from the passage? Gunzo assumes that everyone will be familiar with the kind of poetry his presumptuous antagonist composes to disrespect him. Analogues could be found in the ninth-century "Terence and His Mocker" or in the challenges that Froumund of Tegernsee (second half of the tenth century) issues to boys, calling upon them to respond in verse.[34] Though Gunzo does not quote the verses, he states that his unnamed mocker lacked not only an overall grasp of poetry but also the sense of decorum essential to good rhetoric. In an egregious violation of that decorum, he overused borrowings from classics, to the point of committing plagiarism.

Training in the verbal arts of grammar, rhetoric, and dialectic was pugilistic in at least two ways. As the reaction to Gunzo's *lapsus linguae* at the end of a long day suggests, the grammar school encouraged and even inculcated eristic approaches to learning and teaching. Education entailed a

---

[32] Gunzo, *Epistola ad Augienses*, III (ed. Manitius, 22.18-23.12); the translation is mine.

[33] On pacts to speak only in Latin, see Winterbottom, "On the *Hisperica famina*," esp. 129, 131-2.

[34] For the text of "Terence and his Mocker" (*Terentius et delusor*), incipit "Mitte recordari monimenta vetusta, Terenti," see Strecker, *Poetae Latini aevi Carolini*, 4.3, 1088-90. For that of Froumund of Tegernsee, see Strecker, *Die Tegernseer Briefsammlung (Froumund)*, carmen 19, 53-5, and carmen 32, 80-3. For an exploration of these passages and other related ones, see Ziolkowski, "Medieval Latin Beast Flyting."

threat of violence: in representations of grammar masters and Lady Grammar, the inalterable attributes are the book and the rods. The rods were not ornamental. From Augustine's earliest prayers to God — to spare him a whipping by his teacher — through the burning of St. Gall on 26 April 937 — when in the hope of staving off such punishment one of the schoolboys set fire to the storeroom where the rods were kept — to many centuries beyond, beatings belonged to the routine of basic education.[35] But as in boxing, the combat followed rules.

A splendidly detailed, if probably idealized, tableau of schoolboys as they are engaged in the competitiveness of the trivium can be found in a description of London in the time of Thomas Becket:

> Disputant scholares, quidam demonstrative, dialectice alii; hi rotant enthymemata, hi perfectis melius utuntur syllogismis.... Pueri diversarum scholarum versibus inter se conrixantur; aut de principiis ártis grammaticae vel regulis praeteritorum vel supinorum contendunt. Sunt alii qui in epigrammatibus, rhythmis, et metris utuntur vetere illa triviali dicacitate; licentia Fescennina socios suppressis nominibus liberius lacerant; loedorias jaculantur et scommata; salibus Socraticis sociorum vel forte majorum, vitia tangunt, vel mordacius dente rodunt Theonino audacibus dithyrambis.
>
> [The scholars dispute, some in demonstrative rhetoric, others in dialectic. Some reel off enthymemes, others make better use of full syllogisms.... Boys of different schools compete against one another in verse; or they contend about the principles of grammar or the rules of past tenses or supines. There are others who employ the old crude wit of the trivium in epigrams, rhythmic poems, and metrical poems; with Fescennine licence they excoriate their fellows freely (though under concealed names); they hurl abuse and taunts; with Socratic witticisms they touch on the faults of their peers or even of their superi-

---

[35] See Augustine, *Confessiones*, 1.9.14 (ed. O'Donnell, 1:8), and Ekkehard IV of St. Gall, *Casus Sancti Galli*, chap. 67 (ed. and trans. Haefele, 142).

ors, or more bitingly, with Theonine tooth, they tear with daring dithyrambs.][36]

William fitz Stephen (d. 1190), the author of this wonderful vignette, devotes considerable space to description of the rap-like verse insults exchanged by the boys. His reference to "Fescennine license" may betray knowledge not just that this Roman ritual involved abusive verse but also that the abusive verse was extemporized.[37]

Formal rhetoric indicated that extemporaneous speaking had three prerequisites: talent [*ingenium*], command of rhetoric [*ars*], and practice [*exercitatio*].[38] Once again, we are fortunate in having an enumeration of the classroom activities that would have granted its adepts ease in extemporizing in prose and poetry. In this case our source is John of Salisbury (ca. 1115-1180), who gives in his *Metalogicon* a full account of the training Bernard of Chartres (d. 1124-1130) gave his followers:

> Et quoniam memoria exercitio firmatur, ingeniumque acuitur, ad imitandum ea quae audiebant, alios admonitionibus, alios flagellis et poenis urgebat. Cogebantur exsoluere singuli die sequenti aliquid eorum quae praecedenti audierant.... Quibus autem indicebantur praeexercitamina puerorum in prosis aut poematibus imi-

---

[36] *Descriptio nobilissimae civitatis Londoniae*, in *Vita Sancti Thomae, Cantuariensis archiepiscopi et martyris* (in J. Robertson, *Materials*, 3:4-5); trans. (from *licentia*) by Rigg, *History of Anglo-Latin Literature*, 189. Also trans. by Butler, "Description of London."

[37] William's source of information would be Horace, *Epistles* 2.1.145-6 (ed. Goold, 408/409):
> Fescennina per hunc inventa licentia morem
> Versibus alternis opprobria rustica fudit
> libertasque recurrentis accepta per annos
> lusit amabiliter....

[Through this custom came into use the Fescennine licence, which in alternate verse poured forth rustic taunts; and the freedom, welcomed each returning year, was innocently gay....]
Information is also at hand to modern scholars in Livy, Book 7.2.

[38] Lausberg, *Handbook of Literary Rhetoric*, 500 (§1145). All three terms are treated extensively in Ueding's splendid *Historisches Wörterbuch der Rhetorik*, s.v.

tandis, poetas aut oratores proponebat et eorum iubebat uestigia imitari, ostendens iuncturas dictionum, et elegantes sermonum clausulas. Siquis autem ad splendorem sui operis alienum pannum assuerat, deprehensum redarguebat furtum, sed poenam saepissime non infligebat. Sic uero redargutum si hoc tamen meruerat inepta positio, ad exprimendam auctorum imaginem modesta indulgentia conscendere iubebat, faciebatque ut qui maiores imitabatur, fieret posteris imitandus.... Historias, poemata, percurrenda monebat, diligenter quidem et qui uelut nullis calcaribus urgebantur ad fugam, et ex singulis aliquid reconditum in memoria diurnum debitum diligenti instantia exigebat.

[In view of the fact that exercise both strengthens and sharpens our mind, Bernard would end every effort to bring his students to imitate what they were hearing. In some cases he would rely on exhortation, in others he would resort to punishments, such as flogging. Each student was daily required to recite part of what he had heard on the previous day.... He [Bernard] would also explain the poets and orators who were to serve as models for the boys in their introductory exercises in imitating prose and poetry. Pointing out how the diction of the authors was so skillfully connected, and what they had to say was so elegantly concluded, he would admonish his students to follow their example. And if, to embellish his work, someone had sewed on a patch of cloth filched from an external source, Bernard, on discovering this, would rebuke him for his plagiary, but would generally refrain from punishing him. After he had reproved the student, if an unsuitable theme had invited this, he would, with modest indulgence, bid the boy to rise to real imitation of the [classical authors], and would bring about that he who had imitated his predecessors would come to be deserving of imitation by his successors.... Bernard used also to admonish his students that stories and poems should be read thoroughly, and not as though the reader were being precipitated to flight by spurs. Wherefor he diligently and insistently demanded from each, as a daily debt, something commmitted to memory.]³⁹

Although writing roughly two centuries after Gunzo's ill-fated visit to St. Gall, John grants us entry into a world with practices and values very similar to those of the tenth century. The constant is that the ability to compose is achieved through imitation, which means rereading and reworking exemplars to such an extent that they become incorporated lastingly into the imitator's memory.⁴⁰ The imitation is sometimes so close as to border on (mis)appropriation: the metaphor underlying *text* is fabric, and the risk of *imitatio* is that poor imitators would produce nothing but a patchwork.

As John's reminiscences about the classroom of Bernard of Chartres would imply, Gunzo was far from the last to have experience of spur-of-the-moment Latin versifying. In the remaining pages of this essay, I would like to examine instances involving three different poets in the eleventh and twelfth centuries.

The earliest is the least certainly extemporaneous. The Norman Latin poet Warner of Rouen wrote (sometime between 996 and 1026) one of his satires against an Irishman named Moriuht who, after a concatenation of grotesque misadventures, is freed from slavery and reunited with his wife and child. According to Warner, this Moriuht pretended to great erudition in Latin. Consequently, Warner feels entitled to pull no punches in deriding Moriuht for having committed metrical howlers

("Fōribus en clausis mōratur pontifēx Hugo") in a poem he produced, to all appearances impromptu.⁴¹ As in the incident in which Gunzo was em-

---

³⁹ John of Salisbury, *Metalogicon*, Book 1, chap. 24 (ed. Hall and Keats-Rohan, 52.59-53.92); trans. McGarry, *Metalogicon*, 68-9. For references to scholarship on this passage, see D. Kelly, *Arts of Poetry and Prose*, 50-1.

⁴⁰ See further the related notion of "formulaic reading" O'Brien O'Keeffe advances in *Visible Song*, esp. 23-76.

⁴¹ The line in question appears in McDonough, *Moriuht*, as line 341, which is repeated in 451 and discussed recurrently in the satire. McDonough, who analyzes the satire with marvelous details and insights, speaks, *Oxford Poems of Hugh Primas*, 4, in terms of the poem with the prosodic errors as having been published, but Warner's use of the verb "ructare" to describe the production of the verse

Oral-Formulaic Tradition and the Composition of Latin Poetry 143

broiled, a foreign interloper who claims to be learned receives his come-uppance for mistakes in Latinity, here especially in prosody.

In the twelfth and thirteenth centuries the versifier Hugh Primas — whose nickname memorialized his stature as *numero uno* among poets — achieved a legendary reputation for his facility in devising impromptu poetry. A passage appended (ca. 1171) to the *Chronicle* by Richard of Poitiers, but apparently pertaining to 1144 or 1145, tells of a famous poet named Hugh Primas:

> Hiis etenim diebus viguit apud Parisius quidam scolasticus Hugo nomine a conscolasticis Primas cognominatus, persona quidem vilis, vultu deformis. Hic a primeva aetate litteris secularibus informatus, propter faceciam suam et litterarum noticiam fama sui nominis per diversas provincias divulgata resplenduit. Inter alios vero scolasticos in metris ita facundus atque promtus extitit, ut sequentibus versibus omnibus audientibus cachinum moventibus declaratur, quos de paupere mantello sibi a quodam presule dato declamatorie composuit. De Hugone lo Primat Aureliacensi. "Hoc indumentum tibi quis dedit? An fuit emptum?"

> [In those days there flourished in Paris an academic named Hugh — whom his colleagues nicknamed "the Primate" — wretched of aspect, misshapen of face. He had been imbued with secular literature from his earliest years, and the renown of his name grew radiant in diverse provinces, because of his wit and literary sensibility. Among his colleagues he was most eloquent and quick-witted (*promtus*) in making verses, as we can see from the ones he composed by way of declamation (*declamatorie composuit*), making all who heard them laugh aloud, about a poor cloak that a certain bishop had given him: "From

---

(lines 337, 339, 454) and his description of Moriuht's movements as he delivers the poem suggest oral delivery (and even composition).

Hugh, Primate of Orléans: *Hoc indumentum tibi quis dedit? An fuit emptum?*"][42]

The argument has been advanced that this passage, like the *vidas* about the lives of poets who wrote in Old Occitanian, was fabricated on the basis of Primas's poetry rather than on the basis of any independent historical evidence.[43] Even if — for the sake of argument — we concede that there is no evidence Hugh Primas himself extemporized any of his poetry, we are left to explain on what basis the author of this later passage would have believed that Latin rhythmic verse had been improvised a few decades earlier.[44] The passage implies not that improvisation was inherently unusual, but rather that Hugh was exceptionally good at it.

The *Chronicle* of Francesco Pipino (ca. 1270–after 1328), before offering two examples of Hugh Primas's ability to compose witty invective and marvelously concise poetry, relates that "Huius ingenium fuit ultra humanum versificari elegantius et repente" [His genius was to versify with superhuman elegance and rapidity].[45] Unfortunately, neither anecdote indicates exactly how long Hugh took to craft his poems, although the first one suggests that he might well have composed "on the spot." Further evidence can be found for a later belief that Hugh Primas, like Virgil before him and at least one further Latin poet after him, could complete half-verses extemporaneously: a late thirteenth-century collection of *exempla* contains one that tells how while in Orléans Primas was challenged to round off the two incomplete verses "Istud jumentum cauda caret..." [This beast of burden has no tail...] and "Claudicat hoc animal..." [This animal

---

[42] Text in MGH, Scriptores, 26.81. Quoted by W. Meyer, *Die Oxforder Gedichte*, 80; repr., 6; quoted by Rigg, "Golias and Other Pseudonyms," 73, and quoted by McDonough, *Oxford Poems of Hugh Primas*, 2; translation quoted from Adcock, *Hugh Primas and the Archpoet*, xvii. Meyer, followed by Adcock, gives the year as 1142; Rigg, "Golias," 73, has the typo of 1152.

[43] The *vidas* are assembled in English translation in Egan, *Vidas of the Troubadours*.

[44] For the argument about fabrication, see Cairns, "Addition to the 'Chronica.'" For the suggestion about Primas's reputation for composing impromptu, see Adcock, *Hugh Primas and the Archpoet*, xvii–xviii.

[45] *Chronicon*, Liber 1, cap. 47 (in Muratori, *RIS*, 9.628), quoted in Latin by W. Meyer, *Die Oxforder Gedichte*, 4 [78], who is quoted in turn by Rigg, "Golias," 74-5.

is limping...]. To the first he gave the ending "Or la lia t'on" [Since someone tied it to you] to the second "quia sentit labore pedi mal" [Because its foot hurts when there's work].[46] These two supposedly spontaneous line endings conjure up an interesting setting, in which a poet has a feel for both Latin and his own mother tongue, as well as for the audiences that might respond very differently to the two languages, that enables him to respond just as freely with a *bon mot* as with a *bonum verbum,* or with a hybrid of both.

Later in the twelfth century Gerald of Wales (1147–1223), himself a prolific author of Latin works, relates an anecdote that reveals how widespread the knack for Latin versifying had become during the so-called Twelfth-Century Renaissance. According to Gerald, a scholar named Maurice of Glamorgan — presumably a cleric himself, certainly from a family with members in the clergy — had a vision:

> Illo nimirum in sceptris agente, immo revera furente, accidit in australis Kambriae finibus et provincia maritima quae terra Morgani vulgo vocatur, parum ante interdictum Angliae tam diuturnum, quod viro cuidam bono et copiose litterato, cui nomen Mauricius, qui et frater fuit venerabilis abbatis de Neth Clementis, apparuit in visu persona militis cujusdam de partibus eisdem, longe ante defuncti, qui et in hujusmodi verba prorupit: "Magister Maurici, versum hunc finias, 'Destruet hoc regnum rex regum.'" Cui ille respondisse sic videbatur: "Immo et tu, qui versum fere perfecisti, finem apponas." Miles enim ille litteratus fuerat et, dum vixit, solebat saepius alternis versibus, et nunc incipiendo nunc finiendo, sociali quadam recreatione tanquam colludendo conferre. Hoc autem dicto, miles subjecit: "Quoniam hebes es plus solito senioque confectus, versus sic finiatur et perficiatur: — 'Destruet hoc regnum rex regum duplice plaga.'"

> [Moreover, during his government, or rather in his reign of madness, it happened in South Wales, in a certain

---

[46] First noticed by Delisle, "Notes sur quelques manuscrits de la Bibliothèque de Tours"; quoted partially by Rigg, "Golias," 75. The translations are mine.

> maritime province, commonly known by the name of Morgan's Land, a little before the interdict in England, which continued so long, that to a certain good and deeply learned man named Maurice, who was also the brother of Clement, the venerable abbot of Neth, there appeared in a vision the person of a certain knight of those parts, long since dead, who also broke forth into words like these, "Master Maurice, finish this verse: 'The King of kings shall destroy this kingdom.'" To whom the other replied, as it seemed, thus, "Rather do you put an end to it, for you have almost completed the verse." For the knight was a learned man, and whilst he was alive was very frequently accustomed, by way of amusement and social recreation, to converse with him in alternate verses, sometimes beginning and at other times finishing them. But when he had said this, the soldier added, "Since you are more slow of comprehension than you were formerly, and are worn out with old age, the verse may be thus finished and completed, 'The King of kings shall destroy this kingdom by a two-fold plague.'"][47]

This incident takes for granted not only that a cleric might have a vision in Latin but also that he would be unsurprised to meet in it a knight ["miles"] who could play parlor games in spoken Latin, even in verse.[48]

At the end of a late twelfth-century manuscript that comes from the Cistercian abbey of Aulne, in what was the diocese of Liège, there survives a text of another vision involving Latin poetry.[49] The text describes the apparition of a friend who had recently died to his living friend. The reve-

---

[47] Gerald of Wales, *De principis instructione*, Distinctio 3, cap. 28 (ed. Warner, 310-11); trans. Stevenson, *Instruction of Princes*, 104 (pagination of 1991 reprint). I have modified Stevenson's translation by twice replacing "soldier" with "knight" (to translate "miles"). The passage has been considered by Rigg, *History of Anglo-Latin Literature*, 348 n. 105 and 368 n. 116.

[48] The game here is not technically "capping verses," which is defined as "reply[ing] to one previously quoted with another, that begins with the final or initial letter of the first, or that rimes or otherwise corresponds with it": see Knowles, *Oxford Dictionary of Phrase and Fable*, 178.

[49] Leclercq edits this text in "Virgile en enfer d'après un manuscrit d'Aulne."

nant tells the living friend that in death he has earned eternal damnation. His friend, apparently unconcerned about his friend's afterlife, asks him about Virgil and expresses the particular hope that the Roman poet will explicate for him two verses. A little while later, the dead friend brings back Virgil's reply: the poet exhorts the living friend to renounce the idle fictions of literature, which had led to the everlasting punishment of his deceased companion. The surviving friend accepts this encouragement, abandons the classics, and renounces the world.

The two visions form an unintended diptych. The latter depicts the zeal with which the Latin literate perused the canonical authors, especially the poets. The former delineates the related ease in producing poetry afresh on the basis of such readings; for at its heart is the phrase "rex regum," which had been a stock component of hexameter verse since late antiquity.[50]

At the end of my first term teaching classical Latin, I received the usual stack of completed course evaluation forms. One buoyed me, as I read under the heading "Strengths of the Course" the response "made me dream in Latin." As my eye continued down the form, this initial exuberance diminished because under "Weaknesses of the Course" the same student had scrawled "The dreams are all nightmares."

The acquisition of any foreign language requires work, at least for most mortals. Over the centuries Latin teachers devised methods, involving stout doses of both what could be termed positive and negative reinforcement. For all the anxieties that these methods stirred among pupils, they succeeded in many cases.[51] Augustine came away from grammar school with Latin but only small Greek. The fulcrum of study in the grammar school was repetition with variation. Hear a poem, recite a poem, repeat its words in normal prose word order, abridge its contents, expand its contents. Such repetition was the mother of all learning. Although incontrovertibly book-centered — that is part and parcel of the Latin side of diglossia — the remembrance that came of it could bear a powerful resemblance to the remembrance that undergirds oral-formulaic traditional composition. Maybe this circularity should surprise no one. The rhetoric that underlay medieval Latinity fused the oral and the writ-

---

[50] Schumann, *Lateinisches Hexameter-Lexikon*, 4:522–3.

[51] A succinct characterization of their methods can be found in Murphy, "Teaching of Latin."

ten, as had all rhetoric from the beginning: Aristotle may take his time in building up to citing poetry in his *Rhetoric*, but his first three explicit examples are all drawn from the *Iliad*.[52] The same complex paradox is evident in the peculiar orality of extempore versification in the Latin tradition. The orality is more than academic, and the ramifications of its effects on poetic composition are more than an academic question.

---

[52] *Iliad* 1.255, 2.160, 2.298, cited in *Rhetoric*, Book 1, 1362b1, line 36, 1363a1, line 5, and 1363a1, line 7 (ed. and trans. Barnes, 2167).

KATHERINE O'BRIEN O'KEEFFE

Deaths and Transformations: Thinking through the 'End' of Old English Verse

The last two works that the Anglo-Saxon Poetic Records recognizes as poems in the Anglo-Saxon Chronicle are memorials for the last surviving sons of Æthelred, works as dissimilar as the fates of the brothers they commemorate. Beyond their obvious advantage in being closely datable, the *Death of Alfred* (1036) and the *Death of Edward* (1065)[1] are unlikely candidates through which to explore the viability of Old English verse in the middle of the eleventh century. As any bibliographical survey will attest, these works are now little read and less commented upon. Though both pieces are preserved in two eleventh-century manuscripts of the Chronicle,[2] they are absent from the twelfth-century Peterborough Chronicle, where the death of Edward receives only perfunctory notice (s.a. 1066 "Her forðferde Eaduuard king"), and the untimely end of Alfred Ætheling receives no mention at all.[3] If the Peterborough Chronicle, in its

---

[1] Dobbie, *Minor Poems*, 24-6. Translations are my own unless otherwise indicated.

[2] In the C-text, London, British Library, Cotton Tiberius B. i (Ker, item 192, s. xi¹-xi²) and in the D-text, London, British Library, Cotton Tiberius B. iv (Ker, item 193, s. xi med.-xi²). For the former see now *Anglo-Saxon Chronicle, MS C*, ed. O'Brien O'Keeffe, and for the latter see *Anglo-Saxon Chronicle, MS D*, ed. Cubbin.

[3] The E-text. See Plummer, *Saxon Chronicles*. None of the six texts edited as verse by Dobbie in *Minor Poems* is transmitted in E. The D-text transmits all except *The Coronation of Edgar* and *The Death of Edgar*, for which, like E, it offers in the first instance a prose summary (s.a. 972) and in the second a brief parallel account which Plummer prints as verse, but which is better understood as prose. A num-

brusque prose redactions of the Chronicle verse, is symptomatic of a larger contemporary refusal of classical Old English forms, it would appear that the moment for the *Death of Alfred* and the *Death of Edward* was brief indeed. Their present obscurity is in one sense richly deserved. Lacking the triumphant immediacy of *Brunanburh*, the narrative urgency of *Maldon*, or the lapidary profusion of epithets in Caedmon's *Hymn*, they strike a modern eye as a journeyman's performance — perfunctory, gestural, and dull. But it is important not to draw from our aesthetic responses to these small works a larger conclusion about the viability of Old English verse in the mid-eleventh century. While the *Death of Alfred* and the *Death of Edward* in retrospect may be seen to mourn the end of the Cerdicing dynasty in England, they do not mourn the passing of Old English verse.[4] While I do not intend to mount an argument for their recuperation (an argument better not attempted), I suggest that these two pieces, for all their obvious shortcomings, speak clearly, if in complementary ways, to the work that traditional verse forms were seen to perform around the middle of the eleventh century. What follows explores the vitality as well as the limits of traditional verse in the mid-eleventh century by attending to the political aesthetics of commemoration.

The Death of Alfred
Elliott Van Kirk Dobbie's main criterion for inclusion in *The Anglo-Saxon Minor Poems*, "sufficiently regular meter," though tolerably broad, produced such embarrassment in the case of the *Death of Alfred* that he was constrained to add a small apology: "[it] is not regularly alliterative, like the other five poems, but is partly prose and partly irregular rimed verse. It is,

---

ber of other texts with clear rhetorical elaborations are printed as verse by early editors, but do not qualify as such by "classical" standards. See Dobbie, *Minor Poems*, xxxiii n. 1, and Fulk, *Old English Meter*, ¶301. Bredehoft's *Textual Histories: Readings in the Anglo-Saxon Chronicle*, was published after this essay was submitted. His chapter 4 treats the multiply-occurring poems of the Chronicle and argues for recuperating as poetry the non-classical "verses" of the Chronicle, especially in versions D and E. For his treatment of the *Death of Alfred* and the *Death of Edgar* see 110-13.

[4] Though such a reading is implied when the *Cambridge History of Medieval English Literature* begins what it is pleased to call "The Afterlife of Old English" with the E-text's 1087 "Rime of King William" — funeral baked meats coldly furnished indeed. See Lerer, "Old English and its Afterlife."

Deaths and Transformations 151

however, included here, following the practice of earlier editors."[5] That is, it is a "poem" only on sufferance and by appeal to a modern editorial tradition that prints it as verse. In the wake of such uncertainty about the generic identity of the *Death of Alfred* there has been (perhaps understandably) virtually no work on it.[6] Part of the difficulty of approaching the text lies squarely in the puzzle of its form. Daniel Abegg, in his consideration of the verse of the Chronicle, inferred from a comparison of the two witnesses that the *Death of Alfred* was an "ursprüngliches Gedicht," later inserted into the Chronicle and recast with a prose introduction.[7] What that original may have resembled was beyond the scope of his early study, hampered as it was by its publication before the appearance of Charles Plummer's introduction and notes to the Chronicle.[8] Speculation on what the "original" appearance of *Death of Alfred* might have been had to wait for a brief note by Ferdinand Holthausen, who ventured a number of emendations to improve the appearance of the "poem" (there mordantly described as "kein Meisterwerk").[9] Holthausen's suggestions, though printed simply as a list, offer a thought experiment on the ways in which we choose to understand Old English verse at the end of the tradition. I print this imaginary text below by inserting Holthausen's "leichte

---

[5] Dobbie, *Minor Poems*, xxxii. He omits, xxxiii, n. 1, several other passages from the Chronicle that other editors chose to print as verse as not being in "regular metrical form": see s.a. 959 DE, 975 DE, 975D, 979E, 1011E, 1057D, 1067D, 1075DE, 1086E, 1104E.

[6] Fulk, *Old English Meter*, 258, uses *Death of Alfred*, line 8 as an illustration of the principle that the presence of rhyme indicates "unreliable witnesses to metrical developments." A recent study of the metrical technique of the Chronicle poems by Townsend, "Metre of the *Chronicle*-verse," 143, declines to consider the meter of *Death of Alfred* at all, on the grounds that it "eschews the alliterative model and employs rhyme as its main structural feature."

[7] Abegg, *Entwicklung der historischen Dichtung*, 68: "dass unsere Erzählung nicht selbständig von einem Worcester Annalisten verfasst ist, sondern dass C und D als gemeinsame Quelle ein Gedicht hatten, das sie auf verschiedene Weise verwerteten" [that our story was not written independently by a Worcester annalist, but that C and D had as a common source a poem which was used in different ways].

[8] Plummer, *Saxon Chronicles*, II.

[9] Holthausen, "Zu dem ae Gedichte von Ælfreds Tode," 157.

Änderungen" (in highlight) in the relevant places of my edition of the text:[10]

> M.xxxvi. Her com Ælfred se unsceðöiga æþeling Æþelrædes sunu cinges hider inn 7 wolde to his meder þe on Wincestre sæt, ac hit him ne geþafode Godwine eorl ne ec oþre men þe mycel mihton wealdan, forðan hit hleoðrode þa swiðe toward Haraldes, þeh hit unriht wære.
> Ac Godwine hine þa gelette 7 hine on hæft sette
> 7 his geferan he todroh[a] 7 sume mislice ofsloh.
> Sume hi man wið feo sealde, sume hreowlice acwealde,
> sume hi man bende, sume hi man blende,
> sume hamelode, sume hættode.
> Ne wearð dreorlicre dæd gedon on þison earde <ær>[b]
> syþþan Dene comon 7 her frið namon.
> Nu is to gelyfenne to ðan leofan Gode <ðenne>[c]
> þæt hi blission <swiðe>[d] mid <Jesu>[e] Criste bliðe[f]
> þe wæron butan scylde swa earmlice acwealde.
> Se æþeling lyfode þa get;[g] ælc yfel man him gehet,
> oð þæt man gerædde þæt man hine lædde
> to Eligbyrig <on fenne>[h] swa gebundenne.
> Sona swa he lende on scype man hine blende
> 7 hine swa blindne brohte to ðam munecon <softe>,[i]
> 7 he þar wunode ða hwile þe he lyfode.
> Syððan hine man byrigde swa him wel gebyrede,

---

[10] *Anglo-Saxon Chronicle*, MS C, ed. O'Brien O'Keeffe, 105-6. Translation follows the manuscript, not Holthausen.

[a] todroh: Ms. *todraf.*
[b] ær: not in Ms.
[c] ðenne: not in Ms.
[d] swiðe: not in Ms.
[e] Jesu: not in Ms.
[f] bliðe: before *mid.*
[g] get: Ms. gyt.
[h] on fenne: not in Ms.
[i] softe: not in Ms.

Deaths and Transformations 153

<þæt wæs>^j ful wurðlice <gedon>,^k swa he wyrðe wæs <to fon>,^l
æt þam westende   þam styple ful gehende,
on þam suðpo<r>tice;   seo saul is mid Criste.

[1036. In this year Alfred, the guiltless aetheling, son of King Æthelred, came here into the country and wished to go to his mother, who was living at Winchester, but Earl Godwine did not permit him to do this, nor did the other men who had great power, because sentiment was going very much to Harold, although that was not right. But Godwine prevented him, and put him in captivity, and he destroyed his companions and slew a number of them in various ways. Some were sold for money, some were cruelly cut down. Some were put in fetters, some blinded, some hamstrung, some scalped. A bloodier deed has not been done in this land since the Danes came and made peace here. It must be believed now at the hands of God that they rejoice with Christ, who were without guilt so wretchedly cut down. The aetheling still lived, threatened by every evil, until it was advised that he be led to Ely, so bound. As soon as he landed he was blinded on shipboard, and so blinded he was brought to the monks, and he dwelled there while he lived. Afterwards, he was buried, as befitted him well, very worthily, as he was worthy, at the west end, very near the steeple, within the *suðportic*. His soul is with Christ.]

Holthausen's ingenious emendations, proposed to give "eine bessere Gestalt" than the manuscripts provide, seek to return the *Death of Alfred* to a recognizable form. Such a maneuver presupposes, not unreasonably, that the kernel of the Chronicle entry for 1036 appeals to a recognizable tradition, whether it was an independent poem (as Abegg assumed) later inserted in the Chronicle, or whether it was composed in the first instance for the Chronicle itself. Through a "restoration" of sorts, Holthausen's

---

^j þæt wæs: not in Ms.
^k gedon: not in Ms.
^l to fon: not in Ms.

regularizations, particularly of rhyme, reproduce the *Death of Alfred* as a kind of *Riming Poem*. The results of such an adjustment are instructive, if only by pointing away from the direction they are meant to lead us.

The examples of rhyme in Old English traditional verse are generally local and isolated, like "swiðe swingeð and his searo hringeð" describing the agitated movements of the Vasa Mortis, a sinister and bizarre creature described in *Solomon and Saturn II* (267).[11] The *Phoenix* has a two-line burst of rhyme in a *ne*-catalogue:

> ne forstes fnæst   ne fyres blæst,
> ne hægles hryre,   ne hrimes dryre.[12]
>
>   (15-16)

Cynewulf employs prominent runs of sustained rhyme in *Christ II* (591-6) and in the epilogue of *Elene* (1236-50).[13] Its relative infrequence may well have been owing to a kind of prudence in avoiding a metrical Siren. R. D. Fulk observes that "even Cynewulf sacrifices metrical niceties for the sake of rhyme" and that rhyme "impose[s] a different sort of form from that of normal Old English verse."[14] That said, the most determined use of rhyme in the surviving corpus is the distinguishing mark of the *Riming Poem*, whose form is *sui generis*.[15] Its rhymes (where they survive) result in a cranky, often obscure, set of verses. The eye of the deviser of the *Riming*

---

[11] For a useful discussion of rhyme in Old English verse see Macrae-Gibson, *Old English "Riming Poem,"* 21-5. E. G. Stanley surveys the incidence and types of rhyme in Old English in "Rhymes in Medieval Verse," treating the "impure rhymes" of the Chronicle verse at 28-30.

[12] Line 54, "ne synne ne sacu   ne sarwracu" exhibits rhyme, but the following line, with "gewin" and "onsyn" is not exact.

[13] See also "Latin-English Proverbs" in Dobbie, *Minor Poems*, 109, and Dobbie's discussion, cx-cxii.

[14] Fulk, *Old English Meter*, ¶301 and ¶389. Dobbie, *Minor Poems*, xxxiii n. 1, lists the *Chronicle* passages falling "between irregular meter and rhythmical prose" that Plummer prints as verse. A tendency to rhyme is not prominent in the early passages, appears at points in 1067D, 1075E (1076D), but is fairly regular in 1086E.

[15] Fulk, *Old English Meter*, 365-6, on the substitution of Anglian forms to restore rhyme.

Poem was always trained on form, hence the poem's maddening double rhymes, tight alliteration, and jingly meter. For example:

> Swa nu world wendeþ,   wyrde sendeþ
> ond hetes henteð,   hæleþe scyndeð:
> wencyn gewiteð,   wælgar sliteð
> (flahmah fliteþ;   flan man hwiteþ);
> borgsorg biteð   (bald ald þwiteþ,
> wræcfæc wriþað),   wraþ að smiteþ.[16]
>
> (59-64)

[So now the world changes, sending fate on hatred's heels to ruin noble men. The kindred of joy is gone, the spear tears and slaughters, contention is set on evil, arrow fletched by malice, good faith consumed by distress and oath fouled by anger, brave men crabbedly foiled, a flourishing of affliction.]

This poem rejoices in the most daunting of formal constraints: double alliteration in the a-line, internal rhyme extended often to multiple lines (e.g., 61-4), double rhyme within a line (62, 63, 64), in addition to the normal alliterative and rhythmical constraints of classical Old English poetry. These lines are by no means exceptional within the poem. Sacrificed on the altar of the formal, of course, is sense, and the *Riming Poem* has exercised the wits of several generations of academic readers attempting to resolve the crossword-style lexical deformations that the poem's formal experimentation produced. Quite clearly, the *Riming Poem* does not appeal to the traditional word stock of Old English poetry, and despite its observation of the norms of alliteration and meter, it remains an oddity within the Exeter Book and, indeed, within the larger corpus. In a 1987 essay, James W. Earl advances an intriguing argument for reading this Old English poem within the context of the hermeneutic Latin poems of the tenth century, as well as other Latin rhymed hexameters and rhymed and alliter-

---

[16] Text and translation from Macrae-Gibson, *Old English "Riming Poem,"* 34-5.

ating iambic dimeters.[17] It is doubtful that the *Riming Poem*'s pressure on Old English words is closely analogous to the Grecisms and neologisms of Latin hermeneutic poetry, saturated as that is in the language of Aldhelm's works.[18] Nonetheless, the formal experimentations of the *Riming Poem*'s combination of polysyllabic rhymed couplets and alliteration find a closer analogue in Aldhelmian Latin octosyllables than in any surviving Old English verse.[19] While the moment for such octosyllables was confined to the late seventh and early to mid eighth centuries, they reappear (lacking alliteration) in the tenth century in two extended sets of rhymed octosyllabic couplets in Lantfred's *Translatio et miracula S. Swithuni* (c. 975) — a work that clearly post-dates the *Riming Poem*[20] — and in some later Anglo-Latin work.[21] Looking to the *Riming Poem* for a formal model for the *Death of Alfred* produces pointed, negative results: just as the *Riming Poem* appears to look away from traditional Old English verse for its models, so does the *Death of Alfred*, though for opposite reasons.

The *Death of Alfred* resists identification with the *Riming Poem* not merely because its rhymes are sporadic and its meter deficient. Given liberal appeal to anacrusis and resolution, many lines can be fitted into the

---

[17] Earl, "Hisperic Style," esp. 187, 190. Earl insists on "Hisperic," despite acknowledging the almost universal use of "Hermeneutic" for this poetry following upon Lapidge's ground-breaking essay, "Hermeneutic Style."

[18] See Lapidge, "Hermeneutic Style," 67-8. The seventeen surviving lines of *Aldhelm*, a macaronic poem preserved in a manuscript of Aldhelm's prose *De virginitate* (CCCC 326), are unique in including Greek words with the Latin and Old English. See Dobbie, *Minor Poems*, 97-8.

[19] In an apparent inversion of the influence Old English alliteration clearly had on Aldhelm's (and later) Latin verse. On the vernacular influences on Aldhelm's octosyllables see Orchard, *Poetic Art of Aldhelm*, 19-72, esp. 52-3. See also Lapidge, "Aldhelm's Latin Poetry," 218-23.

[20] Ker, *Catalogue*, item 116, dates the Exeter Book to s. x^2. Gameson, "Origin of the Exeter Book," 166, refines that dating to 960-970. For an argument on the Exeter provenance of the manuscript (disputed by Gameson) see Conner, *Anglo-Saxon Exeter*.

[21] See now Lapidge's edition of the *Translatio et miracula*, c. 26, "Alme Deus munificens," and c. 34, "Auctor o rerum prepotens," in *The Cult of St Swithun*, esp. n. 130. I am grateful to Michael Lapidge for drawing these poems to my attention.

Deaths and Transformations 157

standard classical arrangements of dips and lifts.[22] The collocation of meter with alliteration is another matter. Alliteration is entirely missing in eight lines (5, 6, 7, 12, 15, 16, 21, 24);[23] when it is arguably present, it is often not correctly distributed (as in, for example, lines 8, 22, etc.); and often the finite verb alone carries alliteration (lines 14a, 20b, 22a, 22b) rather than a noun or adjective. And yet there are unmistakable runs of alliterative effects (lines 11-12 on *d*; 16-17 on "man"; 19-20 on *b*; 23-4 on *w*) which work across lines rather than within them. Despite its shortcomings in alliteration and meter when measured against the requirements of classical Old English poetry, it is clear that the *Death of Alfred* strives for heightened aesthetic effect. This is no clearer than in lines 7-10, where a *sum*-catalogue is set up to commemorate the terrible fates — death, enslavement, or mutilation — endured by the men in Alfred's retinue:

> ....7 sume mislice ofsloh.
> Sume hi man wið feo sealde,   sume hreowlice acwealde,
> sume hi man bende,   sume hi man blende,
> sume hamelode,   sume hættode.
> (7b-10)

[and some he killed in various ways. Some were sold for money, some were cruelly cut down, some were fettered, some blinded, some hamstrung, some scalped.]

While the internal rhyme in line 10 is simply an instance of homeoteleuton, those in lines 7 and 8 are true syllabic rhymes. In addition to the rhetorical heightening produced by anaphora on "sume," the lines also achieve libration between the a- and b-lines in lines 9 and 10. There is, additionally, the cross-alliteration on *s*, *m*, and *b* in line 9 and *s*, *h* in line 10. The intensity of the effect is not produced by meter, but rather by rhythm, rhyme, and an anaphora that does its work primarily from the metrical dip. (The exception is line 10, where presumably there is cross-alliteration on *s* and *h*.) It would be possible to argue that the *Death of Alfred* models its usage on the example of *sum*-catalogues elsewhere in the

---

[22] Additionally, a lift is missing from 14a; 23a ("ful" is short), 23b ("wæs" is short).

[23] Unless, of course, one admits alliteration on the pronouns "hit" or "hine" in lines 5 and 6.

canon,[24] but there is another tradition in Old English to which the entry for 1036 makes both aesthetic and political appeals.

To look backward to the Exeter Book, either to *Fortunes of Men* or *Gifts of Men* or to the *Riming Poem*, as Holthausen appears to do in rehabilitating the *Death of Alfred*, is to look precisely away from the well from which the poem drinks. The lexicon for representing Alfred and his men comes not from the heroic conventions of the hall, but from the hagiographic conventions of the church. What we blandly call the *Death of Alfred* is a work the ambitions of which exceed those of epitaph and look rather to the promotion of a cult of the dead prince. The development of a cult seems to have been the expectation of the *Encomium Emmae*, which concludes its account of Alfred's murder with the observation that

> In loco autem sepulcri eius multa fiunt miracula, ut quidam aiunt, qui etiam se haec uidisse saepissime dicunt. Et merito: innocenter enim fuit martyrizatus, ideoque dignum est ut per eum innocencium exerceatur uirtus. Gaudeat igitur Emma regina de tanto intercessore, quia quem quondam in terris habuit filium nunc habet in caelis patronum.[25]

> [However, many miracles occur where his tomb is, as people report who even declare most repeatedly that they have seen them. And it is justly so: for he was martyred in his innocence, and therefore it is fitting that the might of the innocent should be exercised through him. So let Queen Emma rejoice in so great an intercessor, since she now has as a patron in the heavens him whom she formerly had as a son on earth.]

The claim of miracles at the tomb is also made by the twelfth-century *Liber Eliensis*, though a fully articulated cult seems not to have developed for the

---

[24] See, for example, *Fates of Men*, lines 15-16, and 66-70 for catalogues with *sumum* where "sumum" is in the dip. The *sum*-catalogue in *Elene* lines 131-6 on the deaths of the army facing Constantine is less balanced. See Howe, *Catalogue Poems*.

[25] Campbell, *Encomium Emmae Reginae*, 46, his trans., 47. Earlier in the passage, 44, Alfred is referred to as "iuuenis ... beatissimus" [most blessed youth].

Deaths and Transformations   159

ætheling.[26] The culting of murdered royal saints was a development peculiar to Anglo-Saxon England, and one which gave itself to political maneuvering, since the claim of martyrdom might be used to emphasize the guilt of the killers.[27] The interests of the Old English passage along these lines are immediately signaled by its lexicon with the uneasy pairing in line 1 of "se unsceðeðiga" [the guiltless] with "æþeling." *Æþeling*, of course, may be found throughout the corpus of verse in the general sense of 'prince' or 'hero.' It is at home in the descriptions of heroes, villains, or Christ himself (e.g., "wuldres æþeling" [*Christ* 158a] [prince of glory]). Its use in the Chronicle, however, is by contrast technical and political in the further specification that the murdered prince is "Æþelrædes sunu cinges" [son of King Æthelred].[28] Such specification clarifies that the lexicon the chronicler is drawing on comes primarily from royal politics, not heroic convention. And it is this lexicon that makes the pairing with "unsceððiga" surprising, since words built on *unsceðð-* (adjectives and substantives) are overwhelmingly confined to religious discourse. Ælfric, for example, uses it of sacrificial doves, of Christ's redemptive death, and as a gloss for *innocens*.[29] Even more interesting, the word appears in a later eleventh-century list of relics given to the monastery of Exeter by King Athelstan (d. 940).[30] The notation for the relics of St. Satiuola observes that she "wæs un-

---

[26] Blake, *Liber Eliensis*, 160.

[27] On the politics of murdered royal saints see Rollason, "Cults of Murdered Royal Saints," 16.

[28] On the meaning of *ætheling* and its particular sense in the eleventh century see Dumville, "The Æthelings," esp. 13.

[29] The adjective form (regardless of orthography) is confined to *Death of Alfred*; Ælfric, in *Catholic Homilies*, ed. Clemoes, I.9.110, "Culfran sint swiðe unsceððige fugelas" [doves are very innocent birds]; ibid., I.14.170, "þurh his unsceððian deaðe wurdon we alysede" [through his guiltless death we were saved]; Ælfric, *De duodecim Abusivis* (ed. Morris, *Old English Homilies*, 304, l. 12), "Gif þu unsceððig si" [if you are guiltless]; Ælfric, *Grammar* (*Aelfrics Grammatik*, ed. Zupitza, 253, l. 16) "innocens unsceððig is æfre nama" ["innocens," guiltless, is always a noun]; Hertzfeld, *Old English Martyrology*, 213, ll. 26-7; Kotzor, *Der altenglische Martyrologium*, 2.263, ll. 20-1, "on þa wrace hyre þæs unsceððian blodes" [in vengeance for her guiltless blood]; Förster, *Reliquienkultus*, 244 [of St. Edward's relics], "þe wæs unsceððig acweald" [who guiltless was killed].

[30] Ker, *Catalogue*, item 291c, describes the entries as written in "a large ill-formed hand" "somewhat later" than c. 1070.

sceððiglice acweald" [guiltless, she was killed].[31] Of particular interest is its use in the entry on the relics of the dead child king, Edward the Martyr (d. 978), murdered in an intrigue for control of the throne: "Of sanctus Eadwardes reliquion þæs cyninges, þe wæs unsceððig acweald" [of the relics of St. Edward, the king, who, guiltless, was killed].[32] Edward the Martyr was the older half-brother of King Æthelred, Alfred's father. After the murder, Edward's body was interred without ceremony at Wareham, reinterred with appropriate honors in the following year at Shaftesbury, and finally translated within Shaftesbury Abbey in 1001, when Edward was culted as a saint.[33] While Alfred was no child at his untimely death, he was cut down, as the entry for 1036 makes clear, in a treacherous power struggle for the throne. Not killed outright, he was blinded instead to prevent his succession to the throne and spent the brief remainder of his days in the care of the monks of Ely. Upon his death, he was buried at Ely within the *suðportic*, a structure, in Anglo-Saxon church architecture, that housed the bodies of bishops and kings as well as the relics of saints.[34] The shocking facts of Alfred's death — his blinding and the enslavement or mutilation of the men in his retinue — presented the chronicler with a set of difficult rhetorical and formal problems in representing Æthelred's youngest son. As an exiled pretender to the throne, Alfred could not be comfortably described within the lexicon of kingship or lordship. Not killed in battle (and so not qualifying for tropes of the heroic available to the *Maldon*-poet), he survived for a while with ruined eyes, the scars from which would have been indistinguishable from those inflicted on common criminals.[35] The recuperation of Alfred (and the vilification of Godwine's party) trumps the *dom* of heroic poetry by appealing to cult. In so doing, the lexical and stylistic tradition upon which the *Death of Alfred* draws in its hybrid form is the homiletic discourse of martyrdom, its mode less verse than prose.

---

[31] Förster, *Reliquienkultus*, 244.

[32] Förster, *Reliquienkultus*, 129.

[33] For detail on the development of the cult see Fell, *Edward King and Martyr*, xx–xxv. In "Anglo-Saxon Hagiographic Tradition," 6, Fell describes the Chronicle as "a quite extraordinarily interesting study of the development of what one might perhaps call 'hagiographic awareness.'" See also Ridyard, *Royal Saints*, 44–50 and 154–75.

[34] On the meaning of OE *portic* see Biggs, "The Exeter *Exeter Book?*" 65.

[35] See the discussion in O'Brien O'Keeffe, "Body and Law," esp. 213–14.

Deaths and Transformations

The *sum*-catalogue of lines 7b-10, the most rhetorically heightened passage in the entry, commemorates the mutilations inflicted on Alfred's men, and insists the dead among them rest with Christ. These outrages, it claims, were not exceeded by anything done since the wars that put Cnut on the throne on England. That this passage draws on a trope of commemorating martyrs becomes clearer when placed in a context of homiletic prose:

> We sceolon geþencan hu geþyldige hi wæron
> þa þe for cristes naman gecwylmede wæron.
> hi man swang mid swipum . and on sæ adrincte [sic].
> oððe on fyre forbærnde . oþþe forðwyrftum limum
> to wæfersyne tucode . mid gehwilcum witum.
> and on ælcum wawan hi wæron geþyldige.
> and ælcne hosp hi forbæron . for þæs hælendes naman.[36]

> [We must think how patient they were who were killed for the name of Christ. They were beaten with whips and drowned in the sea, or burned in a fire or tormented with mutilated (?twisted) limbs as a spectacle; with such torments and in such miseries they were patient and they endured each insult for the name of the Savior.]

In drawing the lesson from the angelic reception of the souls of St. Maurice and his companions, Ælfric urges the patience of martyrs in tribulation as an example to the faithful. In this instance the enumeration of painful deaths (including the breaking or twisting of limbs to produce a spectacle) is made in Ælfric's signature alliterating rhythmical prose. In a more extended passage on martyrdom, here from the homily for the feast of All Saints, we see the same trope of thought in an extended catalogue of modes of death leading up to the assurance that the martyred souls have been proved as friends of God:

> Æfter þam apostolican werode we wurþiað þone sige-
> fæstan heap godes cyþera þe þurh mislicum tintregum
> cristes þrowunge werlice geefenlæhton. 7 þurh martyr-

---

[36] *Ælfric's Lives of Saints*, ed. Skeat, 2:166, lines 125-30.

dome þ<æt> upplice rice geferdon; Sume hi wæron mid wæpnum ofslegene; sume on lige forswælede; Oþre mid swipum ofbeatene. oþre mid stengum þurhðyde; Sume on hengene gecwylmede. sume on widdre sæ besencte; Oþre cuce behylde. oþre mid isenum clawum totorene; Sume mid stanum ofhrorene. sume mid winterlicum cyle geswencte. | sume mid hungre gecwylmede; Sume handum 7 fotum forcorfene folce to wæfersyne for geleafan 7 halgum naman hælendes cristes; ða sind þa sigefæstan godes frynd þe ðæra forscyldgodra ealdormanna hæse forsawon. 7 nu hi sind gewuldorbeagode mid sige | heora þrowunga on ecere myrhþe; Hi mihton beon lichamlice acwealde ac hi ne mihton fram gode þurh nanum tintregum beon gebigede; heora hiht wæs mid undeadlicnysse afylled þeah þe hi ætforan mannum getintregode wæron; Hi wæron scortlice gedrehte. 7 langlice gefrefrode. for þan þe god heora afandode swa swa gold on ofene. 7 he afunde hi him wyrþe. 7 swa swa halig offrung he hi underfeng to his heofenlicum rice....[37]

[After the apostolic band we honor the glorious host of God's martyrs who through various tortures imitated Christ's suffering courageously and through martyrdom attained the heavenly kingdom. Some were slain with weapons, some consumed in flame, others beaten with whips, others pierced with rods, some were killed on the cross, some drowned in the wide sea, others were flayed alive, others torn apart with iron hooks, some were stoned, some tormented with wintry cold, some were starved, some as a spectacle for the people were deprived of hands and feet for their faith and for the holy name of

---

[37] *Ælfric's Catholic Homilies* I, ed. Clemoes, Homily 36, "Natale omnium sanctorum," 488-9, lines 71-88, in a passage reworked from an earlier homiletic source. (See Cross, "Legimus in ecclesiasticis historiis," 115-16, ll. 124-32, 142-6. For a sourcing of individual lines see *Fontes Anglo-Saxonici*: http://fontes.english.ox.ac.uk/.) For an example of Ælfric's crafting of a prose *sum*-catalogue without extensive rhetorical elaboration, see, by contrast, *Ælfric's Catholic Homilies*, ed. Godden, "In natale unius confessoris," 323-4, lines 165-75.

the Savior, Christ. These are the glorious friends of God who despised the command of guilty rulers, and now they are gloriously crowned with the victory of their sufferings in eternal joy. They could be killed bodily but they could not be turned away from God by any tortures; their hope was fulfilled by immortality although they had been tormented before men; they were afflicted for a short time and comforted for a long time, because God tried them like gold in the furnace and he found them worthy of him, and just as a holy offering he received them in his heavenly kingdom.]

In this passage, Ælfric's rhetorical elaboration of the sufferings of the martyrs links bodily suffering with eternal reward. By contrast to the alliterating four-stress rhythmical prose of the earlier passage, the passage from *Catholic Homilies* I.36 relies for its effect on a more fluid deployment of repetition, alliteration, balance, and rhythm. In this passage, alliterative effects transcend rhythmical units. This strategy appears most effectively in the first five clauses of the catalogue proper (with structural repetition on "sume," "sume," "oþre," "oþre," "sume"). Here the rhythm is established through the parallel structures of preposition, noun, past participle, and alliteration on *s* (and in Ælfric this may include *s*-clusters[38]) sweeps across the clauses, reconnecting phrases formally severed by interrupting the anaphora on "sume." While the passage works to avoid homeoteleuton,[39] it admits the rhyme "totorene" with "ofhrorene" in subsequent clauses. While Ælfric's aesthetic effects are immediately recognizable, such effects work with something already in the prose tradition.[40] In her recent study of tradition in homiletic writing, Clare Lees points out that "alliteration often signals that which is culturally significant or memorable; this can be the case for the laws, prayers, proverbs, and homilies or saints' lives as well

---

[38] *Homilies of Ælfric*, ed. Pope, 1:127–8 and nn. 1, 2.

[39] Note the separation of "ofslegene," "ofbeatene," "hengene."

[40] See *Homilies of Ælfric*, ed. Pope, 111. In a private communication Paul E. Szarmach notes the integration of verse forms within prose in Vercelli Homilies 2 and 21. See his edition of Homily XXI in *Vercelli Homilies IX–XXIII*. Scragg, *Vercelli Homilies*, prints the homilies as prose throughout. For a helpful discussion of the "borderland between verse and prose" see E. G. Stanley, "Judgement of the Damned," esp. 390–1.

as the poetry, even though prose alliteration is not as rigorously metrical as poetic and does not deploy a poetic vocabulary."[41]

In suggesting that the *Death of Alfred* draws for some of its effects on the lexicon and aesthetic resources of Ælfric's homiletics, I am not arguing that the entry for 1036 either imagines itself as a homily or even produces a particularly theological sentiment; rather I suggest that what we call the *Death of Alfred*, finding itself necessarily between genres and, as a result, in the "borderland between verse and prose," uses a tradition of thinking to produce a particular aesthetic and political result. Just as the *Battle of Maldon* called on the forms and traditions of Germanic heroic verse to give meaning and honor to a crushing defeat, the *Death of Alfred* calls on an equally powerful tradition to confer meaning and honor on a humiliating death. Mutilated by his enemies but not killed, Alfred could not sustain the heroic pairing of *dom* and *deað* that was the pivotal fiction in *Maldon*.[42] What his suffering and death might sustain, however, is treatment within the rhetoric of the suffering of the martyrs as part of a movement to cult him. The aesthetic appeal in this commemoration is in the eleventh century more homiletic than heroic, more prose than verse, when measured by the standards of classical Old English verse. But we are mistaken if we regard this puzzling work as a sign of the end of Old English poetry. As a *tertium quid* it walks the generic borders with a number of homilies, including Ælfric's metrical prose. With its weakened grammatical endings, privileging of rhyme, and fluid alliteration, it is an emergent form, looking forward, not back.

The Death of Edward
By contrast, the *Death of Edward* is a poem that looks backwards for its forms. By this I do not mean to suggest that the poem is 'antiquarian' in any sense, but rather to argue that the poet recognized the power inherent in a formulaic appeal to lordship.[43] For clear political reasons, the *Death of Edward* is a self-consciously traditional poem and uses what amounts to

---

[41] Lees, *Tradition and Belief*, 23.
[42] See O'Brien O'Keeffe, "Heroic Values," 123.
[43] Irvine overlooks the Chronicle's strategic political use of the form ("Medieval Textuality," 202–8) in dismissing the Chronicle poems as "an act of poetic nostalgia" (202).

traditional referentiality[44] in the service of Harold's succession. This choice suggests that the tradition still had life and work to do at the end of Edward's reign.

The *Death of Edward*, copied in both the C- and D-texts under the year 1065,[45] appears in each at the end of a larger entry. In C, the earlier of the two manuscripts, the entry must have been copied after September 1066, since it seems to suggest by "7 he lytle stillnesse þar on gebad þa hwile þe he rices weold" [and he lived there in little peace while he ruled the kingdom] that at the time of writing Harold was already dead. It is, of course, possible, though incapable of proof, that the writing of the entry underlying the C- and D-texts was done in three parts: the opening prose, to which the verse was added afterwards, and the final comment as a further addition.[46] If so, then we have an interesting development within the entry for 1065, where the verse actually calls on the tropes of lordship and heroic verse to shore up Edward's image and to assist in legitimating Harold as Edward's heir. Unlike the elusive form of the entry for 1036, that for 1065 makes a clear distinction between the prose and the verse. The introduction to the verse ("And Eadward kinge com to Westmynstre.... 7 hyne man bebyrigde on Twelftan Dæig on þam ylcan mynstre swa hyt her æfter seigð" [And King Edward came to Westminster.... And he was buried on the Feast of Epiphany (6 January 1066) in that same minster as it says here afterwards][47]) marks that difference formally ("swa hyt her æfter seigð") but also, by inadvertence, conceptually, since the verses lack the punctual date that the prose directs us to find in it. In contrast to Chronicle practice of giving years *ab incarnatione*, the poem offers the clumsy calculation of Edward's date of death as twenty-three years after his accession.[48] The poem's complex relationship with time and history is figured in its gestural use of "her." In the earlier Chronicle poems, the adverb of space *her* recapitulates the opening of the prose entries by pointing to time

---

[44] On which see Foley, *Immanent Art*, 6–9, 203–5.

[45] Edward died 5 January 1066. Both the C- and D-texts use for 1065 and 1066 a reckoning that begins the year in the spring.

[46] For a discussion of the writing of the entries for 1065 and 1066 in MS C see *Anglo-Saxon Chronicle, MS C*, ed. O'Brien O'Keeffe, lxxii.

[47] O'Brien O'Keeffe, *MS C*, 118. The differences between the C-text and D-text at this point is orthographic. For a comparison see Conner, *Abingdon Chronicle*, 34.

[48] The C-text has ".xxiii....7 healfe tid"; the D-text gives twenty-three years.

as a date written (or in the present instance not written) in the margin. In the Chronicle poems for 937 and 942, both self-standing entries, "her" was the non-metrical introduction that integrated them formally into the Chronicle and signaled their function as annals in their own right. The *Death of Edward*, given its position in the middle of an entry, does not need such a temporal marker. However, the first half-line of the poem requires "her" metrically, given the monosyllabic "kingc" in the final position in 1a.[49] In making "her" part of the shape of the half-line, the poem seems to follow the practice of 973 and 975, though they were independent entries.

The opening prose of the entry records two disasters: Caradog's raid against Portskewett with the slaughter of most of its workmen and overseers, and the subsequent seizure of stores; and the related (and more consequential) uprising of the Northumbrians against earl Tostig and his replacement by Morcar of Mercia.[50] While both events affected Harold's position, the Northumbrian's revolt showed Edward to be significantly

---

[49] A b-verse. See Townsend, "Metre of the *Chronicle*-verse," 149. It would be interesting to speculate on whether "her" in *Death of Edward* indicates that the poem was meant at some early point to be an independent entry in the fashion of the verses s.a. 937, 942, 973, and 975. The entry for 1065 was written in a single hand (hand 6) responsible for fol. 160 and the first seven lines of the following 162ʳ (on the correct order of leaves in the final quire see *Anglo-Saxon Chronicle, MS C*, ed. O'Brien O'Keeffe, xxi). Hand 6 has fitted the whole of the prose beginning of the entry on fol. 160ʳ, omitting the annal number (presumably for later rubrication). Space for some eight letters is left blank on line 27 of 160ʳ, suggesting that the scribe wished to keep the verses intact. He begins them at the left margin of line 1 on the verso, writing "[ ]er" with space left for the capital h, again, presumably for rubrication. The verses are written across the lines, disregarding the right hand margin (as does hand 4). After the last word of the poem, "þeodkyninges," there is a simple point and the rest of the line is left blank, leaving space for several words, some twenty letters. The last prose lines of the entry are begun flush left on the next line with the nota for "ond" written in the margin. The physical condition of the entry suggests that it was entered all together, though without the level of care of earlier entries. There is no material evidence, beyond the ambiguous evidence of the formatting of the verses, to suggest that the annal for 1065 consists of three discrete parts. On the metrical pointing of the entry see *Anglo-Saxon Chronicle, MS C*, ed. O'Brien O'Keeffe, xlix–l, and her *Visible Song*, 135.

[50] See also Darlington and McGurk, *Chronicle of John of Worcester*, 2:596 (s.a. 1065), and Barlow, *Edward the Confessor*, 233–4.

weak, since he was compelled to confirm the Northumbrians' selection of Morcar as earl, apparently against his expressed wish.[51] Indeed, the *Vita Ædwardi regis* blames the king's death two months later on his distress over the banishment of Tostig.[52]

In the C-text, King Edward is barely in the prose portion of the entry at all: he is mentioned as part of Harold's plans for a hunting party in the spring, and he is mentioned as being at Britford with Tostig that fall. His single activity in the prose portion is the dedication of Westminster Abbey on 28 December 1065, after which he dies a week later on the eve of Epiphany.[53] Two questions arise, then, about the verses in the entry for 1065: what work do they perform at this stage in the writing of the Chronicle, and how does this work draw upon traditional Old English verse?

The answer to both questions begins with an assessment of form – its meter and structure of half-lines. One of the remarkable features of the *Death of Edward* is its metrical regularity. Although a small percentage of its seventy-eight half-lines are problematic (indeed one is deficient), the poem is sufficiently regular to lead Thomas Cable to consider the Old English verse form, in the almost four centuries from *Caedmon's Hymn* to the *Death of Edward*, to have been "transmitted in a highly regulated, technically precise, essentially monolithic, continuous tradition."[54] The poem shows a

---

[51] See Barlow, *Vita Ædwardi regis*, 80 "merens nimium quod in hanc impotentiam decideret" [profoundly distressed at the powerlessness that had come upon him (trans. Barlow, 81-3] with the further suggestion, 82, that his unhappiness contributed to his death "ex contracta animi egritudine languescens ..." [languishing from the mental illness he had contracted (83)]. See also DeVries, *Norwegian Invasion of England*, 180-1; Stenton, *Anglo-Saxon England*, 578-9. See also A. Williams, "Land and Power," 171-87, 230-4; Fleming, "Domesday Estates."

[52] Barlow, *Vita Ædwardi regis*, 80: "Quo dolore decidens in morbum, ab ea die usque in diem mortis sue egrum trahebat animum" [Sorrowing at this, he fell ill, and from that day until the day of his death he bore a sickness of the mind (81)].

[53] The king plays a somewhat more prominent role in D, where the king himself is shown granting the Northumbrians' demands, reaffirming the laws of Cnut on their behalf, and receiving in reply the further raiding and looting of the Northumbrians before they returned north. See *Anglo-Saxon Chronicle, MS D*, ed. Cubbin, 78.

[54] Cable, *English Alliterative Tradition*, 55: "despite the extra syllable in 28a, the poem as a whole can be said to be in the classical meter." Townsend, "Metre

marked fondness for a- and d-type verses (63%, with a correspondingly low occurrence of c- and e-verses), a preference that ensures a fairly predictable rhythm stressing the first syllable of a half-line.[55] The metrical accomplishments of the *Death of Edward* assume greater point in the present instance when read in conjunction with the poem's appeal to and manipulation of traditional formulas. An examination of the Appendix below shows how many of the verses replicate formulaic structures found elsewhere in the corpus. In a limited number of instances there are verses identical to half-lines elsewhere (e.g., "on Godes wæra" [in God's protection]; "land ond leode" [land and people]; "wide geond eorðan" [widely over the earth]), and there is a noteworthy number of repeated lines within the poem: "wintra gerimes" (7a, 21a) [by count of years], "hyrdon holdlice" (14a) [they obeyed him loyally]; "hyrde holdlice" (32a) [he obeyed loyally], "weolan britnode" (7b), "welan brytnodon" (21b) [he (they) shared out wealth]. However, most half-lines can be shown to belong to recognizable formulaic systems (e.g., xx *swegles leoht*; *deore* Xx; xx *lange ær*). This is not to suggest that the *Death of Edward* was composed orally, but merely to observe how carefully the poem conforms to the traditional shape and content of half-lines. The poem was meant, I suggest, to sound traditional.

In the thirty-four lines of the poem, Edward is described in the traditional language of lordship as well as of kingship: "Engla hlaford" (1b) [lord of the English]; "freolic wealdend" (6b) [glorious ruler], "hæleða wealdend" (8b) [ruler of warriors], and "Her Edward kingc" (1a) [In this year King Edward], "æðelum kinge" (13b) [noble king], "bealuleas kyng" (15b) [innocent king], "kyningc kystum god" (23a) [a king good in his virtues]. The crafting of this poem in the pattern of its Chronicle predecessors is clear from a comparison of the epithets used in the commemorations of Kings Athelstan, Edmund, and Edgar. The first line of the *Death of Edward* might well have been patterned on the opening line of *Capture of the Five Boroughs* — "Her Eadmund cyning   Engla þeoden" — for they are identical in meter and formulas. The *Battle of Brunanburh* begins with the identical "Her Æþelstan cyning" (1a). The *Coronation of Edgar*'s "Engla

---

of the *Chronicle*-verse," 156, notes that only four half-lines (including 28a) "give difficulty," though she finds (158) that "the *Death of Edward*-poet seems the least skilful of all the poets [i.e of the ASC]."

[55] Townsend, "Metre of the *Chronicle*-verse," 156 and Table 8. She speculates, 158, that the regularity of the meter in the *Death of Edward* might "indicate a shift towards rhythmic verse."

Deaths and Transformations 169

waldend" (1b) is metrically identical and is part of the same system.[56] The a-type formula *engla Xx* has a much larger life in the corpus, where its referents are religious, and it is only the later, Chronicle poems in which "Engla" refers to the English and not to angels.[57]

In *Death of Edward* the distinction between "Englum" and "Sexum" points us less to the present of the poem than to the poetic past. These words echo the ending of *Brunanburh*, where Athelstan's triumph is compared with the founding victory in which the *Engle* and *Seaxe* overcame the *Brytene* and *Wealas*.[58] In the eleventh century, *Engle* normally meant 'English' not [continental] 'Anglian,' and when *Seaxe* is used in the Chronicle, except for references to the continental Saxons, it is normally modified by 'East,' 'West,' or 'South.'[59] Similarly, the geography of Edward's rule is alluded to only in a brief clause ("swa ymbclyppað   cealde brymmas" (12) [so far as the cold seas encompass]) dependent on "oretmæcgum" (11b) [warriors],[60] a primarily poetic word summing the peoples over whom Edward is said to have ruled. The historical referents of "Englum" and "Sexum" impart a strong temporal dimension to the representation of Edward in his memorial poem. To the extent that they look back to *Brunanburh* and the historical framework of Athelstan's victory, Edward is made to embody and figure his line. Hence the importance of "byre Æðelredes" (10b) [son

---

[56] *Death of Edgar's* "Eadgar, Engla cyning" (2a) uses the epithet in a larger line.

[57] See: 1 Exo 432b, 559b; 1 Xst 198b, 518b, 562b; 2 And 278b, 290b, 900b, 1007a; 3 Chr 332b, 791b; 6 SnS 462b; 6 Crd 21b; 6 CFB 1b; and 6 EgC 1b.

[58] And *Menologium* 185b. See also *Widsith* 62a ("Mid Seaxum ic wæs ond Sycgum" [I was with the Saxons and the ?Secgan]). For an account of Edward's relation with the Scots and the Welsh see Barlow, *Edward the Confessor*, 201–12.

[59] An exception is the Peterborough Chronicle s.a. 649 which has "Sexena biscopdomas" for the Parker Chronicle's "Wesseaxna bisc<op>domes" (s.a. 650). It should be noted that the Latin term *Saxones* for *English* was not uncommon. See Lapidge, "Hermeneutic Style," 81 n. 2. For an argument on the political development of "Angelcynn" see Foot, "The Making of *Angelcynn*." On the political origins of "Englishness" see Wormald, "*Engla Lond*: The Making of an Allegiance," 10–11.

[60] The word occurs in *Andreas* 664b ("orettmæcgas"); *Beowulf* 332a, 481b, 363b; and *Judith* 232b. Its use is confined to poetry except for two glosses: in London, British Library, Cotton Cleopatra A. iii: Wright-Wülker, *Anglo-Saxon and Old English Vocabularies*, 1:338.2, Agonista: oretmæcga and I.342.13, Anthletæ: oretmæcgan.

of Æthelred] and the double use of *æðele* (as "æðelum kinge" (13b) [noble king] and "Eadward se æðela" (24a) [Edward the noble]) in referring to Edward.

But another people in the poem emerge from the more recent, and more troubling, past. When the *Dene*, in the person of Cnut, are introduced as the conquerors of Æthelred's "kynn" [(here) people], Edward is portrayed once again as a traditional figure. He treads the paths of exile (much like the *Wanderer*), but he does so with patience ("a bliðemod") in the twenty-eight years of his absence. Edward's accession is important here as a restoration of Æthelred's line. Where in exile he was "lande bereafod" (15b) [deprived of his land], upon his return he "eðel bewerode" (24b) [defended his native land]. In this delicate balancing act between past and present, "Edward" acts as a place marker for the power of English rule. It is not too much to say that the most important work in the poem is done by the word "befæste" (29b) [entrusted]. Indeed, everything before leads up to it, and everything following is meant to justify it. If the twenty-eight-year disruption in English rule was put to right by Edward's accession, Edward's action in securing a succession must be underscored. And so much in Harold's description mirrors that of Edward: Harold's description as "heahþungenum" (30a) [illustrious, or of high rank] echoes Edward's "geþungen" (9b) [excellent, distinguished]. Edward's description as "æþelne" (27a) and "æðela" (24a) is recapitulated in Harold's description as "æþelum eorle" (31a). Just as when Edward was alive, all men "hyrdon holdlice" (14a) [obeyed him loyally], so too his chosen successor "hyrde holdlice" Edward, who in the following half-line is described in the traditional poetic word as his "hærran" [lord].

The *Death of Edward* is not a poem that permits itself the luxury of much mourning. For all its regret at bitter death and its double mention of Edward's soul and his heavenly rest, the work of the poem is firmly in its present and focuses on Harold, who begins and ends the entry for 1065. The chronicler responsible for drafting the entries for 1065 called on the elliptical syntax of traditional verse to produce an account of Edward that could elide the seamy politics of Godwine's ascendency by virtue of two appeals: a political appeal through family and descent (with the descriptor "kynn Æðelredes" (18b) and a religious appeal (through "clæne and milde" [23b] [chaste and merciful]), showing the first shoots of his later cult. It is a poem from which every trace of Edward's collaboration with Godwine is erased, in marked contrast to the impassioned anti-

Godwinism of the C-entries in the years betwen 1036 and 1053.[61] Appeal to the injury done to Edward through his exile is made by calling on the traditional language of exclusion (lines 16-17) and of blood ties (line 18). The construction of Edward as a traditional lord makes it possible to naturalize the selection of Harold as successor in the absence of a heir of Æthelred's line.[62] Edward, figured as "se froda" (29a) [the wise], commits (with the alliterating verb "befæste") the kingdom to Harold, who is linked to Edward by his nobility (31a) and his loyal service (31b-4).[63] Both the form of classical Old English verse and its traditional diction are exploited in the *Death of Edward* for their political possibilities to shape both past and present.[64]

The *Death of Alfred* points less to the death of Old English verse (a death knelled either by dismissing the text as the product of a doltish poetaster or tin-eared scribe, or by dismissing the tradition itself as exhausted) than to something emergent. The entry for 1036, so puzzling in its hybrid form, opens up an alternative generic space in response to the foreclosure of the standard forms for a royal person – praise poem or epitaph – in the wake of the circumstances of Alfred Ætheling's murder. To transform the humiliation of Alfred's blinding and the scandal of the mutilation of his retinue, the *Death of Alfred* draws on homiletic prose in its most rhetorically elaborate state. It uses the fluid alliteration and looser metrics associated with Ælfric's rhythmical prose and incorporates the end rhyme and true rhyme that appear sporadically throughout the canon. For

---

[61] The C-text at this point is the product of a different perspective than that in the earlier entries. See the discussion in *Anglo-Saxon Chronicle*, MS C, ed. O'Brien O'Keeffe, lxxi–lxxiii, xc–xci.

[62] For an overview of the unsuccessful attempt to secure Edward "the Exile" for the throne see Barlow, *Edward the Confessor*, 218-20. See also Dumville, "The Æthelings," 33, and Hooper, "Edgar the Ætheling," 202-3.

[63] See Barlow, *Vita Aedwardi regis*, 122: "'Hanc,' inquit, 'cum omni regno tutandam tibi commendo...'" [I commend this woman and all the kingdom to your protection (trans. Barlow, 123)] and Plummer, *Saxon Chronicles*, 1:197 (E-text): "⁊ Harold eorl feng to Engla landes cynerice. swa swa se cyng hit him geuðe. ⁊ eac men hine þær to gecuron" [And Earl Harold succeeded to the kingdom of England, just as the king had granted to him and also as men had chosen him for it].

[64] For the political claims of traditional heroic language in *Brunanburh* see Thormann, "Matter of History," 8.

this reason, printing this work with the lineation of verse continues to be useful: it allows the modern reader to see more readily the rhetorical elaborations otherwise occluded by the visual conventions of printed prose. In the cross-wise workings of its alliteration and rhyme the *Death of Alfred* shows us the future (for example in the Peterborough Chronicle's rhyming lines on the death of William s.a. 1086) even as the *Death of Edward* puts the past to work in the service of contemporary politics. The appearance of classical Old English verse in the Anglo-Saxon Chronicle in forms so closely allied with the royal house of Wessex suggests two related conclusions: that classical forms could still be written in the later eleventh century, and, more important, that they were still perceived to have work to do. The *Death of Edward* with its accurate meter and its traditional formulas was incorporated into the Chronicle precisely because it was understood to do political work. But its moment was brief. Old English poetry was not dead by the middle of the eleventh century, nor did it die of itself when Edward died. Religious verse, certainly, continued to have an audience. But with the death of Harold and William's effective neutralization of the Anglo-Saxon aristocracy, conditions for a classical praise poem or epitaph vanished. Quite simply, the grammar of that form, so closely identified with royal politics, became incoherent in the absence of an English king.[65]

---

[65] I should like to thank Andy Orchard and Paul E. Szarmach for their kindness in reading the essay as it was written and for their many useful suggestions.

Deaths and Transformations 173

Appendix: *Traditional Formulas in* Death of Edward[66]

1. \<H\>er Eadward kingc, Engla hlaford,	a: –. 6 Brb 1a (Her Æþelstan cyning); 6 CFB 1a (Her Eadmund cyning). b: –. engla | X x appears: 1 Exo 432b, 559b; 1 Xst 198b, 518b, 562b; 2 And 278b, 290b, 900b, 1007a, 1064b; 2 Ele 1230b; 3 Chr 102b, 332b, 651b, 791b, 1342b, 1520a; 3 Glc 325a, 782a, 1314b, 1319b; 3 OrW 92b; 5 P148.2 1b; 6 SnS 462b; 6 Crd 21b; 6 EgC 1b; 6 Pra 54b.
2. sende soþfæs\<te\> sawle to Criste	a: — . b: —. Compare 6 LP2 8a (sawle of synnum); cf. DEw 28a.
3. on Godes wæra, gast haligne.	a: 3 Glc 690b, 746b; 6 Mnl 39b, 217b: (in [on] Godes wære). b: 6 P50 96b.
4. He on worulda her wunode þrage	a: –. 5 MB 4 47b (nu on worulde her); 1 XSt 500a (þæt on worulde wæs); 2 Ele 561a (hu on worulde ær); 6 PCE 3b (ðæt on worulde forð). b. -. 1 Gen 1931b; 5 MB 26 68b (wunode siððan); 5 P54.7 2b; 5 MB 28 80b (wunode lange).
5. on kyneþrymme, cræftig ræda.	a: 5 P95.12 5b. 1 Dan 705b

---

[66] Abbreviations are those used in Bessinger and Smith, *Concordance*, xiii–xv. There are two levels of information in the appendix. The first entry for each half-line gives the location of exactly matching half-lines, if any exist. The next set of entries gives half-lines with the identical alliterating word and the same formula, or, in the absence of the alliterating word, simply the same pattern.

		(mid cyneðrymme). b: –. In an a-type line *cræftig* appears in second position only: 2 Ele 419a, 3 GfM 81a; 3 Whl 24b, 72b; 4 Bwf 1962b; 6 SnS 292b.
6. .xxiiii.	freolic wealdend	a: –. 2 And 114b (seofon ond twentig); 6 EgC 18a (nigon ond twentig); see 6 DEw 20b. b: –. 1 Gen 1189a (freolic frumbearn).
7. wintra gerimes	weol<an> brytnode	a: 1 Xst 500b; b: See line 21b below.
8. 7 healfe tid,	hæleða wealdend,	a: —. 1 Gen 804b; 3 Phx 77b; 3 Sfr 124b (on [in] ealle tid); 2 And 1091a; 3 R74 2b (in [on] ane tid); 3 Chr 406b (in ælce tid). b: 1 Gen 2139b + 32 instances of gen. + wealdend.
9. weold wel geþungen	Walum 7 Scottum	a: –.[67] Cf. 4 Bwf 1927a. b: –. see line 11a below.
10. 7 Bryttum eac,	byre Æðelredes,	a: –. ond Xx eac is a fairly common pattern, e.g., 5 P104.22 3a (and Aaron eac). b: –. 4 Bwf 2907b, 3110b (byre Wihstanes).
11. Englum 7 Sexum	oretmægcum.	a: 6 Brb 70a; 6 Mnl 185b (as Engle and Seaxe). b: 2 And 664b (orettmæcgas).
12. Swa ymbclyppað	ceald<e> brymmas,	a: –. b: 4 Bwf 1261a (cealde streamas); 2 And 1212a (cealdan clommum); 2 SB1 15b (cealdan reorde).
13. þæt eall Eadwarde,	æðelum kinge,	a: –. b: æðelum Xx: 1 Exo 186b; 2 And 230b, 636a,

---

[67] See Townsend, "Metre of the *Chronicle*-verse," 156.

Deaths and Transformations 175

	882a; 3 Phx 586b; 3 R43 1b; 4 Bwf 1949a; 5 P75.4 2b; 5 P79.1 1b; 5 P143.15 3b; 6 DEw 31a.
14. hyrdon holdlice hagestealde menn.	a: 6 DEd 32a. b: Compare 6 DEw 30a (heahþungenum menn); 2 And 257a (macræftige menn), 814a (modblinde menn); 2 FAp 24a (æglæawe menn); 3 SB2 85a (firenfulle menn); 3 R28 13a (wisfæstum men); 4 Bwf 2189a (tireadigum menn).
15. Wæs a bliðemod bealuleas kyng,[68]	a: –. 1 Dan 712a (ða wearð bliðemod). b: –. See 3 Mx1 39 (Bliðe sceal bealoleas heorte).
16. þeah he lange[69] ær lande bereafod,	a: –. 2 SB1 123b (þæt <he> lange ær); 3 SB 2 118b (þæt he longe ær); 3 Chr 115b (þa þe longe ær); 3 DHl 54a (þa þe longe ær); 5 MB 13 38b (þe hi lange ær). b: –. 1 Gen 859b (blæde bereafod); 3 Chr 168b (dome bereafod); 4 Bwf 2746b (since bereafod), 2825b (ealdre bereafod), 3018b (golde bereafod).
17. wunode wræclastum wide geond eorðan,	a: –. 1 Xst 120a; 3 Wan 5a (wadan wræclastas). b: 3 Mx 1 199b; 4 Bwf 266b, 3099b; 5 P65.2 2b; 5 P109.6 3b; 5 P137.6 1b; 6 Mnl 176b.

---

[68] On this short verse see Townsend, "Metre of the *Chronicle*-verse," 156.

[69] Ms. C: lang. See Dobbie, *Minor Poems*, 151, note to line 3.

18. syððan Cnut ofercom kynn Æðelredes	a: –. b: There are 14 examples of genitive + cynn (i.e., e-types only; no d-types).
19. 7 Dena weoldon deore rice	a: –. b: –. 3 Glc 1059a (deore frætwe); 4 Bwf 2236a (deore maðmas); 5 P69.1 1b; 6 F69.1 1b (deore fultum); 5 P115.8 3b (deore syndan); 5 P118.1 2b (deore gangað); 6 Run 74b (deore mannum).
20. Engla landes .xxviii.	Engla Xx is ubiquitous. In this formula *engla* means 'angels' except where it occurs in 6 CFB, 6 EdC.
21. wintra gerimes welan bry<t>nodan.	1 Xst 500b; 6 DEw 7a. b: 1 Gen 2179b (welan bryttian); 1 Dan 690b (welan brytnedon); 6 Wld 2 30b (welan britnian); cf. line 7b above.
22. Syððan forð becom freolice in geatwum	a: –. xx X becom: 1 XSt 243b, 385b; 2 And 1666b; 4 Bwf 115b; 5 P72.6 1a; 5 MB 13 70b. b: –. 3 Rim 38b (freolic in geatwum).
23. kyningc kystum god, clæne 7 milde,	a: –. 3 Prc 2a (maga cystum eald); 4 Bwf 2178a (guma guðum cuð). b: –. 6 Gll 16a, 53a (clæne and cræftig); 3 Chr 331a; 3 Phx 541a; 3 Jln 613a (clæne ond gecorene); 6 LP2 53a (clæne and gecorene); 3 Glc 536a (clæne and gecostad); 5 P78.9 3b (sefte and milde).
24. Eadward se æðela eðel bewerode,	a: –. b: –.
25. land 7 leode oð þæt lung<re>[70] becom	a: 2 And 1321a. b: cf. 26b below.

---

[70] Ms. C: lunger. Dobbie, *Minor Poems*, 151, note to line 25, emends to

Deaths and Transformations 177

26. deað se bitera   7 swa deore genam — a: –. b: cf. 25b above.
27. æþelne of eorðan.   Englas feredon — a: –. b: 3 Glc 1306b (englas feredun).
28. soþfæste sawle   innan swegles leoht, — a: –. 1 Xst 306a (soðfæste men); 2 Ele1289b (soðfæste bioð). b: –. xx swegles leoht 1 Xst 28b; 3 Glc 486b; 3 Phx 288b.
29. 7 se froda swa þeah   befæste þæt rice — a: –. 1 Exo 339b (he wæs gearu swa þeah); 2 And 1250b (he wæs Criste swa þeah); 2 Hm1 5b (ond þæt facen swa þeah); 3 Glc 940b (He on elne swa þeah); 4 Bwf 972b (No þær ænige swa þeah), 1929b (næs hio hnah swa þeah). b: –.
30. heahþungenum menn, Harolde sylfum, — a: –. 2 SB1 159b (heahþungene beon). b: –. 2 SB1 78b (dryhtne sylfum); 3 Chr 1222b (Criste sylfum).
31. æþelum eorle,   se in ealle tid — a: –. æðelum Xx: 1 Exo 186b; 2 And 230b, 636a, 882a; 3 Phx 586b; 3 R43 1b; 4 Bwf 1949a; 5 P75.4 2b; 5 P79.1 1b; 5 P143.15 3b; 6 DEw 13b. b: –. (x)x ealle tid: 1 Gen 804b; 3 Phx 77b; 3 Sfr 124b; 5 P105.3 3a; P118.20 3a.
32. hyrde holdlice   hærran sinum — a: 3 Glc 604a (hyran holdlice); 3 Chr 430a (hergen holdlice); 3 R 34 4a (hiþeð holdlice); 5 P101.16 4a (herað holdlice). Cf. LawVI

"lungre" *metri causa.*

	Atr1 (holdlice hyran). b: –. 1 Gen 567a (herran þines); 1 Gen 586b (herran minum).
33. wordum 7 dædum, wihte ne agælde	a: 2 And 596b; 3 Glc 619b. b: –. 5 P94.11 1b (wihte ne oncneowan).
34. þæs þe þearf wæs[71] þæs þeodkyninges.	a: –. b: –. 6 Jg2 162b (and þeodcyningas).

---

[71] On this verse type see Townsend, "Metre of the *Chronicle*-verse," 156.

MARK C. AMODIO

Res(is)ting the Singer: Towards a Non-Performative Anglo-Saxon Oral Poetics

The oral poet is a figure well known to students of the English Middle Ages.[1] Although his title changes from '*scop*' (pl. *scopas*) in Anglo-Saxon England to 'minstrel' by the early Middle English period and although the language in which he composed undergoes dramatic changes during that same time period, his job description seems to have remained fairly constant: as the extant medieval literary and historical documents reveal, the poet is charged with entertaining and perhaps edifying his audience — the vast majority of whom may well have been non-literate — through the performance (perhaps with musical accompaniment) of vernacular narrative poetry on a wide variety of secular and religious topics. While we know little about the day-to-day life and practices of the Anglo-Saxon *scopas* (were

---

[1] The literature devoted either directly or in passing to the medieval English oral poet is far too voluminous to rehearse here. An important recent discussion of this figure can be found in Frank, "Oral Poet," who also offers a detailed survey of how the *scop*/minstrel/bard has been viewed from the seventeenth to the twentieth century. Other studies of the *scop* can be found in Niles, *Poem and Its Tradition*, 31-65; Kendall, *Metrical Grammar*, 1-12; and more widely in Opland, *Oral Poetry*, 189-266. Although he mentions the medieval English oral poet only in passing, Lord's discussion of oral singers, *Singer of Tales*, 13-29, remains the *locus classicus* for studies of this figure. He discusses the medieval English oral tradition in the same study, 198-202. For studies of oral singers from a variety of traditions and time periods, see Finnegan, *Oral Poetry*, 170-213; Opland, *Xhosa*, 57-89, Reynolds, *Heroic Poets*, and, most recently, Foley, *How to Read an Oral Poem*.

they non-literates? were they trained in vernacular and Latin letters?[2] were they professional poets attached to the court of a particular lord? were they amateurs, perhaps even warriors, with a gift for poetry? were they itinerants who roamed about the countryside selling their poetic wares as best they could? were their ranks exclusively male?), and not much more about the minstrels who fill the literary landscape later in the period,[3] they remain firmly entrenched in the literary-critical landscape as figures who played an important, though not clearly defined and largely unsubstantiated, role in medieval English society, as they are apt to suggest in their literary (self-)representations and as their representation in the pages of contemporary chroniclers and other commentators often confirms. In *Beowulf*, the *scop* is called upon on several significant occasions to sing celebratory and commemorative songs before the noblemen and women who populate that poem, and although the Middle English minstrel seems to enjoy less prestige on the whole than does his Anglo-Saxon forebear, he not only continues to keep company with kings and courtiers throughout the period but also counts among his kind a number of actual and fictional kings as well as a few ecclesiasts. Roberta Frank has recently shed considerable light upon the dark corner of medieval English culture which the Anglo-Saxon oral poet occupies,[4] but unlike most other commentators, she begins her insightful and witty 'search' for this notoriously shadowy figure by offering the caveat that virtually everything written on the

---

[2] In his discussion of what he labels "the literate mentality," Clanchy, *From Memory*, 185-334, notes that for most of the medieval period, the term *litteratus* applied only to those schooled in Latin letters while the *laici* (a group which included those schooled in vernacular letters) were, by definition, categorized among the *illiterati*. As late as the reign of Edward I (1272-1307), if "a person ... had learned to read in English or French but not in Latin, he could never have become *litteratus*, nor could he have understood the majority of writings circulating in his own lifetime because these were in Latin" (233).

[3] On the oral poet in the Middle English period see Taylor, "Myth"; Crosby, "Oral Delivery" and "Custom"; and Baugh, "Improvisation" and "Question."

[4] The medieval English oral poet is not alone in occupying *terra incognita*: as Baldwin, "Image of the Jongleur," 635, notes, "In the pages of the Latin chroniclers writing around 1200 the jongleur appears as a gray, furtive shadow. His existence was acknowledged by the broad term *joculator*, but his functions were too suspect to deserve further comment." On the difficulty of determining just what the terms *ménestral* and *jongleur* mean, see Vitz, *Orality and Performance*, 51-2.

subject is doomed to remain "no more than hopeful speculations hallowed by repetition" because "nothing can be proven, not even that such a poet never existed."[5]

Although a popular figure in the critical consciousness of scholars from the eighteenth century onwards,[6] the Anglo-Saxon oral poet remained chiefly a romanticized and idealized one — a bard (in the view of many earlier scholars he is a warrior-bard) strumming his harp and producing verse that was primitive and picturesque — until the middle decades of this century when he (or much less likely she), under the impetus of oral-formulaic theory, suddenly seemed to emerge from the mists that had long covered him to be revealed clearly and finally as what he truly was: a singer of tales who, along with Homer, twentieth-century South Slavic *guslari*, and more contemporary performers, was part of a virtually unbroken continuum of performing oral poets stretching from at least the eighth century B.C.E. to the present day. That the Anglo-Saxon oral poet should have quickly (and rather uncritically) become the darling of oral-formulaicists is not at all surprising: the exclusively performative tradition which Milman Parry and Albert B. Lord, the two chief architects of the theory of oral-formulaic composition, encountered in then-Yugoslavia in the 1930s and which forms the bedrock upon which the highly influential Parry–Lord theory rests appears to parallel rather closely the tradition recorded in Old English verse and prose. From the moment the figure of the Anglo-Saxon oral poet first appears in the written records in the Venerable Bede's eighth-century *Historia ecclesiastica* through the end of the Anglo-Saxon period some three and a half centuries later, he is always situated within the highly performative matrix which the Parry–Lord theory argues is the *sine qua non* of oral poetry.[7] Further, the *scopas*, like the South Slavic singers Parry and Lord recorded, articulated poetry which depends heavily, if not exclusively, upon a widely shared, highly formulaic, highly traditional register, one that remains remarkably stable over the course of several centuries and is also marked off in significant ways from the register

---

[5] Frank, "Oral Poet," 12.

[6] And perhaps even earlier. See Frank's authoritative survey in "Oral Poet," 14-28.

[7] See Lord, *Singer of Tales*, 3-29.

of everyday discourse.[8] In part because of these very parallels and in part because differences between the traditions were either overlooked or elided, the picture of the Anglo-Saxon oral poet that has come to dominate is, not surprisingly, virtually indistinguishable from that of his South Slavic descendant: one can easily imagine that the Anglo-Saxon oral poet theorized by contemporary scholars would be as comfortable strumming a *gusle* in a twentieth-century *kafana* as he would be plucking a lyre in an eighth-century *meduheall*.[9] So compelling did Francis Peabody Magoun, Jr. find the parallels between the South Slavic and Old English traditions that he subtitled his influential 1955 examination of Bede's story of the cowherd turned oral poet Cædmon, "The Case History of an Anglo-Saxon Oral Singer."

Although the field of oral studies has been undergoing an important and far-reaching reconfiguration over the past few years, a reconfiguration which promises to give it a much sturdier foundation as well as greater currency, the ways in which oralists view the singer, in general, and the Anglo-Saxon oral poet, specifically, have remained so constant that the *scop* who continues to peer out at us from the pages of much recent criticism is remarkably similar to the one who sprang so convincingly to life in the pages of Lord's and Magoun's studies: he is variously someone who as a youth heard and "absorbed the recurrent formulae of the *scopas* and, with practice, learned to fashion similar expressions of his own,"[10] someone who, at the prompting of an outsider, "s[a]ng a song or recite[d] a poem in the presence of a scribe,"[11] or someone who may have lived in a monastery and who did not need to "read in order to have acquired the

---

[8] For a full and important discussion of oral-traditional registers, see Foley, *Singer of Tales in Performance*, 7-30. Parry early on noted just how separate the Homeric *Kunstsprache* was: as Parry, "Homer and Homeric Style," 314-15, notes, "we know that the Homeric diction was centuries making. The linguists have shown us that the language of the Homeric poems, which was once given the mistaken name Old Ionic, is an artificial language, made up of words and forms taken from the current Ionic, from Aeolic, even from Arcado-Cyprian dialects; and along with these are artificial forms which could never have existed in the speech of any people."

[9] For studies that assume the Anglo-Saxon *scop*'s similarity to the South Slavic *guslari*, see Kendall, *Metrical Grammar*, and Niles, "Oral Poetry Acts."

[10] Kendall, *Metrical Grammar*, 3.

[11] Niles, "Oral Poetry Acts," 137.

knowledge that he seems to have had" to compose oral songs based on written sources.[12] The continuing appeal of the performative model of poetic composition so fundamental not just to oral-formulaic theory but to oral theory in general may be attributed to the vital and sustaining link between performance and oral poetry in pre-literate cultures: as Walter J. Ong and Eric Havelock, among others, have argued, in cultures with no access to the technology of writing, the performance and dissemination of poetry are, as both logic and necessity dictate, coterminous activities entirely dependent upon a specially trained poet who (re-)composes during performance. In pre-literate cultures, there can be neither song nor poetic tradition without the singer because both 'exist' only while the singer is singing. Once the song is sung, the song and the tradition which gives it a meaningful context and which determines its form reside only in the collective memory of those who heard it sung.

Although a number of arguments have been put forth to explain the performative – and putatively oral – features of the vernacular verse produced in Anglo-Saxon England, the performance-based theory upon which they rest remains unable to address a central (and, for many, crippling) paradox: namely that all the extant Old English poems whose 'orality' has been a source of discussion and often heated dispute for more than forty years survive only *in writing* on the mute surfaces of manuscript pages.[13] While performance rightly remains an integral component of contempo-

---

[12] Lord, *Singer Resumes the Tale*, 112. See also Lord, "Cædmon Revisited." Foley has recently turned his attention to the nature and function of the "legendary singer" in ancient and more recent oral traditions and argues, "Individual Poet," 149, that singers such as Homer and Ćor Huso are best understood as mythic figures "designating the poetic tradition." Additionally, although she is chiefly interested in investigating the cultural materiality of Anglo-Saxon manuscripts and scribal rather than authorial compositional practices, O'Brien O'Keeffe's model of scribal recomposition can easily be extended to encompass poets/authors as well. See her *Visible Song*, as well as Pasternack, *Old English Poetry*.

[13] In "Literary Character," Benson responded to the early, often polemical, claims oralists were making for the 'orality' of Old English verse texts by noting that Old English poetry based on indisputably written sources evidenced precisely those characteristics which oralists claimed established the 'orality' of much Old English poetry. Cf. Parks, "Song, Text," 104, who addresses the question of how an "oral traditional perception of literary discourse differ[s] from that of a textualized society."

rary oral theory as a whole,[14] the exclusively performance-based model which has so long been applied to ancient and medieval literatures is beginning to be questioned by scholars who are constructing a radically different paradigm for those supposedly oral poetries which survive only in written form from the ancient and medieval periods, a paradigm in which textuality is neither elided nor silently (and awkwardly) passed over and in which performance is viewed as a local, tradition-specific and tradition-dependent feature which may well be nonessential to the production of verse, rather than a *sine qua non* of poetic composition. What is emerging, in the work of scholars such as Katherine O'Brien O'Keeffe and John Miles Foley, among others, is a non-performative oral poetics that is employed not by an oral poet in the crucible of performance but rather by a literate poet who composes pen-in-hand.

As a first step in exploring the complex issue of how an oral poetics survives and continues to function once it is no longer part of a (putatively) pre-literate culture but a component of a more varied cultural milieu, one in which oral and literate poetics intersect with and help shape one another,[15] I would like to revisit the figure of the Anglo-Saxon *scop* and consider the ways in which he is employed by the literate authors who present him to us in a variety of texts, all of which are indisputably literate productions, dating from the eighth to the tenth centuries. The time is at hand for us to consider resting, if not absolutely resisting, the medieval English oral poet who has been kept so busy by scholars over the past forty years and to acknowledge that those reports of scopic activity that survive

---

[14] Recent studies of performance in contemporary oral traditions include Bauman and Ritch, "Informing Performance"; Astakhova, "Sound Shaping"; and Finnegan, *Oral Poetry*, as well as the essays edited by Lee Haring in *Oral Tradition* 9.1, a special issue devoted to African oral traditions. See also Foley, *Singer of Tales in Performance*; Bauman, *Verbal Art* and *Story, Performance*; Hymes, "Breakthrough" and "Breakthrough Revisited"; and Niles, *Homo narrans*.

[15] As Stock, *Listening*, 145, has noted, "[d]uring the Middle Ages, the high point of orality after archaic Greece and Mesopotamia, texts almost vanished from view, but never the model or memory of them, which continued to guide expression and behavior through the so-called Dark Ages (whose darkness is merely a metaphor for the disappearance of writing). The written word did not rule *in absentia*, nor the spoken *in praesentia*. They governed together, and this fact must be remembered despite the oral or written traditions provided by different disciplines such as literature and law."

in the *written* records do not document contemporary Anglo-Saxon cultural praxis but are rather idealized and fictionalized accounts of how legendary figures composed vernacular poetry.

To put it another way, the performing *scopas* who infrequently appear in the Anglo-Saxon literary landscape have much more in common with legendary figures such as Homer and Ćor Huso than they do with the actual poets and scribes who composed and preserved Old English poetry.[16] The *scopas* instance the tradition and serve much the same purpose that *sêmata* do in Homeric epic: just as the *sêmata* "index traditional meanings" and call forth "worlds of implication" through signs that are readily apprehensible to a properly attuned audience,[17] so too do the Old English *scopas* whose performances are reported in the verse and prose index the entire oral tradition. As Foley has demonstrated, in a tradition with a demonstrably performative oral poetics, such as the one Parry and Lord encountered in then-Yugoslavia, the figure of the legendary singer serves as "a representational strategy that allows *guslari* to talk about what they and their peers jointly inherited and continued to practice."[18] The line of descent from legendary avatar to contemporary practitioner is clear and relatively straightforward in the South Slavic tradition. Although only the latter's output can be attested, both articulate poetry only within the performance arena and both rely on a demonstrably performative oral poetics to compose vernacular verse. In Anglo-Saxon England, the line of descent from oral *scop* to Anglo-Saxon poet is, by way of contrast, both clear and cloudy, simple and complex: both are situated within a unified, determining poetics, one that governed poetic articulation in England for some seven hundred years, but the *scop*, like his legendary and real counterparts in the former Yugoslavia, composes orally and only within the performative matrix while the Anglo-Saxon poet composes within a very different matrix, one that is literate and largely, if not exclusively, non-performative.[19] "Performance is," as Foley has aphoristically put it, "the

---

[16] For a full discussion of the legendary singer in the ancient Greek and South Slavic oral traditions, see Foley, "Individual Poet."

[17] Foley, "Individual Poet," 172.

[18] Foley, "Individual Poet," 152.

[19] Although poetry is composed outside of the performance arena in Anglo-Saxon England, the performative features of the register remain crucial to it because throughout the Anglo-Saxon period (and the Middle English period as well), poetry is received chiefly through the ear and not the eye.

enabling event" for living oral traditions because it is the only means by which both native participants and external observers can gain access to the tradition.[20] But in a tradition such as the one we find in Anglo-Saxon England where oral and literate cultures interpenetrate, performance is no longer the sole pathway for negotiating the tradition, but is rather one of several such pathways. Audiences engage in what Elizabeth Robertson labels "Aural reading (reading with the ears)"[21] when they hear a poet compose in performance or when they hear poems read from manuscripts, and some of them can also read texts privately, silently or aloud.[22] In turning now to consider the role of the *scop* in Anglo-Saxon poetics, we need to remember that all the extant reports of scopic activity are filtered through the literate sensibilities of authors (and scribes) for whom the performative model they are presenting may be nothing more than a fiction.

The Anglo-Saxon oral poet makes one of his earliest recorded appearances, if not indeed his earliest, in the twenty-fourth chapter of the fourth book of the *Historia ecclesiastica* when Bede relates his famous story of the cowherd Cædmon, a story fundamental to the widely-held argument that performance and poetic articulation are deeply intertwined in the Anglo-Saxon vernacular tradition. In so placing Cædmon and his poem squarely within the richly textured and complex performative matrix modern scholars have long recognized as a central component of oral cultures and of traditional oral poetic articulation, Bede "seems to affirm those nineteenth-and twentieth-century cultural notions of the oral nature of archaic literature and the spontaneity of poetic performance."[23] But for Cædmon – and perhaps Bede –, this performative matrix is a locus of considerable anxiety: the cowherd's initial insecurity over performing (for reasons that neither he nor Bede ever makes explicit) drives him from the "gebeorscipe" [drinking party] in which all those present were apparently expected to produce poetry. They had to, Bede informs us, "þurh endebyrdnesse be

---

[20] Foley, *Homer's Traditional Art*, 6.

[21] E. Robertson, "Female Literacy," 14.

[22] On reading practices in ancient and medieval times, see Saenger, "Silent Reading" and *Space Between Words*. For a discussion of oral poetics in the Middle English period, see Amodio, "Tradition, Performance, and Poetics" and most recently, *Writing the Oral Tradition*, chaps. 3 and 4.

[23] Lerer, *Literacy and Power*, 33.

hearpan singan" (342) [all in order sing to the harp].[24] But Cædmon's hasty departure from the group before the harp reaches him provides him only temporary respite: shortly after retreating from the "gebeorscipe" he is confronted in a dream by a figure (an angel?) who not only twice commands him to sing but who also dictates what the cowherd's subject matter should be. Upon awakening, Cædmon produces his famous nine-line hymn to the creator:

> Nu sculon herigean   heofonrices weard,
> meotodes meahte   and his modgeþanc,
> weorc wuldorfæder,   swa he wundra gehwæs,
> ece drihten,   or onstealde.
> He ærest sceop   eorðan bearnum
> heofon to hrofe,   halig scyppend;
> þa middangeard   moncynnes weard,
> ece drihten,   æfter teode
> firum foldan,   frea ælmihtig.[25]

[Now we must praise the Guardian of Heaven, the Measurer's might and His thoughts, the work of the Glorious Father in that He, the Eternal Lord, in the beginning was the author of all wonders. In the beginning He created the earth for the sons of men, heaven as a roof, the Holy Creator; then He afterwards, the Eternal Lord, the Guardian of mankind, created middle-earth, the world, for men.]

Through his narrative of Cædmon as reluctant performer, Bede effectively models the power and pervasiveness of the vernacular performative matrix, for all Cædmon needs to do to become a successful creator of Old English poetry is to step within the "performance arena" of traditional oral verse[26]

---

[24] *Ecclesiastical History*, ed. T. Miller, 342. I cite the Old English version of the *Historia* throughout from this edition. Unless otherwise noted, all translations are mine.

[25] Dobbie, *Minor Poems*. I cite Dobbie's West-Saxon version of the *Hymn* throughout.

[26] Foley, *Singer of Tales in Performance*, xv. See his discussion, 8-11.

— a cultural locus that, so Bede would have us believe, the others gathered at the "gebeorscipe" habitually and successfully negotiated — and sing. The Old English version of Bede places Cædmon's subsequent, reportedly prolific (but significantly unrecovered) poetic production[27] in an even more complex cultural matrix and makes even more explicit the division between his exclusively oral and performative mode of producing verse and the literate technology by which the monks are able to preserve (and, presumably, transmit) it: his teachers in the monastic community, we are told, "æt his muðe wreoton 7 leornodon" (346) [wrote from his mouth the words he spoke and learned them].[28] They inscribe the words Cædmon utters and perhaps even commit his poems to memory but, significantly, Bede makes no mention of whether the literate members of the monastic community at Whitby who were charged with preserving the vernacular verse on religious topics that Cædmon produced ever attempted to appropriate or had any desire to appropriate his mode of production.[29]

---

[27] In addition to the poem that Bede paraphrases, he tells us, *Ecclesiastical History*, ed. Colgrave and Mynors, 419/418, that Cædmon "Canebat autem de creatione mundi et origine humani generis et tota Genesis historia, de egressu Israel ex Aegypto et ingressu in terram repromissionis, de aliis plurimis sacrae scripturae historiis, de incarnatione dominica, passione, resurrectione et ascensione in caelum, de Spiritus Sancti aduentu et apostolorum doctrina; item de terrore futuri iudicii et horrore poena gehennalis ac dulcedine regni caelestis multa carmina faciebat" [He sang about the creation of the world, the origin of the human race, and the whole history of Genesis, of the departure of Israel from Egypt and the entry into the promised land and of many other of the stories taken from the sacred Scriptures: of the incarnation, passion, and resurrection of the Lord, of His ascension into heaven, of the coming of the Holy Spirit and the teaching of the apostles. He also made songs about the terrors of future judgement, the horrors of the pains of hell, and the joys of the heavenly kingdom]. All quotations from and translations of Bede's Latin text are from Colgrave and Mynors's edition.

[28] Bede's Latin text, 419/418, similarly focuses on the performative aspect of Cædmon's career as a poet: his verse is "so sweet" [carmen dulcissimum] "that his teachers became in turn his audience" [suauiusque resonando doctores suos uicissim auditores sui faciebat].

[29] Although as Lerer, *Literacy and Power*, 34, correctly notes, the "vernacular version of the Caedmon story [and, I would add, the Latin version as well] brings out the ... distinctions between the new Christian literate community and the old oral world of performance," Bede's story of the cowherd is also, and paradoxically, an attempt to bridge the very distinctions it highlights.

Bede, of course, writes the *Historia* in Latin prose and offers in his text what he identifies as only a paraphrase of the Old English poem Cædmon is supposed to have produced. While Bede stresses that "This is the sense but not the order of the words which he sang as he slept. For it is not possible to translate verse, however well composed, literally from one language to another without some loss of beauty or dignity,"[30] the parallels between his Latin prose and the earliest Old English version of Cædmon's poem suggest a far different, much closer, and more problematic relationship. Although we will never be able to establish to any real satisfaction the priority of one version over the other, the Old English version of the *Hymn* written into the bottom margin of folio 107ʳ of the St. Petersburg Bede[31] in a scribal hand virtually indistinguishable from the one responsible for copying this section of the Latin text may well be a poetic translation of Bede's prose text.[32] Although it is generally and rightly considered to be the earliest documented oral poem in Old English, the Old English version of the *Hymn* further complicates, rather than clarifies, Bede's representation of the cowherd's engagement with the vernacular tradition and should perhaps not be read, as it frequently is, as an accurate and objective depiction of contemporary cultural praxis but rather as the vehicle through which "Bede argue[s] a cultural thesis" as he attempts to establish an originary myth for the composition and dissemination of vernacular verse on Christian topics.[33] Cædmon and his *Hymn*, both of which survive only within the confines of Bede's carefully constructed and highly literate 'history,' represent not so much Anglo-Saxon pre-literate cultural practice as the way that culture was perceived and manipulated by literate culture. While there is, of course, no way of knowing whether or not the illiterate cowherd Bede describes ever truly existed, it is clear that if he did not exist, Bede would have invented him.

---

[30] *Ecclesiastical History*, ed. Colgrave and Mynors, 417/416: Hic est sensus, non autem ordo ipse uerborum, quae dormiens ille canebat; neque enim possunt carmina, quamuis optime conposita, ex alia in aliam linguam ad uerbum sine detrimento sui decoris ac dignitatis transferri.

[31] St. Petersburg, Saltykow-Ščedrin Public Library, Q.v. I. 18.

[32] See Kiernan, "Reading," 162.

[33] Frantzen, *Desire for Origins*, 138. For other discussions of this issue, see Kiernan, "Reading"; O'Brien O'Keeffe, *Visible Song*; and Dumville, "Beowulf Come Lately" and "'*Beowulf*' and the Celtic World."

Another figure who is frequently invoked in discussions of Anglo-Saxon oral poets is Aldhelm, the abbot of Malmesbury and later bishop of Sherborne. Although no surviving Old English poetry can be confidently attributed to Aldhelm, and although he nowhere in his voluminous Latin writings (both prose and verse) mentions any vernacular works that he composed, his reputation as a vernacular oral poet has been secure from at least the late ninth century when King Alfred the Great relates in his *Handboc* — a work now lost to us — the famous anecdote of Aldhelm performing vernacular verse on a bridge near his church. William of Malmesbury, who relied on Alfred's *Handboc* for the version of this anecdote he offers in his twelfth-century *Gesta Pontificum Anglorum*, lends it credibility by carefully explaining that Aldhelm was as adept at producing vernacular poetry (presumably without recourse to writing) as he was at producing Latin verse (in writing). As William succinctly notes, Aldhelm may have been a universally acknowledged master of Latin prose and verse, but the cleric "also did not neglect songs in his native language."[34] While Niles cautions that William's report of Aldhelm's ability to perform vernacular verse is "probably no more historical than the story of Gunnar's playing the harp with his toes,"[35] it has nonetheless often been cited to establish both the fundamentally performative nature of Anglo-Saxon poetics and Aldhelm's status as an oral poet.[36]

But even if Aldhelm were able to enter the performance arena of Anglo-Saxon oral poetics, as his fictional near-contemporaries present at the "gebeorscipe" with Cædmon were apparently able to do, both his indis-

---

[34] *Gesta*, ed. Hamilton, v. 336: nativae quoque linguae non negligebat carmina. I cite the *Gesta* throughout from Hamiltion's edition. I am indebted to J. K. McDonough for his advice on my Latin translations.

[35] Niles, *Poem and Its Tradition*, 71.

[36] Despite his acknowledgment, *Anglo-Saxon Oral Poetry*, 125, that William's report is "at best a twelfth-century summary of a ninth-century account of a series of seventh-century performances," Opland, 120-7, argues strongly for seeing Aldhelm as a *scop*. Other similar views can be found in Schofield, *English Literature*, 16, who equates Aldhelm with an early Germanic bard when he claims that "Even bishops, such as St. Aldhelm of Salisbury ([d.] 709) and St. Dunstan of Canterbury ([d.] 988), took delight in the harp," and in Zesmer, *Guide*, 22, who describes Aldhelm as "a skillful writer of Latin verse (and of songs in English…)." For more recent and more nuanced views of Aldhelm, see esp. Orchard, *Poetic Art*, and Lapidge, "Aldhelm's Latin Poetry."

putable literacy and the context within which he reportedly performed his poetry – William reports that Aldhelm was able to compose poetry in his native language and that he offered/sang vernacular poetry on a bridge near his church as a way of enticing the population to enter the holy spot where they were, presumably, offered more doctrinal fare in Latin – establish him as a traditionalistic rather than traditional poet.[37] Brian Stock, from whom I borrow the term 'traditionalistic,' argues that traditional action "consists of the habitual pursuit of inherited forms of conduct, which are taken to be society's norm" while traditionalistic action, in contrast, "is the self-conscious affirmation of traditional norms" that are "consciously selected from the fund of traditional knowledge in order to serve present needs."[38] In chanting "profane poetry interspersed with biblical phrases at the bridge at Malmesbury for the behoof of his congregation,"[39] Aldhelm consciously manipulates the oral tradition in precisely the way that Bede manipulates the story of Cædmon. Bede stresses the performative matrix more insistently in his account of Anglo-Saxon oral poetics than William does in his, but Bede, Aldhelm, and even William, all of whom are members of the literate clerical culture, employ the oral tradition to serve their literate culture's present needs. What Bede's story of Cædmon and William's story of Aldhelm ultimately reveal about the Anglo-Saxon oral tradition is the degree to which it intersected with and intermingled with literate culture. Literacy, rather than closing off its practitioners from the world of traditional oral composition, as was long believed to be the case,[40] seems not to have prevented either Bede or Aldhelm from successfully navigating the *terra cognita* of vernacular oral culture.[41] The episodes

---

[37] William tells us, *Gesta*, v. 336, that Aldhelm "Poesium Anglican posse facere, cantum componere, eadem apposite vel canere vel dicet" [was able to make English poetry, compose a song, likewise fittingly either sing or speak it].

[38] Stock, *Listening*, 164.

[39] Lapidge and Herren, *Aldhelm: The Prose Works*, 19.

[40] Beginning with Lord's statement in his highly influential *Singer of Tales*, 129, that the techniques of oral and written composition are "contradictory and mutually exclusive," the belief that the oral and written worlds were fundamentally opposed came to be a cornerstone of oral-formulaic theory as originally formulated.

[41] The anonymous tenth-century poet who penned the fragmentary poem prefixed to a copy of Aldhelm's *De Virginitate* underscores the complexity of the Anglo-Saxon oral-literate matrix and suggests the ease with which authors could

related by Bede and William further witness the degree to which oral culture was, from very early in the period, imbedded within the fictions (originary and otherwise) of literate culture. Bede, Aldhelm, and William, we must remember, were not fieldworkers seeking to preserve, transmit, or ultimately valorize oral culture but devoted their lives to advancing the doctrines and cultural practices of literate, Latin culture.

Although slender, the evidence regarding the Anglo-Saxon oral poet's existence and cultural situation offered by the extant corpus of Old English poetry follows the paradigm Bede, Alfred, and William lay out by firmly linking poetic articulation with performance. The depictions of poetic activity in *Beowulf*, for example, are carefully anchored to a strictly performative matrix by the poet and so fit quite comfortably within the model of seventh-century Anglo-Saxon oral poetics Bede offers in the *Historia ecclesiastica*, but as with Bede's story of Cædmon and Alfred's and William's anecdote about Aldhelm, we must not lose sight of the fact that the depictions of scopic activity in *Beowulf* occur within the poem's literate framework, and so, on the simplest level, must be considered as offering something other than an unobstructed view into the praxis of oral culture. In what follows, we will consider the *Beowulf*-poet's presentations of the Anglo-Saxon performative matrix and the *scopas* who occupy it, bearing in mind that Old English "verse is poetry, not social history"[42] and that accordingly, we should not treat the poetic texts extant from the period as if they were the Anglo-Saxon equivalent of anthropological field notes.

The figure of the oral poet first appears very early in *Beowulf* when Hrothgar's *scop* is called upon to situate the newly constructed hall Heorot – the Danes' most recent, and their socially and architecturally most glorious, accomplishment – within the confines of sacred history. Just as Bede employs the story of the cowherd Cædmon to legitimize and valorize the process of composing vernacular verse by singing a creation song, so too does Hrothgar employ a Danish *scop* to legitimize the construction and establish the social significance of Heorot in a "swutol sang" (90a) [clear

---

move between the oral and literate worlds when he describes Aldhelm as a "beorn boca gleaw, bonus auctor, / ... æþele sceop" (2-3a) [a good author, a man skilled in books, ... a noble poet]. I quote the poem Dobbie titles *Aldhelm* from *Minor Poems*, 97. See Opland, *Anglo-Saxon Oral Poetry*, 230-56 for a thorough discussion of the words used by the Anglo-Saxons to refer to poets and poetic activity.

[42] O'Brien O'Keeffe, "Performing Body," 49.

song] of creation,[43] a song which the *Beowulf*-poet, like Bede, paraphrases:[44]

> Sægde se þe cuþe
> frumsceaft fira   feorran reccan
> cwæð þæt se Ælmightiga   eorðan worh(te)
> wlitebeorhtne wang,   swa wæter bebugeð,
> gesette sigehreþig   sunnan and monan
> leoman to leohte   landbuendum,
> ond gefrætwade   foldan sceatas
> leomum and leafum,   lif eac gesceop
> cynna gehwylcum   þara ðe cwice hwyrfaþ.
>   (90b-8a)

[The one who knew, who could relate the origins of men, said that the Almighty made earth, a bright field surrounded by water, set up in triumph the sun and the moon as lights for the land dwellers, and adorned the surfaces of the earth with branches and leaves, created also life for each of the races that move about alive.]

Beyond their similar meta-narrative functions and their thematic and lexical parallels,[45] there are two noteworthy points of contact between Bede's representation of Cædmon's poem and the *Beowulf*-poet's representation of the fictional Danish *scop*'s poem: neither one purports to be an actual instance of Anglo-Saxon oral poetic production, and neither one offers much support for the doctrine of composition-in-performance which has been fundamental to the way in which the *scop*'s role has been constructed

---

[43] All quotations from and citations to *Beowulf* are from Klaeber's edition of the poem.

[44] Bede similarly offers not an example of Cædmon's art but rather what he claims is simply a rearrangement of the word order of the first song Cædmon produces, a detail which the Old English translator of Bede omits. See above, 189 and n. 30. While some consider Bede's text a literal translation of Cædmon's Old English poem, Kiernan, "Reading," 157-64, reminds us that the relationship of Bede's Latin prose rendition of Cædmon's Old English verse is complex and much less clear than Bede and many of his modern commentators admit.

[45] See further Lerer, *Literacy and Power*, 30-48.

and understood by contemporary oral theorists. Both episodes do invoke quite explicitly a socially dynamic performative matrix consistent with that put forth in oral theory, and both do present figures who successfully negotiate this crucial matrix, but as is explicit in the case of Cædmon (in both the episode under consideration and the later history of the cowherd which Bede goes on to relate) and implicit in the case of the Danish *scop*, the poems performed are not unmediated engagements with traditional oral poetics and its attendant thematics, but rather emerge from the performers' knowledge of sacred history, a history grounded in the Latin literate tradition, not the vernacular oral one. Although Cædmon follows the prompting of his spectral visitor and produces "verses which he had never heard before,"[46] his topic is one which even the most casual of Christians was likely to have known well in the eighth century. Similarly, the Danish *scop* sings a song which thematizes not vernacular traditional matter but literate, sacred history, matter that he draws upon either through his direct acquaintance with sacred history (by reading the texts himself) or, as was the case with Cædmon, through a literate mediator who reads the texts aloud and so makes the written material available for aural reception by non-literate auditors.[47]

The second and third instances of poetic performance in *Beowulf* fit somewhat more comfortably into the categories that contemporary scholars have developed for Anglo-Saxon oral poetry. The feast that follows the Geats' arrival at Heorot is punctuated by the words of Hrothgar's *scop*: "Scop hwilum sang / hador on Heorote" (496b–7a) [At times a *scop* sang, clear-voiced in Heorot]. The *Beowulf*-poet does not even hint here at the contents of the *scop*'s song, but it clearly contributes a great deal to the "hæleða dream" (497b) [joy of brave men] central to this occasion. Just as he did earlier, the *Beowulf*-poet here carefully situates the *scop* within a clearly performative matrix, one that appears, further, to be located completely within oral culture. But while this performative matrix aligns itself with the one central to performance-based oral theory in that the *scop* apparently composes a song (or perhaps songs) spontaneously in the hall, the

---

[46] *Ecclesiastical History*, ed. Colgrave and Mynors, 417/416: uersus quos numquam audierat.

[47] For Stock, the latter situation, one in which non-literates gain access to the world of literacy through public readings of written texts, forms the very foundation of the "textual communities" that arose in the Middle Ages. See further, Stock, *Implications*, 88–240 and *Listening*, 140-58.

utter lack of information regarding the song's content should prevent us from arguing that this performance is completely removed from textual culture. The Danish *scop* may have sung a song rooted in oral tradition, that is, a song which had never been recorded in writing and the subject matter of which is not based on written records, but he may also have drawn upon a literate source or sources for his subject matter, as Anglo-Saxons poets habitually did.[48] The point of such speculation is not to try and establish what can never be established — the content of the song — but simply to acknowledge that the *scop*'s performance, despite its close adherence to the model of performance laid out in oral theory, cannot be taken as an entirely unambiguous example of oral-traditional composition untainted by the world of letters.

Thematically and culturally, the third song sung by a *scop* parallels the second. An integral part of the celebrations which occur on the morning after Beowulf's defeat of Grendel, the third song allows the *scop* both to commemorate Beowulf's victory and to disseminate news of it. Amidst the racing of horses and other celebratory activities, the *Beowulf*-poet informs us that

>   Hwilum cyninges þegn,
> guma gilphlæden,   gidda gemyndig,
> se ðe ealfela   ealdgesegenga
> worn gemunde,   word oþer fand
> soðe gebunden;   secg eft ongan
> sið Beowulfes   snyttrum styrian,
> ond on sped wrecan; ....
>
> (867b-74a)

[At times a thane of the king, a proud man mindful of songs, the one who could recall many old stories found other words truly joined; he began with wisdom to recite Beowulf's adventure, and skillfully to utter it; ....]

This episode performs precisely the type of cultural work we expect oral poetry to perform. The song appears to be the spontaneous production of

---

[48] For an important recent discussion of how Anglo-Saxon poets drew upon written sources, see Orchard, "Both Style and Substance."

a singer in praise of the great deeds of a hero, deeds which the singer immediately anchors to a very comfortable and traditional foundation by following his recitation of the young Beowulf's actions with a full account of those of a much more established hero, Sigemund. The *scop*, the *Beowulf*-poet informs us, "welhwylc gecwæð, / þæt he fram Sigemunde[s]   secgan hyrde / ellendædum,   uncuþes fela" (874b-6) [said everything that he had heard concerning Sigemund's brave deeds, many a strange thing]. Just as the creation song sung to commemorate Heorot's completion carefully situates that event within a clear cultural context, so, too, does the *scop*'s song of Beowulf's deeds clearly situate them in the West-Germanic heroic context. In equating Beowulf's deeds with Sigemund's, the *scop* places the Geatish hero among the ranks of the greatest of Germanic heroes. Narratively and meta-narratively, then, the song sung on the morning following Grendel's defeat functions as contemporary oral theory predicts oral poems should function.[49]

But despite its apparent adherence to the model oral theory puts forth, the evidence this episode in *Beowulf* offers concerning Anglo-Saxon oral poetics is as problematic as it is tantalizing. As in the instances we have considered above, the *Beowulf*-poet only reports the substance of the poem and does not attempt to present the song itself because he is engaged in creating a piece of poetic fiction and is not presenting anthropological evidence. Furthermore, the *Beowulf*-poet's representation of the performative aspects of the *scop*'s presentation is frustratingly sparse. The poet does not seem to suggest that the *scop* performed his song all at once; syntactically, the construction "Hwilum... Hwilum..." (864ff.) suggests that the *scop* steps forward during what may simply be slack times in the horse racing, whether by design or necessity.[50] Could the *scop* step forth to give a portion of his poem after one race has been completed and before

---

[49] So close is the fit between this episode and oral-formulaic theory's claims regarding the nature of Anglo-Saxon oral composition that I once witnessed an informal but heated debate between two well-respected scholars over whether the *scop* performed his songs on horse-back as one scholar suggested, something which the other argued would have called for near-superhuman vocal capacity if the *scop* were to be heard above the noise of horses, and so on, and similarly near-superhuman acrobatic skill if he accompanied himself on a lyre.

[50] Similarly, the "hwilum" (496b) in the report of the second episode of scopic activity suggests that the *scop* sings at various times during the course of the feast, perhaps during lulls in the other activities.

the next one begins? Were there intervals when the horse races were suspended to give both horses and riders a rest, and did the *scop* step forth and provide some sort of entertainment in the meantime? If the horse racing were less rather than more organized, did the *scop* seize whatever moment he could to sing as much of his song as he could before he lost his audience? Was he in direct competition with the other celebratory activities and did he simply hold forth to whoever cared to give him their attention?[51]

There is little doubt that the *scop*'s performance in this third episode is clearly segmented. The *Beowulf*-poet makes explicit that the *scop* starts and stops at least one time during the celebration when he tells us that the *scop* "eft ongan / sið Beowulfes snyttrum styrian" (871b-2) [again began to recite with wisdom Beowulf's exploit], but he gives no clear signal of when the *scop*'s tale finally ends and his own resumes. The song, we might surmise, should conclude with the presentation of the negative exemplum of Heremod, who, unlike Sigemund, betrays his people and uses his great abilities for evil purposes. Given the context of the song — the celebration of a remarkable young hero's deeds — and the cultural work songs perform in oral cultures where they not only serve as entertainment but also preserve codes of behavior and offer instruction in them,[52] the narrative structure the *scop* employs in first recounting Beowulf's deeds, then turning to Sigemund's, and finishing with Heremod's as a negative example seems sound and logical. However, the line between the voice of the fictional *scop* and that of the *Beowulf*-poet blurs dramatically because the latter does not sharply mark out the conclusion of the fictional *scop*'s performance but rather seems to finish it in his own voice when he relays to us the future fortunes of Beowulf, not as the *scop*'s projection of what would be a fitting trajectory for Beowulf's career to take, but as a known fact: "He þær eallum wearð / mæg Higelaces manna cynne, / freondum gefægra; hine fyren onwod" (913b-15) [He, the kinsman of Hygelac, be-

---

[51] Baker, "Inland Ship," 88, has recently suggested that the rhapsode may have occupied a similarly non-central position in ancient Greece: "the full recitation of an *Iliad* or *Odyssey*, taking up the bulk of three days, would have competed with many other distractions, such as processions, athletics, and contests in other musical forms: rhapsodic contests never dominated the program of the Panathenea in the way that drama held center stage at the Dionysia, or Wagner at Bayreuth...."

[52] See further, Robb, *Literacy and Paideia in Ancient Greece*.

came dearer to his friends, to all mankind; crime possessed (Heremod)]. In so breaking down the distinction between the rhetorical structure of the *scop*'s performance and his own production, the *Beowulf*-poet also conflates his aim with his fictional *scop*'s so that they both praise Beowulf, not just in what is for the *scop* the narrative present but also in the narrative future (a future wholly unknowable to the fictional Danish *scop* but well known to the *Beowulf*-poet) as well. Situated as it is firmly within the narrative contours of *Beowulf*, the performance arena which the *Beowulf*-poet invokes in this instance stands, finally, not as further proof of a performative Anglo-Saxon oral poetics but as one more element of the subtle fiction the literate poet is (re-)creating about the cultural praxis of these northern tribes.

The fourth time a *scop* appears in the poem is similarly situated within the performance arena that is integral to other scenes of feasting and celebration in the poem and elsewhere in Old English poetry. At the feast celebrating Beowulf's victory over Grendel, the *Beowulf*-poet reports that "Þær wæs sang ond sweg samod ætgædere / ... gomenwudu greted, gid oft wrecen" (1064-6) [there was song and music mixed together ... the harp touched, song often sung.] But even though the *Beowulf*-poet's invocation of the performance arena is here once again only general and sweeping – as we have seen him do several times earlier in the poem –,[53] the episode concerning Finn which follows appears to be the only instance in which he may or may not do more than paraphrase the song which a fictional *scop* sings. When recounting all the other instances of scopic activity in the poem, the *Beowulf*-poet either alludes briefly and sketchily to the performances – "Scop hwilum sang / hador on Heorote" (496b-7a) [At times a *scop* sang, clear-voiced in Heorot] – or he clearly marks his paraphrases as such by referring to the fictional performing *scop* in the third person, as we saw above: "Sægde se þe cuþe / frumsceaft fira feorran reccan, / cwæð þæt se Ælmihtiga eorðan worh(te)" (90b-2) and "wel-

---

[53] He offers no details concerning these performances and there is no indication whether these songs are offered by professional entertainers or by participants at the feast who feel themselves moved (or compelled) to sing or by some *tertium quid*. Similarly, the lament which Hildeburh sings in the Finn episode, the lament the nameless woman sings beside Beowulf's pyre (of course, owing to the damaged state of the manuscript this reading must remain conjectural), as well, perhaps, as the elegy which the twelve riders utter ("wrecan" [3144a]) are all merely mentioned and/or loosely and briefly paraphrased.

hwylc gecwæð / þæt he fram Sigemunde[s]   secgan hyrde / ellen-dædum" (874b-6a).

The Finn episode, in contrast, contains no such markings but simply begins, *in medias res*, in a voice which is not differentiated from the voice of the *Beowulf*-poet: "Ne huru Hildeburh   herian þorfte / Eotena treowe" (1071-2a) [Indeed, Hildeburh had no need to praise the good faith of the Jutes]. Although many students of the poem take the tale told about the strife between Hnæf and Finn to be the performance of the *scop*, a reading that the *Beowulf*-poet's treatment certainly encourages, what we witness in the Finn episode is not the performance of a *scop* at all, or even the recounting of scopic activity, but the *Beowulf*-poet reaching into *his* repertoire of heroic poetry. In drawing into *Beowulf* material from the broader tradition of heroic poetry which undergirds and gives shape to his narrative, he does just what Bede and Aldhelm do when they incorporate the oral tradition into their own indisputably highly literate one. Although the performance of the Danish *scop* provides the background against which this portion of Finn's tale is related, the *scop* disappears from the *Beowulf*-poet's vision because he serves the poet chiefly as a fictional device through which to present the material of the Finn episode, material taken from any of a wide variety of sources, either (or both) oral and written. Indeed, this long, highly elliptical, and narratively dense tale of betrayal and revenge further stands out from the rest of the poem in that it may well be related, perhaps closely, to another piece of Anglo-Saxon secular heroic poetry, the *Fight at Finnsburg*.[54] But as the *Fight at Finnsburg* survives only in George Hickes's transcription in his *Linguarum Vett. Septentrionalium Thesaurus*, its authenticity must remain suspect and whatever light it might shed upon *Beowulf* must remain dim. More important to the present purposes, what we can determine about the Finn episode, however, is that whether its narrative substance has been imported into *Beowulf* from another Old English poem that has not survived or whether it is the unique creation of the *Beowulf*-poet, it is entirely of a piece with the rest of *Beowulf*: if its source is an external one, it is a source that the poet has internalized as fully as he had his source(s) for *Beowulf*. Indeed, the episode's

---

[54] As Klaeber, *Beowulf*, 231, notes "Of the two fights alluded to in the Episode (B. 1069 f.; 1151 f. [1068]) it is clearly the former which the fragmentary poem describes, so that the events of the Episode must be considered to follow those of the Fragment."

beginning is so thoroughly woven into the fabric of *Beowulf* that scholars and editors have long disagreed over precisely where the narrative of *Beowulf* leaves off and the song of Finn begins.[55] No such problems attend the end of the Finn episode because the *Beowulf*-poet carefully and clearly marks it by announcing "Leoð wæs asungen, / gleomannes gyd" (1159b-60a) [the song was sung to the end, the song of the *scop*]. Both in his introduction of it and more clearly (and successfully) upon its conclusion, the *Beowulf*-poet goes to some lengths to set the Finn episode apart from its surrounding narrative, something that is striking because he does not in any way mark the conclusions to either of the two song paraphrases he offers earlier. After paraphrasing the song sung at Heorot's creation the *Beowulf*-poet simply turns his attention back to his narrative's action, something he does as well following his paraphrase of the *scop*'s song celebrating Beowulf's victory over Grendel. The *Beowulf*-poet is also careful to point out that the *scop*'s song is followed by the *resumption* of joyous noise in the hall in lines that suggest that the *scop* had the hall's full (and perhaps silent) attention during his performance — "Gamen eft astah / beorhtode bencsweg" (1160b-1a) [Joy rose again, the bright bench-noise].

But rather than suggesting that the Finn episode stands out as some sort of independent component of *Beowulf*, one clearly and directly linked to the tradition of Anglo-Saxon heroic verse and that it further presents the voice of a *scop* as he composes traditional oral verse, I would suggest that this episode reveals more about the complex and interdependent oral

---

[55] Klaeber takes lines 1063a to 1070b as one sentence spoken by *Beowulf*'s narrator and marks the inception of the Finn episode by beginning a new sentence at 1071 ("Ne huru...") and by indenting 1071; Sedgefield similarly punctuates it but without indentation (as do Dobbie and Wrenn). Because he (as does Tolkien, *Finn and Hengest*, 92ff.) believes that a line is missing after 1067b, he adds ellipses at the end of 1067b and begins a new sentence, which he indicates is spoken by the Danish *scop* through the use of single quotation marks, at 1068a, despite the grammatical and syntactical problems this causes. Dobbie follows Klaeber in taking 1063a-70b as one sentence, as does Wrenn although Wrenn adds further to the confusion by punctuating the passage with a colon followed by a dash after 1067b. In his recent edition of the poem, Jack chooses to begin a new sentence at 1068b and one at 1071a. Mitchell and Robinson opt for a colon at 1068b and comment in a note to this passage, 83, that "The syntax of this half-line is dubious and something seems to be missing between ll. 1067 and 1068." For fuller discussions of this editorial crux, see Jack's note to 1066-70 and esp. Dobbie's extended note to 1068-70.

and literate poetics underlying the composition of *Beowulf* than it does about the actual composition and dissemination of heroic (and other) verse in the ancient Germanic past or the Anglo-Saxon present in which our copy of *Beowulf* was penned.[56]

As are the other depictions of scopic activity in the poem, the one contained in the narrative of his adventures Beowulf relates upon his return to Geatland is firmly anchored to the performative matrix. After concluding his account of his fight with Grendel, Beowulf briefly mentions the rewards he received for defeating Grendel before commenting at greater length upon the "gidd ond gleo" (2105a) [song and mirth] which marked the feast held to celebrate his accomplishment. In recounting the feast for Hygelac and the other members of the Geatish court, Beowulf mentions the fitting tales which were performed and he also notes that the "hearpan wynne" (2107b) [the joy of the harp] resounded throughout the hall. Like the *Beowulf*-poet, Beowulf does not attempt to recreate the substance of what is performed but simply reports that a "gomela Scylding / felafricgende feorran rehte" (2105b-6) [an old, wise Scylding, spoke of old times]. The song of this nameless old singer situates Beowulf's victory within the continuum of Danish history and so commemorates and valorizes the event in precisely the way that both the song sung upon Heorot's completion and the one sung near Grendel's mere do. As was true of some of the earlier performances we have encountered in the poem, the one Beowulf reports on also appears not have been presented continuously from start to finish: rather, Beowulf tells us four times in the space of ten lines of verse that songs and music were offered "hwilum" [at times] during the feast.

While it aligns itself in many ways with the other reports of scopic activity in the poem, Beowulf's depiction of the Anglo-Saxon performative matrix stands apart from them because it is the only one in which multiple participants perform. In addition to the nameless old Scylding,[57] Hrothgar and perhaps at least one other character also enter the performance arena to offer songs "soð ond sarlic" (2109a) [true and sad], or "syllic spell / reh-

---

[56] Niles, *Poem and Its Tradition*, 38, takes a rather different view of these matters and argues that the "ease with which the *Beowulf* poet slips into and out of the persona of an oral singer suggests that he saw little distinction between these singers and himself."

[57] Who may or may not be Hrothgar; see n. 58 below.

te æfter rihte" (2109b-10a) [strange tales told correctly], or ruminations on departed "gioguðe" (2212b) [youth] and (now faded) "hildestrengo" (2213a) [battle-strength].[58] Elsewhere in the text a single, presumably highly-trained and perhaps professional singer is the only one who negotiates the performance arena. By way of contrast, Beowulf presents an open and accessible performative matrix which recalls the one in which Bede situates Cædmon. Beowulf does not go so far as to suggest that anyone can negotiate the performative matrix – the characters who do are set apart by virtue of their social standing, age, and/or accomplishments and are far removed from the non-literate cowherd and his cohort –, but his representation of it more closely approximates the idealized and fictionalized one Bede creates than any other that survives from the Anglo-Saxon period.

While Beowulf's narrative reflects the cultural dynamic of Bede's story, we should not place undue weight upon it, in part because the poet's initial depiction of the celebration (1008ff.) mentions only one performer, who is explicitly identified as a "scop" (1066b) and whose responsibilities, we are told, include the expected ones of playing the "gomenwudu" (1065a) [harp] and relating "healgamen ... / æfter medobence"

---

[58] There is general agreement that at least two different characters, the "gomela Scylding" of line 2105b and the "rumheort cyning" [great-hearted king] of 2110b, step into the performance arena and perform during the feast, although the passage is sufficiently ambiguous that we cannot discount the possibility that at least one more character who attends the feast also enters the performance arena. A random sampling of how translators handle this passage reveals the following: Donaldson suggests, 36, that two men performed, the old Scylding, whom he loosely equates with Hrothgar, and someone described as "a brave one in battle"; Greenfield, 107 n. 78, allows for the possibility of more performers when he suggests that the old Scylding "refers to the 'king's thane' of line 867, and 'the man proved in war' of line 2107 to the scop who tells the Finn Episode" although he readily concedes that "these may be one and the same." He agrees with Donaldson that the "'generous king' of line 2109 and the 'old warrior' of line 2111 clearly seem both to refer to Hrothgar." D. Wright, 76-7, wants us to see Hrothgar as the primary performer and even goes so far as to put the harp in his hands but even in his somewhat skewed presentation he leaves a little room for other participants when he tells us that "Now and then some true and unhappy ballad was sung" without assigning them explicitly to Hrothgar; Hieatt suggests, 65, that three different men, Hrothgar, "a warrior," and "the great old warrior" perform in sequence; and, finally, Heaney, 67, identifes four singers: "an old reciter," "some hero," "the king," and "a battle-scarred veteran."

(1066a–7a) [hall-mirth among the mead-benches]. The poet does not single out any other performer during this episode, and, indeed, he relegates all other performances (if indeed there were any) to the general "sang and sweg" (1063a) [song and music] — the usual background noises — that attend feasts in Old English poetry. This discrepancy between the two accounts notwithstanding, we should also approach Beowulf's account cautiously, for he presents an idealized and fictionalized account of the performative matrix which serves to establish the importance of the feast, something which, in turn, reflects directly and very positively upon his newfound cultural status. Indeed, by placing the king, as well as another old, tried, and respected warrior in the performance arena and by removing all traces of the performance anxiety so central to Bede's story of Cædmon, Beowulf actually creates a more fully idealized, if much less fully realized, picture of the Anglo-Saxon performative matrix than Bede does. The social standing of the performers in Beowulf's account adds significantly to the import of their presentations, ones that are seamlessly interwoven into the very cultural fabric of the feast. The *Beowulf*-poet, of course, stands squarely behind everything Beowulf says or does, but this fact should not prevent us from noting that Beowulf (and by extension the *Beowulf*-poet) manipulates the Anglo-Saxon poetic tradition to suit his present needs in just the way Bede manipulates it to serve his needs in the *Historia*.

The few extant contemporary accounts of Anglo-Saxon *scopas* have proved to be both a blessing and a curse. Although they provide invaluable commentary on poetic production and have thus long been regarded as important touchstones in the mapping of Anglo-Saxon poetics, the model of poetic articulation they present — that of spontaneous (or in Cædmon's case nearly spontaneous) composition-in-performance — has been generally accepted as *the* model of Anglo-Saxon poetic production. As a result, oral theorists have unduly privileged the binarist model of poetic production and inscription which emerges explicitly in Bede's account and implicitly in the others. The depictions of poetic articulation that Bede and the *Beowulf*-poet offer no doubt reflect what was *at some point* in Anglo-Saxon literary history the common and necessary mode of producing poetry. But instead of taking the accounts of Bede, the *Beowulf*-poet, Alfred, and others — most notably Widsith and Deor — as evidence of the widespread currency of composition-in-performance in Anglo-Saxon England, we should recall that they all invoke a temporally removed, and hence fictionalized and idealized, performative matrix which may well represent not a contemporary practice but rather a dying or defunct one. The nature of the surviving evidence is such that we will never be able to determine with any degree of certainty just when the pen became the primary conduit for poetic articulation or when the performative matrix invoked in the poetry ceased to be functionally significant. But the extant poetry does strongly suggest that evidence of written composition in no way precludes the continued presence of oral poetics. Sharing the same tectonics and depending upon the same specialized idiom, the two modes of expression appear to have co-existed throughout the period, despite the growing importance of literacy and literate means of producing, preserving, and receiving poetry.

The close connection between performance and the transmission and continued survival of traditional oral art has been a central tenet of oral theory from Parry onward, and it is clear that the characteristic contours of such things as verbal collocations, type-scenes, specialized syntax, larger narrative structuring (ring composition, story-patterns, etc.), in short, all the constituents of the specialized registers evident in ancient Greek, Anglo-Saxon, and South Slavic traditional oral poetries developed diachronically as aids to the rapid composition of verse in performance.[59] The survival and transmission of these registers are also generally seen as reflecting their continued utility within a dynamic performative matrix; once they are no longer necessary to the production of verse, one influential argument runs, they wither and soon disappear altogether. But while certain aspects of traditional oral registers undoubtedly evolved in response to the immediate pressures attendant upon composing during performance, they do not exist solely in symbiosis with performance. In the South Slavic tradition, for example, performance appears to play a far more central role than it does in either the ancient Greek or Anglo-Saxon tradition.[60] Of the three, only the South Slavic tradition can be demonstrated as having produced unambiguously oral texts. For the others, we must speak in terms of oral-derived texts, texts whose poetics emerges from a complex

---

[59] Foley, reacting to the reductivism inherent in this view, has argued incisively against the mechanistic view of traditional oral poetic articulation which was (and in some quarters still is) widely promulgated. See esp. his *Singer of Tales in Performance*.

[60] See Finnegan, *Oral Poetry*, 88–133, and, more recently, Foley, *How to Read an Oral Poem*, for considerations of the many varied roles performance plays in different oral traditions.

and complicated cultural milieu, the contours of which have only recently begun to come into focus. Removing the performative component from oral poetics surely sounds the death knell of traditional *oral* poetry – that is, poetry that is both composed and disseminated exclusively during performance by non-literate singers –, but the effect of its removal on the traditional oral register is neither so dramatic nor so pronounced. The mode of presenting poetry shifts radically once it is severed from the performative matrix, but the channels through which it is articulated and received do not necessarily undergo a concomitant change because the traditional oral register remains a powerful and flexible significative idiom.[61] Because the expressive economy of oral poetics is much more than the sum of its formulaic verbal collocations, metrical conventions, typical scenes, and story-patterns, *how* the poetry is articulated, *how* it means, and *how* it is received remain stable once the pen replaces the tongue as the primary avenue for poetic expression.[62]

But given the remarkable stability that results from the combination of the oral-traditional register's specialized structural constituents and highly metonymic idiom, how can we see the poet who (performatively or non-performatively) engages oral poetics as more than the prisoner of an extremely deterministic tradition? The answer lies in the nature of the dedicated register of oral poetics, a highly specialized and "idiomatic version of the language that qualifies as a more or less self-contained system

---

[61] Foley, "Word-Power," 293, further notes that "[t]he integers of expression and perception, the cognitive categories that function optimally only within the enabling event of performance, retain in their textual forms a rhetorical vestige of that performance that cannot be ignored," a position that O'Brien O'Keeffe, "Performing Body," 53, endorses when she argues that "[w]riting does not alienate a text from traditional meaning immediately – early written texts will still appeal to immanent meaning despite their written condition."

[62] The view that Anglo-Saxon oral poetics is a richly associative, highly significative idiom can be traced back at least as far as Creed, "Criticizing Old English Poetry," 101, who argued that "every time a singer performs the same theme he and his audience hear and appreciate that performance against the music of all other performances of that theme." He continues by stating that the "audience – singer included – hears each new performance of a theme *counterpointed* against all the old performances it has heard" (his emphasis). Some thirty years later, one of Creed's former students, John Miles Foley, was to offer in his *Immanent Art* the most fully realized account to date of the deeply metonymic character of the traditional oral register hinted at by Creed.

of signification specifically because it is the designated and sole vehicle" for articulating poetry.[63] Seen in this light, the register of oral poetics is no more limiting, restrictive, or deterministic than are the grammar and syntax of natural languages. If this were not so and the traditional oral register were truly the mechanistic, confining force it is often surmised to be,[64] our manuscript records would show none of the flexibility of expression, suppleness of narrative patterning, or originality that they do. The formulaic tectonics of the register would not function metonymically but would rather be stripped of its significative powers in just the ways that formulas, clichés, and dead metaphors largely are in contemporary literate poetics.

If we compare the phrase "in geardagum" [in days of yore] which occurs at *Beowulf* 1b[65] with the formula "once upon a time" which regularly occurs throughout children's literature, we discover that they both function as diective temporal referents in setting the ensuing narrative in the distant, perhaps mythical or fictional past. But this similarity aside, these formulas diverge sharply. Formulas such as "once upon a time," like most formulas in a literate poetics, "have lost all evocative power and are merely used because they save people the trouble of inventing phrases for themselves"[66] while "in geardagum," by way of contrast, is firmly imbedded in a highly metonymic referential system and is, especially when used at or near the beginnings of poems, demonstrably part of a larger traditional "I heard" narrative pattern. In addition to alluding "characteristically ... to

---

[63] Foley, "Word-Power," 287. Although for Foley this register is inextricably linked with "the act of traditional oral performance," his observations apply equally well to the register of a non-performative oral poetics, as he argues at length in *Singer of Tales in Performance*, 60–98.

[64] Consider, for example, Parry's highly influential remarks, in "Homer and Homeric Style," 317, that the formulaic diction of the Homeric poems reflects "not only the desire for an easy way of making verses, but the complete need of it." He continues and suggests that "Without writing, the poet can make his verses only if he has a formulaic diction which will give him his phrases all made, and made in such a way that, at the slightest bidding of the poet, they will link themselves in an unbroken pattern that will fill his verses and make his sentences."

[65] "In geardagum" finds close parallels in the phrase "on fyrndagum" of *Andreas* 1b and *Vainglory* 1b.

[66] Orwell, "Politics," 159.

the world of oral discourse and oral tradition,"[67] the "I heard" pattern, which metonymically signals the beginning of a heroic narrative, constitutes an important moment of traditional recovery in that it allows the poet to recreate the past by making past utterances present once again.

In contrast to the fixed epithets in oral and oral-derived literatures which, despite the regularity of their appearance (and their oftentimes apparent narrative inappropriateness), "reach outside of individual instances to larger-than-textual realities and stand *pars pro toto* for complexes of ideas too evanescent for commitment to the single occurrence,"[68] the alliteration and chiastic structure of a fixed epithet such as "brave and bright, bright and brave" which is regularly attached to a character in Jane Yolen's children's story *Commander Toad in Space* serve an exclusively mnemonic rather than significative function. When we learn of Commander Toad that he is "brave and bright, bright and brave," an assessment consistently and simplistically confirmed throughout the series of tales devoted to his exploits, the epithet bears only minimal, non-systematic significative weight. In contrast, a fixed, distinctive epithet such as *podas ôkys Achilleus* [swift-footed Achilles] belongs to a rich, complex, associative web of reference which is called forth indeterminately but powerfully with each occurrence of the epithet.[69]

The lexical, metrical, syntactic, and narrative contours of medieval English oral poetics were undoubtedly all shaped in the crucible of performance, and at some point and doubtless for a long time poetry was transmitted and preserved solely within the performative matrix. As a result, performance and traditional oral poetic articulation have throughout the development of oral theory been seen as necessarily interdependent. But this view depends upon logic that needs reconsideration. A poem evidencing oral poetics must be an *oral* poem, so one important, but ultimately circular, argument goes, because oral poetics is the hallmark of orally composed and transmitted poems. The non-performative poetics towards which I have gestured here does not demand that we reject outright the crucial and necessary interdependence of oral poetics and performance, but instead challenges the application of a performance-based

---

[67] Parks, "Traditional Narrator," 47.

[68] Foley, *Immanent Art*, 23.

[69] For an in-depth treatment of the noun-epithet phrases in Homer, see Foley, *Immanent Art*, 139–50.

model to the oral poetics which survives in *demonstrably written* Old English poetry, a set comprised of, by definition, all the extant Old English poetry.[70] Removing the necessity of performance from Anglo-Saxon oral poetics does not preclude the continued practice of producing poetry orally under the exigencies of performance; it rather offers up another, more flexible and more responsive way of understanding those poetic records that have come down to us as written texts which nevertheless evidence oral poetics.

---

[70] Finnegan, *Literacy and Orality*, 124-5, stresses the interdependence of oral poetics and performance in arguing that the "style of delivery (tempo, mood, dynamics or tone, to mention just some aspects), the drama and characterization conveyed by the performer, the audience's involvement through interjections, responses, verbal interplay or choral participation in response to the main performer's lead — all these are not extra, optional embellishments, as they might seem if we follow a written paradigm, but a central constituent of the literary act." In this, she joins Foley, Bauman, Tedlock, and Ben-Amos as part of a growing group of scholars who increasingly and profitably are bringing ethnopoetics and the ethnography of speaking to bear on oral and oral-derived literatures.

JONATHAN WATSON

Writing Out "Óðinn's Storm": The Literary Reception of an Oral-Derived Template in the Two Versions of Laȝamon's *Brut*

> Hvernig skal kenna orrostu? Svá at kalla veðr vápna eða hlífa eða Óðins eða valkyrju eða herkonunga eða gný eða glym.
>
> [How should battle be named? It should be called the storm of weapons or of shields or of Óðinn or of a valkyrie or of chieftains or tumult or noise.][1]

A witness to both a Germanic past and an Anglo-Norman present, Laȝamon's *Brut* represents a crucial resource for understanding how oral and written systems converge in post-Conquest England. As a late twelfth-century or early thirteenth-century work, based on Wace's *Roman de Brut* but composed in a native verse style, Laȝamon's *Brut* necessarily harbors a high degree of tension between a residual orality and an emerging literacy.[2] In recent years, Mark C. Amodio has underscored this tension in the Caligula version of *Brut* (the standard version of the poem), noting how resonant pre-Conquest structures persist — and are often transformed — in the *Brut* narrative: if Laȝamon renders Wace's *Roman de Brut*, he also "rec-

---

[1] *Skáldskaparmál*, 194, §61. I cite the text from G. Jónsson, *Edda*. Unless otherwise noted, all translations are mine.

[2] On the date of *Brut*, see LeSaux, *Poem and Its Sources*, 10, who places the composition of the poem between 1185 and 1216.

reates" it in "the only poetic idiom at his disposal, that which descends from the English oral tradition"; by doing so, Amodio adds, the early medieval poet taps into "a simultaneously determining and enabling oral poetics."[3] Drawing on an inherited oral-derived discourse, Laȝamon thus perpetuates the pre-formed textual world of earlier Germanic culture. Freeing Laȝamon from his "antiquarian sentiments,"[4] highlighting resilient oral-derived features, and locating *Brut* on the oral-literate continuum, Amodio has made an invaluable contribution to Laȝamon scholarship and laid the groundwork for a further consideration of Laȝamon's oral poetics: how oral-derived features inform the *two* extant versions of Laȝamon's *Brut*.

In this essay, I would like to embark on this comparative investigation, considering how the two *Brut* texts receive a single traditional unit: an oral-derived template, which I label "Óðinn's Storm."[5] This unit, described in detail below, draws its name from Old Norse court poetry, where "Óðins veðr" [Óðinn's Storm] occurs as a kenning for "battle." Of course, the inherent cognitive leap that characterizes this kenning (storm = battle) is not peculiar to the early Germanic world. Yet at a textual level, as evident in eddic and skaldic verse, in *Beowulf* and other Old English works, this battle–storm correlation is a highly stylized, distinctive trope: birds attending battle will be dewy-feathered; trees on the war-field will be hung with hail; a ship transporting troops will have a frost-covered prow. What marks this battle-storm template as distinctive is that the storm imagery is typically accompanied by a shaking object – a horse, a warrior's chainmail, a bird's feathers – and/or an aural detail, such as a screaming eagle or a resounding sword. So, too, core lexical items underpin this textual environment, becoming associative cues in this stable, yet protean, unit.[6] As I will demonstrate, Óðinn's Storm serves as a useful tag for this template, because as a kenning it functions metonymically and thus mirrors the metonymic signification of the oral-derived template: just as the kenning depends on an oblique and distinctive poetic landscape to realize its evocative potential, so the stylized template keys broader "anaphoric

---

[3] Amodio, "Introduction," 18.
[4] E. G. Stanley, "Antiquarian Sentiments," 23-37.
[5] See Watson, "'Óðinn's Storm.'"
[6] For a more expansive treatment on the specific features of the "Óðinn's Storm" template, see Watson, "'Óðinn's Storm,'" esp. 32-3.

fields"[7] — an audience's cumulative experience with the traditional element and, at least originally we might presume, its knowledge of a distinctive mythological framework.

Having encoded his narrative in a traditional Germanic register, Laȝamon occasionally invokes reflexes of Óðinn's Storm in his battle sequences. Yet, as we shall see, the two thirteenth-century transcribers of Laȝamon's poem respond with ambivalence and even, no doubt, with genuine confusion to this waning textual device sprung from a pre-Viking mythological and textual world. As a consequence, the *Brut* texts reveal degrees of *metonymic encoding* and *metonymic erosion*, for at least one scribe seeks to displace or "write out" this increasingly obscure template with the more voguish poeticisms of Anglo-Norman culture. Ultimately, the two texts enact cultural transition, entwining vestiges of an early Germanic worldview with the emerging fashions of an Anglo-Norman textual community.

Composed as early as the late twelfth century, Laȝamon's *Brut* survives in two thirteenth-century copies, London, British Library, Cotton Caligula A. ix and London, British Library, Cotton Otho C. xiii (which I hereafter refer to as "Caligula" and "Otho"). Caligula, an early thirteenth-century West Midland version, has long been considered the superior text; Otho, a later Southern production, has been viewed as an inferior reflection of the original. H. C. Wyld's famous judgment voices an earlier generation's response to the poetic relations of the two:

> The later version is more compressed than the other; the younger scribe has cut out many picturesque lines, and in others has omitted characteristic words and phrases, often replacing them by something more commonplace. This is partly due to his not always understanding the old language of the original, but also partly to his being a less poetically minded person. A careful comparison of the two versions leaves the impression that the scribe of O. had before him a MS. practically identical with C., and perhaps actually C. itself.[8]

---

[7] See also Keith, "Literary Differences"; and Gibbs, "Literary Relationships."
[8] Wyld, "Laȝamon as an English Poet," 4.

Though the burden of being a "less poetically minded person" has long saddled the Otho-poet, modern scholarship has dramatically revised the view of the texts Wyld articulates. In terms of their textual relations, Françoise LeSaux concludes that Caligula and Otho derive from either a common lost exemplar or "extremely close originals,"[9] rather than the scribe of Otho necessarily having a copy of Caligula before him. In terms of their literary relations, Christopher Cannon has begun shifting the textual relationship away from issues of genealogy and manuscript chronology (which has become less certain) toward questions of audience.[10] Thus, in an important recent article, he perceives in Otho "a consistent plan" to re-fashion the poem into "something like a romance."[11] Indeed, speculating that Laȝamon himself might be responsible for both versions and was perhaps "involved in a Langlandian process of *re*-making," Cannon proposes that "the Otho and Caligula texts are not simply two different copies of a single poem";[12] rather, they represent Laȝamon's attempt "to bridge a cultural divide," to respond to two different audiences, with Caligula appealing to those who relish Old English poetry, and Otho to an audience eager for Anglo-Norman romance, for literature that is *"au courant."*[13]

For the purpose of extending the oral poetics of *Brut*, we can yoke this revised textual and literary understanding of the two versions with the implications of Amodio's work. LeSaux's conclusion that the two versions derive from a common lost exemplar or extremely close originals lets us surmise that we have two readings of the same text — or virtually the same text — screened through two different sensibilities. We might expect, then, divergent, even competing, responses to traditional structures: as the two scribe-poets receive their "message," they reshape ("decode" and "encode") this material according to their own particular formulaic conditioning (or lack of it). To some extent, this aligns with the "double Laȝamon" theory of Cannon: reading his exemplar, the Caligula-poet encodes his text with epic features (presumably found in the original), whereas the Otho-poet

---

[9] LeSaux, *Poem and Its Sources*, 13.

[10] Cannon, "Style and Authorship"; see also Bryan, *Collaborative Meaning*, esp. 47-60.

[11] Cannon, "Style and Authorship," 188, 193.

[12] Cannon, "Style and Authorship," 200-3.

[13] Cannon, "Style and Authorship," 203.

displaces these for romance decoration. If Cannon stresses the infusion of romance into epic structures, then Amodio stresses the infusion of epic-resonance into an emerging romance milieu; in other words, the two scholars take an obverse approach to *Brut*, one emphasizing the romance-based potential (Cannon), the other the epic-based potential (Amodio). My methodology, toward formulating an "oral poetics" for *Brut* – Caligula *and* Otho – seeks to harness both these promising but, until now, independent approaches to the poem. In order to clarify the complementary aspects of these two approaches, I must pursue them briefly in more detail, prior to setting forth a methodological model for relating Laȝamon's two texts.

In sharp contrast to Amodio, Cannon sees Laȝamon's Old English idioms as largely unproductive and stresses the connotative potential of individual word substitutions in Otho. For instance, Cannon notes that the frequent use of *knight* – perhaps the term "most emblematic of romance"[14] – serves as a revision in Otho for an entire set of Old English terms for warrior (*bern, erl, gome, kempe, thein*, etc.). Displacing the more archaic Old English phraseology, these individual word substitutions, Cannon contends, with their romance-steeped associations (such as *knight*), effect a "connotative" (or "symbolic") change.[15] Amodio's epic-based approach, on the other hand, excavates echoic phraseologies and contexts on the precedent of Anglo-Saxon verse, especially *Beowulf*, the work perhaps closest to *Brut* in spirit and form in the Old English poetic canon. Looking, for example, at the occurrences of the term *gebolgen* [enraged] in *Beowulf*, Amodio demonstrates that the Middle English reflex *abolȝen* retains much of its affective impact in *Brut*. In both *Beowulf* and *Brut*, the word harbors contextual overtones: it both describes a combatant's enraged state of mind and can signal imminent battle or slaughter.[16] We can conclude, then, that if Amodio's oral poetics do not pursue both versions of *Brut*, Cannon does not avail himself of oral traditional theory. For in his fancying Laȝamon a poetic belletrist – a poet capable of summoning at once the "antiquarianism that defines the style

---

[14] Cannon, "Style and Authorship," 197.
[15] Cannon, "Style and Authorship," 197–8.
[16] Amodio, "Oral-Formulaic Tradition," 10, also notes crucial differences between the use of these terms in *Beowulf* and *Brut*, the result perhaps of "comparative decay." See his comments, 10ff.

of Caligula" and, at the same time, the "romance style of Otho"[17] – Cannon offers a view of authorship which does not accord with what we know of oral-derived texts: that oral and written elements often fuse in complex ways and that an author may not always be cognizant of deploying traditional textual signals. When we combine these two approaches, however, a promising synthesis emerges: in recasting the inquiry by looking at the oral poetics between Caligula and Otho, we seek meaning in not only what is "written in," such as the romance terms privileged by Cannon, but what is "written out" – what resonant traditional structures are excised.

Extending the continuum of orality and literacy to include both Caligula and Otho, we find that a more dynamic hybrid of orality and literacy will emerge, one that reveals cognitive and linguistic tensions embedded in the text. These tensions, as I will demonstrate, often defy genre categories such as "epic" and "romance" and, especially, "oral" and "literate": in Otho, for instance, we encounter hybrids of fragmented epic elements peppered with a romance lexicon. The picture of transitional literacy that *Brut* affords is thus a complex one. In terms of oral theory, what we encounter in the *Brut* texts is a fracturing interpretive matrix, wherein reperformance invites (or requires) supplementation from competing textual and semantic fields.

By way of illustrating the ubiquity of Óðinn's Storm and clarifying the distinction between metonymic and semantic information, I will cite two passages from artistically distant but genetically linked traditions: the first is from *Brut*, featuring a young King Arthur, who enters battle wolf-like; the second is a *helmingr* [four line stanza] from an Old Norse skaldic poem by Arnór Þórðarson (c. 1047) portraying a young King Magnús sailing toward Sweden in his dragon-headed longship. In these two passages, and in those which follow in this essay, I use boldface to highlight the stock lexical items of Óðinn's Storm and italics to denote phraseology, lexical items which occur in at least one other surviving example of Óðinn's Storm. In translating the Arthur and Magnús passages below, I use an asterisk (*) to denote those phrases that belong to the traditionally conditioned context:

Vp bræid Arður his sceld: foren to his breosten

---

[17] Cannon, "Style and Authorship," 204.

[and] he gon to **rusien**: swa þe **runie** wulf
þenne he cumeð of holte: **bi-honged mid snawe**
and þencheð to biten: swulc deor swa him likeð.[18]
(10040-3)

[Up raised Arthur his shield in front of his chest, and he began to *shake* like the *rime-covered* wolf when he comes from the holt *hung with snow* intending to devour whatever animal he wishes to.]

Vafðir lítt, enn vendir bifðusk;
varta hrøkk, enn niðr nam søkkva;
geystisk hlýr, enn **hristi** bára
hrími stokkin búnar **grímur**.[19]

[Little did you waver, though the masts trembled. The *rime-splattered* prow pressed on and submerged; the bow of the vessel dashed ahead, and the sea-swell *shook* the decorated ship beaks.]

In terms of semantic content, what these images evoke is very different, indeed: on the one hand, Arthur, readying for battle, shakes like a frost-covered wolf emerging (so we can assume for the moment) from a snow-draped wood in expectation of slaughter; on the other hand, King Magnús dashes onward in the sea, his Viking-ship prow sheeted with ice and tossed by waves that rattle the golden figureheads. In terms of metonymic content, however, the images deploy the shared Óðinn's Storm template, highlighting the collocation of a shaking object and a wintry (or dew-covered) aspect.[20] As I will demonstrate in more detail below, this textual environment is generally marked by a set of lexical features. In the

---

[18] Unless cited otherwise, all passages from *Brut* are reproduced from *Laȝamon: Brut*, ed. Brook and Leslie.

[19] F. Jónsson, *Skjaldedigtning*, 333. All skaldic poetry excerpted is based on Jónsson's text. I have silently modernized his orthography and occasionally emended his readings, either on the basis of Kock, *Skaldediktningen*, or from the helpful advice of Kari Ellen Gade.

[20] As stated earlier, it may also include an aural element, though this feature will not be as relevant for the present study.

examples above, for instance, the traditionally conditioned space (marked * * in the translations) is cued by the collocation of "rusien"/"runie" (ON "hristi"/"hrimi").[21] Whereas a modern audience would probably see vast differences in these images, processing only the semantic information — we see a wolf *and* a longship (with overlapping winter imagery perhaps) — an early Germanic audience would have recognized a shared metonymic base, one that intoned imminent battle and a Valhallian presence. Of course, this claim may seem rather tenuous at this point, posited solely on the basis of two distant images, and so I will need to pursue a more detailed analysis of their common subtext — their oral-derived template — below. First, however, it will be useful to clarify further the distinction between *metonymic* and *semantic* as these terms relate to the oral and written mind; then I will demonstrate the semantic presuppositions of modern readers by considering past readings of Laȝamon's wolf image excerpted above.

Metonymy, as John Miles Foley has already established, is the primary mode of signification for oral-derived verbal art.[22] The language of any single oral-derived performance necessarily encodes an inherent, acquired value dependent on previous performances:

> What passes down through the generations is ... not simply an idiom that allows convenient oral composition, but the equivalent of a critical methodology, evolved and practiced by a 'school' or 'interpretative community' unified by the act of (re-) making and (re-)'reading' traditional verbal art.[23]

Of particular interest for this study is the phenomenon of lexical clustering, which Foley construes as collective meaning-laden signals capable of evoking an immanent context — an extratextual field formed by an audience's cumulative experience with a motif or theme. More recently, Foley configures the inherent potential of these lexical items as *word-power*

---

[21] The word *grímur* referring to the dragon-faced figureheads often occurs in this conditioned textual milieu as well, and likely also contributes to the passage's affective impact.

[22] See Foley, *Immanent Art*, esp. 1-60, and *Singer of Tales in Performance*, esp. 1-98.

[23] Foley, *Immanent Art*, 45

and the interpretive zone in which word-power functions, the *performance arena*.[24] Both these terms will be useful for our discussion at hand. Returning to our two images above — the wolf and the figurehead — we can recast the proposed resonant lexical items — *rusien/runie* (*hrista/hrimi*, *stokkin/grimur*) as a core group capable of word-power, of summoning anaphoric contexts or fields. Essential for word-power, the performance arena involves competence, the ability for an interpretive community to encode and decode a message.[25] As I have already observed and will demonstrate below, Laȝamon's two versions represent, to some degree, a shifting performance arena and differing levels of competence in processing oral-derived idioms. In sum, then, we can say that, whereas a contemporary audience would seize on the images of the wolf and the Viking ship, an early audience would approach these vastly different images as relatively transparent: they would have seized upon the resonant textual cues invoking Óðinn's Storm.

Because of this gap between modern and medieval sensibilities, the image of Laȝamon's wolf excerpted above has not been seen as a traditionally-based image; rather it has always been perceived either as the product of Laȝamon's sheer imagination or as the by-product of a Wacian or Latinate influence upon him.[26] Only recently, in a passing comment, has it been suggested that this wolf might owe something to the *wulf mære* [glorious wolf] or *úlfheðinn* [wolf-coat] tradition of early Germanic culture and thus be the lupine equivalent of the *berserkr*.[27] Because Laȝamon

---

[24] On these important terms, see Foley, *Singer of Tales in Performance*, 42-9, et passim.

[25] For a discussion of Laȝamon's performance competence, see Amodio, "Introduction," 19-20.

[26] See, for instance, Dickins and Wilson, *Early Middle English*, 169, who note that "This type of simile appears to be unknown in OE, and is first noted in Layamon who may have derived it from Latin epic." For Wacian influence, see Barron and Weinberg, *Laȝamon's Arthur*, xli-xlii.

[27] See Deskis and Hill, "Wolf Doesn't Care." They focus on the most elaborate wolf simile in *Brut*, in which Arthur figures himself a wolf chasing down a pack of hilltop goats (10624-36), but offer some oblique light in their discussion on the shorter Arthur-wolf simile under consideration. Their primary purpose, 42, is to demonstrate "the process of poetic elaboration and amplification which characterizes Lawman's art." An illuminating study, and not only for their mentioning Lawman's indebtedness to early Germanic verse, it nevertheless relegates

scholars have failed to recognize the traditional underpinnings of this image, they largely misread it. This "misreading" arises not only from philological oversights but also from the modern reader's encounter with a metonymic structure. To illustrate my point, I excerpt below the treatment of this passage in the popular translations of *Brut*, which can be divided into two camps: those who see the *wolf* as covered with snow ("bi-honged mid snawe") and those who see the *forest* covered in snow. For ease of comparison, I excerpt the passage once again:

> Vp bræid Arður his sceld׃ foren to his breosten.
> 7 he gon to **rusien**׃ swa þe **runie** wulf.
> þenne he cumeð of holte׃ **bi-honged mid snawe**.
> and þencheð to biten׃ swulc deor swa him likeð.

snow-covered wolf:
Up caught Arthur his shield, before his breast, and he gan to rush as the howling wolf, when he cometh from the wood, behung with snow, and thinketh to bite such beasts as he liketh.[28]

Arthur raised his shield in front of his breast and rushed forward like a mad wolf who comes from the woods, hung with snow, thinking to ravage the flocks at will.[29]

snow-covered wood:
Arthur raised his shield before his chest and went rushing like the savage wolf when he comes from the snow-hung wood, bent on devouring whatever prey he pleases.[30]

---

the shorter Arthur-wolf simile to a footnote (see 42 n. 4), with no translation. As I hope to demonstrate, the shorter Arthur-wolf simile depends less on an elaborative style than the more extended wolf-goat simile: its more compressed poetics depends on metonymic signification.

[28] Mason, *Wace and Layamon*, 185.
[29] Bzdyl, *Layamon's Brut*, 195.
[30] *Laȝamon's Arthur*, ed. and trans. Barron and Weinberg, lines 10040–3. In their translation of the entire poem, which appeared in 1995, the line is translated as "frost-grey wolf," rather than "savage wolf."

> Arthur caught up his shield, covering his breast,
> And began rampaging like the rime-grey wolf,
> When it comes loping from the snow-laden woodland.[31]

Much of the broad semantic range here can be clarified philologically. For instance, the term "runie" should mean what the most recent translators have taken it as: "frost-gray" or "rime-gray"; "runie" is simply a confused form of *rimie* [frost-gray]. The reason for the error, which to my knowledge has not yet been pointed out, probably results from scribal confusion of ligating minims in the manuscript.[32] The scribes have "mis-read" the minim cluster, resulting in a false joining of minims; hence, the manuscript reading "R]]]]] E" becomes "runie" (R]]]]] E) instead of "rimie" (R]]]]] E).

The word "rusien," too, needs clarification. As evident in the translations above, past readers have usually construed this verb as 'to rush,' with only Rosamund Allen's translation offering a variant: "rampaging." Though it is tempting to render this verb as 'to rush,' it is actually a separate verb meaning 'to tremble, shudder, shake, or rattle.' The confusion arises from two ME verbs which share the identical ME infinitive form, *resen*, but derive from two distinctive Old English verbs: OE *hrisian* [to tremble or shake] and OE *ræsan* [to run or rush] (MED, s.v., 1, 2). *Rusien*, the verb used by Laʒamon in this passage, with its *-ien* ending (OE *-ian*), is clearly related to the Old English verb *hrisian*, not OE *ræsan*. The usage, as I will discuss below, is akin to the shaking chain-mail of Beowulf's troop arriving in Denmark ("syrcan *hrysedon*, / guðgewædo" [226b-7a] [their chain-mail rattled, their war-dress]; emphasis added). My suggested translation above, when comparing the wolf simile with Magnús's longship, incorporates these insights, making the cognate connection with ON *hrista* and *hrím*. Despite having resolved some of these philological issues, we are left with one remaining uncertainty: is the *wolf* "bi-honged mid snawe" or is the *wood*? This poses a *locus desperandus* for the modern reader, a "gap of indeterminacy" in Iserian terminology, that should be approached in terms of word-power; that is, it probably did

---

[31] *Lawman: Brut*, trans. R. Allen, lines 10040-3.

[32] For a fuller treatment of scribal confusion of minims, see Watson, "Minim-istic Imagination."

not matter to an early medieval audience *what* was snow-covered, only that *something* was snow-covered.

Even a selective survey of early Germanic analogues bears out this ambiguity of snow-covered animal and snow-covered landscape. The detail, as these analogues will suggest, is simply a part of Óðinn's Storm, the stylized textual locus through which Laȝamon's wolf moves. In the Old English *Riddle 89*, for instance, an antler that has been fashioned into an inkhorn describes his glorious past atop the head of a stag, a stag who lives on a mountain crag but occasionally seeks his "duguþe" [troop] on the frost-hardened plain:

> hwilum stealc hliþo   stigan sceolde
> up in eþel   hwilum eft gewat
> **in deop dalu**   duguþe secan
> strong on stæpe,   stanwongas grof,
> **hrimig**hearde,   **hwilum hara scoc**
> **forst of feaxe.**[33]
>
> (9–14a)

[At times (the old one, i.e., the stag) had to climb up the steep slope to his dwelling; but, at other times, when the strong-stepping one would go to seek his troop in the deep dales, digging into the rime-crusted fields, then he would shake the hoary frost from his coat.]

The language of the riddle delights in a playful context: leaving his crag home, the stag simply descends to find his herd, yet the conventional language invokes his going to battle. Not only does he seek out his "duguþe" but also his vigorous movements, the digging with his hooves and the shaking of his coat, function as a circumlocution for fighting in battle. 'Once in a while,' the antler says in effect, 'my lord sought out battle.' But to say this he uses the traditional imagery of Óðinn's Storm (covering the grounds and the animal's coat with rime), and this is borne out by the lexical cluster as well: "hrimig," "scoc," "in deop dalu," "hara forst" — all these, as we shall see, find frequent usage in the battle-storm complex.

---

[33] I cite the Riddle from Williamson, *Old English Riddles*, 119.

In *Beowulf*, *Exodus*, and *Andreas*, the template functions in a context more closely aligned with its manifestation in *Brut*, occurring as it does in heroic narratives and in scenes of imminent battle. We must therefore consider these the closest genetic analogues. In these examples we find as well the blurring of wolves and warriors, a tendency deep-seated in early Germanic warrior culture, as attested to by the "Torslunda die" wolf-warrior and the poetic accounts of *úlfheðnar* in battle. In *Beowulf*, Óðinn's Storm trails the warriors all the way to Heorot. As Beowulf's sea-band arrives on the Danish shore, "syrcan hrysedon, guðgewædo" [mail-shirts rattled, war-garments] (226b-7).[34] Through its mention of the single detail of shaking armor, the phrase introduces Óðinn's Storm into the narrative. Its more full-blown treatment comes soon after, when the troops arrive at the hall and come closer to their rendezvous with Grendel. Setting their war-equipment against the wall, the troop sits along a hall-bench, and, lest the audience assume this is a breathless, weary host, the poet encodes their battle-readiness:

> Setton sæmeþe   side scyldas,
> rondas **regn**hearde   wið þæs recedes weal;
> bugon þa to bence,   **byrnan hringdon**,
> *guðsearo gumena*;   garas stodon,
> sæmanna searo   samod ætgædere,
> **æscholt ufan græg**;   wæs se irenþreat
> wæpnum gewurþad.   Þa ðær wlonc hæleð
> oretmecgas   æfter *æþelum* frægn:
> "Hwanon ferigeað ge   fætte scyldas,
> **græge syrcan**,   ond *grimhelmas*,
> heresceafta heap?"
>
>   (325-35a)

[The sea-weary ones placed their great shields — their shields godlike in their strength — against the wall, and sat down on a bench. The chain-mail resounded, the war-gear of men; the spears of the skilled seamen stood gathered together, an ash-forest gray from above: the iron-troop was adorned with weapons! Then the proud soldier asked the

---

[34] I cite *Beowulf* throughout from Klaeber's edition.

warriors about their descent: "From where do you carry gold-plated shields, gray battle-shirts, masked helmets, and the host of battle-shafts?"]

Though the troop rests temporarily, their weaponry and armor convey their seriousness of purpose and the approaching fight: their spears are transformed into an ash-forest; the gray details — spears and mail-shirts — satisfy the wolfish, frost-covered component of the template. We may also have an invocation of the gods in the adjective describing the shields in line 326, "regnheard." *Regn-* is cognate with ON *Regin*, a term designating 'the ruling powers, or gods.' Friedrich Klaeber would render the line as "shield-bosses wondrously strong," so that the force of the gods is only implied in "wondrously." But we might translate this more literally as "*Regin*-hard shields," with the force being either "shields made strong by the gods" or "shields godlike in their strength." If this is a reference to ON *Regin*, it would certainly suit the context, for the gray spear-forest and the "græge syrcan" can be firmly placed within the matrix of Óðinn's Storm.

Consider, for instance, an account of an *úlfheðinn* in battle from a skaldic verse (c. 985) attributed to Eyvindr Skáldaspillir:

> Ok sá halr
> at Háars veðri
> **hösvan serk**
> **hrísgrímnis bar.**[35]
>   (stanza 222, 1–4)

[And that warrior bore in Óðinn's storm (i.e., battle) a gray sark of the wolf (i.e., a wolf-coat)].

Like the phrase "hösvan serk," worn in Óðinn's Storm, "græge syrcan," juxtaposed with the aerial view of a gray ash-spear forest, will be seen as quite typical of the Óðinn's Storm template. What we have in these tandem examples from *Beowulf* can be likened to a glimpse of varying surface realizations of a single "deep structure": a linguistic and conceptual

---

[35] G. Jónsson, *Edda*, 194, §61. The passage is cited by Snorri in *Skáldskaparmál*; another version of the stanza appears in Eyvindr's poem *Háleygjatal*, which can be found in F. Jónsson, *Skjaldedigtning*, 69.

fund that produces varying and partial "surface structures." Not all details, therefore, must be included for the deployment of Óðinn's Storm, and not all details will be recoverable, given the chance survival of early Germanic verse. But we can continue building the lexemic fund of this storm imagery, which has been marked above in boldface and italics.

Exodus offers a cousin passage of wolves, grayness, and shaking in the approach of Pharaoh's host. Even though the clash will be avoided, the poet musters Óðinn's Storm, building suspense, we may surmise, as well as demonstrating his virtuosity:

> *guðweard gumena   grimhelm gespeon,*
> cyning cinberge   (cumbol lixton)
> wiges on wenum,   **wælhlencan sceoc**,
> het his hereciste   healdan georne
> fæst fyrdgetrum...
> . . . .
> Ymb hine wægon   wigend unforhte,
> **hare heorawulfas**,   hilde gretton,
> þurstige þræcwiges,   þeodenholde.[36]
>
> (174-82)

[The war guardian of men fastened his masked helmet, the king his cheekguard, in expectation of war. The standards shone. The king shook his coat of armor, commanding his select warriors to hold strong in their battle formation.... About the king hoary sword-wolves, faithful to their lord, anticipated battle, thirsty for violent combat.]

In both the *Beowulf* and *Exodus* examples the armor shakes and warriors are tinged with a gray, wolfish aspect. Thus in the *Exodus* excerpt above "hare heorawulfas" surround their Egyptian leader, who encodes the battle-shiver ["wælhlencan sceoc"]. Recurring lexical features would seem to confirm a bond between the *Beowulf* and *Exodus* passages, with the following key phrases marking Óðinn's Storm:

---

[36] I cite *Exodus* from Lucas's edition.

B: guðsearo gumena ... grimhelmas
E: guðweard gumena grimhelm gespeon

Grim-, already noted earlier in the Viking longship example, would appear part of the deep structure of Óðinn's Storm, at least from what we can recover from surviving instances of this template. But what we observe is a system of "substitution" and "highlighting,"[37] a generative deep structure (of a finite or defining set of lexemes) which produce variable surface structures. This will not strike oral theorists as new, for it simply confirms the view of oral-derived verbal art posited by contemporary oral theory.

If we compare the passage from *Andreas* — in which a man-eating Myrmidonian host rouses itself — we see more clearly the compositional principles at work:

Duguð samnade,
hæðne hild*frecan*, heapum þrungon,
(guðsearo gullon, **garas hrysedon**),
bolgenmode, under bordhreoðan.[38]
(125b-8)

[The raging troop gathered under shield-cover, the heathen battle-wolves[?] thronged into a group (war-gear screamed, the spears shook.)]

While this scene represents perhaps a more elliptical deployment of the battle-storm template than the previous two passages, it nevertheless draws on its metonymic potential, with the mention of shaking spears ("garas hrysedon") and a quiet wolfish presence in "hildfrecan" [battle-wolves].[39] Despite its limited scope, the passage does offer a further glimpse of the substitutional field attached to "hrysedon": the subject of the verb, in these surviving examples, points to a favored variation of war-armor *or* weapons (such as spears). This will be especially suggestive for Laȝamon's treatment of the theme.

---

[37] Griffiths, "Convention and Originality," 179-99.

[38] I cite Krapp's edition of the poem in *Vercelli Book*.

[39] However, this semantic force is usually considered expended in the Anglo-Saxon period and the word comes to bear the more general meaning 'warrior.'

Writing Out "Óðinn's Storm"

Across the North Sea, we also find the shaking animals, spears, and iron in wintry contexts, and these motifs, unlike those in the Old English tradition, would seem linked more specifically to a Valhallian presence on the battlefield, to Óðinn's dispatch of the Valkyries. Among these "choosers of the slain" are the often paired "Hrist and Mist" [Shaker and Mist], whose figures may be the mythological inspiration for the tandem shaking/snow or dew battle-details. In *Helgaqviða Hundingsbana in fyrri* 47,[40] for example, we are told that amid dewy fields and warriors fighting "scalf Mistar marr" [the horse of Mist (=earth) shook]. This template coincides, lexically and imagistically, with the Old English passages cited above. So we find the hail-strewn trees, dew-coated fields, shaking (also dew-coated) animals:

> marir **hristuz**, stóð af mönom þeira
> **dögg í diúpa dali,**
> **hagl í háva viðo.**
> (stanza 28, 3-5)
>
> [horses shook, from their manes
> there came dew in deep dales,
> hail in tall woods.]

Gray spears mark Óðinn's Storm:

> ván qvað hann mundo veðrs ins micla
> **grára geira** oc gremi Óðins.
> (stanza 12, 3-4)
>
> [he said he would expect the great storm
> of gray spears [battle] and the wrath of Óðin.]

A warrior fighting is likened to a dew-slung creature:

> Svá bar Helgi af hildingom
> sem ... sá dýrkálfr, **döggo slunginn.**
> (stanza 38, 1-3)

---

[40] Neckel, *Edda*, 146.

[So Helgi rose above heroes
as the stag, slung with dew.]

Ravens and eagles move through battle hail-splattered or shaking:

Hlakkar **hagli stokkinn**
hræs es kømr at sævar
móðr krefr morginbráða
már valkastar báru.[41]

[The raven (seagull of the wave of the corpse-heap), besprinkled with hail, shrieks when it comes to blood (the corpse-sea); the tired one craves the morning food.]

valgammr skók í vápna rimmu
viðr Helganes blóðugt fiðri.[42]

[The slaughter-vulture (eagle) shook its bloody feathers in the weapon-fray near Helganess.]

And, of course, the warriors — in wolf-skins and bear-shirts — commence battle as iron shakes:

Grenjuðu berserkir,
Guðr vas þeim á sinnom;
Mjuðu **Ulfheðnar**,
ok ísörn **dúðu**.[43]

[The Bear-sarks bellowed;
battle was upon them;
the Wolf-coats howled
and the iron (spears?) shook.]

---

[41] F. Jónsson, *Skjaldedigtning*, 96.
[42] Kock, *Skaldediktningen*, 157.
[43] Aðalbjarnarson, *Heimskringla*, 116.

Even a selective survey, then, yields this heavily stylized portrayal of imminent or pitched battle. And just as Joseph Harris has illustrated the "ventriloquism of tradition" at work in *Beowulf* by culling analogues from early Germanic sources,[44] so we can do for *Brut* in this particular instance. What sticks to Laȝamon's wolf is a textual environment: snow-canopied trees, frost-covered animals, and battle-shivers mark its territory. So does a specific set of lexemes: OE *hrimig*, *hrisian*, and *grim* (or conceptual equivalents such as *græg* or *sceacan*), as well as the phrase "in deop dalu."

What will interest Germanicists and oral-theorists, though it cannot be explored fully in this limited study, is how Óðinn's Storm overlaps with the "hero-on-the-beach" and the "beasts-of-battle" type-scenes. In an incisive recent article on the beasts of battle, Mark Griffith observes that in Old English literature, just as the beasts of battle often exhibit human characteristics, so warriors frequently exhibit "beast-like" qualities.[45] Moreover, what often establishes this beast-like quality is the blurring of animal coats and armor, wherein the dewy-feathered bird's plumage and the hoary coat of the wolf "can be seen to function as analogues of the armour or warriors."[46] This applies readily, as we have seen above, to those instances in which the grayish component vacillates among armor, weapons, and wolf-coats. But I suspect, too, that this theriomorphic edge works within the frame of Óðinn's Storm: the details of snow, mist, and shaking point to a Valhallian or, perhaps more specifically, a valkyrian presence. Regardless of these potential ambiguities, the Germanic subtext recovered should catalyze the dormant metonymic charge of Laȝamon's wolf image: we might now hear Arthur's rattling armor in the snow-shiver of the wolf; we might better sense the extraordinary power of this initiate warrior, whose ferocity recalls metamorphic wolf-warriors; and we might envision a larger battle-storm topography, one filled with snow-hung trees, beasts of battle, and gray-mailed hosts.

Having now established this traditional template, we can return to Laȝamon's wolf simile and other instances of Óðinn's Storm, to compare their uses of the template in the two versions of *Brut*. As will become evident, the Otho-poet is less comfortable with the inherited battle-storm template; but his response is neither necessarily uniform, nor necessarily

---

[44] J. Harris, "Literary History," 32.
[45] Griffith, "Convention and Originality," 190.
[46] Griffith, "Convention and Originality," 191.

indicative of someone unfamiliar with the stock oral-derived element. On the contrary, on at least one occasion he shows evidence of participating in the kind of "formulaic reading" that likely perpetuated this narrative template.[47]

Both versions of *Brut* feature two deployments of the wolf similes, the Arthur-wolf comparison which we have been considering throughout this paper and an earlier Corineus-wolf simile (below "A") that also invokes a "rimie wulf." What becomes evident in these passages is that the Otho-poet displaces, in part, the snow-covered wolf in favor of a more Mediterranean-based model: he reinscribes a savage sheep-attacking wolf that would probably have had more resonance for his Anglo-Norman audience:

>(A) C: Corineus heom rasde to: swa þe **rimie** wulf
> þane he wule on **scheapen:** scaðe-werc wrchen.
> (Caligula, 774-5)

[Corineus rushed at him like a rime-covered wolf when it wishes to attack sheep.]

>O: Corineus him resde to: ase þe **wilde** wolf
> wane he wole ama[ng] **seep:** eni harm wirche.
> (Otho, 774-5)

[Corineus rushed at him like a wild wolf when it wishes to work harm against sheep.]

>(B) C: Vp bræid Arður his sceld: foren to his breosten.
> 7 he gon to rusien: swa þe **runie** wulf.
> þenne he cumeð of holt: bi-honged mid snawe.
> and þencheð to biten swulc: **deor** swa him likeð.
> (Caligula,10040-3)

>O: Vp brayd Arður his seald: forn to his breoste.
> and he gan to rese: so þe **wode** wolf.

---

[47] See further O'Brien O'Keeffe, *Visible Song*, 47-76, *et passim*, and Watson, "Affective Poetics."

>   wane he comeð of holte: bi-honge mid snowe.
>   and þencheþ to bite: woch **seap** þat him likeþ.
>
>   (Otho, 10040-3)

> [Up raised Arthur his shield in front of his chest, and he began to shake like the mad wolf when he comes from the holt hung with snow intending to snare whichever sheep he pleases.]

Whether a "frost-gray wolf" may have ceased being a productive cue for his audience, or whether he simply did not understand the word "rimie"/ "runie," the Otho-poet "writes out," in part, the inherited template: the revisions here are not merely single word substitutions ["rimie" > "wilde"; "runie" > "wod"; "deor" > "seap"]; the words displace an entire cognitive world, supplanting it with a rival lupine school. Of course, it is difficult to say whether this lupine school derives from Christian rhetoric or from proverbial usage, where mad wolf/sheep collocations are rife; but we do know that such mad-wolf similes had currency in thirteenth-century southwestern England, the environment in which *Brut* was produced. The *Life of St. Katherine* (c. 1225), for instance, attests to such wolf-idioms:

>   Bigon [Maxence] anan **asa wed wulf**
>   to weorrin hali chirche.
>
>   (31-2)

> [Maxence, like a mad wolf, began to war against the holy church.]

>   Under þis, com þe þurs Maxence,
>   **þe wed wulf**, þe heaðene hund
>   aȝein to his kineburh.[48]
>
>   (1857-9)

> [At this time, the giant Maxence — the mad wolf, the heathen hound — returned to his kingdom.]

---

[48] I cite Einenkel's edition of the poem.

The Caligula-poet is evidently not free from such discourse: his Corineus simile forms an odd hybrid as well: a frost-covered wolf chasing sheep. What we see here is, ultimately, the loosening ancient identification of wolf and warrior (indeed, even the movement to a similaic rather than a metaphoric space enacts this movement [cf. OE "hare heorawulfas"]; nevertheless, one can still perceive a glint of the Germanic "wulf mære" — the creature's "noble tenacity" which the *Germani* clearly venerated[49] — or what W. R. J. Barron and Carole Weinberg have called La3amon's "contempt for the harried sheep" and "half-reluctant awe of the wolf."[50] La3amon's "reluctant awe" need not be understood as an abstract ambivalence, for the lupine conflict is preserved in language, in the hybrid responses of the Caligula- and Otho-poets.

Despite joint erosion of the metonymic template in the two versions of the *Brut*, Caligula is clearly more fluent in the Óðinn's Storm idioms. For instance, just before the armies of Hengest and Aurelien clash in Scotland, La3amon triggers the battle-storm template with his metonymic detail: awaiting Hengest's forces, Aurelien constructs a "sceld-trume" [shield-formation] that the Caligula-poet likens to a hoary wood:

> him-seolf he nom his eorles: 7 his **aðele kempes**.
> 7 his holdeste men: þa he hæfde an londe.
> 7 makede his sceld-trume: swulc it weoren an **hær** wude.
> (Caligula, 8168–70)

> him-seolf he nam his eorles: and his **stronge cnihtes**.
> . . . .
> and makede one soltrome: ase hit were a **wilde** wode.
> (Otho, 8168–70)

Not only does the Otho-poet struggle with the image of the "hær wude" (or simply prefers the more romance-familiar "wilde wode"), but the most recent translators of *Brut* seem divided, once again, on the semantic force of the image, one envisaging a "thicket of bare tree-trunks," the other "a winter-hoary wood":

---

[49] Glosecki, *Shamanism*, 190.
[50] *La3amon's Arthur*, ed. and trans. Barron and Weinberg, line 843.

> He himself, choosing his chieftains and his noble warriors and the most trusty men in arms he had there, so formed his phalanx that it was **like a thicket of bare tree-trunks.**[51]

> He himself took his earls and his excellent warriors,
> And the most loyal men whom he had in his land,
> And he formed up his shield-wall **like a winter-hoary wood.**[52]

Based on what we have already discovered about Óðinn's Storm, one must champion the latter reading (R. Allen's). More a marker of the traditional milieu, the "hær wude" carries inherent meaning, which does not allow for much denotative license, for the evocation of bare tree-trunks, lyrical though it may be. The power here rests not with a lyric semanticism but with an oral-derived word-power. Conventional matter is most likely intended with the Byrhtnoð-like Aurelien, who musters his troops into the shield-wall, surrounding himself with his most loyal ("holdost") men.[53] We find also in the *Exodus* example mentioned earlier, with the shaking armor and hoary battle-wolves, the same stock idea: the king ordering his "hereciste" [select warriors] to stand in their "fyrdgetrum" [battle-formation].

Indeed, one can locate Caligula's stylized image of the hoary-wood battle aspect along a textual and temporal continuum. The image has its prototypes in the *Beowulf* troop's spear-cluster, "æscholt ufan græg" (330a) [an ash-holt gray from above], the eddic "hagl í hava viðo" [hail in tall woods], extends through Laȝamon's *Brut*, and persists into later alliterative verse. In *The Wars of Alexander*, for instance, a kindred "hare wode" [hoary wood] image — one that will recall the example of Magnus's frost-sheeted

---

[51] *Laȝamon's Arthur*, ed. and trans. Barron and Weinberg, lines 8168-70.

[52] R. Allen, *Lawman: Brut*, 8168-70.

[53] Cf. *Maldon* 22-4:
  Þa he hæfde þæt folc fægere getrymmed,
  he lihte þa mid leodon þær him leofost wæs,
  þær he his heorðwerod holdost wiste.
  [Then he had the troops neatly arrayed. He alighted among the host, where it was dearest to him, where he knew his most faithful hearth-band to be.]
I cite Dobbie's edition of the poem from *Minor Poems*.

prow mentioned above — lends texture to a looming sea-battle. As the *Wars*-poet paints his scene with "grete schipis full of grym wapens" (65) [great ships full of grim weapons] and "full of breneid bernes" (66) [full of mail-clad warriors], he says of the awesome navy portrayed:

> Slik was þe multitude of mast so mekil & so thike
> Þat all him þo3t bot he treis **a hare wod it semyd**.
> (69–70)[54]

[Such was the multitude of masts so great and so thick, that all of them thought the boat[s] trees — a hoary wood it seemed.]

Hence, when the Otho-poet writes out this traditional battle idiom of shield-walls and winter-hoary trees, he discards a usage that is linked to a continuum of performances. Such revisions presume an editor at work whose intent would accord with Cannon's romance-reviser: the Otho-poet *does* seem to recognize traditional matter and *does* like to excise it. This raises the question of his fluency, or "competence," with formulaic idioms: if we can exclude his being a "less poetically minded person," as I think we can, then the Otho-poet elides either from difficulty with the language (as Cannon suggests in part) or from a knowledge of traditional oral-derived composition.

While we cannot exclude the possibility of his struggling with arcane diction and concepts, one passage at least suggests he may have been more fluent in formulaic composition than has been acknowledged in the past. In the only other occurrence of the verb *rusien* in the entire *Brut* narrative, we find this verb keying Óðinn's Storm once again, as a Roman troop moves in for an ambush on Arthur's men. Strikingly, the substitution here is less the signature of romance revision than of formulaic reading, as Caligula has burnies shaking, and Otho weapons:

> Þa riden Rom-leoden: **riseden burnen**.
> **quahten** on hafden: helmes he3en.
> seldes on rugge: ræ3e Rom-leoden.
> (Caligula, 13435–7)

---

[54] I cite the *Wars* from Skeat's edition.

Writing Out "Óðinn's Storm" 233

[Then the Roman troop rode forth, their chain-mail shook; they shook their high helmets on their heads and the shields on their backs — the bold Roman-host!]

þo ride Romleode: **rusede wepne.**
setten (an h)ire h..(e)des heȝe hi(re he)al(mes).
(Otho, 13435-7)

[Then the Roman troop rode forth, their weapons shook; they put their high (helmets on their heads).]

Though the Otho text is damaged in part, the damage has not affected the relevant substitutions ("burnen" > "wepne"; "quahten" > "setten"). Like the *Exodus* king who shakes his mail-coat and like the Beowulfian sea-band whose "syrcan hrysedon" [mail-corslets shook], Caligula's Roman troop shake their raised helmets and shields in anticipation of battle, while their "riseden burnen" (the phrase "ane deope dale" occurs less than ten lines after this action [13444]). In characteristic fashion, the Otho-poet mutes the metonymic dimension by stilling the helmet-shivering, shield-rattling troop. But his use of "wepne" does not strike me as happenstance; rather, his usage points toward formulaic reading, a dip into the traditional lexemic and conceptual reservoir. For as was apparent from our Germanic subtext reconstruction, the favored subjects of *rusien* (or another verb conveying the shaking) were either the armor (as in *Beowulf* and *Exodus*) or the weapons (cf. "garas hrysedon" and "ísarn dúðu").

Indeed, looking to an analogous instance, we find further evidence that the Otho-poet may have been formulaically productive. Even though he can write with denotative precision, supplanting the epic-based forms with romance terminology, he is also capable of entering an elastic compositional mode characteristic of oral-derived verbal art: as is evident in his weapon-for-armor swap, the Otho-poet can be compositionally productive with the Óðinn's Storm unit. Generally speaking, he is quite precise when it comes to armor and weapons; he may occasionally substitute the word "wepne" for another term, but it displaces a semantically comparable term, e.g., "wi-æxe" [war-ax] (3349). "Burne" (or "brune") is most often retained in Otho, though we find a few exceptions: Caligula: "mid burne bihonged" [clad in chain-mail] > Otho: "mid stele bi-honge" [clad in steel] (13306) and Caligula: "þah he hefde brunie on" [though he was clad in chain-mail] > "þeh he bere yre an" [though he was clad in iron] (778). In both instances, the armor is replaced with a comparable quality, i.e., steel or iron, but not with a new image. At only one other time does the Otho-poet substitute "wepne" for "burne," and, again, Óðinn's Storm looms. Before the Briton King Wither is treacherously killed by Hamun (a Roman disguised as a Briton soldier), he is said to have retreated from a fight in his sweaty armor:

> Þe king wende forð-rihtes: bihælues þan fihte.
> he wes swiðe of-hæt: þat al his **burne wes bi-swæt**.
> he lette his burne of his rugge eorne.
> (Caligula, 4645-7)

[The king turned away from the fight. He was overheated, so that all his armor was covered in sweat. He let his armor fall from his back.]

Otho has some textual damage in these lines, but the passage in which the substitution occurs is not affected:

> . . (king) wende forþ-rih... .(i-ha)lue þan fihte.
> and (lete hi)s brunie of his rug(ge val)le.
> for he was swiþe afe(a)t: and his **wepne al bi-swat**.
> (Otho, 4645-7)

[the king turned away from the fight and he let his armor fall from his back, as he was overheated and his weapon covered in sweat.]

Of course, one expects soldiers to sweat in the heat of battle; but the *Brut* renderings above have a peculiar ring: the sweat clings not to the king's person, as it were, but to his war-gear — his armor (Caligula) and his weapon (Otho). Though we must be cautious about overgeneralizing the possibilities of Óðinn's Storm, lest it lose its distinctive qualities, it is worth noting that such external battle "sweats" are well attested in earlier Germanic verse. Like dew and snow, ON *sveiti* [blood, or sweat] cloaks items in the battle milieu: horses, warriors, and ships. In Old Norse poetry, the word *sveiti* often occurs as part of a set phrase, "sveiti stokkin," which is usually understood as 'covered in blood.' In the eddic verse, for instance, "sveita stokkinn" occurs three times, invoked at the start or close of battle. In *Fáfnismál* 32, Sigurðr, "sveita stokkinn," roasts Fáfnir's heart after killing the man-dragon; in *Guðrúnarkviða önnor* 4, Sigurðr's horse Grani retreats from battle and is said to be coated in blood (or sweat?): "öll vóro söðuldýr sveita stoccin"; and, in a final instance from *Reginsmál* 16, the phrase is clearly placed within the context of Óðinn's Storm. Given a boat to avenge his father, Sigurðr (along with his companion Reginn) sails into a great storm, which accompanies Óðinn's sudden appearance on a promontory. As the ship struggles in the high waves much like King Magnús's Viking longship, Óðinn asks who goes through the storm in the "seglvigg ero sveiti stoccin" [blood- (or sweat-?)covered wave-horse]. The detail of blood or possibly sweat sticking to the ship may satisfy the requisite moisture-laden item that encodes the Valhallian presence, just as the posited flashing-light element of the hero-on-the-beach type-scene can have a variable denotative source — the sun, a gleaming helmet, a shining sea-cliff, and so on. For an audience familiar with the conventions of Germanic verse, Laȝamon's sweat-covered armor and weapons might have portended the king's imminent slaughter (which, indeed, follows in the next few lines). But we must wonder also if the Laȝamon texts, with their odd images of sweaty armor and weapons, reflect a debased formula: is this "bi-swæt" (which is the only occurrence of this word-form in the *Brut* texts) a corruption of a traditional metonym?

That the Otho-poet enters a more elastic space — a formulaically conditioned mode — is not only evident in the armor-for-weapon substitution but also in the uncharacteristic looseness and rearrangement of the ideas. His inversion, for instance, of Caligula's lines 4646–7 can be read in one of two ways: he either leaves textual exactness behind or improves the causative force of the passage (i.e., he includes "for"). Either scenario, I propose, witnesses formulaic reading. He either re-performs the conventional passage (with little textual dependence on Caligula) or concentrates on revising the causative relation of the clause (a literate strategy?), while, at the same time, drawing — perhaps unwittingly — from the traditional deep structure. In each case, we find the exchangeable image that characterizes the metonymic, oral-derived mind: it does not really matter whether it is a frost-covered longship or a frost-covered wolf, and it does not really matter whether it is a sweat-coated mail-corselet or a sweat-coated spear. What matters is that the metonymically productive detail is present. That the "battle-sweat" image, which may originally have been associated with a dew- or blood-soaking, is attributed to a warrior being overheated might be evidence of scribal reinvention: a textual moment in which a scribe tries to make sense of unfamiliar, formulaic vestiges.[55]

As thirteenth-century scribal-poetic recomposers of the late twelfth-century *Brut*, the two Laȝamons combine oral-derived and literate sensibilities to read and produce their individual texts. And while each can decode and encode some oral-derived content — as is evident in their treatment of the Óðinn's Storm template — their responses vary: the Caligula-poet is generally more receptive to the epic-based features, whereas the Otho-poet often elides these resonant components in favor of a romance (or more contemporary) idiom. Throughout much of my argument, I have presumed that the two Laȝamons draw from a common manuscript or closely related exemplars, as is generally assumed by contemporary *Brut* scholarship. But it should be observed that, because the exemplars may not be exact replications, what I have called the "formulaically productive" styles of the Caligula- and Otho-poets (as evident in their variance of "burne" and "wepne") may reflect the divergent readings of the two *earlier* cousin exemplars. In this case, we must ascribe the formulaic productivity to an earlier generation and not to our thirteenth-century transcribers. Yet, allowing for this possibility, our argument concerning the convergence of oral and written in post-Conquest England does not change in its essential form: there is evidence that scribes could both perpetuate the formulaic reading habits of pre-Conquest verse and simultaneously reconfigure a text to accord with a more semantically precise, literate standard. This oral–literate nexus is at the core of Laȝamon's two texts, and the cognitive tensions evident in it provide us with a window onto a shifting world.

---

[55] For further examples of scribal reinvention in *Brut*, see Watson, "Affective Poetics."

JOSEPH FALAKY NAGY

A Leash and an *Englyn* in the Medieval Welsh Arthurian Tale *Culhwch ac Olwen*

Whether or not there was a pipeline operating in medieval Celtic literatures between venerable and ongoing oral traditions and what we find in the surviving manuscripts from medieval Ireland and Wales, the vast majority of these texts make the claim that there was, and that what emanated from native tradition onto the manuscript page was perhaps comparable to but still different in content and form from what the medieval Celtic *literati* encountered there in the first place, namely, biblical and classical/late-antique texts. This is a conceit we have to take seriously if we are to understand the modes of validation by which the Irish and Welsh vernacular text presented itself as a legitimate document to its contemporary audience and to a hypothetical posterity, and as a link in a chain of authentic representations of the past that extended down through the ages. There is no challenge issued anywhere in medieval Celtic literary traditions to the underlying assumption that the commemoration of what *was* in the past, and what was *known* in oral tradition, is the primary goal of literature, as it is the goal of most if not all other nascent literary traditions.

An earlier version of this paper was given as a presentation in a panel on medieval oral tradition organized by Mark C. Amodio at the annual meeting of the Pacific Ancient and Modern Language Association, held at the University of California, Irvine, November 1996.

But (and this is perhaps where the diversity characteristic of medieval Celtic literatures comes most impressively into view), there *is* much doubt expressed in our texts as to the efficiency of the process of grafting by which an oral tradition comes to be incorporated into, represented in, and even superseded by writing. This doubt manifests itself in the numerous medieval Celtic literary myths (I would call them) that are overtly about the origins of literature or of particular texts, but also in many stories circulating in literary tradition that only implicitly but no less informatively address issues having to do with their provenance and affiliation. Especially in narratives having to do with a heroic search for the unknown or the otherworldly, often a search is simultaneously launched for knowledge and its fabled possessor, a figure located in legendary space and time. When these prove elusive, the text calls its ability to locate and handle such knowledge into question; when the knowledge and its possessor are found, they usually prove to be too much for the text to process or contain properly, by the text's own admission. The much-celebrated confidence of medieval Celtic *literati* in their ability to generate a vernacular written style and corpus, and their embracing everything from the Bible and the remains of classical literature to native stories as grist for their past-producing mill, are balanced by a nagging worry about the integrity, accuracy, and efficiency of their texts.

This worry frequently manifests itself in a juxtaposition to be found in many of our medieval Celtic texts, a bringing together of discursive registers that have traditionally been seen by Celticists as forming a generally harmonious whole, namely, the medium of *prosimetrum*. According to some scholars attuned to comparable texts in Vedic and Classical Sanskrit literature, the predilection for the prosimetric is another reflection of the Celts' Indo-European heritage.[1] Narration in medieval Irish and Welsh literature is a job almost always carried by prose, but narrative texts often feature poetic passages, which in quantity typically amount to far less than the prose. (Poetry in all its generic variety is also to be found in manu-

---

[1] A description of *prosimetrum* in medieval Celtic literatures and a critical evaluation of scholarly approaches to it, including the theory of Indo-European origins, are usefully presented in MacCana, "Prosimetrum." J. Harris and Reichl's *Prosimetrum*, a collection of surveys of prosimetric composition in various oral and literary traditions, including the valuable introduction by the editors, is a *sine qua non* for any comparative consideration of the mixing of discursive registers in narrative texts.

scripts by itself, with a brief prose introduction or frame, or embedded in non-narrative texts, such as law tracts.) The prominence of *prosimetrum* in early literary discourse in Irish and Welsh is an overlooked "given" in readings of this literature, which are occasionally enlivened by the controversial assertion that behind the manuscript manifestations of *prosimetrum* lie a native performative style and the domain of practicing professional storytellers. In the study of medieval Welsh literature a cottage industry arose in the last century centered on the speculative process of reconstructing purportedly lost prose narrative frames for a considerable body of early poetry, on the assumption that these were not recorded since they were supposed to be improvised by the storyteller.[2] In fact, at least one scholar very much of our time has thrown a good deal of salutary cold water on such attempts at reconstruction, pointing out that much of this poetry could have had value for the original audience even outside a narrative frame.[3]

Still, while there may be argument over the original performative or textual setting of certain poems that have survived in manuscripts, the pervasive assumption remains unchallenged among scholars that, when there are what can be described as a prose frame and poetry embedded in it, a basic cooperation between the prose and the poetry is to be expected, even if the composition of one is chronologically anterior to that of the other. The aesthetics of the tradition, according to this assumption, demand of the competent composer/compiler that he arrange for a fit as close as possible. Prose as frame forms an overarching referent which the embedded signs of the poems bolster and embellish. These are the notions I would like to challenge in this paper, where a not untypical case is presented in which the combination of prose and poetry not only creates *formal* tension but signals a *thematic* tension in the text as well, a tension that reflects a profound mistrust of the process of textualization itself. The voice raised in song within the prose narrative text often resists that text, presenting a completely different point of view on the origins, proceedings, and direction of the story.

---

[2] Rowland, *Early Welsh Saga Poetry*, builds upon the scholarship of Sir Ifor Williams and others who grappled with these seemingly disembodied poetic texts earlier in the century.

[3] See Ford, *Poetry of Llywarch Hen*, 48-62.

But how do we distinguish the poetry from the prose, and did our medieval Celtic *literati* verifiably distinguish the two themselves? In *prosimetrum* as it appears in both Irish and Welsh texts, the language (prosody, syntax, diction) of poetic utterance is not only more marked than that of prose but also tends to be explicitly indicated. What we would call the poetic insert is usually set off and characterized by the impersonal prose narrator by means of one of the various words for "poem" or "sing, versify" available to him. What we as readers "see" as a poetic text (especially as presented in editions and translations) is not simply labeled as such but typically introduced by the narrator as a poetic performance. X, a character in the story, spoke, composed, or sang P, the poem X "performs." That this is meant to be understood as genuinely an individual's performance, and a musical one at that, is demonstrated in both Irish and Welsh by the frequent use of the verb *canaid* (Irish)/*canu* (Welsh) 'sing' (cognate with Latin *cano*) to designate the action of the character to whom the poem/song is attributed, whether he/she plays a role in the story or is an after-the-fact commentator on it. Moreover, the semantic field of Celtic *can-, including compounded forms, includes both the concept of "compose" and that of "perform," both of which apply to the characteristic poetic utterance of *prosimetrum*, which is presented as spontaneously composed – that is, reactive and commemorative, as opposed to predetermined and fixed in memory. In other words, the markedness of poetic discourse as it appears in *prosimetrum* resides to a considerable degree not only in its meaning being a function of context (you, the listener/reader, had to be there) but also in the attribution of its very existence to that context (*it*, the poem, had to be there).

All of this, however, is not to say that the song embedded in the story simply reiterates or amplifies what the story has to say. Unlike the designs of narration as they are fleshed out in the prose of the literary text, the song in *prosimetrum* accidentally "happens," sometimes precipitating out of the situation at hand, but also sometimes seeming to come out of nowhere, a disembodied voice that challenges the impersonal storytelling intelligence that frames the text. As one recurring device in the the medieval Irish heroic tale *Táin Bó Cúailnge* [*Cattle Raid of Cúailnge*] for introducing poetry puts it, even when there is no doubt who is speaking poetically, "co cloth ní" [and then something was heard].[4]

---

[4] E.g., *Táin Bó Cúailnge*, ed. O'Rahilly, 34-5.

A Leash and an Englyn

How can something "that is heard," to quote the Irish cueing device, do anything but disturb the surface of the written page? And how can the cultural forces that license the song as an authoritative performance and a means of negotiating distance between an audience and a performer be restrained from running amok if they are allowed to seep into an artifact that aspires to break free of the tyranny of the moment, and the tyranny of the necessity for constant, delicate negotiation between audience and performer, that is, the artifact of the written text? If song, understood as taking shape in the context of oral performance, is allowed into the realm of written prose, can we expect anything less than a war of words, a *logomachia* that inevitably drags in the words' referents as well?

Of course, the song that throws down the gauntlet to prose and casts what has just happened in the narrative in perhaps a drastically different light can equally well cast doubt on the assumptions underlying the sense the prose is trying to make of the entire series of events it strings together as narrative. A remarkable example of song that threatens to overturn the text and the project it embodies can be found in a medieval Welsh text that, like the ancient Greek *Iliad* and the medieval Irish *Táin*, presents to the modern reader, as it probably did to its original audiences, a dual-purpose template, demonstrating both the standards of heroic behavior and speech that obtain in heroic narrative and the standards governing the production of story out of the various local traditions known to the oral storyteller and subsequently the literary composer.

The tale, commonly known today as *Culhwch ac Olwen*, is the earliest surviving example of extended Arthurian narrative, running to 1246 lines of almost all prose in the available critical edition. Typically in medieval Welsh manuscripts there is no difference in the presentation of poetry and prose as text. The brief shift from prose to poetry in *Culhwch ac Olwen* to be discussed below is not marked visibly in either manuscript that contains the text. The text is preserved in two fourteenth-century manuscripts each of which preserves the eleven tales, essentially what has survived of medieval Welsh non-historical narrative, that have come to be known collectively as the *Mabinogion*. These sources, the White Book of Rhydderch (the earlier manuscript, containing only two thirds of our text) and the Red Book of Hergest, clearly are not dependent on each other; they appear to have derived the text of *Culhwch ac Olwen* from a third (lost) source, or perhaps they even represent two different lines of transmission for this particular tale, the language of which points to the eleventh or twelfth century as the period of composition. Designed almost like a time capsule, *Culhwch ac Olwen* provides a great deal of evidence for scholars in search of what Arthurian tradition was like before the dissemination of Geoffrey of Monmouth's highly popular and influential portrait of Arthur in *Historia Regum Britanniae*, but it is also a text that ends up teasing more than satisfying a modern reader. A work crammed with names and details from what are by now mostly obscure stories from the pre-*Historia* Arthur cycle, *Culhwch ac Olwen* has been read by critics as the closest approximation we have to medieval Welsh oral tradition, the last gasp of the heroic tale, an everything-but-the-kitchen sink parody of the genre, or a botched and bookish attempt to tell what is in essence a rather simple story, penned by a writer who bit off far more than he could chew.[5] The plot has to do with Arthur and his men accomplishing the tasks set for Arthur's cousin and protégé Culhwch (whose birth and youth are recounted in the first part of the text) by the giant Ysbaddaden, father of Olwen, loved sight unseen by Culhwch as the result of a curse-like destiny imposed upon the young hero by his resentful stepmother. At the end of the story, with the accomplishment of a sampling of the forty-odd tasks, the giant is slain, Culhwch wins Olwen, and the heroic company of Arthur (who is more a leader of hunts and expeditions than a king here) disperses, presumably to be reassembled on the occasion of the next adventure.

Culhwch ac Olwen might seem a curious choice to those familiar with medieval Celtic literatures as an example of *prosimetrum*, since it contains only one explicit instance of switching from prose to poetry in the course of the story. In general, the tales of the *Mabinogion* offer slim pickings, quantitatively speaking, for the exploration of prosimetric composition. Apart from the one in *Culhwch ac Olwen*, there are only two other examples of explicit switching from a prosaic to a poetic register, in the second and fourth branches of the Mabinogi. In all three cases the verse utterance is in the form of the *englyn*, consisting of three or four lines with fixed numbers of syllables and end rhyme, a form used for epigrammatic or gnomic comment. Altogether, then, there are only five stanzas' worth of poetry in the body of the *Mabinogion*, three of these *englynion* forming a chain in the episode of the fourth Branch where the breakthrough into

---

[5] See, for example, Edel, *Helden auf Freierfüssen*; Radner, "Interpreting Irony"; Roberts, "*Culhwch ac Olwen*, the Triads, Saints' Lives"; Davies, *Crefft y Cyfarwydd*, 63–71, and elsewhere.

poetic language occurs. And yet, I would argue, it is precisely the paucity of poetry in these texts that makes these breakthroughs all the more conspicuous, meaningful, and representative of what *prosimetrum* seeks to accomplish in medieval Celtic texts.

Specifically in *Culhwch ac Olwen*, a singular, centrally placed *englyn* emanating from Arthur, who provides the narrative's base of operations, cynically wreaks havoc with established heroic convention and reputation, and strikes a discordant note as plangent as any to be found elsewhere in European medieval literature. We "hear" this note after the tale has shifted its focus from Culhwch to Arthur and to the job of obtaining the forty *anoethau* [wonders] requested by Ysbaddaden, a considerable undertaking that Arthur has assumed on behalf of his cousin. Before the episode featuring the solitary *englyn*, the search for the *anoethau*, with one exception, proves to be a smooth operation, exemplary of the courage, persistence, and generosity thanks to which Arthur and his retinue retain pride of place in posterity. In a definitive statement he makes early on in our text, Arthur himself expresses his awareness of the need for him and his men to take on and conduct such adventures according to the high standards tradition has set for them. He responds thus to the objection of Cei, his right-hand man and a key figure in this as well as other early Welsh Arthurian texts, to allowing the persistent Culhwch into Arthur's court after their meal has started:

> Na wir, Kei wynn. Ydym wyrda hyt tra yn dygyrcher. Yd ytuo mwyhaf y kyuarws a rothom, mwyuwy uyd yn gwrdaaeth ninheu ac an cret ac an hetmic.

> [Not so, fair Cei. We are nobles as long as anyone seeks us out; the greater the favor we bestow, the greater shall be our nobility, our fame, and our honor.][6]

In the course of Arthur's company getting a good start on the *anoethau* and living up to this consciously cultivated reputation, valiant figures of

---

[6] Bromwich and Evans, ed., *Culhwch and Olwen*, 5-6; translation from Ford, *Mabinogi*, 125. I thank my old student Vimal Duggal for having pointed out to me the centrality of this statement to the ethos the text strives both to exemplify and to critique.

legend long held prisoner and thought lost are rescued; the oldest of animals is found and interviewed; a female and her children mysteriously turned into wolves in a cave are located by Arthur and returned to their natural forms by God himself, for Arthur's sake; and, in an episode charmingly redolent of the märchenesque air that pervades the tale in general, a fire threatening to destroy an anthill is removed by Gwythyr, a member of Arthur's court, and subsequently the ants offer their services to Arthur – a valuable contribution to the larger task, since it is they, the text tells us, who will later provide the exact amount of linseed required by Ysbaddaden as one of the *anoethau*, a task that would otherwise have been impossible for Arthur and company to obtain.

In Celtic tradition heroes are deemed to be at their most heroic not only when they are fighting nobly and invincibly but also when they are recovering and upholding the "truth" of the tradition by which they are deemed heroic. Hence the recovery of the prisoners Eidoel and Mabon, missing since the beginning of historical time and by implication in possession of long-lost lore, the identification of the oldest of animals, and having the chance to hear their stories about ancient times all add considerable lustre to the accomplishments of Arthur's men as they methodically tackle the tasks at hand. Their pursuit of the *anoethau*, however, starts out with an unexpected find, in an adventure that does not come about as the result of any planning on the part of Arthur or his men, and that shows how devious their methods can be. This episode forms a pair with the one featuring the poetic breakthrough at the end of this sequence of episodes, insofar as each features a *cawr* [giant] and his undoing through trickery. Culhwch, Cei, and the other companions who have made the journey to Ysbaddaden's court (but not including Arthur himself) serendipitously come upon the dwelling of the giant Wrnach, whose sword constituted the last in the sequence of *anoethau* stipulated by Ysbaddaden. Cei, going incognito, pretends to be merely a disinterested sword repairman who would be happy to fix the sword of the *cawr*, but, while pretending to be sheathing it, he uses the sword to decapitate Wrnach. The weapon, with the taint of the circumstances through which it was obtained, is presented to Arthur without further comment from the text or the principals in the story. Then the pursuit of the other *anoethau* continues, as summarized above, until another giant who possesses something needed for the getting of Olwen is found, also by happenstance.

Seemingly in between assignments, Cei and his perennial companion Bedwyr (the Welsh original of the later figure of Sir Bedivere, just as Cei is the prototype for Sir Kay) come upon a giant roasting a pig in the wilderness, a figure that Cei recognizes as Dillus Farfawg [Dillus the Bearded]. Cei explains his significance to Bedwyr, referring back to a task imposed by Ysbaddaden:

> Nyt oes yn y byt kynllyuan a dalyo Drutwyn keneu Greit uab Eri namyn kynllyuan o uaryf y gwr a wely di racko. Ac ny mwynhaa heuyt onyt yn vyw y tynnir a chyllellprenneu o'e uaraf, kanys breu uyd yn uarw.
>
> [There is no leash that can hold Drudwyn, the whelp of Greid son of Eri, except a leash made from the beard of the fellow you see there. But it will be of no use unless the hairs are plucked with wooden tweezers while he is yet alive, for they'll be brittle when he's dead.][7]

A leash is needed for the dog Drudwyn, the obtaining of whom is another task, so that the great wild boar Twrch Trwyth can be hunted down with the hound's participation, so that the comb and scissors on the boar's head may be obtained, so that with these implements Ysbaddaden, per his request, may be given a proper haircut for his daughter's wedding. Here we have a typical example of the interlinkedness of the *anoethau* that are the serial goals of this multi-stage quest.

Cei obtains the giant's whiskers by stealth. He waits until the giant falls asleep after his meal, then digs a giant-size pit into which he pitches the unsuspecting Dillus, and together with Bedwyr plucks out the beard follicle by follicle while the giant, stuck in the pit, sits helplessly. Cei and Bedwyr finally slay the depilated *cawr* and proceed to Arthur's residence with the leash, made out of whiskers paradoxically gathered while their owner was still alive, but in their detatched state telling evidence that he is dead. Grimly evident in the Dillus episode, as in the previous giant epi-

---

[7] Bromwich and Evans, *Culhwch and Olwen*, 34-5; Ford, *Mabinogi*, 150. The rare word "kyllellprenneu" [wooden tweezers] is also used in connection with Wrnach's sword (Bromwich and Evans, *Culhwch and Olwen*, 30). While the meaning of this word is not altogether clear in this context, its presence establishes yet another link between these "tricked giant" episodes.

sode, where Cei sharpens Wrnach's sword only to use it against him, and in the grand finale of the brutal shaving and decapitation of Ysbaddaden,[8] slain by a hero who is named and comes to prominence in the adventure of Wrnach's court,[9] is a motif of trimming giants or their possessions, even to the point of removing their hair and head.

It has been noted that the incident of Arthur's encounter with the giant Retho in Book Ten of Geoffrey of Monmouth's *Historia*, where it is the beard-collecting giant who threatens to remove's Arthur's facial hair, was probably inspired by stories in Welsh tradition such as this one about Dillus.[10] In the latter text, the incident with Retho and the adventure of Arthur's fight with the monstrous giant on St. Michael's Mount, within which the reference to Arthur's earlier encounter with Retho is embedded, form a refreshingly different intrusion of "folk" and popular Arthurian elements into Geoffrey's narrative, serving to enliven his account of Arthur's campaign on the continent. The giants in *Culhwch ac Olwen* may serve a similar function, evoking the vast oral tradition that both inspires the content of the literary text and militates against the strictures of acceptable behavior and narrative content that it aspires to impose. Gigantism is in fact one of the characteristics of ancient knower figures in Celtic traditions. In medieval Irish literature, for instance, the revived Fergus, who tells the story of the *Táin* to the storytellers of Ireland (who have let it slip from their repertoire),[11] the old Fenian heroes who encounter St. Patrick on his mission to convert Ireland and tell him all they know about the

---

[8] Bromwich and Evans, *Culhwch and Olwen*, 42; Ford, *Mabinogi*, 157.

[9] Bromwich and Evans, *Culhwch and Olwen*, 30; Ford, *Mabinogi*, 146. The naming of Goreu as a result of his being able to penetrate the dwelling of Wrnach is parallel to the ritual hair-cutting Arthur gives Culhwch after the latter successfully forces his way into Arthur's court (Bromwich and Evans, *Culhwch and Olwen*, 6-7; Ford, *Mabinogi*, 126; on the parallelism between Goreu and Culhwch, see Bromwich and Evans, *Culhwch and Olwen*, liv-lv). Both actions define and socialize the hero, but are of course much more moderate and friendly acts of "cutting" and "trimming" than the instances of giant abuse in the text.

[10] Bromwich and Evans, *Culhwch and Olwen*, lvi-lvii; Tatlock, *The Legendary History of Britain*, 388-9. An overview of Welsh giant lore is offered in Grooms, *Giants of Wales*.

[11] Fergus is so tall that he has to sit down in order for his dictation to be heard (K. Meyer, "Neue Mitteilungen aus irischen Handschriften," 4; see J. Nagy, *Conversing with Angels and Ancients*, 315).

A Leash and an Englyn 247

past,[12] and the mysterious figure of Trefhuilngid Treochair who can teach the men of Ireland a thing or two about the primeval history of Ireland that even the antediluvian sage Fintan does not know,[13] are all described as superhuman in stature. Closer to home, in *Culhwch ac Olwen* the Oldest (and the Wisest) of the Animals, the Salmon of Llyn Llyw, who knows where the prisoner Mabon has been kept since ancient times, is large enough to carry Cei and Bedwyr on his back.[14] Interpreting the giants as symbols of intimidatingly venerable tradition seems especially appropriate in the case of Ysbaddaden, who at first is unknown and cannot be found (not unlike many Celtic figures symbolizing ancient knowledge), but once he is located threatens to become the controlling force for the rest of the tale, the game-master setting Arthur and his men through their paces, interminably it seems.[15] But what the giant requests, Arthur and his men shape into a weapon to use against him, just as Wrnach's sword after receiving Cei's expert treatment becomes the instrument of its giant owner's death. The *anoethau* dictated by Ysbaddaden form a chain, *a very long story in the making*, which the giant is certain Culhwch and his allies cannot realize because the links are so difficult to piece together, and because there are so many of them. Like a mantra, Culhwch repeats after the giant's statement of each prerequisite to the winning of Olwen, "Hawd ys genhyf gaffel hynny, kyd tybyckych na bo hawd" [It is easy for me to accomplish that, though you may not think so], to which Ysbaddaden responds with

---

[12] Stokes, *Acallamh na Senórach*, 3: "Ocus atconncatar na cléirigh dá n-indsaighi iat-sum, 7 ro ghabh gráin 7 egla iat roimh na feraibh móra cona conaibh móra leo, uair nír' lucht coimhré na comhaimsire dóibh iatt" [(Patrick's) priests, seeing Caílte and his men approaching, were seized with fear and horror at the sight of these enormous men, the warriors of an earlier age, together with their great dogs] (trans., Dooley and Roe, *Tales of the Elders of Ireland*, 5).

[13] Best, *Settling of the Manor of Tara*, 138: "Donbert ingantas mór méd a delba. Comard fri fid máel a dá gúaland, ecnach nem 7 grían fo gabal ara fhot 7 ara cháime" [We wondered greatly at the magnitude of his form [says Fintan]. As high as a wood was the top of his shoulders, the sky and the sun visible between his legs, by reason of his size and comeliness] (trans., ibid., 139).

[14] Bromwich and Evans, *Culhwch and Olwen*, 33; Ford, *Mabinogi*, 149.

[15] Dillus is similarly hard to find, until he is found: he is said in our text to be "y rysswr mwyaf a ochelawd Arthur eiryoet" [the greatest warrior who had ever avoided Arthur] (Bromwich and Evans, *Culhwch and Olwen*, 34; Ford, *Mabinogi*, 150).

his own mantra, prefacing the next request: "Kyt keffych hynny, yssit ny cheffych" [Though you accomplish that, here is something you won't accomplish].[16] In fact, Arthur's team and/or the narrative pay attention to only fourteen of the set tasks, upon the successful completion of which Culhwch gets the girl, and Ysbaddaden receives his deadly hair/headcut. The heroes' outwitting and besting the giant comes about sooner than expected thanks to the author's editing the details of the story. So too, finding expeditiously the means of "trimming" Ysbaddaden, namely the comb and scissors on the boar's head and Wrnach's sword (if it is the unnamed weapon used on Ysbaddaden by Goreu),[17] is equivalent to figuring out how to cut corners on the project of finding all of the *anoethau*. These incidents may well constitute cheating, like trapping Dillus unawares and obtaining his whiskers that way, but giants, it would appear in *Culhwch ac Olwen*, are regularly tricked by heroes, and, vast though it may be, oral tradition as manipulated in this text turns out to be easy prey for the wiles practiced by literary composers.

But does the trick really work? And is there no price at all to pay for playing fast and loose with giants, with their vulnerability (paradoxical, given their size), and with oral tradition? There is an ominous answer to be found in the follow-up to Cei's exploit with Dillus, a coda that throws up a formidable roadblock to the progress of the search for the *anoethau*, and to the continuation of the text itself.[18]

Upon the presentation of the leash to him by Cei and Bedwyr, Arthur, and the prose text, shift gears dramatically, thereby perhaps winning for Arthur the otherwise mysterious reputation of being one of the three "oferfeirdd" [scurrilous bards] of Britain, as recorded in the medieval collection of Triads:[19]

---

[16] Bromwich and Evans, *Culhwch and Olwen*, 21-2; Ford, *Mabinogi*, 137-8.

[17] As speculated in Bromwich and Evans, *Culhwch and Olwen*, liv.

[18] It should be kept in mind that the Dillus episode occurs well before the end of the text. In the Bromwich and Evans edition, which consists of 1,246 lines, the Dillus episode occupies lines 953 to 984. Furthermore, the episode that follows it, having to do with the truce arranged by Arthur between the demonic Gwyn ap Nudd (whose participation in the hunt of Twrch Trwyth is another of Ysbaddaden's stipulations) and his enemy Gwythyr, also disrupts the heroic and textual master plan, as I hope to show in a future study.

[19] Bromwich, *Trioedd ynys Prydein*, 21. In the editor's survey of the few other surviving allusions to Arthur as an amateur composer of satirical verse in later lit-

A *Leash and an* Englyn 249

>Ac yna y kanei Arthur yr eglyn hwnn:
>>Kynnllyuan a oruc Kei
>>O uaryf Dillus uab Eurei.
>>Pei iach dy angheu uydei.
>
>Ac am hynny y sorres Kei hyt pan uu abreid y uilwyr yr Ynys honn tangneuedu y rwng Kei ac Arthur. Ac eissoes, nac yr anghyfnerth ar Arthur nac yr llad y wyr, nyt ymyrrwys Kei yn reit gyt ac ef o hynny allan.
>
>[Thereupon Arthur sang this *englyn*:
>>"A leash was made by Cei
>>From the beard of Dillus son of Eurei;
>>If he were hale, 'tis you he'd slay."
>
>And Cei became so indignant at that, that the warriors of this Island could barely make peace between him and Arthur. And yet from that time on neither Arthur's need nor the killing of his men could induce Cei to join in battle with him.][20]

Even apart from the context in which it was composed/performed and the identity of the composer/performer, this ditty casts serious aspersions on the heroism of one of the major figures of early Welsh narrative, the everready battler Cei, whose reduction to a disputatious cog in the Arthurian

---

erature, two of these build on the connection between Arthur's poetizing and hair: an *englyn* attributed to him in which he addresses a giant named Cribwr and puns on his name ("crib" [comb]), and the poet Gruffudd Llwyd's comparing the impossibility of his plucking a single hair from his patron's beard even if he had Cei's grip to the impossibility of obtaining one from the beard of Arthur the *oferfardd* (*Trioedd ynys Prydein*, 21-2). Bromwich's conclusion is that the triad refers to figures of legend who are better known as leaders and/or warriors but are also known for their improvisation of (perhaps specifically satirical) *englynion*. It is fitting and perhaps not altogether coincidental that the poetry in this singular instance of a breakthrough of verse into prose in this particular text is what we would call "satire" (corresponding to Welsh *dychan* or *gogan*, both compound forms of *canu* [sing]), the source of which word, *satura* from classical Latin, originally designated what we would now call *prosimetrum* (see Ziolkowski, "Prosimetrum in the Classical Tradition," 46-7).

[20] Bromwich and Evans, *Culhwch and Olwen*, 35; Ford, *Mabinogi*, 151.

wheel is a later, non-Welsh development.[21] Earlier in our text it is even said that "ny byd gwasanaythur na swydvr mal ef" [there shall never be a server or officer like] this indispensable pillar of Arthurian exploit.[22] But especially given the context in which the *englyn* is uttered — that is, within a momentum-gaining series of complicated, intertwined heroic exploits requiring the utmost efforts and concentration of Arthur and his men, in a tour-de-force demonstration of the strength of the bond that exists among them — and given the attribution of this *englyn* to the usually prosaic Arthur, who here as elsewhere in Welsh tradition depends upon Cei to get the job done, the impact of this poetic breakthrough upon the original audience of the text must have been as stunning as it was devastating to Cei, who from the moment he heard the poem ceased to be Arthur's matchless "server and officer." True, the performance of the tasks continues after this point, even without Cei, just as the text regains its poise and finishes the story. Still, the Arthurian milieu will just not be the same any more, and the old gang, which in many ways is the focus of *Culhwch ac Olwen*, won't ever be the same again.[23]

For us as for Cei, Arthur's *englyn* is hard to swallow, since it contains more than a grain of truth. Cei indeed could not and would not face this giant in face-to-face combat. The way Cei trapped Dillus smacks more of tricksterish stratagem than the lofty valor on display in the other tasks, the ones not involving giants. Cei, however, was not simply motivated by cowardice in the case of Dillus. To pluck the beard fresh, he had to pin down the giant without killing him, not an easy assignment to carry out without resort to extraordinary measures, including deception. Still, Cei's and our

---

[21] The characterization of Cei in this and other early Welsh texts and the development of Cei into the *Caius* of Geoffrey's *Historia* and the Kay of continental Arthurian romance are the subject of Gowans, *Cei and the Arthur Legend*.

[22] Bromwich and Evans, *Culhwch and Olwen*, 10; Ford, *Mabinogi*, 129. The words are those of Cei's father, recorded in the list of the members of Arthur's court.

[23] In the list of the members of Arthur's court (given in the text well before the episode of the giant's beard), we are told of Gwyddawg son of Menestyr that he was the one who slew Cei, and was in turn slain along with his brothers by Arthur in revenge (Bromwich and Evans, *Culhwch and Olwen*, 10; Ford, *Mabinogi*, 129). Thus, while Cei abandons Arthur, the latter does not forget his obligation to Cei. Of course, this demonstration of their lasting bond could take place only after Cei had departed from life altogether, not just from Arthur's company.

hearing this *englyn* in the midst of a series of heroic exploits building up (we hope) to a successful conclusion breaks the story's stride and forces a re-evaluation of what lies behind as well as beyond these (we thought) doughty deeds.

A closer examination of just what Arthur says in his pithy bipartite verse brings out even more just how subversive this *englyn* is to the project of the text as a whole. In the first part (two lines), he acknowledges the presented object and restates what has transpired: Cei succeeded in making a leash out of Dillus's beard. In the last line of the *englyn*, however, where the "punch line" resides, Arthur proposes a hypothetical situation, the continued existence or revival of Dillus, and builds upon it an unflattering outcome for Cei: he would be bested by the still-living giant, just as he would have been unable to defeat Dillus if he had not tricked him. Arthur's playing for poetic purposes with the possibility of the dead coming back to life, or of a dead person still being a formidable contender, takes on additional significance in light of what the main referent of the *englyn* is, and how it was obtained. The leash is the product of pulling out someone's beard while he is still alive, and hence has a living, supple quality to it, as opposed to the brittle bristle that would have been extracted from the face of a dead giant. Arthur's performing this *englyn* in Cei's presence is metaphorically an act of beard-pulling, perhaps even more shameful than that inflicted on Dillus,[24] and it marks Cei as an anomaly who should be dead even though he is alive — parallel to the leash, an object that is both living and dead, and to the text itself, cobbled together deviously from the remains of giant lore and other deposits of oral tradition. Like the beard-leash, the song is a still-living part of a corpse-like product of textual memorialization,[25] disruptively introducing spontaneous oral

---

[24] On the mortifying aspects of beard-pulling and shaving in Irish tradition, see Sayers, "Early Irish Attitudes."

[25] Dillus's is not the only corpse featured and recycled in our tale. The last feat accomplished by Arthur and his men before they head triumphantly back to Ysbaddaden's court involves obtaining the blood of the Y Widon Ordu [Very Black Hag] who is sliced in half by Arthur himself, in one of the few instances in the tale where he takes a hand in the accomplishment of the task in question. The blood is needed for the stretching of Ysbaddaden's hair in preparation for its cutting, an act that, as we have seen, is equivalent to his execution (Bromwich and Evans, *Culhwch and Olwen*, 24, 41-2; Ford, *Mabinogi*, 140, 157). In one of the oddest and most striking passages in *Culhwch ac Olwen*, the hero Culhwch himself

performance into the prescribed story, and a dynamic flash-point in our understanding of it. The *englyn*, coming in a sense out of nowhere yet also going to the heart of the matter, thrashes about in the body of the tale, allowing Arthur to step out of character, spreading dissolution instead of consolidation, pointing out the inconsistency in the ethos of the heroic protagonists, and even proposing a reversal of the inexorable course of events in the tale *and* provoking a preview of the Cei-less future beyond the time-frame of the tale, all in one deft stroke. And, of course, it stands out as the single island of poetry marked as such in a sea of prose.

There are other, larger-than-life reminders in *Culhwch ac Olwen* of the power of oral performance, of the reliance of the text for its matter on oral tradition, and of the analogy between the action of the tale and the act of telling the tale itself. Examples of these embedded references to oral tradition and performance are the voluminous list of the members of Arthur's retinue, recited by Culhwch in order to enlist them as guarantors for his request (significantly, this listing is not presented as direct discourse but is reported by the text, as if it to conjure the cast of characters, and to emphasize that the virtuosity on display is really that of the composer of the text and/or his sources); the extended dialogue between Ysbaddaden and

---

is described as a corpse washed ashore, the fairest he has ever seen, says the herdsman Custenhin, who is lying for no apparent reason upon being asked by his wife to explain whence he obtained the ring given to him by Culhwch (Bromwich and Evans, *Culhwch and Olwen*, 16; Ford, *Mabinogi*, 134).

Moreover, all the other *englynion* to be found in the surviving corpus of medieval Welsh prose narrative, like the one featured in our text, similarly refer to beings that are both alive and dead. Efnisien's *englyn* in the Second Branch of the *Mabinogi* refers to the Irish concealed in bags – enemies whom Efnisien is squeezing to death – as "blawd" [flower(s)/flour] (Thomson, *Branwen uerch Lyr*, 13; Ford, *Mabinogi*, 68-9). In the Fourth Branch, Gwydion's *englynion* are composed/performed so as to lure close to him the eagle into which his nephew Lleu was transformed after he was slain; the stanzas describe him and the tree in which he resides, from which his flesh drops. The rotting detritus is characterized in one of the *englynion* as "blawd" [flowers] (Ford, *Mabinogi*, 107; *Math uab Mathonwy*, 18-19). Even the singular instance of *englyn* composition that is not introduced as such in the text and is not said to be "sung," Math's listing of the three sons of his nephew Gilfaethwy, has to do with creatures born of exiled criminals turned into animals and changed in their sex – arguably, figures who are metaphorically if not literally dead (Ford, *Mabinogi*, 98; *Math uab Mathonwy*, 8); on the identification of this passage as an *englyn*, see I. Williams, *Pedeir Keinc y Mabinogi*, 268.

Culhwch resulting in the seemingly interminable catalogue of *anoethau*; and the lament of Mabon in his prison, the words of which are not supplied (or the lament may have been wordless), and which like a distress signal finally brings him to the attention of the Oldest of Animals and later to the Arthurian party in search of Mabon. While it is unlikely that these passages — or the text as a whole — are actually the product of oral composition, they all evoke vividly the milieu of oral performance and demonstrate the power of the heard voice. But these demonstrations highlight the potential length and volume of oral performance, and of the memories that generate it: the court list and the catalogue of *anoethau* verge on the fulsome, while poor Mabon has been lamenting for a long, long time, according to the story. Arthur's *englyn* provides another demonstration of the power of the virtuosically spoken word, but in this case the product is brief, concentrated, and as sharp as any weapon wielded in Arthurian story. Succinctly weaving together the categories of living/dead, ally/foe, and oral/written, leashing the text in its sometimes unscrupulous pursuit of tradition, and simultaneously serving as a memento of past deed and token of things to come, this single stanza constitutes the most subtle of the many reflexive contrivances at work and at play in this most remarkable of Welsh Arthurian texts.

LORI ANN GARNER

The Role of Proverbs in Middle English Narrative

From its opening lines, *Havelok the Dane* marks its dual participation in oral as well as written traditions of medieval England. The pages of the surviving twelfth-century manuscript (Oxford, Bodleian Library, Laud Misc. 108) beckon an immediately present listening audience:

> Herknet to me, gode men —
> Wiues, maydnes, and alle men —
> Of a tale þat Ich you wile telle,
> Wo-so it wile here and þer-to duelle.
> (1–4)

> [Listen to me good men — wives, maidens, and all people — to a tale that I will tell you, whoever wants to hear it and remain thereto.][1]

Its manuscript versions also dating from the twelfth century, *King Horn* likewise opens with the speaker's (written) promise that "alle beon hi blithe / That to my song lithe!" (1) [all will be happy who listen to my song]. The sorrowful speaker of Chaucer's *Troilus and Criseyde* more openly acknowledges the act of writing his narrative as he asks for help from Thesiphone to "help me for t'endite / Thise woful vers, that wepen as I write"

---

[1] Unless otherwise indicated, all citations and numberings of *Havelok* are from Smithers's edition; citations of *King Horn* are from Sands's edition; and citations of Chaucer are from Benson's edition. Translations throughout are my own, unless otherwise noted.

(I.6-7) [help me to write these woeful verses, which weep as I write them]. Yet he also participates in the illusion of performance for an immediately present audience, promising his listeners that "ye may the double sorwes *here* / Of Troilus in lovynge of Criseyde, / And how that she forsook hym er she deyde" (I.54-6; emphasis mine) [you may hear the double sorrows of Troilus in his love for Criseyde, and how she forsook him before she died].

The extent to which these narratives' speakers associate themselves with written and oral expressive forms is only one among many ways the respective poems demonstrate their varying degrees of participation in oral and literate modes of communication. The complex interplay of oral and literate cultures in Middle English narratives raises many important issues, among them implications for how we are to understand medieval concepts of genre. Understanding how layers of orality and literacy are employed to create meaning is critical to how we interpret component parts of the narratives and the narratives as a whole. Chaucer's Pandarus speaks to the complexity of the situation by explicitly observing the dual provenance of proverbs as witnessed in daily life and as read in written narrative, proverbs that "Men sen alday, and reden ek in stories" (III.1063) [men see all the time and also read in stories]. Focusing specifically on the genre of proverbs, this paper explores how two romances[2] situated at different points along the medieval orality/literacy continuum — *Havelok the Dane* and *Troilus and Criseyde* — employ traditional genres within narrative to create meaning in very different ways.

---

[2] What constitutes the generic category "romance" has been a much debated question in scholarship surrounding the texts generally included under this heading. As Bradbury, *Writing Aloud*, notes, the category is very amorphous, and "each text is in a sense its own category; each new text makes the old definition obsolete" (9). She argues further that "tracing generic transformation is likely to be a more productive approach to the romances than division and classification" (9). While the comparative points to be made in this paper depend more on the status of works addressed here (*Havelok the Dane* and *Troilus and Criseyde*) as narratives rather than specifically as romances, occasionally they will be referred to as romances, in keeping with most scholarship dealing with both poems. See, for example, Bradbury, *Writing Aloud*, 5, who considers *Havelok* and *Troilus* romances; Windeatt, *Oxford Guides to Chaucer*, 144-53, on elements of romance in *Troilus*; and Fewster, *Traditionality and Genre*, 19-20, 31-3, on *Havelok* as romance.

Crucial to this endeavor is an awareness that traditional modes of composition and reception were not instantly supplanted with the advent of writing. Rather, as John Miles Foley has observed, medieval texts present themselves to us as a "spectrum of expressive forms," allowing us to see the persistence of certain traditional structures — such as proverbs — in even highly textual works.[3] An awareness of multiple influences, "popular" as well as "learned," upon Middle English writers will also be critical to understanding how traditional proverbs operate within longer narratives, narratives that are now textualized but that nonetheless demonstrate, in various ways and to different degrees, their relationship to oral tradition.[4]

The genre of Middle English romances offers a wide range of texts with varying degrees of participation in oral and literate traditions. Nancy Mason Bradbury's approach to the body of Middle English romances as a continuum representing different levels of "reliance on written modes of thought and expression" provides a very useful construct for comparative study of works within the genre.[5] Employing such a model, Dave Henderson demonstrates that protagonists in romances "closer to a hypothetical oral provenance" are far more clearly aligned with traditional codes of behavior than characters in less traditional works, which tend toward greater narrative ambiguity and psychological complexity.[6] So much

---

[3] Foley, *Homer's Traditional Art*, 17, and *Singer of Tales in Performance*, 79. On the oral and manuscript transmission of Middle English romances, see Baugh, "Improvisation," and Holland, "Formulaic Diction." On the scribe's participation in oral traditional modes of thought, see McGillivray, *Memorization*, 27, who contends that "There is no sure way ... to tell scribal recasting from minstrel recasting, scribal introduction of formulas from minstrel introduction of formulas, scribal editing from minstrel alterations with the same effects."

[4] See further Bradbury, "Gentrification," 307. For an examination of oral and written modes of transmission in the Canterbury Tales, see Kellogg, "Oral Narrative." See also Wolf, "Medieval Heroic Traditions," 67, who argues that "in the Middle Ages orality and literacy ... merged and supported each other."

[5] As Bradbury explains, *Writing Aloud*, 9, such a construct provides "a way of seeing more clearly the relationship of the texts in this corpus to oral and literary traditions" and should not be seen as a chronological history in which Middle English romance evolves from oral performance into manuscript culture.

[6] Henderson, "Tradition and Heroism," 91. See also Ong, *Orality and Literacy*, esp. chap. 6, in which he discusses character development in relation to the technology of writing. He observes that as discourse moves from "primary orality" toward a culture of print, "the flat, 'heavy' or type character yields to characters

has complexity of character come to be associated with modern fiction, and written narrative more generally, that narratives falling within more immediately recognizable literary traditions (such as Chaucer's) have in the past been seen as the culmination of an evolutionary path toward superior narratives.[7]

While literary influences are certainly not to be overlooked, they do not have to be accepted at the expense of traditional influences. As Foley, Bradbury, and Henderson, among others, argue, we must explore these narratives in all their complexities rather than applying standards based on exclusively literary models. In what follows, we will consider the ways in which proverbs embedded within a more traditional work, such as *Havelok the Dane*, create meaning in ways different from those appearing in a less

---

that grow more and more 'round'" (151-2). "Round" characters, exhibiting greater complexity of motivation and capacity for psychological growth, tend to employ proverbs in ways that contribute to this character development as opposed to "flat" characters in more oral-traditional texts.

[7] Whiting, for example, praises Chaucer's innovative use of proverbs saying, *Chaucer's Use of Proverbs*, 3, that "no other poet had ever used [proverbial material] so skillfully and effectively," his measure of skill being the extent to which proverbs serve "to heighten characterization." A certain degree of distaste for traditional tales has affected much of the scholarship on *Havelok*. See, for example, Mehl, *Middle English Romances*, 164, who defends the narrative against those who might see the style as "simple and artless," but in doing so continues to reinforce the assumption that artistic merit is the exclusive domain of a literary culture: "Though the subjects described are often ordinary enough, the method of description clearly betrays the poet's familiarity with the art of rhetoric." He further privileges the literary over the oral in his argument, 165, that though the repetitions in *Havelok* often "sound like the primitive mannerisms of an oral style..., they also belong to a rhetorical tradition and show a degree of conscious artistry which accords very little with the picture, often drawn, of a popular minstrel entertaining a group of illiterate peasants in a market-place or a tavern." See also Smithers, "Style of *Hauelok*," who ascribes every stylistic trait he observes in *Havelok* to the influences of what he assumes to be a French original and Latin rhetorical conventions employed in more literary Middle English writings. The maxims in the poem, for instance, he sees, 209, as the author's inclusion of *sententiae*; the periphrasis he translates, 195, as the "rhetorical colour" *interpretatio*. In his edition of the poem, Smithers, lix, is equally careful to distance the narrative's artistic merit from oral traditional influences: "Analysis of the author's literary style shows that he was an unobtrusively sophisticated writer, and certainly not a minstrel."

traditional work, such as Chaucer's *Troilus and Criseyde*.[8] Specifically, proverbs in the more traditional *Havelok* speak with the full authority of traditional wisdom while proverbs in *Troilus* become rhetorical tools employed by characters within the narrative. The "modes of meaning" shift, and in order to come closer to a fuller understanding of the surviving texts, we must first understand how meaning is made.

Proverbs within Havelok the Dane

A number of studies have made note of the proverbs employed in the Middle English *Havelok the Dane*. B. J. Whiting comments on the "number of interesting proverbs, sententious remarks, and proverbial phrases which it contains."[9] Anne Scott also observes a high proportion of proverbs in her discussion of the poem's style.[10] G. V. Smithers claims that the ratio of approximately one proverb for every 300 lines is "somewhat higher than is usual" in the *chansons de geste* with which he compares the poem.[11] Scholars have largely focused on the sources of the proverbs, as is the case with Smithers who seeks Old French equivalents and equates the proverbs in the narrative with the "rhetorical colour" *sententiae*. Whiting likewise views the poem as a translation of a French original but argues that the proverbial material "was added by the English author."[12]

Owing to the presence of local details not present in the French versions, the native English rather than French names, and the substantially greater length of the English text in relation to the French, Bradbury convincingly argues against views that claim a French original, suggesting that we "recognize local legend as the primary inspiration for the Middle English poem" and "allow for 'contamination' from a French literary ver-

---

[8] On *Havelok*'s placement nearer the traditional end of the spectrum and *Troilus and Criseyde*'s situation as a work rooted in the more literate tradition of European canonical poetry that is nevertheless influenced by minstrel-style romance, see Bradbury, *Writing Aloud*, 5.

[9] Whiting, "Proverbs," 111.

[10] A. Scott, "Word and Deed," 149.

[11] Smithers, "Style of *Hauelok*," 209. Smithers cites lines 307, 601, 648-9, 1339, 1353, 1636, 1694, 1713-14, and 2462. Whiting, "Proverbs," does not include 1713-14 in his list of proverbs or sententious remarks. Likewise, Smithers does not include 166ff. in his list.

[12] Whiting, "Proverbs," 113.

sion."[13] Such evidence demonstrates that we should be very careful not to underestimate the importance of oral traditions for concurrent written texts. In the study of the poem's proverbs, the need to be aware of the poem's connections with oral traditions seems especially important, since seeing them as translations of or additions to French originals risks losing the context within which they function and create meaning.[14]

Following is an examination of eight proverbial statements[15] (all acknowledged by Smithers as well as Whiting), focusing not on possible sources but on the function of these statements, regardless of their origin, within an oral traditional context. The use of proverbs in this poem does contribute to character development and narrative progression but does so in ways substantially different from those in Chaucer's *Troilus and Criseyde*. The first two proverbs to be discussed, both employed by the narrative voice, serve to direct audience response and to sanction events in the narrative. Examples three and four work together to help explain and validate a seemingly inexplicable shift in the motives of two characters, Grim and his wife. Examples five and six are both spoken by Goldeboru and function to reinforce the authority of her commands to Havelok. The seventh example sets forth a proper code of conduct between leaders and their men, the authority of which is reinforced at several points during the

---

[13] Bradbury, *Writing Aloud*, 67.

[14] While I do find Bradbury's arguments more convincing than those claiming a French original, determination of this as fact is not necessary for the purposes of this paper. Smithers and Whiting both concede an English influence for the proverbial matter and agree that what they see as a translation has been adapted for an English audience in significant ways. Thus, whether a French translation or an English original, the poem as we have it is — in ways important to the understanding of the poem — traditional.

[15] Smithers, "Style of *Hauelok*," 209, noting a distinction in medieval rhetoric between *sententiae* (instructive) and *proverbs* (useful), refers to the group of "gnomic statements" as *maxims*. Whiting likewise makes a distinction between "proverbs" and "sententious remarks." According to Whiting, "Nature of the Proverb," 302, a proverb is "an expression which, owing its birth to the people, testifies to its origin in form and phrase. It expresses what is apparently a fundamental truth." He notes further, 306, that a "sententious remark" is "a piece of wisdom which has not crystallized into specific current form." In order to allow for the generic comparisons among cultural traditions, in this paper "proverbs" will refer to the larger group of statements expressing traditional wisdom rather than Whiting's or Smithers's sub-groups within a larger category.

events of the story. The eighth and final example presents an interesting case: ironically, it is spoken by one of the story's two villains, not a character we might naturally expect to embody the voice of traditional wisdom. Although it is evident that the proverb has been grossly misapplied to suit the speaker's own needs, the proverb's ultimate truth is borne out clearly by the events of the narrative.

Our first two examples occur at lines 1636 and 2462. Maintaining the frame of a speaker with an immediately present audience, the narrator in *Havelok* frequently directs audience emotional response in a number of ways: with curses against villains – "Haue he þe malisun today / Of alle þat eure speken may" (426-7) [May he have the curse today of all who ever may speak] –, references to traditional figures (e.g., by comparing Godard to Judas [319] when he breaks his oath to King Athelwold), and threats against those who sympathize with the villains (for example, "Daþeit hwo recke" [Cursed be he who cares] – at Godard's death [2512]). To this end, he also employs proverbs. Havelok's gift of a ring upon meeting the earl Ubbe is approved by the narrator with the proverb "He was ful wis þat first yaf mede" (1636) [He who first gave a reward was very wise]. The transition back to the narrative and the explicit comparison with Havelok is made with "and so":[16] "And so was Hauelok ful wis here" (1637) [And so was Havelok very wise here]. The transaction now sanctioned by the voice of traditional wisdom, an attuned audience knows to recognize the legitimacy of the bond between Havelok and Ubbe and to trust in the good will of both.

The justification of Godard's punishment for his previous heinous acts – specifically the murder of Havelok's sisters and the intention of having Havelok, the future king, murdered as well – is also provided by a proverb: "Old sinne makes newe shame" (2462) [Old sin makes new shame]. Lest we as an audience feel any sympathy for Godard as he is dragged from the tail of a scurvy horse before being flayed alive and then hanged, traditional wisdom reminds us that such shame and punishment are warranted for crimes such as his. Through such proverbs the speaker evokes traditional authority to align himself with the hero and against the

---

[16] The usage of "and so" parallels the use of *swa* in transitions to and from proverbs in the Old English *Beowulf*, e.g., lines 20a, 1534b, 2166b, and 2291a. I cite Klaeber's edition of *Beowulf*.

villain. In this way, proverbs serve to sanction certain events of the narrative and to indicate appropriate audience response.

Directing audience response in a slightly different way, our third and fourth examples sanction a reversal of character sympathies that would be inexplicable if we applied more literary models that demand consistency of characters' psychologies. The proverb at line 601 marks one of the most significant, and potentially problematic, shifts in the development of the narrative. A number of readers have noted Grim's sudden conversion from villain to lifelong, loyal friend.[17] Just a few lines before Dame Leve sees the telltale light emanating from Havelok's mouth, Grim has explained how he plans to "beren him to þe se" (582) [carry him to the sea] and "drenchen him þer-inne" (584) [drown him therein]. Hired by Godard to carry out the crime, Grim is acting entirely in his own self-interest in hopes of attaining wealth, and his wife is in full agreement with the plan. However, after recognizing the light as a sign that Havelok is the rightful heir to the throne, the two approach him, unbind him, and help him from that day forward even at the risk of their own lives. The proverb at line 601 asks us not to question the transition: "For man shal god wille haue" [for man must have good will]. The authority behind the proverb, rather than an explanation of Grim's inner thought processes, tells us we can now trust him.[18]

The proverb quoted by Dame Leve herself at lines 648-9 reinforces the inevitability of their providing aid for Havelok: "Soth it is, þat men seyt and suereth: / Þer God wile helpen, nouth ne dereth" [True it is, as men say and swear: where God will help, nothing will cause harm]. Her use of this proverb further sanctions her actions as noble by allying her with the authority of traditional wisdom. Just as the narrative voice at 601

---

[17] Bradbury, *Writing Aloud*, 76, explains that "the oral art of traditional narrative relies heavily on the immediate emotional impact of each scene as it comes along, and places far less emphasis on the need for realistic consistency from scene to scene." She notes further that Grim's function is thus "facilitator of action" and "whether Grim acts in a cruel or a kind way varies by the needs of the scene in question." On other theories behind Grim's brutality and subsequent kindness, see Mills, "Brutal Fisherman."

[18] Cf. Foley, *Immanent Art*, 210-14, for a discussion of the phrase "þæt wæs god cyning" [That was an excellent king] in Old English poetry. Foley demonstrates here the power of this phrase to evoke the traditional ideal of kingship and thereby to certify the authority of individual kings to whom the phrase is applied.

justifies Dame Leve's extreme change in sympathies through the use of a proverb, Dame Leve also explains the unlikely order of events that contribute to Havelok's success with traditional wisdom. The prefatory phrase, "þat men seyt and suereth," underscores her alliance with tradition.

Such reinforcing of points is employed by other characters as well. Our fifth and sixth examples, both spoken by Goldeboru, serve to lend authority to her directives. Shortly after Goldeboru comes to understand Havelok's identity through the sign of the light coming from his mouth, the angel's telling her that he will be king of England, and Havelok's sharing his dream with her that together they would one day rule Denmark as well as England, she sets forth a plan by which such a prophecy could actually come to pass. Twice in her speech she reinforces her commands to Havelok with proverbs that call for swift action. She says that they must call together troops and that Havelok "nouth on frest þis fare" (1338) [must not put off this journey], a command reinforced by the proverb, "Lith and selthe felawes are" (1339) [Help and success are fellows].[19] A similar proverb closes this lengthy, important speech, further reinforcing the urgency of Havelok's need to act. Her command "þat þou dwelle nouth" (1352) [that you delay not at all] is followed immediately by the proverb "Dwelling haueth ofte scaþe wrouth" (1353) [Delay has often caused harm].

Our seventh example illustrates how proverbial wisdom can encompass an entire narrative rather than remain limited to a specific situation. We are first able to witness the wisdom of the proverb at line 1694 in its immediate context. At later points in the narrative, however, the same piece of traditional wisdom is more implicitly invoked. In the first instance, William Wendut's unfailing courage in defending Ubbe's property is explained in part with the proverb "Wel is him þat god man fedes" [Well is it for him who feeds a good man]. The proverb's truth is certainly confirmed here: the narrative devotes fourteen lines to the description of the food that Ubbe served to Havelok and his men, among them William Wendut. The food was "þe beste mete / Þat king or cayser wolde ete" (1725-6) [the best food that a king or emperor would want to eat], but the

---

[19] Sands, *Verse Romances*, 92 n., explains that the meaning of "lith" is uncertain but translates the saying as 'Speed and prosperity are fellows.' Smithers translates "lith" as 'traveling,' leaving the sense of the statement — take action — the same. See further, Whiting, *Proverbs, Sentences*, 350.

narrator is careful to point out that *all* present shared in the great feast: "Was þer-inne no page so lite / That euere wolde ale bite" (1731-2) [There was no page so small that he would ever drink ale there] because in Ubbe's household there was the preferable "win hwit and red, ful god plente" (1730) [white wine and red, a very good abundance]. During the night after such a feast Havelok and his small group of three conquer a band of "mo þan sixti þeues" (1957) [more than sixty thieves].

Later in the narrative we see a battle from Godard's perspective in which men have not been treated as graciously and fight more out of fear than out of loyalty. As a result, these men "fledden" (2417) as soon as they realized that danger was at hand. In an attempt to gain their loyalty, Godard appeals to the traditional code referred to in the proverb discussed above:

> "Mine knithes, hwat do ye?
> Sule ye þus-gate fro me fle?
> Jch haue you fede and yet shal fed —
> Helpe me nu in þis nede,
> And late ye nouth mi bodi spille,
> Ne Hauelok don of me hise wille!"
>
> (2419-24)

["My knights, what are you doing? Must you flee from me in this manner? I have fed you and yet shall feed you — Help me now in this need, and do not let my body be destroyed or let Havelok inflict his will on me."]

Somewhat shamed, the men return and "slowen a knit and a sweyn / Of þe kinges oune men" (2428-9) [slew a knight and a swain of the king's own men], but the king's (now Havelok's) men, fiercely loyal,

> Scuten on hem, heye and lowe,
> And euerilk fot of hem slowe,
> But Godard one....
>
> (2432-4)

[rushed on them, high and low, and slew every foot of them except for Godard alone....]

Just prior to the battle Havelok's men had taken part in the greatest feast of all in the narrative, the celebration of Havelok's being dubbed king and the knighting of Red Robert, William Wendut, and Hugh Raven. At this feast there "was neuere yete ioie more / Jn al þius werd þan þo was þore" (2335-6) [was never yet more joy in all this world than then was there], and their success in the subsequent battle further reinforces the wisdom of the proverb, establishing that leaders who treat their men well have loyal retainers.

The eighth and final example, at line 307, provides an interesting crux; because it is spoken by the villain Godrich, it might seem that we should not trust the words spoken even though they bear all the marks of traditional wisdom and authority. Just as above we saw Godard participating very selectively in traditional wisdom, appealing to the men's code of honor because he had fed them when his rule was actually based on fear, we see Godrich much earlier making selective use of proverbial wisdom. As Goldeboru approaches the age at which — according to the oaths Godrich made to Athelwold at the king's untimely death — she should rule England herself, Godrich decides that "shal sho it neuere more haue" (297) [she shall nevermore have it] and refers to Goldeboru as a "fol" (298) [fool]. To justify his decision in going against Goldeboru's rightful expectations, he quotes the proverb "Hope maketh fol man ofte blenkes" (307) [Hope often deceives a foolish man]. Once again, we see proverbial wisdom misapplied as Goldeboru proves herself to be anything but a fool throughout the course of the poem, immediately understanding the significance of Havelok's light and making a plan for action that does in fact lead to the couple's reclaiming of their respective lands. The truth of the proverb itself is thus never truly challenged. Rather, Godrich's villainy is underscored by his misappropriation of traditional wisdom.

The proverbs above have been used in very different ways — by the narrator (to direct audience response and sanction narrative events), the heroine (to strengthen the authority of her commands), and even the villains. In all situations, however, the proverbs — even when applied inappropriately — retain their authority. Even the proverb employed by Godrich that "Hope maketh fol man ofte blenkes" bears out its truth in the end: the two villains of the poem do harbor false hopes of retaining kingdoms unjustly and in the end are undone as a result, proving themselves, rather than their victims, fools.

The ways that proverbs are applied in this narrative parallel in important ways the use of proverbs within narratives performed in a number of living oral traditions. Isidore Okpewho distinguishes between proverbs employed in a variety of contexts in African oral traditions: in everyday discourse, in performances such as storytelling, and in rituals and chants. In all of the situations that Okpewho describes, including storytelling, the proverbs always retain the authority of tradition. For example, Charles Simayi from the village Ubullu-Uno in southwestern Nigeria employs many proverbs in his narratives:

> he tells us at one point how he was entertained by the formidable federal soldiers and how he fell heartily to the feast: the proverb "the chameleon is never beset by ants" is used both to establish the point that he is equal to any situation in which he finds himself (like the chameleon that adapts its color to any surrounding) and that the soldiers are too small ("ants") to subdue him.[20]

In fact, in almost every story recorded from this singer, Okpewho explains, "Simayi uses proverbs to enliven the tale and to reinforce the significance of the points he makes."[21]

In South Slavic epic, proverbs also serve significant functions similar to those we saw in *Havelok*. Foley has demonstrated a number of ways that proverbs "carry with them value-added, idiomatic meanings that allow the singer and his audience to engage in a highly economical communication."[22] For example the proverb "U bećara nema hizmećara" [For a bachelor there is no maidservant] in the epic *Ženidba Bećirbega Mustajbegova* [*The Wedding of Mustajbeg's Son Bećirbega*] is "both structurally and indexically resonant," functioning to identify the protagonist Djerdelez Alija as a lone hero and as a "transitional marker."[23]

Other examples of proverbs within narratives of living oral traditions can be found in Fa-Digi Sisòkò's performance of the West African *Epic of Son-Jara*. At several points, for instance, the need for action is expressed

---

[20] Okpewho, *African Oral Literature*, 232.
[21] Okpewho, *African Oral Literature*, 232.
[22] Foley, "Proverbs," 89.
[23] Foley, "Proverbs," 82.

Proverbs in Middle English Narrative 267

with the proverb "What sitting will not solve, / Travel will resolve" (e.g., 470-1, 944-5, 1668-9).[24] Here, as in *Havelok*, proverbs are a defining feature of the narrative's "multigeneric structure"[25] and serve to direct audience response by sanctioning actions and events with the authority of traditional wisdom. Proverbs can evoke a web of associations within the specific narrative by appealing to the overarching authority of the tradition at large.

Proverbs in Troilus and Criseyde
The proverbs in Chaucer's *Troilus and Criseyde* have been discussed far more extensively than those in *Havelok the Dane*. In fact, Wolfgang Mieder includes Chaucer among a list of authors that have been the subject of the world's "best literary proverb studies."[26] The earliest work that attempts comprehensive treatment of the subject is Whiting's *Chaucer's Use of Proverbs*, in which a full chapter is devoted to *Troilus and Criseyde*. As in the study on *Havelok* discussed earlier, Whiting distinguishes between "proverbs" and "sententious remarks." In *Troilus and Criseyde*, Whiting notes sixty-one proverbs and sixty-seven sententious remarks, a total of 128 statements asserting traditional wisdom.

The first indication that proverbs function differently in Chaucer's text from the way they do in *Havelok the Dane* involves sheer numbers: even when the poems' relative lengths are taken into account, Chaucer's proverbs more than triple the number found in *Havelok*. If we accept Whiting's count for proverbs and what he terms "sententious remarks," there is one such statement for every sixty-four lines in *Troilus*, compared with one per three hundred lines in *Havelok*. According to Whiting's counts, this proportion is higher than in anything else Chaucer wrote.[27] Further, the ratio is far higher than in the Troilus's source, Boccaccio's *Il Filostrato*. Whiting explains that Boccaccio's poem contains a total of only

---

[24] I cite Johnson's translation of *Son-Jara*.
[25] Johnson, trans., *Son-Jara*, 10.
[26] Mieder, "Proverbs," 526.
[27] Whiting, *Chaucer's Use of Proverbs*, 49.

twenty-six proverbs and sententious remarks and that even these do not have direct parallels in Chaucer's.[28]

More important than the statistics are *how* these proverbs are used. The ways in which proverbs function in *Troilus and Criseyde* are significantly different from the ways they function in *Havelok*. Proverbs in *Troilus and Criseyde*, rather than carrying the full weight of their traditional authority — as in *Havelok* — become to an extent a tool for characterization, as each character (as well as the narrator) employs proverbs for different rhetorical purposes, such as resolving internal debate in the case of Criseyde or swaying the decisions of others in the case of Pandarus. Chaucer's choices become even more significant when we consider that the relatively small number of proverbs employed in Boccaccio's version did not function as a means of characterization.[29] Chaucer's rhetorical use of proverbs reminds us that medieval culture cannot be divided into mutually exclusive categories of elite versus popular.[30] Traditional proverbs often acquired specialized usages in literary culture, such as being translated into and out of Latin as part of classroom exercises.[31] An awareness of proverb usage within two cultures allowed Chaucer multiple ways of creating meaning in narrative. Though the number of proverbs employed by Chaucer is far greater than the number we saw in *Havelok*, the ultimate authority of individual proverbs is far less certain. Proverbs serve a number of different important functions in *Havelok the Dane*, but the truths of the proverbs themselves are never challenged. In *Troilus and Criseyde*, however, the traditional authority of proverbs is subordinated to their rhetorical functions in several ways. First, conflicting usages of the same proverb (or a pair of similar proverbs) can negate any ultimate truth a given proverb might otherwise reflect. Second, juxtaposition of two proverbs conveying

---

[28] Whiting, *Chaucer's Use of Proverbs*, 58-9. See further Windeatt, who in his edition of the poem presents *Troilus and Criseyde* alongside Boccaccio's *Filostrato*, its principal source.

[29] Whiting, *Chaucer's Use of Proverbs*, 49, and Lumiansky, "Proverbial Monitory Elements," 6.

[30] See further Bradbury, "Gentrification," who argues, 307, that "Chaucer's folkloric materials" were not "otherwise alien materials that he gathered by listening to churls, but language and lore that he and his small, cultivated primary audience shared with the wider society." See also Lindahl, *Earnest Games*, 1-15, on Chaucer's role as storyteller and on his familiarity with folkloric practices.

[31] Bradbury, "Gentrification," 317.

contradictory messages sometimes challenges the authority of both. And third, proverbial wisdom is often countered by events that unfold in the narrative itself.

For the initial portion of *Troilus and Criseyde*, however, proverbs are invested with as much traditional authority as they are in *Havelok*. Even before the entrance of Pandarus midway through Book I, we encounter at least nine proverbial statements.[32] While these statements perhaps draw attention to themselves because of their high numbers, their authority is not questioned. For example, we are told that "alday faileth thing that fooles wenden" (I.217) [things always happen that fools do not expect] and we know before the narrative begins that Troilus's belief in his immunity from love will soon prove false. And shortly afterward the narrator gives advice to his audience, saying that "the yerde is bet that bowen wole and wynde / Than that that brest" (I.257-8) [the staff that will bow and bend is better than the one that breaks]. Troilus's role here within the proverb as the staff that refused to bend and was eventually broken certainly plays out within the narrative as his love for Criseyde all but incapacitates him. To reinforce his point that being near Criseyde made Troilus's pains all the worse, the narrator employs the proverbial statement that "the ner the fir, the hotter is" (I.449) [the nearer the fire, the hotter it is].

The narrator employs several sayings describing the characteristics of love through various metaphors, again none of which the narrative outright contradicts. For instance, the saying "love is he that alle thing may bynde" (I.237) [love is he who can bind all things] here reinforces the narrator's assertions that no one — even one as steadfastly opposed to love as Troilus — is impervious. The presence of the saying "Love to wide yblowe / Yelt bittre fruyt, though swete seed be sowe" (I.384-5) [Love blown (made known) too widely yields bitter fruit, even though sweet seeds may be sown] serves the immediate purpose of describing Troilus's thoughts, but for the poem's intended audience the proverb here also suggests that Troilus's fears are in fact valid, and it further points to the inevitability of his downfall should he proceed and share his secret. Then, midway through

---

[32] As with *Havelok*, Whiting's designation will serve as a base, as his methodology for proverb collections is widely accepted, in the words of Meider, "Proverb," 663, as "*the* model for any national language collection" (his emphasis). A discussion of all statements identified as proverbial, however, is beyond the scope of this study. For a more comprehensive analysis, see Whiting, *Chaucer's Use of Proverbs*, and Lumiansky, "Proverbial Monitory Elements."

Book I, into a world in which thus far proverbs carry at least a certain degree of truth, steps Pandarus, a character whose development has long been linked to his use of proverbs.[33]

A topic that has been less fully explored involves the implications for the genre itself when proverbs become tools for characterization. As an examination of selected proverbs of Pandarus shows, their underlying authority in *Troilus and Criseyde* cannot be taken for granted because proverbs are often employed rhetorically by characters to bring about specific ends rather than to reflect an absolute truth. In places Pandarus employs remarkably similar proverbs to bring about completely different ends: in encouraging Troilus to trust his judgment, Pandarus tells Troilus that he should wait rather than act rashly, "for every thing hath tyme" (II.989) [there is a time for everything]. When talking to Criseyde later, however, Pandarus tells her to act on her feelings for Troilus at once because "alle thyng hath tyme" (III.855) [there is a time for all things].[34] Beyond illustrating Pandarus's manipulative nature, these opposing usages of the same saying undercut the proverb's authority, forcing an audience to look for the proverb's meaning in its specific and immediate narrative context rather than in the larger, traditional context within which it is usually deployed.

Similar proverbs employed by Pandarus and by the narrator further illustrate how proverbs function differently from the way they do in *Havelok*. Again, we see similar sayings employed for quite different rhetorical ends. In justifying his authority to Troilus, Pandarus — who has apparently been no more successful in love than those to whom he gives counsel — assures Troilus that he might benefit from Pandarus's own mistakes. Pandarus then employs a lengthy string of proverbs to convince Troilus to take him as his guide, among them "A fool may ek a wis-man ofte gide" (I.630) [A fool can often guide a wise man]; "A wheston is no kervyng instrument, / But yet it maketh sharppe kervyng tolis" (I.631-2) [A whetstone is no carving instrument, yet it makes sharp carving tools]; "Thus of-

---

[33] Many have observed the role proverbs play in developing Pandarus's character. For example, Lumiansky, "Proverbial Monitory Elements," 14, notes the way Pandarus employs proverbs to extract information from Troilus. Likewise, Whiting, *Chaucer's Use of Proverbs*, 48, has argued that Pandarus's use of proverbs contributes to his character's being "one of the great comic characters of all time."

[34] For a brief discussion of both proverbs, see Whiting, *Chaucer's Use of Proverbs*, 52-3.

ten wise men ben war by foolys" (I.635) [Thus wise men are often warned by fools].³⁵ In the proem to Book II, the narrator employs a number of proverbs, among them one that excuses his alleged lack of skill by his own lack of experience in the subjects about which he is writing. He asks not to be blamed if he speaks of love "unfelyngly" [unfeelingly] because "a blynd man kan nat juggen wel in hewis" (II.21) [a blind man cannot judge well between colors]. The proverbial blind man referred to by the narrator seems *syntactically* parallel to the fool (and the whetstone) of Pandarus's proverbs, yet one proclaims wisdom to be gained from inexperience and the other apologizes for it. As the conflicting proverbs employed by Pandarus implicitly challenge the authority of the proverbs in general, so do the differing rhetorical usages of these two similar remarks cast doubt on the ultimate truth of both.

A second way in which traditional authority of proverbs is undercut in this narrative is by the juxtaposition of proverbs that send contradictory messages. Shortly after he is introduced into the narrative, for example, Pandarus begins the process of extracting Troilus's secrets. The following proverb is employed to illustrate for Troilus the wisdom of sharing with Pandarus, complete with the typical invocation to traditional wisdom, "men seyn":

> Men seyn, "to wrecche is consolacioun
> To have another felawe in hys peyne."
>
> (I.708-9)

---

³⁵ Other proverbs employed in the same speech to illustrate further Pandarus's point that wisdom can be gained from his own mistakes are as follows: "By his contrarie is every thyng declared" (I.637) [Everything is known by its opposite]; "For how myghte evere swetnesse han ben knowe / To him that nevere tasted bitternesse?" (638-9) [How might sweetness ever have been known to him who had never tasted bitterness?]; "Ne no man may ben inly glad, I trowe, / That nevere was in sorwe or som destresse" (640-1) [No man may be entirely happy, I trust, who never was in sorrow or some distress]; "Eke whit by blak, by shame ek worthinesse, / ech set by other, more for other semeth, / as men may se, and so the wyse it demeth" (642-4) [As white by black, so shame by worthiness; each thing set by the other is more visible because of the other, as men can see and so the wise judge it]; and "Of two contraries is o lore" (645) [From two contraries is one lesson].

[Men say, "to a wretched person it is a consolation to have another fellow in his pain."]

To further show the aptness of this proverb to their particular situation, Pandarus then proceeds to describe to Troilus how he does in fact share Troilus's suffering: "So ful of sorwe am I, soth for to seyne" (I.712) [I am so full of sorrow, truth to tell]. In protesting the alleged wisdom of sharing secrets, Troilus employs another saying, again appealing to the authority of tradition with "it is seyd":

> For it is seyd, "Men maketh ofte a yerde
> With which the maker is hymself ybeten
> In sondry manere."
> (I.740-2)

[For it is said, "In various ways men often make a rod with which the maker himself is beaten."]

And, as Pandarus did before, Troilus here explicates the proverb for their specific situation: "as thise wyse treten, / And namelich in his counseil tellynge / That toucheth love that oughte ben secree" (I.742-4) [as these wise men explain, especially with regard to telling one's counsel in matters concerning love that ought to be kept secret]. The close placement of two proverbs with such opposing sentiments offers possible challenges to the advice in both by allowing for a rhetorical notion of truth, one that is negotiable and that hinges on the rhetorical skills of competing authorities.

Understanding the tensions between traditional expectations of proverb usage and the usages employed by Pandarus can also help explain the seeming contradiction between Troilus's distancing himself from Pandarus's proverbs and his own usage of such wisdom. During his first conversation with Pandarus on the subject of Criseyde, long before Pandarus has exhausted his supply of proverbs, Troilus protests that "thy proverbes may me naught availle" (I.756) [your proverbs cannot help me at all]. Whiting connects Troilus's relatively sparing use of proverbs with this statement;[36] Troilus is reserved in his use of proverbs, however, only in relation to Pandarus and possibly Criseyde, not to the tradition at large. We know

---

[36] Whiting, *Chaucer's Use of Proverbs*, 65.

from *Havelok* that as few as one proverbial statement per 300 lines is considered a high number, and by such standards Troilus ranks high in his proverb usage. His objection seems to be specific to *Pandarus's* excessive use of proverbs — "thy proverbes may me naught availle" — not necessarily to proverb usage in general. The negotiable notion of truth that Pandarus's use of proverbs reflects also stands at odds with the conception of truth embodied by Troilus. Troilus, guided less by circumstances than by unshifting ideals of love and fidelity, evokes proverbs as ultimate truths — much in the tradition of *Havelok* — rather than as rhetorical tools adapted to fit specific circumstances.

A third way that the authority of proverbs becomes less universal in the narrative is seen in the proverbs that the events of the plot do not affirm. In Book III, for example, after Criseyde learns that she is to be returned to her father, she laments bitterly. The narrator gives the reader hope that all will turn out well with the following string of wise sayings, sayings that have traditional and written authority as they were heard and read:

> For I have seyn of a ful misty morwe
> Folowen ful ofte a myrie someris day;
> And after wynter foloweth grene May;
> Men sen alday, and reden ek in stories,
> That after sharpe shoures ben victories.
>
> (III.1060-4)

> [For I have very often seen a pleasant summer's day follow a very misty morning; and after winter follows green May; men see all the time and also read in stories that after fierce assaults come victories.]

The use of this proverb here is doubly ironic because not only are Troilus and Criseyde ultimately deprived of the joy promised by proverbial wisdom, but the narrator, who has referred repeatedly to the sorrow in his source text, knows full well what the unhappy outcome for the lovers will be and that "grene May" will not follow this particular winter.

The contradictions cited above that prevent wholesale acceptance of proverbial wisdom stand in stark contrast to the deployment of proverbial wisdom in *Havelok the Dane* and in proverb usage within narratives performed in living oral traditions. A proverb can be contradicted by itself depending on its usage, as Pandarus shows; two contradictory proverbs can be juxtaposed as characters (such as Pandarus and Troilus) debate their respective notions of truth; and events of the narrative can go against the predictions of the proverbs that precede them. From these discrepancies, however, we need not conclude that the difference reflects Chaucer's contempt for proverbs or a distancing from oral traditions. The difference rather parallels the differences in character development noted above. As the attention in narratives turns towards characters with more complex psychologies and away from more idealized or vilified characters who function more to propel narrative developments, characters, as Walter J. Ong notes, appear more like "real" people. In Pandarus's, Criseyde's, Troilus's, and even the narrator's use of proverbs, Chaucer is perhaps demonstrating a keen awareness of proverb usage in daily, non-narrative contexts. In daily life — the "performance arena" of proverbs[37] — proverbial sayings are generally employed by speakers toward very specific ends and are often contradicted by other proverbs or challenged by actual situations or events.

In this regard, Barbara Kirshenblatt-Gimblett's argument that "a proverb can be made to express more than one meaning, that sometimes these meanings are contradictory, and that a proverb's meaning ... is indeed contextually specified"[38] allows us to see that Chaucer was possibly reflecting, rather than commenting upon, proverb usage in the culture around him. What we see in the examples from *Troilus and Criseyde* is exactly the sort of contradiction Kirshenblatt-Gimblett cites. The multiple meanings available in the proverb "every thing hath tyme" [or "alle thyng hath tyme"] exploited by Pandarus in Books II (989) and III (855) parallel the possibilities that Kirshenblatt-Gimblett has noted in actual usage of the proverb "A rolling stone gathers no moss." Like Pandarus's proverb, this saying has been shown to have completely opposite meanings, depending on situational context — in this case whether moss is seen culturally as a positive or negative trait. In Scotland, where moss is undesirable, she notes, the interpretation is to "keep abreast of modern ideas, keep your

---

[37] In *Singer of Tales in Performance*, Foley, 47, defines the "performance arena" as "the locus where the event of performance takes place, where words are invested with their special power."

[38] Kirshenblatt-Gimblett, "Proverb Meaning," 112.

brain active."[39] In England, where moss is seen to have desirable qualities, the proverb affirms stability.

Likewise, the pair of contradictory proverbs employed by Troilus and Pandarus in their debate over the wisdom of sharing secrets with close friends (I.708-9; I.740-2) reflects the possibilities the genre offers in actual speech. Proverbs that contradict one another are also abundant, as Kirshenblatt-Gimblett points out. A few select pairs can illustrate: "You are never too old to learn" and "You cannot teach an old dog new tricks"; "Nothing ventured nothing gained" and "Better safe than sorry"; "Haste makes waste" and "Strike while the iron is hot."[40] Such contradictions illustrate her point that proverbs express "relative rather than absolute truths."[41] Chaucer further reflects actual proverb usage by employing sayings that the narrative does not go on to affirm. Just as the usage of a given proverb in actual speech cannot guarantee a specific outcome, the narrator's assertion that "after sharp shoures be victories" (III.1064) does not necessarily foreshadow a happy outcome for the lovers. In Chaucer's narrative, as in real life, the authority of proverbs is situation-specific. In *Havelok the Dane*, as in other oral-derived texts and in living oral traditions, the context within which proverbs have authority — the point of relativity — may encompass the entire narrative rather than being limited to a specific situation within the story. Just as characters' roles as heroes or villains are fairly clear-cut, so do sources of authority remain largely unambiguous. Thus the contradictions that we see across the wide spectrum of proverb usage in everyday discourse (or in Chaucer's writings that in significant ways reflect such discourse) do not occur in *Havelok*. The point of relativity shifts in Chaucer's writings: truths here are relative to the very immediate narrative context, perhaps only to be contradicted a few lines later by another character or when the dramatic situation changes. The wide range of possibilities allows Chaucer to play off audience expectations. Proverbial signs point toward traditional authority, but what we see in *Troilus* are competing authorities and multiple notions of truth.[42]

---

[39] Kirshenblatt-Gimblett, "Proverb Meaning," 112.

[40] Kirshenblatt-Gimblett, "Proverb Meaning," 114-15.

[41] Kirshenblatt-Gimblett, "Proverb Meaning," 112.

[42] See further Niditch, *Folklore and the Hebrew Bible*. She compares, 69, proverb usage in biblical texts that exhibit varying degrees of participation in traditional wisdom, specifically Proverbs and Ecclesiastes: "The author of Ecclesiastes

Proverbs like those seen in *Havelok* and *Troilus* represent only one of many traditionally-encoded genres embedded in narrative oral traditions and oral-derived texts. In a discussion of epics and narrative traditions world-wide, Lauri Honko has explained that most such narratives "contain other genres: proverbs, praises, prayers, incantations, laments, descriptions of ritual, etc., all also appearing independently in oral tradition."[43] Gopala Naika, singer of the Tulu *Siri Epic*, also recognizes the component parts that create meaning within longer narrative songs:

> You see, it goes knitting together, look!
> . . . .
> One piece joins another in sequence.[44]

The underlying tradition that gives powerful meaning to the pieces (in this case, proverbs) "knit" into the fabric of narratives is not lost with the technology of writing. Rather, meaning is created in substantially different ways.

Proverbs in *Havelok the Dane* direct emotional responses by sanctioning certain actions and characters while condemning others. As readers attuned to the genre's traditional implications, we can trust the words of wisdom to bear truth throughout the narrative. Chaucer, however, clearly operating within a literate tradition — the narrator of *Troilus and Criseyde* repeatedly refers to his own responsibilities as translator of a fixed text — evokes all the wisdom in proverbs but strips the representatives of these genres of their automatic authority by placing them in the mouths of unpredictable, and often unreliable, characters. The ambiguity evoked in these passages is potentially heightened for an audience familiar with the oral traditional register, one that can recognize the contrasts between what

---

uses a typical saying structure to challenge his own and his audience's learned belief system. The ear and the mind expect different 'fill in the blanks' ... and thus instead of reinforcing the status quo, the sayings challenge it." For example, compare the expected usage of the following saying in Proverbs 22:1, with the adaptation in Ecclesiastes, 7:1: "Preferred is a reputation than great wealth, than silver and gold is favor better" (Prov.); "Better a good reputation than fine oil and the day of death than the day of birth" (Eccles.): Niditch, trans., *Folklore and the Hebrew Bible*, 69.

[43] Honko, *Textualising the Siri Epic*, 28-9.
[44] Honko and Gopala, *Siri Epic*, 2, 493.

tradition leads us to expect and what the narrative actually provides. Recognizing the interplay between oral and literate expressive modes in Middle English narratives and the ways that genres employed within these narratives operate differently can potentially lead to a heightened awareness and appreciation of the artistry involved in *Havelok*, *Troilus*, and the body of Middle English romances as a whole.[45]

---

[45] I am especially grateful to John Foley, Martin Camargo, Mark Amodio, and Scott Garner for their assistance during the preparation of this paper.

TIM WILLIAM MACHAN

Writing the Failure of Speech in *Pearl*

Since transitions from an oral to a textual culture and then a print one are gradual, it has become axiomatic to note the survival of earlier cultural forms in later cultural practices. Though extant Homeric, Anglo-Saxon, and Middle Welsh literatures thus obviously exist in written form, for example, their aesthetics bear traces of oral traditions, just as literature from the early days of print sometimes embodies the aesthetics of manuscript culture. For Middle English literature, composed with Anglo-Saxon oral traditions in the recent past and early modern print culture in the near future, studies of orality initially focused on an aesthetic residue of formulas and type scenes that appear frequently in romances of the period. Such studies had limited success, for however formulaic a particular phrase in a particular work may be, the work in its entirety and medieval transmission by minstrels and *disours* undermine any claim that composition could be explained by the Parry–Lord hypothesis.[1] Yet if the transition from the oral to the textual, like that from the chirographic to the typographic, is gradual and sustained, the clearest residue of orality may lie not in the most obvious features of composition but in subtler and more fundamental features of poetics and transmission.[2] Unexamined aesthetic assumptions and strategies in a textual culture, that is, may reproduce oral prac-

---

[1] The literature on orality and the composition of Middle English romances in particular is vast. The seminal thesis, now much qualified, can be found in Waldron, "Oral-Formulaic Technique."

[2] See, for example, Amodio, *Oral Poetics*; Machan, "Editing, Orality"; McGillivray, *Memorization*; and, more generally, Renoir, *Key to Old Poems*.

tices in ways that had become naturalized, even inevitable, for those who clearly saw themselves as writers and, just as clearly, cultivated certain features of written aesthetics. The critical difficulty then becomes distinguishing the patterns of conversation and styles of speech that reflect spontaneous oral practices or composition from those that reflect studied, textual cultivation.

As written remains, extant Middle English works certainly do not offer transcriptions of natural speech. Particularly in the case of poetry, Middle English writings are fundamentally rhetorical exercises that are constrained by various social factors and conditioned by medieval discursive practices (e.g., the demands of genre) as well as by strictly sociolinguistic impulses. In some instances, such as in works traditionally considered belletristic, the rhetorical stylizing may owe to the demands of meter or genre. For legal, ecclesiastical, or historical works, traditional expressions, narrative conventions, or ideological imperatives may overlie any genuine spoken usage. In this way, the speech of lower-rank individuals like millers or women from Bath (say) is not only always a written representation of that speech but also often the work of a fairly narrow social group — male, courtly, and devout — that might well have a vested interest in the character and content of this speech.

At the same time, all language, written or spoken, figures in the semiotics of social practice. Legal publications, bank statements, and advertisements may do so rather obviously in the way they fashion social identities and relations, but poetry and fiction participate in the production of social meaning as well. On a purely technical level of grammar and usage, the language of literature is not fundamentally different from the language of daily life, for spoken language is characterized by the presence of the same tropes and rhetorical strategies as literary language and therefore responds to the same kinds of study.[3] The primary differences between literary and daily language lie in the use to which such strategies are put and in the degree to which they are used at all. Conversation can be considered in this regard. When speech acts contribute to the mimetic aspirations of a work's fictional world — as they typically do to at least some extent — they succeed or fail in accordance with how well they reproduce the linguistic

---

[3] See, for example, Fludernik, *Fictions of Language*; Tannen, *Talking Voices*; and Biber, *Variation Across Speech*. Recent criticism on this topic thus rejects the Prague School of Linguistics's claims about the peculiarity of literary language.

semiotics of the reader's social world. Put another way, if writers seek to represent conversations, then the conversants, speech acts, and discursive strategies that they depict must bear enough resemblance to real-life conversations for their readers to perceive the connection. To be recognized as a trial, for instance, even in the topsy-turvy world of Alice's Adventures in Wonderland, a speech event needs to contain the speech acts and speaking roles characteristic of a trial, and one might therefore use Alice's trial as a partial model for language use in real Victorian courtrooms,[4] just as, more generally, one might use real-life utterances and pragmatics as ways to evaluate fictional ones. By the same token, when medieval morality plays are criticized for the woodenness of their characters and artificiality of their dialogue, this criticism emerges at least in part from the disparity between a reader's experience of conversations and the plays' representations of them.

My focus in this essay is Pearl, a late-fourteenth-century poem that tells the first-person story of a man who one day, while asleep on his daughter's grave, has a fantastic dream in which the girl appears to him and offers him consolation about grace, divine justice, and her salvation. Though the girl was not even two when she died, she materializes as the fully grown adult much medieval thought predicted for resurrection,[5] conversant with Scripture and firm in the orthodoxy of her faith. For much of the poem, the Dreamer struggles to comprehend the changes his daughter has experienced, and he is insistently puzzled by the fact that one so young, who did not yet know even the Lord's Prayer, has not only gained entrance to heaven but also, by her own admission, been crowned a queen. Whether the Dreamer ever learns the lessons the Maiden teaches is in fact one of the central critical issues of scholarship on Pearl, with the poem's conclusion offering evidence for mutually conflicting positions. On the one hand, when he awakes the Dreamer strongly affirms God's power by declaring, "'Now al be to þat Prynseȝ paye'" (1176) ["Now all may be as that Prince may please"];[6] but on the other, he has awakened only because he has attempted to cross the river that separates him from the Maiden, de-

---

[4] Carroll, Alice's Adventures, 132–49.

[5] Bynum, Resurrection of the Body.

[6] All quotations of Pearl are from Gordon's edition and, unless otherwise noted, the translations are Tolkien's.

spite her continuous implicit and explicit assertions that it would be impossible for him to join her.

In some ways, *Pearl* is one of the most cultivated, textual poems of the late medieval period, for it embodies perhaps the most complex metrical scheme in the whole of the Middle English canon and demonstrates detailed familiarity with the Bible.[7] At the same time, the poem's emphasis on conversation renders *Pearl* a work imbued with oral concerns. Of the 1212 lines, indeed, perhaps seven hundred are devoted to a conversation between the Maiden and the Dreamer, and once the two meet, they do little else but talk as they stand or walk beside the river that divides them. Coming from a gray area of transition from primary orality to primary textuality, *Pearl* is thus itself an aesthetically transitional work, one responding both to medieval textual culture and to the mimetic demands of representing speech. My interest is not with any putative connection between the poem's aesthetics and traditional oral-formulaic theory, nor simply with how conversation contributes to the poem's meaning. Rather, I want to use the poem's rhetorical effects as a platform for examining how written literature, however stylized it may be, can – perhaps must – nonetheless bear traces of a literally oral context of ordinary speech; or, to put the matter another way, how these traces can help to account for some of a written poem's distinctive aesthetic achievement. In pursuing such an examination, I will use features of contemporary discourse analysis to assess the topic, structure, and success of the conversation in *Pearl* as well as its implications for medieval cultural practices.

For many readers, the heart of *Pearl*, both thematically and narratively, is the contrast between the bereaved father's limited understanding of faith, salvation, and heaven, and the transcendent and theologically unimpeachable explanations of his transformed daughter. John M. Hill, for example, suggests that the Maiden, "conveying celestial truth, speaks skillfully and in highly figurative mode. Her role, essentially, is one of revelation: she points to divine logic and truth on the one hand and the dreamer's insufficient cognition on the other."[8] In the way the Maiden offers this revelation, Derek Pearsall sees her as reproving the Dreamer "like a stern school-mistress for his incorrigibly worldly habits of mind," while

---

[7] For a brief account of the poem's metrical structure, see Gordon, ed., *Pearl*, 87-91. The secondary literature on this structure and its effects is extensive.

[8] Hill, "Middle English Poets," 166.

W. A. Davenport describes the cognitive contrast between the Dreamer and the Maiden as the vehicle for the poem's instruction: "as the Dreamer speaks briefly and ignorantly and the Maiden with knowledge and at length, Dreamer and reader are simply presented with a series of carefully pre-packaged instruction parcels."[9] Elizabeth D. Kirk, however, has diverged from this critical consensus on the poem's pedagogical orientation. She suggests that *Pearl* presents a fundamental opposition between reasoned theology and affective humanity. In this sense, though the Dreamer lacks the ability to understand the Maiden, she, too, lacks the ability to understand him:

> Unlike the Lamb to whom they have a common allegiance, she has never been a real human being and can have no idea what it is like. Consequently she has no ability to engage with why he finds any of her teaching difficult. Her voice, indeed, is an extrapolation of all those answers he already knew before he fainted onto her grave and they can not help him here any more than they did then.[10]

Kirk sees the Dreamer finally reconciling himself to his condition and the Maiden's transformation in the Eucharist, which he acknowledges only after the dream has ended.

Though the critics themselves do not put the issue in these terms, all these readings imply that the Dreamer and the Maiden's conversation, however long and intense it may be, is not a success. Until the final fit of the poem, the Dreamer seems unable to comprehend what the Maiden says, and by Kirk's analysis this lack of communication is mutual. In fact, the mimetic qualities of the conversation in *Pearl* suggest that the miscommunication is more extensive and has greater sociolinguistic implications than critics have recognized. As a way into this issue, I begin with two general features characterizing all conversations in which participants

---

[9] Pearsall, *Old English and Middle English*, 173; and Davenport, *Art of the Gawain-Poet*, 17. Also see Stanbury, *Seeing the Gawain-Poet*, 12–41; Gross, "Courtly Language"; Nolan, *Gothic Visionary Perspective*, 191–203; and Milroy, "Verbal Texture."

[10] E. Kirk, "Anatomy of a Mourning," 222.

are not intentionally attempting to mislead one another. First, conversants want to understand what each other says. And second, to this end they typically strive for, and are satisfied with, adequate rather than complete communication.[11] The latter may occur in certain limited circumstances, such as an inquiry about the correct time or a library's ownership of a particular book, but this kind of communication constitutes only a limited portion of everyday conversation. More typically, when we find ourselves discussing politics, education, or even the weather, communication occurs and conversations progress despite the fact that much of what is said is only partially understood. In a discussion of government policy, it is sufficient if listeners recognize only that the speaker disagrees with a particular law on the grounds that it disadvantages a particular group; they need not understand precisely how the speaker disagrees with particular paragraphs of the law. Or when speakers arrange to meet by a particular bench in a particular park, the fact of their meeting obviates whatever differences there may have been between the speakers' conceptions of the bench and its location.

As well-intentioned as both conversants in *Pearl* seem, however, they fail to reach even adequate communication, a failure that is evident already in the details of their initial exchange. When the Dreamer encounters the Maiden at the beginning of this exchange, he has been describing the wonders of the surrealistic landscape in which he finds himself, and he continues by describing the Maiden with the same degree of detail. After eighty lines during which neither of them has spoken, the Dreamer finally declares:

> "O perle," quod I, "in perleȝ pyȝt,
> Art þou my perle þat I haf playned,
> Regretted by myn one on nyȝte?"
>
> (241–3)

> ["O Pearl!" said I, "in pearls arrayed,
> Are you my pearl whose loss I mourn?
> Lament alone by night I made."]

---

[11] Levinson, *Pragmatics*, 17–18.

In asking this question, the Dreamer attempts one of the most common and basic strategies in any conversation — membershipping, in which speakers endeavor to classify each other according to background, social standing, intelligence, and so forth.[12] Membershipping figures prominently in conversations, for it enables speakers to decide who their interlocutors are, the relationship they in turn bear them, the consequent topics that they might have in common, and the attitude each might display towards these topics depending on the degree of intimacy and friendliness each desires. The same individual might be membershipped in different ways in different conversations, or even in different ways in the same conversation, but without membershipping speakers lack a focus and goals for their remarks, so that even the best-intentioned fail (in various ways) to engage their interlocutors in successful conversation. As they membership one another, speakers also classify their conversation as an instance of a particular speech event, such as a lecture from a minister, or a heart-to-heart with a close friend, or a discussion around the family dinner table. Speakers concomitantly essay particular topics according to knowledge that they invoke to provide inferential understanding of an utterance (i.e., frames) or to a sequence of events that they regard as typical for a given situation (i.e., scripts). In short, ordinary conversation works by means of speakers identifying their interlocutors and drawing on analogy with their prior experiences in a particular speech event, and it is for this reason that strange or unique circumstances leave us, proverbially and literally, speechless.[13]

The simple gesture of the Dreamer's greeting thus carries with it an expectation for the direction of the conversation and the characteristics of its speakers. The Dreamer memberships the Maiden as his deceased daughter, a fashion that is at once logical and consistent with the grief he has already expressed. In doing so, he appropriates for himself a paternal role, evinced in his use of the familiar pronoun "þou," and foregrounds the human emotion that he presumes to share with her from their mutual loss — he of her, and she of him. The speech event he attempts is a conversation between father and daughter, the attendant frames of which would

---

[12] Coulthard, *Introduction to Discourse Analysis*, 82.

[13] Brown and Yule, *Discourse Analysis*, 67. The larger issue here involves Idealized Cognitive Models, on which see Lakoff, *Women, Fire, and Dangerous Things*, esp. 68-76.

involve information about their individual characters, their personal life together, and the power and predictability of human emotion. Potential scripts include those involving the display of overwhelming passion at reunion with a lost loved one, in which case one would expect confirmation of identity, the expression of simultaneous sorrow and joy, and the attempt to update each speaker's membershipping of the other through declarations of what they have experienced since they last parted.

Yet the Maiden's brusque answer to the Dreamer indicates that she rejects every conversational strategy he has employed: membershipping, frame, and script. "'Sir, ȝe haf your tale mysetente'" (257) ["Good sir, you have your speech mis-spent"], she responds, and if the title "sir" denotes respect and thereby seems to evoke a speech event similar to the one the Dreamer posits, her rejection of his strategies — and the abrupt syntax of her expression — does not. Indeed, henceforth she uses not the honorific "ȝe" and "ȝow," as one would anticipate from a daughter to a father, but the familiar if not condescending "þou" and "þe."[14] For the Maiden, it becomes clear, the speech event is a theological lecture by the learned and divine for the ignorant and human. The knowledge she evokes accordingly involves concepts of the unchanging and eternal soul in comparison to the transient body, while her script demands a *disputatio* and point-by-point refutation of an erring student's views. As she demonstrates, for example, she is in fact a "pearl," though not in the earthly sense of the Dreamer's beloved daughter but in the theological sense of a soul saved and made divine "þurȝ kynde of þe kyste þat hyt con close" (271) [the casket's virtues that it enclose].

If the Dreamer's and the Maiden's differing conversational expectations enact miscommunication, so, too, does the fact that these differences have no effect on either conversant, for as much as the Maiden has rejected or ignored the Dreamer's conversational strategies, his response to her reveals that he has not qualified his sense of the speech event or script at all. In this initial exchange he continues to foreground the pathos of the situation, the communality of human emotion, and the literalness of the pearl rather than its theological significance:

---

[14] A convenient discussion of the second person pronouns in Middle English is Burnley, *Chaucer's Language*, 18-22. For a more nuanced account of how Middle English pronouns marked asymmetrical status relations and also indicated increased emotional involvement and intimacy, see Lass, "Phonology and Morphology," 148-55.

"Iwyse," quod I, "my blysfol beste,
My grete dystresse þou al todrawe3.
To be excused I make requeste;
I trawed my perle don out of dawe3.
Now haf I fonde hyt, I schal ma feste,
And wony wyth hyt in schyr wod-schawe3."
                                                    (279-84)

["My blissful one," quoth I, "most dear,
My sorrows deep you have all allayed.
To pardon me I pray you here!
In the darkness I deemed my pearl was laid;
I have found it now, and shall make good cheer,
With it dwell in shining grove and glade."]

To put the matter concisely: though the Dreamer and Maiden speak the same variety of Middle English, engage in a well-structured question-and-answer exchange, and even seem to be addressing the same topic — the nature of the Maiden — they do not see themselves in the same speech event and they do not draw on the same consequent frames and scripts. They are not, in fact, talking about the same thing at all, and after only forty-eight lines of dialogue there is already ample indication that the conversation will not succeed.

As even this brief analysis suggests, each speaker brings to the conversation a different set of assumptions and a different set of conversational strategies. Above all, the Dreamer's language is interactional, focusing on social relations and personal feelings, so that his primary speech acts are assertives and expressives — complaints about his unhappiness or the Maiden's lack of sensitivity or expressions of other emotional conditions.[15] Consistent with his skill at describing the vivid detail of his vision,[16] his own utterances to the Maiden are thoroughly literal, and he is in general, both ontologically and linguistically, very much of the physical world. While the Maiden, for example, employs co-referential language that alludes to other texts as well as to her own utterances, the Dreamer's language is nearly exclusively referential, positing relations to his own real

---

[15] On interactional language, see Brown and Yule, *Discourse Analysis*, 1-4.

[16] Stanbury, *Seeing the Gawain-Poet*, 12-41.

world.[17] Further, if metaphors and allusions to Scripture characterize the Maiden's language, the Dreamer alone uses domestic images like weaving (71-2) or plain and common colloquialisms like "'We meten so selden by stok oþer ston'" (380) ["We meet on our roads by chance so rare"] and "'What lyf ȝe lede erly and late'" (392) ["What life you lead the livelong day"]. Of the former A. C. Spearing observes, "As a cliché belonging to earthly meetings and separations it makes us feel the Dreamer's loneliness in the strange world of his dream."[18]

Also characteristic of the Dreamer's language is the fact that his responses typically indicate that he has not understood what the Maiden has said — or, to put the matter in terms of discourse analysis, that he has constructed a reference different from the speaker's meaning as it seems evident to the reader. Such is the case with the example I have just considered, and it remains so throughout the conversation. In the stanzas following this exchange, for instance, the Maiden uses theology to dismiss the Dreamer's belief that he has once more seen his daughter and that he intends to join her across the water. Predicating her response on the central truth and significance of Christ's death and resurrection, the Maiden stresses the priority of faith over literal sight and asserts that the Dreamer may join her only with God's permission and after he has died. The essence of her answer is thus the theological truth that following the mortal death demanded by Adam and Eve's fall, salvation, which is what she has and embodies, comes only through God's grace and belief in what His physical death represents. In effect, the Maiden here utters a directive about what the Dreamer must do to join her, but he hears this as an assertive about the mere fact that they cannot be together:

> "Demeȝ þou me," quod I, "my swete,
> To dol agayn, þenne I dowyne.
> Now haf I fonte þat I forlete,
> Schal I efte forgo hit er euer I fyne?

---

[17] Brown and Yule, *Discourse Analysis*, 204.

[18] Spearing, *The Gawain-Poet*, 154. Also see Davenport, *Art of the Gawain-Poet*, 16. Indicative of this quality of the Dreamer's speech is the simile "I stod as hende as hawk in halle" (184) [I stood as tame as hawk in hall], which he uses, however, in a passage of description.

Why schal I hit boþe mysse and mete?"
(325-9)

["If my doom you deem it, maiden sweet,
To mourn once more, then I must pine.
Now my lost one found again I greet,
Must bereavement new till death be mine?
Why must I at once both part and meet?"]

Having perceived the Maiden's meaning in this fashion, the Dreamer consequently misperceives its implications, for while she addresses transhuman experience — experience that is governed by theological logic rather than human emotion — he sees only a specifically human response to the human situation he has understood:

"When I am partleȝ of perle myne,
Bot durande doel what may men deme?"
(335-6)

["When in my pearl no part is mine,
Only endless dolour one that may deem."]

Similar misperceptions rooted in differing conceptual and conversational strategies occur later in the poem. When the Maiden declares that she is a queen of heaven (415), meaning that she is one of those who has eternally joined the bridegroom of the New Testament, the Dreamer understands the reference in earthly terms and, assuming that there may be only one king and queen at a time, insists that the "'Quen of cortaysye'" (432) ["Queen of Courtesy"] can be Mary alone.

Here and elsewhere the Maiden displays conversational strategies strikingly different from those of the Dreamer.[19] Where he is interactional and given to assertives and expressives, she is transactional and primarily utters directives like commands, requests, advice, and recommendations.

---

[19] In many ways, the conversational differences between the Dreamer and the Maiden parallel those between Jonah and God in *Patience*, another poem uniquely found in the same manuscript that contains *Pearl* (London, British Library, Cotton Nero A. x) and possibly by the same author.

The entire speech event with the Dreamer as she conceives it, indeed, is essentially a directive meant to enlighten him about the significance of her death and the promise of salvation. Even speech acts like her narration of the parable of the vineyard, which is in one sense an assertive meant to report the truth of a Scriptural passage, ultimately function as commands that the Dreamer should simply believe. If the Dreamer's utterances tend toward the literal, further, the Maiden's are frequently metaphorical, using words like "queen" and "courtesy" in evolved senses and depending on allusions to Scripture. As I noted earlier, thus, while the Dreamer's language is referential to the real world that he and all human beings inhabit outside his dream, hers is co-referential, tied to her other utterances, as in her initial rebuke of the Dreamer when she depends on indirect quotation of him. Since the Maiden is so theologically orthodox and bears so little relation to the human girl who "'lyfed not two ȝer in oure þede'" (483) ["Two years you lived not on earth with me"], she is in fact little more than a text herself, declaring the revealed truths of Christianity. Consequently, her frequent references to Scripture – including Genesis, Isaiah, the Gospel of St. John, and Revelations – are essentially co-referential to the same text that has produced her and that she, in turn, utters.[20]

The Maiden's use of scriptural quotations points to another of her distinctive conversational strategies: assumption of a dominant role. Her frequent quotations, particularly the lengthy retellings of the parable of the vineyard in fits IX and X and of Revelations in fit XV, are authorizing gestures used by the Dreamer only at lines 595-6, where he quotes Psalms.[21] It is also the Maiden who typically determines the topics of conversation; even when the Dreamer asks about her dwelling place (917) and thereby seems to redirect the discussion, she transforms the topic by processing the question as not a literal but a theological one, and the remainder of the poem consequently concerns heaven and the beatific vision. Perhaps the surest indicator of the Maiden's dominance strategy, however, is the sheer volume of her utterances in comparison to the Dreamer's. Of the roughly seven hundred lines devoted to their conversation, approxi-

---

[20] For a full list of biblical allusions in the poem, see Gordon, *Pearl*, 165-7.

[21] On other occasions, scriptural allusions seem to underlie the Dreamer's comments, but even these are incidental. His long use of Revelations in fits XVII and XVIII to describe the heavenly Jerusalem is of course narrative and not part of his conversation with the Maiden.

mately four hundred actually involve speech, and of these lines over three hundred are spoken by the Maiden.

One way to read the speakers' differences and misperceptions, again, is the way critical receptions of the poem often read them — as indications of the flawed and limited understanding that typifies human beings. Drawing on the conversation's mimetic qualities, including the way each speaker's interpretation of the other is entirely consistent with their characteristics as speakers, I want to suggest an alternative reading, one that turns on the construction of conversational meaning in general. Though structural linguistics treats reference as something inherent in an utterance, regardless of who produces it and under any circumstances, in J. L. Austin's pioneering work on speech acts, from which much discourse analysis evolves, the illocutionary force of an utterance (what a speaker intends to accomplish by it) depends on the speaker's meaning. John Searle furthered and refined Austin's thinking by maintaining that it is in fact the listener's interpretation of an utterance that defines its illocutionary force.[22] Recent discourse analysis has pushed this line of thinking even further to define reference as an action of speaker and listener together within a particular context, by which meaning is precisely what is being negotiated in conversations. From this view, a conversation is a fundamentally joint action the meaning and structure of which emerge as the conversation progresses, sometimes in ways that none of the participants intends or imagines.[23] A given speaker may have an objective in a conversation as well as an intended meaning, but whether these objectives and meanings are realized depends as much on how the listener processes the speaker's utterances — and consequently responds to the speaker — as it does on the utterances themselves. What is particularly important for understanding the structure of a conversation is recognition of how utterance and interpretation dynamically interact.

From this perspective on conversational structure and success, it is significant that the Maiden seems no more effective at understanding the Dreamer than he is her. After she rejects his sorrow by asserting the omnipotence of God, for instance, and the Dreamer asks the Maiden for for-

---

[22] The classic studies are Austin, *How to Do Things with Words*; and Searle, *Speech Acts*. Also see Petrey, *Speech Acts*; and Coulthard, *Introduction to Discourse Analysis*, 24.

[23] See Clark, *Using Language*, esp. 59-91.

giveness, he expresses his joy at seeing her and describes himself as "'bot mol and manereȝ mysse'" (382) ["but mould and good manners miss"]. Though the "loneliness" (in Spearing's words) that he expresses suggests no emotional or intellectual change from his previous position, the Maiden misinterprets his words as acceptance of her arguments and welcomes him

> "...here to walk and byde,
> For now þy speche is to me dere."
> (399-400)
>
> ["And welcome here to walk and bide;
> For now your words are to me dear."]

The Maiden displays a similar misunderstanding of the Dreamer's own misunderstanding in fit XVI, when, after a lengthy account of heaven that draws heavily on the description in Revelations, the Dreamer asks,

> "Haf ȝe no woneȝ in castel-walle,
> Ne maner þer ȝe may mete and won?"
> (917-18)
>
> ["No home in castle-wall do ye share,
> No mansion to meet in, no domain?"]

The Dreamer's question is almost painfully literal, displaying no comprehension of either the Maiden's immortality or the theological ramifications of John's vision; he goes on to wonder, indeed, where so "'cumly a pakke of joly juele'" (929) ["jewels so lovely"] might live since he sees "'no bygyng nawhere aboute'" (932) ["nowhere about any house"]. Yet the Maiden does not acknowledge the literalness of his comprehension, proceeding instead with a *distinctio* between the earthly and heavenly Jerusalems and then, with God's prior permission, acceding to the Dreamer's request for a glimpse of the latter.

If meaning is what conversants construct together, the Dreamer's interpretations can be wrong — and the Maiden's right — only when the two of them, sharing an understanding of the conversation's structure and purpose, accept this to be the case, and when the conversation in its entirety supports this interpretation. And this does not happen. As much as the Dreamer's reference may be earthly, the Maiden's is theological, and each of them attempts to manage the conversation as a corresponding speech event. From the view of discourse analysis, the Dreamer's misperceptions are his attempts to define not simply her meaning but the meaning of the conversation, and while his attempts certainly do run contrary to hers, hers, equally, run contrary to his. In his speech at lines 323-6 the Dreamer inclusively and eloquently (I think) recounts his pain, for example, but the Maiden, recognizing that his utterance is in no way theologically responsive, can only ask why he sorrows. In response, the Dreamer then excuses his misunderstanding by again processing the Maiden's renewed assertion of God's omnipotence not theologically but emotively and with a characteristically humanizing simile:

"My herte watȝ al wyth mysse remorde,
As wallande water gotȝ out of welle."
(364-5)

["My heart the pain of loss outpoured,
Gushing as water springs from the well."]

And later, when the Dreamer challenges a courtesy that can reward infants with the status of queen, the very form of the Maiden's response — a parable — is discordant with the literal character of his questions.

It is not surprising that two such disparate conversational strategists should produce a conversation marked by other signs of unsuccessful communication. Debate over the precise meaning of words like *queen, courtesy, pearl, jeweler, innocent,* and *right* motivates much of the discussion and thereby structures the poem, which in this sense can be seen as a poem about theological meaning.[24] But though the conversants' differing construals of these concepts are apparent to the reader, neither the Dreamer nor the Maiden — at least during the course of their discussion — become reconciled to one definition or another. When the Dreamer, for instance, suggests that "'Goddeȝ ryȝt'" (591) ["God's justice"] demands that individual reward should be proportionate to the length of service, so that a girl dying before two years of age does not merit such a high posi-

---

[24] See further Milroy, "Verbal Texture."

tion in heaven, the Maiden responds first by asserting that "'þe grace of God is gret inoghe'" (612) ["the grace of God is great enow"] and then by redefining "righteouness": "'And inoscente is saf and ry3te'" (672) ["Innocence is saved by right"]. Though she here asserts the theological equation of righteousness and innocence, the Dreamer gives no indication of having redirected his thinking in this way. He responds to her, indeed, by asking about her beauty, which "'com neuer of nature'" (749) ["was never from nature gained"], and the kind of position she holds in heaven, to which the Maiden responds without commenting on the discordance between his question and their competing senses of righteousness.

If speakers are mutually to negotiate meaning and participate in a successful conversation, they need to adhere to what Herbert Clark calls the Principle of Mutual Responsibility: "The participants in a conversation try to establish, roughly by the initiation of each new contribution, the mutual belief that the listeners have understood what the speaker meant in the last utterance to a criterion sufficient for current purposes."[25] Five ways by which a listener can demonstrate such comprehension, ranked in terms of weakest confirmation to strongest, are: continued attention, initiation of the relevant next contribution, acknowledgment, demonstration, and display. Various social and linguistic forces compel listeners to indicate comprehension, even when it is absent, so that in any successful conversation both speaker and listener pay particular attention to the Principle of Mutual Responsibility. This is especially the case in task-oriented conversations (those that explain a process) or conversations devoted to complex issues. "Generally," Clark observes, "the more complicated A's presentation, or the more demanding the current purpose, the more evidence should be needed to convince A that B has understood."[26] Since even successful conversations sometimes go awry, speakers use strategies like restarts and repairs to clarify their meaning, to the same end as listeners offer phatic utterances like "uh huh" (acknowledgment) or, perhaps in a classroom setting, verbatim repetition of what has been said to them (display). Typically, the place where listeners "initiate most repairs and expansions and offer most replacements is immediately after the presentation and before the next contribution is initiated. It is for this reason that allowing a new contribution to proceed is tantamount to a mutual ac-

---

[25] Clark, *Arenas of Language Use*, 139.
[26] Clark, *Arenas of Language Use*, 153-4.

ceptance of the old one."²⁷ Silence is thus a particularly weak indicator of comprehension, since with it a listener bypasses any opportunity for correction at the most appropriate place in the conversation.

To return to the passage about innocence and righteousness: the Dreamer never addresses the Maiden's definition, though he does, presumably, show continued attention. When he raises the topic of the Maiden's appearance, he might be regarded as initiating the next relevant contribution; but even in this instance he is demonstrating a weak indicator of comprehension, and in any case the relevance of appearance to righteousness is in no way necessary or even intuitive. As insistently theological as her remarks are, so his remain mundane, including, in the passage under consideration, comments about her clothing and, later, the question about where the Maiden lives that occurs after she has paraphrased Revelations on the kingdom of heaven and those who gain entrance to it. The Dreamer's comments and silence here offer little indication that he understands or accepts what is being discussed; given his characteristics as a speaker and the speech event as he evidently understands it, in fact, it is doubtful that he can ever understand the Maiden during the conversation. The Maiden's willingness to move on in the conversation, therefore, would seem to indicate that she, as much as he, has shirked the Principle of Mutual Responsibility, particularly since the complex character of the discussion as she understands it (in effect task-oriented to his instruction) makes it incumbent on her to verify the Dreamer's understanding. Without any restarts, repairs, or verifications, both the Dreamer and the Maiden display no indication that they ever realize they are having difficulty understanding each other.

On a purely formal level, the conversation between Dreamer and Maiden shows still other signs of unsuccessful communication. As the volume of the Maiden's speech implies, there are few adjacency pairs in the discussion, whereby the speakers engage in a sequence of relatively quick turns. Adjacency pairs, such as brief questions and answers, allow speakers a relatively equal voice in conversation and, more importantly and in accordance with the Principle of Mutual Responsibility, are an effective means for the mutual shaping of meaning and the correction of misperceptions. The Maiden's dominance of the interaction indicates that while her meaning is well established (at least for the reader), adequate

---

[27] Clark, *Arenas of Language Use*, 141.

communication is not, with the result that the meaning of the conversation diverges from what either speaker intends.

Another formal feature suggesting infelicitous communication is the Maiden's tone, which, as Pearsall suggests, does indeed sound like that of a "stern school-mistress." Though her tone softens as the conversation progresses, in the beginning her dismissiveness borders on contempt:

> "Wy borde ȝe men? So madde ȝe be!
> Þre wordeȝ hatȝ þou spoken at ene:
> Vnavysed, for soþe, wern alle þre."
> (290–2)
>
> ["Why jest ye men? How mad ye be!
> Three things at once you have said, I ween:
> Thoughtless, forsooth, were all the three."]

Her use of the familiar "þou" here and throughout the remainder of the poem represents a sociolinguistically conflicted strategy. As one of the elect, the Maiden clearly is superior to the Dreamer, and so she certainly is entitled to use the familiar form with him. Yet as the Dreamer's daughter, one could also argue, the Maiden ought rather show respect by using "ȝe," leaving the familiar to him alone. Indeed, this is the pronominal form he uses to her with essentially only one exception, in fit VII, lines 372–96, when in an emotional confession of his sorrow the Dreamer mixes "ȝe" with forms of "þou," and one might well argue that the shift to the plural here constitutes a distancing attempt.[28] The only grammaticalized honorific in Middle English, the second person pronoun serves as a continual reminder that the conversants have been unable to membership each other to mutual satisfaction.[29]

Emblematic of the misformed character of the Dreamer and the Maiden's conversation is the treatment of the greeting and the conclusion.

---

[28] The only other time the Dreamer uses the plural with the Maiden is at line 933, the significance of which is not clear. The preceding passage focuses on the heavenly host, for which "ȝe" is entirely appropriate, and this plural may simply be an accident of the poet's. Indeed, at line 935 the Dreamer resumes with the expected "þou."

[29] Some languages, such as Japanese, do grammaticalize other honorifics. See Levinson, *Pragmatics*, 89–91; and Trudgill, *Sociolinguistics*, 89–91.

Greetings and farewells are among the most complex moments in conversations, since they not only help to define the character and extent of the speech event but also present particular danger for speakers or listeners to produce, unconsciously, face-threatening actions against one other.[30] Beginning a conversation with a stranger can be especially difficult, for speakers risk the embarrassing rebuff of their own attempts at congeniality. At the close of a conversation, conversely, speakers risk terminating the conversation before listeners are ready or in a way that suggests the conversation has been unpleasant. In order to cultivate social relationships, consequently, speakers often employ elaborate rituals of closure, including appeals to some implacable exterior force, such as "I've got to go now," or "duty calls."[31]

The conversation in *Pearl* thus begins inauspiciously, for though the Dreamer relates that the Maiden proffered him speech, inclining "lowe in wommon lore" (236) [low as ladies' ways demand], the first of her words that he records are the brusque "'Sir, ȝe haf your tale mysetente.'" Her rejection of his identification, further, as well as their inability to membership each other properly, means that both speakers, however congenial the rest of the conversation may seem to be, have here exposed themselves to social embarrassment — though admittedly the Dreamer is the only one who is likely to recognize as much. The conclusion of their conversation is even more abrupt. The Maiden instructs the Dreamer to walk parallel with her along the opposite bank of the stream until he sees the new Jerusalem, and then ceases to speak and simply disappears, reappearing seventy lines later in a procession of the elect. The conversation thus provides the Dreamer with no opportunity to commit himself to its (infelicitous) termination, and the proxemics of the speakers — who throughout the conversation are divided by the river and then silently separated — manifests this same infelicity.[32]

---

[30] On face-threatening actions see further below and, more generally, W. Miller, *Humiliation*.

[31] Wardhaugh, *How Conversation Works*, 49, 117, 156.

[32] The Maiden's gaze at the beginning of the poem also has significant proxemic implications. In conversation, Goodwin points out, *Conversational Organization*, 30, "gaze is not simply a means of obtaining information, the receiving end of a communications system, but is itself a social act. Within conversation, the gaze of the participants toward each other is constrained by the social issues, provides for its organization and meaningfulness within the turn." Gazes can in-

In view of these specifics of the failure of conversation in *Pearl* — the participants' inability to membership one another, their use of conflicting frames and scripts, their opposed conversational strategies, and their mutual neglect of the Principle of Mutual Responsibility — I want now to consider the reasons for such failure, and, more generally, how conversations relate to larger social institutions like Christianity in the Middle Ages. What ultimately enables and determines the character of all conversations is common ground, or the conversants' mutual beliefs, mutual suppositions, and mutual knowledge deriving from community membership and physical and linguistic co-presence. This common ground may be communal, meaning it is shared by those belonging to a particular speech community or social group, or it may be personal between two speakers. When speakers meet, it is common ground, in relation to the objectives of a specific speech event, that circumscribes what they say to each other and how — what jokes and allusions they can make, what words and syntax they use, what topics they can successfully raise — and so encounters between two strangers often involve strategies to identify their common ground. In so doing, such conversants construct developing models of one another that they then use as the focus and inspiration of their comments. By Clark's analysis,

> People have selective access to information that is pertinent to each person they talk to. They have a model of what is in the other person's mind, a model they have built up from previous contact and which they continue to update as they go on talking. It is that model that en-

---

dicate submission, as with listeners, who characteristically gaze on speakers more than the latter do on them, or dominance, as when a speaker gazes in order to recover a listener's attention or in animal interactions. The Dreamer first sees the Maiden at line 161, and at line 177 she "vereȝ ... vp her fayre frount" [her forehead fair then up she raises] toward him. He then describes her appearance in detail, until at lines 235-8 he reports that she doffs her crown and greets him. Over sixty lines are thus devoted to the Dreamer's examination of her appearance, during which time the Maiden, presumably, continues to gaze in silence at him, a lengthy gaze that here might well be regarded as a display of dominance. On proxemics see further Wardhaugh, *How Conversation Works*, 78-88; and Argyle and Cook, *Gaze and Mutual Gaze*.

ables people to make and understand references so quickly and accurately.[33]

To understand another's comments, then, we limit ourselves to meanings that reasonably emerge from our common ground.[34]

The source of the conversational confusion in *Pearl*, I suggest, is that having membershipped each other in conflicting ways, the Dreamer and the Maiden accordingly presuppose conflicting common grounds, evidenced in the conflicting frames and scripts that each employs. The Dreamer, seeing the Maiden as his returned earthly daughter, presupposes that they have mutual knowledge of human loss and suffering and, more personally, of their own separation. He further presupposes that she will be as glad to see him as he is to see her, and, on the basis of their linguistic co-presence as he understands it, he believes that they are talking about human feeling, separation, and the general consolation that belief in God provides.

Conversely, the Maiden, no longer knowing human feeling and directly perceiving Christian truth, understands the divine as the source of their communal common ground. While she is correct to recognize that they share a belief in God, she is incorrect to presuppose that they share other kinds of communal mutual knowledge — he is not, after all, a heavenly queen — and she totally rejects the idea that they have any personal mutual knowledge; "'þat þou lesteȝ,'" she tells him early on, "'watȝ bot a rose'" (269) ["what you lost was but a rose"]. Not only can the Dreamer not know what she as one of the elect knows; he cannot know *how* she knows, for his human judgments, as his utterances repeatedly make clear, are inevitably rooted in human feeling. Like the Dreamer, the Maiden uses linguistic co-presence to confirm her assessment of their common ground; as knowledge based on the conversation leading up to a particular moment, linguistic co-presence is perhaps the weakest form of mutual knowl-

---

[33] Clark, *Arenas of Language Use*, 58.

[34] Clark, *Arenas of Language Use*, 61. The use of common ground as the context of interpretation is related to what Brown and Yule, *Discourse Analysis*, 59, consider the Principle of Local Interpretation, which instructs a listener "not to construct a context any larger than he needs to arrive at an interpretation." If someone asks me to shut the door, for instance, I assume it is a door to the room in which I am sitting and not the door to a house down the block. Also see their account of presupposition pools, *Discourse Analysis*, 79–80.

edge,[35] and, as I have already indicated, the Maiden's and the Dreamer's reliance on it accounts for much of the misconstrual in their conversation. Emblematic here is the significance of physical co-presence. For the earthly Dreamer, a remarkable eye for detail of landscape and appearance testifies for his conception of experience as physical, while for the divine Maiden, the physical only serves to obfuscate spiritual reality:

> "I halde þat iueler lyttel to prayse
> Þat leueȝ wel þat he seȝ wyth yȝe."
>   (301-2)

> ["I hold that jeweller worth little praise
> Who well esteems what he sees with eye."]

While each might assume mutual knowledge based on physical co-presence, therefore, each is in fact situated in a strikingly different landscape, and the common ground assumed on this basis, like the common ground assumed on the basis of shared community or linguistic co-presence, is illusory.

Such failures in mutual knowledge, then, belie any presumption of broad common ground between the Maiden and the Dreamer. Though speakers can proceed without regard for the presence of common ground – as woolly academics are often characterized to do in lectures – its absence precludes speakers' construction of accurate models of one another and, hence, successful communication. In *Pearl*, a lack of circumspection about such models compounds the failure of communication. As erroneous as each speaker's model of the other may be, further, these models remain static throughout their conversation, for the Dreamer's final literal questions about the Maiden's housing are, from her viewpoint, still non-sequiturs or are still misunderstood as theological. Because the models are not updated, in fact, I would argue that even at the conclusion of the poem, however much the Dreamer may commend the heavenly "Princeȝ paye," he has not adequately understood the Maiden or the experience. Her abrupt departure for the divine procession serves as a theological response to a human predicament and thereby implies that her model of him has likewise never been updated.

---

[35] Clark, *Arenas of Language Use*, 36-41.

For late medieval culture, the larger issues raised by the conversation in *Pearl* are the relation between the divine and the human and the intelligibility each can have of the other. The most frequent readings of *Pearl* see this intelligibility as one way, with the obtuse Dreamer misconstruing the truths uttered by the nearly omniscient Maiden. To put the matter of such readings more generally, God can understand humans, but humans cannot understand that which by definition surpasses human understanding. Though pointing out the mimetic qualities of the conversation does not exonerate the Dreamer of the charge of obtuseness, it does illuminate the poem's conversation with a different light. In the end the conversation's meaning is not produced by either the Dreamer or the Maiden alone but emerges from their cumulative efforts in what is fundamentally a joint activity, and so their conversation is not simply about either theological consolation or human frailty. Its meaning, rather, embraces these two senses as well as the dissonance between them: as well-intentioned as the Dreamer and the Maiden are, neither can understand the other as a speaker, and both make incorrect presuppositions. Given the role that speech plays in social structure, further, the failure of the conversation in *Pearl* has implications far beyond itself.

Sandy Petrey has observed, "When we do things with words, we enact not only what we name but also the relationship making the name an act. Language is performative of social being as well as illocutionary force; if words fail to do the things they should, social being has failed as well."[36] A conversation structured like that in *Pearl* — in a theologically and socially acceptable fashion, with the divine Maiden offering directives to the earthly Dreamer's assertives and expressives — ought to affirm a well-established hierarchical relation between the divine and the human. The Maiden's meaning ought also to be the conversation's meaning, and this is ultimately how most critics read the poem. But by its failure, their conversation undermines the normative social being it attempts to perform, for even though it is a joint activity articulating unimpeachable Christian beliefs in the traditional format of a dialogue, it also rather non-normatively suggests that humans are fundamentally as obscure and incomprehensible to the divine as the divine is to them and that the two groups are positioned not hierarchically but agonistically. While the poem obviously does not go so far as to turn this conversational dissonance into an indictment

---

[36] Petrey, *Speech Acts*, 20.

against God and the divine, it does in effect (if not in the poet's intention) offer an apology for human intellectual myopia at the same time it makes a faintly early modern statement about the value of human subjectivity. The systematic conversation differences between the Maiden and the Dreamer, indeed, recall similar differences that hinder conversations between cultures in the modern world: varying strategies and expectations — between, say, Navajos and Anglo-Americans — can not only frustrate communication but also result in antagonism and mistrust.[37]

To expand this point I want to turn to a similar *apologia pro humanitate* that emerges from similar discursive practices in a thirteenth-century lyric known as the "Dialogue between our Lady and Jesus on the Cross." This poem belongs to the common lyric genre devoted to an account of Mary at the foot of the cross, here engaged in a conversation with the crucified Christ. Throughout the poem's six-line stanzas, Christ first speaks three lines consoling Mary with theological truths about the necessity of His suffering, death, and resurrection, to which Mary responds with three lines about her own human suffering as a mother forced to watch her son die. The initial stanza, for instance, begins with Christ's conception of His crucified body as a symbol of triumph, while Mary describes the bodily extremities on which, in a quintessentially maternal gesture, she often dotes in visual representations of the Madonna and child:

> Stond wel, moder, ounder rode,
> Bihold þi child wiþ glade mode,
> Moder bliþe miȝt þou be.
> Sone, hou may ich bliþe stonde?
> Ich se þine fet and þine honde
> I-nayled to þe harde tre.[38]
>   (1-6)

[Stand well, mother, beneath the cross; behold your son with a happy disposition — mother, you can be joyful!

---

[37] Trudgill, *Sociolinguistics*, 114-20; and Saville-Troike, *Ethnography of Communication*, 130-3.

[38] Brown, *English Lyrics*, 87-91. Brown prints two versions of the lyric, and others survive. This and the following translation are mine.

Son, how can I stand joyfully? I see your feet and your hands nailed to the hard tree.]

Each stanza thus juxtaposes Christ's theological joy with Mary's motherly distress in a layout that structurally suggests each speaker's separation from and inability to understand the other. In one version of the lyric, this separation and misunderstanding resonate with particular irony as both speakers use images from the other's experience to drive home their points:

> Moder, mitarst þu mith leren
> wat pine þolen þat childre beren
> wat sorwe hauen þat child for-gon.
> Sune, y wot y kan þe tellen,
> bute it be þe pine of helle
> more sorwe ne woth y non.[39]
>
> (37–42)

[Mother, you can learn for the first time what pain those who bear children have — what sorrow they have who lose a child. Son, I know I can tell you that, unless it be the pain of Hell, I don't know any greater sorrow.]

Poignantly, as when the Dreamer and the Maiden both use words like *queen* and *courtesy*, there is no common ground here. To Christ, the pain of childbirth is less a physical experience than a symbolic confirmation of humanity's fall and the promise of the Resurrection. And to Mary, the pain of Hell, which she will never experience, stands as a trope of the worst pain imaginable — a trope used to indicate simply an extreme, rather like the "Arabian sands" (12) and "farthest Hebrides" (16) in Wordsworth's "The Solitary Reaper."[40] As in *Pearl*, the meaning of this conversation diverges from the meaning of either speaker alone and ultimately relates to the mutual intelligibility (or unintelligibility) of the human and the divine. Also as in *Pearl*, this conversationally constructed meaning per-

---

[39] In the other version printed by Brown, Christ merely states that Mary can see His pain but that without His pain "nere no mon" [there would be no one].

[40] I cite the poem from Stillinger, *Selected Poems*.

forms social being in a way that refigures the traditional and inescapable ignorance of human beings contemplating the divine.

Both *Pearl* and the "Dialogue" could thus be characterized as poems in which the conversants overtly fail to achieve adequate communication and in the process reveal larger communicative fissures in the way language maintains the medieval Christian ordering of the universe. At the same time, paradoxically, both poems also affirm the transcendent truths of Christianity — the fact that, in the Dreamer's words, everything happens in accordance with God's desires. Unable to understand one another or the weakness of their dialogue, both the Dreamer and the Maiden lack the broadest kind of communicative competence. Yet precisely because conversation fails in the worlds of *Pearl* and the "Dialogue," faith alone, involving a simple acceptance of meaning, emerges as the only way to conceptualize the divinely determined meaning of history and the universe. In conversation, which is a fundamentally social undertaking, meaning is no longer given but negotiated. To talk about anything, including Christian truth, is necessarily to conceptualize it in human terms, to accept that its signification is the emergent product of a joint activity. Divine meanings are given and not negotiated, however, and thus stand outside of socialized activities like conversations. When a conversation fails, leaving these meanings in dispute, language can sustain social hierarchies and boundaries only by fiat. That it does so in *Pearl* — and did so, more generally, in medieval England — suggests both the power of such hierarchies and the social performance of language.

My intention is not to suggest that the kind of meaning I have here extrapolated from the conversation in *Pearl* is one that the writer intended or would even recognize. The writer's meaning, I suspect, was closer to the Maiden's. That the poem responds to the kind of analysis I have essayed suggests two important conclusions about orality and textuality. First, the oral and the textual always share intimate connections in their strategies and practices. To succeed aesthetically in written form, speech must reproduce characteristics recognizable from spoken form, or dialogue will not appear to be dialogue. The existence of such conversational features in a textual forum is thus not so much a survival or residue of an earlier cultural practice as it is an inevitability. In a good poem, like *Pearl*, these connections dynamically enforce one another for good effect, so that as much as the artificial demands of meter, characterization, and narrative shape the structure of the conversation in *Pearl*, so too are they themselves shaped by it: the Maiden's inability to understand the Dreamer is linked to her conversational limitations, which in turn contribute to the metrical requirements of the poem's form. The second conclusion I wish to draw is this: as aesthetically successful as the intimacy between the oral and the textual can be, it can also mute and even mask the tensions it produces. *Pearl* is a thoroughly orthodox poem, yet in spite of itself it also demonstrates that medieval orthodoxy could be maintained only by severing the human from the divine and human action — like speech — from faith. What the Maiden and Christianity propose must be accepted outside of the terms by which humans ordinarily interact, for when it is subject to them, it becomes a negotiated rather than transcendent way of approaching experience. Speech may be ephemeral and it may be, as Christian exegesis suggests, the gift of God, but as a characteristically human activity it inevitably manifests itself in, and then manages, human activities.

BIBLIOGRAPHY

Primary Sources, Editions, Translations, and Reference Works

Abegg, Daniel. *Zur Entwicklung der Historischen Dichtung bei den Angelsachsen.* Strassburg: Trübner, 1894.

Adcock, Fleur, ed. and trans. *Hugh Primas and the Archpoet.* Cambridge Medieval Classics 2. Cambridge: Cambridge University Press, 1994.

Ælfric. *Ælfric's Catholic Homilies: The First Series.* Edited by Peter Clemoes. EETS ss 17. Oxford: Oxford University Press, 1997.

———. *Ælfric's Catholic Homilies: The Second Series.* Edited by Malcolm Godden. EETS ss 5. London: Oxford University Press, 1979.

———. *Homilies of Ælfric: A Supplementary Collection.* Edited by John C. Pope. 2 vols. EETS os 259, 260. London: Oxford University Press, 1967-1968.

———. *Ælfric's Lives of Saints.* Edited by Walter W. Skeat. EETS os 76, 82, 94, 114. 1881, 1885, 1890, and 1901. Reprinted in 2 vols, London: Oxford University Press, 1966. Reprint, London: Boydell and Brewer, 2003.

———. *Æelfrics Grammatik und Glossar.* Edited by Julius Zupitza. 1880. Reprint, 1966. 3rd ed. with a new introduction by Helmut Gneuss, Hildesheim: Weidmann, 2000.

Allen, Rosamund, trans. *Lawman: Brut.* New York: St. Martin's Press, 1992.

The Anglo-Saxon Chronicle: A Collaborative Edition. Vol. 10: *The Abingdon Chronicle, A.D. 956-1066 (MS C with reference to BDE).* Edited by Patrick W. Conner. Cambridge: D. S. Brewer, 1996.

———. Vol. 5: *MS C.* Edited by Katherine O'Brien O'Keeffe. Cambridge: D. S. Brewer, 2001.

———. Vol. 6: *MS D.* Edited by G.P. Cubbin. Cambridge: D.S. Brewer, 1996.

———. *Two of the Saxon Chronicles Parallel*. Edited by Charles Plummer. 2 vols. 1892-1899. Reissued with a bibliographical note by Dorothy Whitelock, 1952. Reprint, Oxford: Clarendon Press, 1972.

Aristotle. *Aristotelis opera, edidit Academia Regia Borussica*. Edited by Immanuel Bekker. 5 vols. Berlin: G. Reimer, 1831-1870.

———. *The Complete Works of Aristotle: The Revised Oxford Translation*. Edited and translated by Jonathan Barnes. Bollingen Series 71/2. Princeton: Princeton University Press, 1984.

———. *Poetics*. Translated by Leon Golden. Englewood Cliffs: Prentice-Hall, 1968.

———. *On Rhetoric*. Translated by George A. Kennedy. New York: Oxford University Press, 1991.

———. *Rhetoric*. Translated by W. Rhys Roberts. New York: Random House, 1954.

Aðalbjarnarson, Bjarni, ed. *Heimskringla I*. Reykjavík: Íslenzk Fornrit, 1941.

Augustine. *Confessiones*. Edited by James J. O'Donnell. 3 vols. Oxford: Clarendon Press, 1992.

———. *De peccatorum meritis et remissione et de baptismo parvulorum ad Marcellinum libri tres*. Edited by Carl Franz Urba and Joseph Zycha. Corpus Scriptorum Ecclesiasticorum Latinorum 60. Vienna: Tempsky, 1913.

Barlow, Frank, ed. and trans. *Vita Aedwardi regis qui apud Westmonasterium requiescit*. 1962. 2nd ed. Oxford: Clarendon Press, 1992.

Barron W. R. J., and S. C. Weinberg, trans. *Brut, or Hystoria Brutonum*. New York: Longman, 1995.

———. *Layamon's Arthur: The Arthurian Section of Layamon's Brut*. Harlow: Longman, 1989. Rev. ed., Exeter: Exeter University Press, 2001.

Bede. *Bede's Ecclesiastical History of the English People*. Edited by Bertram Colgrave and R. A. B. Mynors, 1969. Reprint, Oxford: Clarendon Press, 1979.

———. *The Old English Version of Bede's Ecclesiastical History of the English People*. Edited by Thomas Miller. EETS os 95, 96, 110, 111. 4 vols. in 2. 1890-1898. Reprint, London: Oxford University Press, 1997.

Beowulf and Judith. Edited by Elliot Van Kirk Dobbie. ASPR 4. New York: Columbia University Press, 1953.

Beowulf: A Student Edition. Edited by Jack George. 1994. Reprinted with revisions and corrections, Oxford: Clarendon Press, 1997.

Beowulf and the Fight at Finnsburg. Edited by Friedrich Klaeber. 1922. 3rd ed. Lexington, Mass.: D. C. Heath, 1950.

Beowulf: An Edition. Edited by Bruce Mitchell and Fred C. Robinson. Oxford: Blackwell, 1998.
Beowulf. Edited by Walter J. Sedgefield. 1910. 2nd ed. Manchester: University of Manchester Press, 1913.
Beowulf with the Finnesburg Fragment. Edited by C. L. Wrenn. Boston: Heath, 1953. 3rd ed. Revised by Whitney F. Bolton. London: Harrap, 1973.
Beowulf: A Prose Translation. Translated by E. T. Donaldson. 1966. 2nd ed. Edited by Nicholas Howe. New York: W. W. Norton, 2002.
A Readable Beowulf. Translated by Stanley B. Greenfield. Carbondale: Southern Illinois University Press, 1982.
Beowulf: A New Translation. Translated by Seamus Heaney. London: Faber and Faber, 1999.
Beowulf and Other Old English Poems. Translated by Constance B. Hieatt. New York: Odyssey Press, 1967.
Beowulf. Translated by David Wright. Harmondsworth: Penguin Books, 1957.
Bessinger, Jess B., Jr., ed. and Philip H. Smith, Jr., progr. *A Concordance to The Anglo-Saxon Poetic Records*. Ithaca: Cornell University Press, 1978.
Best, R. I., ed. and trans. *The Settling of the Manor of Tara*. Ériu 4 (1910): 121-72.
Blake, Ernest O., ed. *Liber Eliensis*. Camden third series vol. 92. London: Royal Historical Society, 1962.
Bromwich, Rachel, ed. and trans. *Trioedd ynys Prydein: The Welsh Triads*. 1961. 2nd ed. Cardiff: University of Wales Press, 1978.
———, and D. Simon Evans, eds. *Culhwch ac Olwen. An Edition and Study of the Oldest Arthurian Tale*. London: University of Wales Press, 1992.
Brook, G. L., ed. *The Harley Lyrics: The Middle English Lyrics of MS Harley 2253*. 1956. 4th ed. Manchester: Manchester University Press, 1968.
———, and R. F. Leslie, eds. *Laȝamon: Brut*. 2 vols. EETS os 250, 277. London: Oxford University Press, 1963, 1977.
Brown, Carleton, ed. *English Lyrics of the XIIIth Century*. Oxford: Clarendon Press, 1932.
Brugnoli, Georgio, and Fabio Stok, eds. *Vitae Vergilianae antiquae*. Scriptores Graeci et Latini. Rome: Typis Officinae Polygraphicae, 1997.
Bzdyl, Donald G., trans. *Layamon's Brut*. Binghamton: MRTS, 1989.
Campbell, Alistair, ed. and trans. *Encomium Emmae Reginae*. London: Royal Historical Society, 1949. Reprinted with an introduction by Simon Keynes, Cambridge: Cambridge University Press, 1998.

Carroll, Lewis. *More Annotated Alice: Alice's Adventures in Wonderland and Through the Looking Glass and What Alice Found There.* Illustrations by Peter Newell, with notes by Martin Gardner. New York: Random House, 1990.

Catullus. *Catullus.* Edited by Elmer Truesdale Merrill. Boston: Ginn and Company, 1893.

Chantraine, Pierre. *Grammaire homérique.* 2 vols. 1958. Reprint, Paris: Éditions Klincksieck, 1997.

Chaucer, Geoffrey. *The Riverside Chaucer.* General editor Larry D. Benson. 3rd ed. Boston: Houghton Mifflin, 1987.

———. *Troilus and Criseyde.* Edited by B. A. Windeatt. 1984. Reprint, London: Longman, 1990.

Cicero. *Rhetorica ad Herennium.* Edited and translated by Harry Caplan. LCL 403. Cambridge, Mass.: Harvard University Press, 1954.

———. *De Oratore Book 3. De Fato. Paradoxa Stoicorum. De Partitione Oratoria.* Edited and translated by H. Rackham. LCL 349. Cambridge, Mass.: Harvard University Press, 1942.

———. *Pro Archia. Post Reditum in Senatu. Post Reditum ad Quirites. De Domo Sua. De Haruspicum Responsis. Pro Cn. Plancio.* Edited and translated by N. H. Watts. LCL 158. Cambridge, Mass.: Harvard University Press, 1923.

Colgrave, Bertram, ed. and trans. *The Life of Bishop Wilfrid by Eddius Stephanius.* Cambridge: Cambridge University Press, 1985.

Cross, J. E. "*Legimus in ecclesiasticis historiis*: A Sermon for All Saints, and its Use in Old English Prose." *Traditio* 33 (1977): 101–35.

Darlington, R. R., and P. McGurk, eds.; Jennifer Bray and P. McGurk, trans. *The Chronicle of John of Worcester.* 3 vols. Oxford: Clarendon Press, 1995.

Dickens, Bruce, and R. M. Wilson, eds. *Early Middle English Texts.* 1951. Reprint, Cambridge: Bowes and Bowes, 1965.

Basileios Digenes Akritas. Edited by Petros P. Kalonaros. 2 vols. 1881. Reprint, Athens: N. Papadema, 1942.

Digenes Akritas. Edited and translated by John Mavrogordato. 1956. Oxford: Clarendon Press, 1999.

Dobbie, Elliot Van Kirk, ed. *The Anglo-Saxon Minor Poems.* ASPR 6. New York: Columbia University Press, 1942.

Dooley, Ann, and Harry Roe, trans. *Tales of the Elders of Ireland.* Oxford World's Classics. New York: Oxford University Press, 1999.

Egan, Margarita, trans. *The Vidas of the Troubadours.* Garland Library of Medieval Literature, Series B, 6. New York: Garland Publishing, 1984.

Einenkel, Eugen, ed. *The Life of St. Katherine*. EETS os 80. London: Trübner, 1884.

Ekkehard IV of St. Gall. *Casus Sancti Galli*. Edited and translated by Hans F. Haefele. Ausgewählte Quellen zur deutschen Geschichte des Mittelalters 10. Darmstadt: Wissenschaftliche Buchgesellschaft, 1980.

Emerton, Ephraim, trans. *The Letters of Saint Boniface*. New York: Columbia University Press, 1940.

Ford, Patrick K., trans. *The Mabinogi and other Medieval Welsh Tales*. Berkeley: University of California Press, 1977.

——, ed. *Math uab Mathonwy*. Belmont: Ford and Baillie, 1999.

——, ed. and trans. *The Poetry of Llywarch Hen*. Berkeley: University of California Press, 1974.

Gerald of Wales. *Concerning the Instruction of Princes*. Translated by John Stevenson. 1858. Reprint with new pagination, Felinfach: J. M. F. Books, 1991.

——. *Giraldi Cambrensis opera*. 8 vols. Vol. 8, edited by George F. Warner. Rolls Series 21. 1891. Reprint, Nendeln: Kraus Reprint, 1964.

Gordon, E. V., ed. *Pearl*. Oxford: Clarendon Press, 1953.

Gunzo. *Epistola ad Augienses*. Edited by Karl Manitius. Quellen zur Geistesgeschichte des Mittelalters. Weimar: Böhlau, 1958. Reprint, Munich: MGH, 1983.

Herzfeld, George, ed. *An Old English Martyrology*. EETS os 116. 1900. Reprint, Woodbridge: Boydell and Brewer, 1997.

Hickes, George. *Linguarum vett. septentrionalium thesaurus grammatico-criticus et archaeologicus*. 1703–1705. Reprint, 2 vols. in 1, New York: Georg Olms, 1970.

Homer. *Homeri Opera, Tomus V, "Hymnos" "Cyclum" "Fragmenta" "Margiten" "Batrachomyomachiam" "Vitas" Continens*. Edited by Thomas W. Allen. 1912. Reprinted with corrections, 1946. Reprint, Oxford: Clarendon Press, 1975.

——. *Homeri Opera, Tomi III–IV, "Odysseae" Libros Continentes*. Edited by Thomas W. Allen. 2nd ed. 1917. Reprint, Oxford: Clarendon Press, 1975.

——. *Homeri Opera, Tomi I–II, "Iliadis" Libros Continentes*. Edited by Thomas W. Allen and David B. Munro. 3rd ed. 1920. Reprint, Oxford: Clarendon Press, 1975.

——. *The Iliad of Homer*. Translated by Richmond Lattimore. 1951. Reprint, Chicago: University of Chicago Press, 1997.

———. *The Iliad*. Translated by Michael Reck. New York: Harper Collins, 1994.

Honko, Lauri, and Gopala Naika, eds. *The Siri Epic*. 2. vols. Folklore Fellows Communications, nos. 265-66. Helsinki: Academia Scientiarum Fennica, 1998.

Horace. *Satires, Epistles, ars poetica*. Edited by G. P. Goold and translated by H. Rushton Fairclough. LCL 194. 1926. Reprint, Cambridge, Mass.: Harvard University Press, 1991.

John of Salisbury. *Metalogicon*. Edited by J. B. Hall with K. S. B. Keats-Rohan. Corpus Christianorum Continuatio Mediaevalis 98. Turnhout: Brepols, 1991.

———. *The Metalogicon: a Twelfth-Century Defense of the Verbal and Logical Arts of the Trivium*. Translated by Daniel D. McGarry. 1955. Reprint, Berkeley: University of California Press, 1962.

Johnson, John William, trans. *The Epic of Son-Jara*. Bloomington: Indiana University Press, 1992.

Jónsson, Finnur, ed. *Den Norsk-Islandiske Skjaldedigtning A I–II*. 1912-1915. Copenhagen: Rosenkilde and Bagger, 1967.

Jónsson, Guðni, ed. *Edda Snorra Sturlusonar með Skáldatali*. Reykjavík: Sigurður Kristjánsson, 1935.

Kelly, Michael, ed. *Encyclopedia of Aesthetics*. 4 vols. Oxford: Oxford University Press, 1998.

Ker, N. R. *Catalogue of Manuscripts Containing Anglo-Saxon*. 1957. Reprint, Oxford: Clarendon Press, 1990.

Knowles, Elizabeth, ed. *The Oxford Dictionary of Phrase and Fable*. Oxford: Oxford University Press, 2000.

Kock, Ernst A., ed. *Den norsk-isländska skaldediktningen*. 2 vols. Lund: Gleerup, 1946-1950.

Kotzor, Günter, ed. *Das altenglische Martyrologium*. 2 vols. Munich: Bayerische Akademie der Wissenschaften, 1981.

Krapp, George Philip, ed. *The Vercelli Book*. ASPR 2. New York: Columbia University Press, 1932.

———, and Elliott Van Kirk Dobbie, eds. *The Exeter Book*. ASPR 3. New York: Columbia University Press, 1936.

Lapidge, Michael, ed. *The Cult of St Swithun*. Winchester Studies 4.ii. Oxford: Clarendon Press, 2002.

———, and Michael W. Herren, eds. *Aldhelm: The Prose Works*. Cambridge: D. S. Brewer, 1979.

Lausberg, Heinrich. *Handbook of Literary Rhetoric: A Foundation for Literary Study*. Edited by David E. Orton and R. Dean Anderson. Translated by Matthew T. Bliss, Annemiek Jansen, and David E. Orton. Leiden: E. J. Brill, 1998.

Leclercq, Jean, ed. "Virgile en enfer d'après un manuscrit d'Aulne." *Latomus* 17 (1958): 731-6.

Levison, Wilhelm, ed. *Vitae Sancti Bonifatii archiepiscopi moguntini*. MGH Scriptores Rerum Germanicarum 57. Hanover: Hahn, 1905.

Lucan. *M. Annaei Lucani Belli Civilis libri decem*. Edited by Karl Hosius. 3rd ed. Bibliotheca scriptorum Graecorum et Romanorum Teubneriana. Leipzig: Teubner, 1913.

Lucas, Peter J., ed. *Exodus*. London: Methuen, 1977.

Macrae-Gibson, O. D., ed. *The Old English "Riming Poem."* Woodbridge: D. S. Brewer, 1983.

Mason, Eugene, trans. *Wace and Layamon: Arthurian Chronicles*. 1912. Reprint, London: Dent, 1986.

McDonough, Christopher J., ed. and trans. *Moriuht: A Norman Latin Poem from the Early Eleventh Century*. Pontifical Institute of Mediaeval Studies, Studies and Texts 121. Toronto: Pontifical Institute of Mediaeval Studies, 1995.

——, ed. *The Oxford Poems of Hugh Primas and the Arundel Lyrics*. Toronto Medieval Latin Texts 15. Toronto: Pontifical Institute of Mediaeval Studies, 1984.

Meyer, Kuno, ed. "Neue Mitteilungen aus irischen Handschriften." *Archiv für celtische Lexikographie* 3 (1950): 1-7.

Migne, Jacques-Paul, comp. *Patrologiae cursus completus*. Series latina. 221 vols. in 212. Paris: Migne, 1844-1891.

Morris, Richard, ed. and trans. *Old English Homilies and Homiletic Treatises of the Twelfth and Thirteenth Centuries*. EETS os 29, 34 in one volume. 1868. Reprint, Woodbridge: Boydell & Brewer, 1998.

Mortier, Raoul, ed. *Les Textes de la Chanson de Roland*. 10 Vols. Paris: Éditions de la Geste Francor, 1944.

Muratori, Ludovico Antonio, ed. *Rerum Italicarum scriptores ab anno aerae Christianae quingentesimo ad millesimum quingentesium*. 25 parts in 28 vols. Milan: Ex typographia Societatis Palatinae, 1723-1751.

Neckel, Gustave, ed. *Edda: Die Lieder des Codex Regius nebst verwandten Denkmälern, I: Text*. Heidelberg: Winter, 1962. 5th ed. Revised by Hans Kuhn, Heidelberg: Carl Winter, 1983.

Odo of Cluny. *Odonis abbatis clvniacensis Occvpatio*. Edited by Anton Swoboda. Bibliotheca scriptorvm medii aevi Tevbneriana. Leipzig: Teubner, 1900.

———. *St. Odo of Cluny. Being the Life of St. Odo of Cluny by John of Salerno and the Life of St. Gerald of Aurillac by St. Odo.* Translated by Gerard Sitwell. New York: Sheed and Ward, 1958.

O'Rahilly, Cecile, ed. and trans. *Táin Bó Cúailnge. Recension I*. Dublin: Dublin Institute for Advanced Studies, 1976.

Parry, Milman, coll. and Albert B. Lord, ed. and trans. *Serbocroatian Heroic Songs*. Vol. 1. Belgrade and Cambridge, Mass.: Serbian Academy of Sciences and Harvard University Press, 1954.

———. *Serbocroatian Heroic Songs*. Vol. 2. Belgrade and Cambridge, Mass.: Serbian Academy of Sciences and Harvard University Press, 1953.

Quintilian. *Institutio Oratoria*. Edited and translated by Donald A. Russell. 5 vols. LCL 124-7 and 494. Cambridge, Mass.: Harvard University Press, 2001.

Rau, Reinhold, ed. *Briefe des Bonifatius. Willibalds Leben des Bonifatius. Nebst Einigen Zeitgenössischen Dokumenten*. Darmstadt: Wissenschaftliche Buchgesellschaft, 1968.

Robertson, James Craigie, ed. *Materials for the History of Thomas Becket*. 7 vols. Rerum britannicarum medii ævi scriptores 67. 1875-1885. Reprint, Wiesbaden: Kraus Reprint, 1965.

Rowland, Jenny. *Early Welsh Saga Poetry. A Study and Edition of the Englynion*. Cambridge: D. S. Brewer, 1990.

Sands, Donald B., ed. *Middle English Verse Romances*. 1966. Reprint, Exeter: Exeter University Press, 1993.

Schaff, Philip, trans. *A Select Library of the Nicene and Post-Nicene Fathers of the Christian Church*. 14 vols. New York: Christian Literature Company, 1887-1892.

Schumann, Otto, ed. *Lateinisches Hexameter-Lexikon: Dichterisches Formelgut von Ennius bis zum Archipoeta*. 7 vols. MGH, Hilfsmittel. 4.1-6. Munich: MGH, 1979-1989.

Schwyzer, Eduard. *Griechische Grammatik I*. 1939. Reprint, Munich: C. H. Beck, 1953.

Scragg, Donald, ed. *The Battle of Maldon AD 991*. Oxford: Blackwell, 1991.

———, ed. *The Vercelli Homilies and Related Texts*. EETS os 300. Oxford: Oxford University Press, 1992.

Skeat, Walter W., ed. *The Wars of Alexander*. EETS es 47. 1886. Reprint, Millwood: Kraus Reprint, 1990.

Smithers, G. V., ed. *Havelok*. Oxford: Clarendon Press, 1987.

Stillinger, Jack, ed. *Selected Poems and Prefaces by William Wordsworth*. Boston: Houghton Mifflin, 1965.

Stokes, Whitley, ed. *Acallamh na Senórach*. Irische Texte mit Übersetzung und Wörterbuch. Fourth Series, Vol. 1, edited by Whitley Stokes and E. Windisch. Leipzig: S. Hirzel, 1900.

Strecker, Karl, ed. *Poetae Latini aevi Carolini*. MGH. Poetarum Latinorum Medii Aevi. Vol. 4, fasc. 2/3. Berlin: Weidmann, 1923.

———, ed. *Die Tegernseer Briefsammlung (Froumund)*. MGH. Epistolae Selectae 3. Berlin: Weidmannsche Buchhandlung, 1925.

Szarmach, Paul E., ed. *Vercelli Homilies IX–XXIII*. Toronto: University of Toronto Press, 1981.

Tangl, M., ed. *Die Briefe des heiligen Bonifatius und Lullus*. MGH. Epistolae Selectae 1. 2nd ed. Berlin: Weidmann, 1955.

Thomson, Derick S., ed. *Branwen uerch Lyr*. Dublin: Dublin Institute for Advanced Studies, 1961.

Tolkien, J. R. R., ed. *Finn and Hengest: The Fragment and the Episode*. Edited by Alan J. Bliss. Boston: Houghton Mifflin, 1983.

———, trans. *Sir Gawain and the Green Knight, Pearl, and Sir Orfeo*. New York: Ballantine Books, 1975.

Ueding, Gert, ed. *Historisches Wörterbuch der Rhetorik*. Tübingen: Niemeyer, 1992–.

Vacca. *Vita Lucani*. In Suetonius, *De poetis e biografi minori*. Edited by Augusto Rostagni. 1944. Reprint, New York: Arno Press, 1979.

Virgil. *The Greater Poems of Virgil*. Vol. 1. *The First Six Books of the Aeneid*. Edited by J. B. Greenough and G. L. Kittredge. Boston: Ginn, 1898.

William of Malmesbury. *De Gestis Pontificum Anglorum, Libri Quinque*. Edited by N. E. S. A. Hamilton. London: Longman & Co., 1870.

Williams, Ifor, ed. *Pedeir Keinc y Mabinogi*. Cardiff: University of Wales Press, 1951.

Williamson, Craig, ed. *The Old English Riddles of the Exeter Book*. Chapel Hill: University of North Carolina Press, 1977.

Wright, Thomas. *Anglo-Saxon and Old English Vocabularies*. Edited and collated by Richard Paul Wülker, 1883. 2 vols. 2nd ed. 1884. Reprint, Darmstadt: Wissenschaftliche Buchgesellschaft, 1968.

Secondary Sources

Allen, Thomas W. *Homer: The Origins and the Transmission.* 1924. Reprint, Oxford: Clarendon Press, 1969.

Amodio, Mark C. "Introduction: Oral Poetics in Post-Conquest England." In *Oral Poetics in Middle English Poetry,* edited by Mark C. Amodio, 1-28. Albert Bates Lord Studies in Oral Tradition 13. New York: Garland, 1994.

———. "Old English Oral-Formulaic Tradition and Middle-English Verse." In *De Gustibus: Essays for Alain Renoir,* edited by John Miles Foley, 1-20. Albert Bates Lord Studies in Oral Tradition 11. New York: Garland, 1992.

———, ed. *Oral Poetics in Middle English Poetry.* Albert Bates Lord Studies in Oral Tradition 13. New York: Garland, 1994.

———. "Tradition, Performance, and Poetics in the Early Middle English Period." OT 15 (2000): 191-214.

———. *Writing the Oral Tradition: Oral Poetics and Literate Culture in Medieval England.* Poetics of Orality and Literacy 1. Notre Dame: University of Notre Dame Press, 2004.

Apthorp, M. J. *The Manuscript Evidence for Interpolation in Homer.* Heidelberg: Winter, 1980.

Argyle, Michael, and Mark Cook. *Gaze and Mutual Gaze.* Cambridge: Cambridge University Press, 1976.

Astakhova, Alla. "'Sound Shaping' of East Slavic *Zagovory.*" OT 7 (1992): 365-72.

Austin, John L. *How to Do Things with Words: The William James Lectures Delivered at Harvard University in 1955.* Edited by J. O. Urmson. 1962. 2nd ed. 1975. Reprint, New York: Oxford University Press, 1986.

Baker, Egbert. "The Inland Ship: Problems in the Performance and Reception of Homeric Epic." In *Written Voices, Spoken Signs: Tradition, Performance, and the Epic Text,* edited by Egbert Baker and Ahuvia Kahane, 83-109. Cambridge, Mass.: Harvard University Press, 1997.

Baldwin, John. "The Image of the Jongleur in Northern France around 1200." *Speculum* 72 (1997): 635-63.

Barlow, Frank. *Edward the Confessor.* 1970. Rev. ed. New Haven: Yale University Press, 1997.

Bassett, Samuel E. "The Structural Similarity of *Iliad* and *Odyssey* as Revealed in the Treatment of the Hero's Fate." *Classical Journal* 14 (1919): 557-63.

Baugh, Albert C. "Improvisation in the Middle English Romance." *PAPS* 103 (1959): 418-54.

———. "The Middle English Romance: Some Questions of Creation, Presentation, and Preservation." *Speculum* 42 (1967): 1-31.

Bauman, Richard. *Story, Performance, and Event: Contextual Studies of Oral Narrative.* 1986. Reprint, Cambridge: Cambridge University Press, 1989.

———. *Verbal Art as Performance.* 1977. Reprint, Prospect Heights: Waveland Press, 1984.

———, and Pamela Ritch. "Informing Performance: Producing the *Coloquio* in Tierra Blanca." *OT* 9 (1994): 255-80.

Bayless, Martha. *Parody in the Middle Ages: The Latin Tradition.* Recentiores: Later Latin Texts & Contexts. Ann Arbor: University of Michigan Press, 1996.

Beaton, Roderick. "Was *Digenes Akrites* an Oral Poem?" *Byzantine and Modern Greek Studies* 7 (1981): 7-27.

Bédier, Joseph. *La Chanson de Roland commentée.* 1927. Reprint, Paris: Édition d'art H. Piazza, 1968.

Benson, Larry D. "The Literary Character of Anglo-Saxon Formulaic Poetry." *PMLA* 81 (1966): 334-41.

Biber, Douglas. *Variation Across Speech and Writing.* Cambridge: Cambridge University Press, 1988.

Biggs, Frederick M. "The Exeter *Exeter Book?* Some Linguistic Evidence." In *The Dictionary of Old English: Retrospects and Prospects,* edited by M. J. Toswell, with a preface by Antonette diPaolo Healey, 63-71. OEN *Subsidia* 26 (1998). Kalamazoo: Medieval Institute, 1998.

Bolling, George M. *The External Evidence for Interpolation in Homer.* 1925. Reprint, Oxford: Clarendon Press, 1968.

Bowra, Cecil M. "Composition." In *A Companion to Homer,* edited by Alan J. B. Wace and Frank H. Stubbings, 38-74. 1962. Reprint, London: Macmillan, 1970.

Bradbury, Nancy Mason. "Gentrification and the *Troilus.*" *CR* 28 (1994): 305-29.

———. *Writing Aloud: Storytelling in Late Medieval England.* Urbana: University of Illinois Press, 1998.

Bredehoft, Thomas A. *Textual Histories: Readings in the Anglo-Saxon Chronicle.* Toronto: University of Toronto Press, 2001.

Brown, Gillian, and George Yule. *Discourse Analysis.* Cambridge: Cambridge University Press, 1983.

Bryan, Elizabeth J. *Collaborative Meaning in Medieval Scribal Culture: The Otho Laȝamon*. Ann Arbor: University of Michigan Press, 1999.
Burnley, J. D. *A Guide to Chaucer's Language*. London: Macmillan, 1983.
Butler, Harold E. "A Description of London by William Fitz Stephen." In *Norman London*, edited by F. M. Stenton, 25-35. Historical Association Leaflets 93-4. London: G. Bell & Sons, 1934.
Bynum, Caroline Walker. *The Resurrection of the Body in Western Christianity, 200-1336*. New York: Columbia University Press, 1995.
Cable, Thomas. *The English Alliterative Tradition*. Philadelphia: University of Pennsylvania Press, 1991.
Cairns, Francis. "The Addition to the 'Chronica' of Richard of Poitiers." *MJ* 19 (1984): 159-61.
Camps, W. A. *An Introduction to Virgil's Aeneid*. London: Oxford University Press, 1969.
Cannon, Christopher. "The Style and Authorship of the Otho Revision of Laȝamon's *Brut*." *MÆ* 62 (1993): 187-209.
Carruthers, Mary. *The Book of Memory: A Study of Memory in Medieval Culture*. Cambridge: Cambridge University Press, 1990.
Cherewatuk, Karen. "Germanic Echoes in Latin Verse: The Voice of the Lamenting Woman in Radegund's Poetry." *Allegorica* 14 (1993): 3-21.
Citti, V. "Le edizioni omeriche 'delle città.'" *Vichiana* 3 (1966): 227-67.
Clanchy, M. T. *From Memory to Written Record: England 1066-1307*. 1979. 2nd ed. Oxford: Blackwell, 1993.
Clark, Herbert H. *Arenas of Language Use*. Chicago: University of Chicago Press, 1992.
———. *Using Language*. Cambridge: Cambridge University Press, 1996.
Combellack, Frederick M. "Some Formulary Illogicalities in Homer." *TAPA* 96 (1965): 41-56.
Comparetti, Domenico. *Vergil in the Middle Ages*. Translated by E. F. M. Benecke. 1895. 2nd ed. 1908. Reprinted with a new introduction by Jan M. Ziolkowski, Princeton: Princeton University Press, 1997.
Conner, Patrick. *Anglo-Saxon Exeter: a Tenth-Century Cultural History*. Woodbridge: Boydell Press, 1993.
Cook, Erwin F. *The Odyssey in Athens: Myths of Cultural Origins*. Ithaca: Cornell University Press, 1995.
Coulthard, Malcolm. *An Introduction to Discourse Analysis*. Hong Kong: Longman, 1977.

Creed, Robert P. "On the Possibility of Criticizing Old English Poetry." *TSLL* 3 (1961): 97-106.
Crielaard, Jan Paul. "Homer, History and Archaeology: Some Remarks on the Date of the Homeric World." In *Homeric Questions*, edited by Jan Paul Crielaard, 201-88. Amsterdam: J. C. Gieben, 1995.
Crosby, Ruth. "Chaucer and the Custom of Oral Delivery." *Speculum* 13 (1938): 413-32.
———. "Oral Delivery in the Middle Ages." *Speculum* 11 (1936): 88-110.
Davenport, W. A. *The Art of the Gawain-Poet*. London: Athlone Press, 1978.
Davies, Sioned. *Crefft y Cyfarwydd. Astudiaeth o dechnegau naratif yn Y Mabinogion*. Cardiff: University of Wales Press, 1995.
Delisle, Léopold. "Notes sur quelques manuscrits de la Bibliothèque de Tours." *Bibliothèque de l'École des Chartes* 29 (1868): 596-611.
Deskis, Susan E., and Thomas D. Hill. "The Wolf Doesn't Care: The Proverbial and Traditional Context of Laȝamon's *Brut* Lines 10624-36." *RES* 46 (1995): 41-58.
Doane, A. N. "Introduction." In *Vox intexta: Orality and Textuality in the Middle Ages*, edited by A. N. Doane and Carol Braun Pasternack, xi-xiv. Madison: University of Wisconsin Press, 1991.
Dronke, Peter. *Women Writers of the Middle Ages: A Critical Study of Texts from Perpetua (†203) to Marguerite Porete (†1310)*. Cambridge: Cambridge University Press, 1984.
Dué, Casey. *Homeric Variations on a Lament by Briseis*. Lanham: Rowman and Littlefield, 2002.
Duggan, Joseph J. *The Song of Roland: Formulaic Style and Poetic Craft*. Berkeley: University of California Press, 1973.
Dumville, David N. "The Æthelings: A Study in Anglo-Saxon Constitutional History." *ASE* 8 (1979): 1-33.
———. "*Beowulf* and the Celtic World: The Uses of Evidence." *Traditio* 37 (1981): 109-60.
———. "*Beowulf* Come Lately." *Archiv* 225 (1988): 49-63.
Earl, James W. "Hisperic Style in the Old English 'Rhyming Poem.'" *PMLA* 102 (1987): 187-96.
Edel, Doris. *Helden auf Freierfüssen. 'Tochmarc Emire' und 'Mal y kavas Kulhwch Olwen': Studien zur frühen inselkeltischen Erzähltradition*. New York: North-Holland Publishing Company, 1980.
Erbse, Hartmut. *Beiträge zum Verständnis der Odyssee*. Untersuchungen zur antiken Literatur und Geschichte, n. 13. Berlin: De Gruyter, 1972.

Fell, Christine. *Edward King and Martyr*. Leeds Texts and Monographs ns 3. Leeds: University of Leeds School of English, 1971.

———. "Edward King and Martyr and the Anglo-Saxon Hagiographic Tradition." In *Ethelred the Unready: Papers from the Millenary Conference*, edited by David Hill, 1-13. BAR British Series 59. Oxford: BAR, 1978.

———. "Some Implications of the Boniface Correspondence." In *New Readings on Women in Old English Poetry*, edited by Helen Damico and Alexandra Hennessey Olsen, 29-43. Bloomington: Indiana University Press, 1990.

Fenik, Bernard. *Studies in the Odyssey*. Hermes Zeitschrift für klassische Philologie Beiheft 30. Wiesbaden: F. Steiner, 1974.

Ferguson, Charles Albert. "Diglossia." *Word: Journal of the Linguistic Circle of New York* 15 (1959): 325-40.

Fewster, Carol. *Traditionality and Genre in Middle English Romance*. Cambridge: D. S. Brewer, 1987.

Fine, Elizabeth C. *The Folklore Text: From Performance to Print*. 1984. Reprint, Bloomington: Indiana University Press, 1994.

———. "Leading Proteus Captive: Editing and Translating Oral Tradition." In *Teaching Oral Traditions*, edited by John Miles Foley, 59-71. New York: MLA, 1998.

Finkelberg, Margalit. "The *Cypria*, the *Iliad*, and the Problem of Multiformity in Oral and Written Tradition." *CP* 95 (2000): 1-11.

Finnegan, Ruth H. *Literacy and Orality: Studies in the Technology of Communication*. Oxford: Blackwell, 1988.

———. *Oral Poetry: Its Nature, Significance and Social Context*. 1977. Reprint, Bloomington: Indiana University Press, 1992.

Fleming, Robin. "Domesday Estates of the King and the Godwines: A Study in Late Saxon Politics." *Speculum* 58 (1983): 987-1007.

Fludernik, Monika. *The Fictions of Language and the Languages of Fiction: The Linguistic Representation of Speech and Consciousness*. London: Routledge, 1993.

Foley, John Miles. "The Challenge of Translating Traditional Oral Epic." In *Dynamics of Tradition. Perspectives on Oral Poetry and Folk Belief (Essays in Honour of Anna-Leena Siikala on her 60th Birthday 1st January 2003)*, edited by Lotte Tarkka, 248-65. Studia Fennica Folkloristica. Helsinki: Finnish Literature Society, 2003.

———. "Folk Literature." In *Scholarly Editing: A Guide to Research*, edited by David C. Greetham, 600-26. New York: MLA, 1995.

———. *Homer's Traditional Art*. University Park: Pennsylvania State University Press, 1999.

———. *How to Read an Oral Poem*. Urbana: University of Illinois Press, 2002. E-companion at www.oraltradition.org.

———. *Immanent Art: From Structure to Meaning in Traditional Oral Epic*. Bloomington: Indiana University Press, 1991.

———. "The Implications of Oral Tradition." In *Oral Tradition in the Middle Ages*, edited by W. F. H. Nicolaisen, 31–57. MRTS 112. Binghamton: CMERS, 1995.

———. "The Impossibility of Canon." In *Teaching Oral Traditions*, edited by John Miles Foley, 13–33. New York: MLA, 1998.

———. "Individual Poet and Epic Tradition: The Legendary Singer." *Arethusa* 31 (1998): 149–78.

———. "Obituary: Albert Bates Lord (1912–1991)." *JAF* 105 (1992): 57–65.

———. "Oral Tradition into Textuality." In *Texts and Textuality: Textual Instability, Theory, and Interpretation*, edited by Philip Cohen, 1–24. New York: Garland, 1997.

———, ed. *Oral-Formulaic Theory and Research: An Introduction and Annotated Bibliography*. New York: Garland, 1985.

———. "Orality, Textuality, and Interpretation." In *Vox intexta: Orality and Textuality in the Middle Ages*, edited by A. N. Doane and Carol Braun Pasternack, 34–45. Madison: University of Wisconsin Press, 1991.

———. "Proverbs and Proverbial Function in South Slavic and Comparative Epic." *Proverbium* 11 (1994): 77–92.

———. *The Singer of Tales in Performance*. Bloomington: Indiana University Press, 1995.

———. "Textualization as Mediation: The Case of Traditional Oral Epic." In *Voice, Text, and Hypertext at the Millennium*, edited by Raimonda Modiano and Leroy Searle, 95–114. Seattle: University of Washington Press, 2003.

———. *The Theory of Oral Composition: History and Methodology*. 1988. Reprint, Bloomington: Indiana University Press, 1992.

———. *Traditional Oral Epic: The Odyssey, Beowulf, and the Serbo-Croatian Return Song*. 1990. Reprint, Berkeley: University of California Press, 1993.

———. "Word-Power, Performance, and Tradition." *JAF* 105 (1992): 275–301.

Foot, Sarah. "The Making of *Angelcynn*: English Identity before the Norman Conquest." *TRHS* 6th ser., 6 (1996): 25-49.
Fordyce, C. J. *Catullus: A Commentary*. 1961. Reprint, Oxford: Oxford University Press, 1990.
Förster, Max. *Zur Geschichte des Reliquienkultus in Altengland*. Munich: Bayerischen Akademie der Wissenschaften, 1943.
Fournet, J.-L. "L'homérisme' à l'époque proto-byzantine: l'example de Dioscore d'Aphrodité." *Ktèma* 20 (1995): 301-15.
Frank, Roberta. "The Search for the Anglo-Saxon Oral Poet." *BJRL* 75 (1993): 11-36.
Frantzen, Allen J. *Desire for Origins: New Language, Old English, and Teaching the Tradition*. New Brunswick: Rutgers University Press, 1990.
Fry, Donald K. "Cædmon as a Formulaic Poet." In *Oral Literature: Seven Essays*, edited by Joseph J. Duggan, 41-61. Forum for Modern Language Studies 10/3. Edinburgh: Scottish Academic Press, 1975.
———. "The Memory of Cædmon." In *Oral Traditional Literature: A Festschrift For Albert Bates Lord*, edited by John Miles Foley, 282-93. Columbus: Slavica, 1981.
Fulk, R. D. *A History of Old English Meter*. Philadelphia: University of Pennsylvania Press, 1992.
Gaisser, Julia H. "A Structural Analysis of the Digressions in the *Iliad* and the *Odyssey*." *HSCP* 73 (1969): 1-43.
Gameson, Richard. "The Origin of the Exeter Book of Old English Poetry." *ASE* 25 (1996): 135-85.
Gibbs, A. C. "The Literary Relationships of Laȝamon's *Brut*." Ph.D. diss., University of Cambridge, 1962.
Glosecki, Stephen O. *Shamanism and Old English Poetry*. Albert Bates Lord Studies in Oral Tradition 2. New York: Garland, 1989.
Goodwin, Charles. *Conversational Organization: Interaction between Speakers and Hearers*. New York: Academic Press, 1981.
Goold, George P. "Homer and the Alphabet." *TAPA* 91 (1960): 272-91.
Gowans, Linda. *Cei and the Arthurian Legend*. Cambridge: D. S. Brewer, 1988.
Green, R. P. H. "Proba's Cento: Its Date, Purpose and Reception." *CQ* 45 (1995) 551-63.
Greenfield, Stanley B. *A Critical History of Old English Literature*. New York: New York University Press, 1968.
Grégoire, Henri. *Ho Digenis Akritas, he byzantine epopoiia sten istoria kai sten poiese*. New York: The National Herald, 1942.

Griffith, M. S. "Convention and Originality in the Old English 'Beasts of Battle' Typescene." *ASE* 22 (1993): 179-99.
Grooms, Chris. *The Giants of Wales*. Lewiston: Edwin Mellen Press, 1993.
Gross, Charlotte. "Courtly Language in *Pearl*." In *Text and Matter: New Critical Perspectives of the Pearl-Poet*, edited by Robert J. Blanch, Miriam Youngerman Miller, and Julian N. Wasserman, 79-91. Troy: Whitson, 1991.
Gunn, David M. "Narrative Inconsistency and the Oral Dictated Text in the Homeric Epic." *AJP* 91 (1970): 192-203.
Hainsworth, Bryan. *The Iliad: A Commentary*. Vol. III. Cambridge: Cambridge University Press, 1993.
Harris, Joseph. "*Beowulf* in Literary History." *PCP* 17 (1982): 16-23. Reprinted in *Interpretations of Beowulf*, edited by R. D. Fulk, 235-41. Bloomington: Indiana University Press, 1991.
———. "Eddic Poetry as Oral Poetry: The Evidence of Parallel Passages in the Helgi Poems for Questions of Composition and Performance." In *Edda: A Collection of Essays*, edited by Robert James Glendinning and Haraldr Bessason, 210-42. University of Manitoba Icelandic Studies 4. Manitoba: University of Manitoba Press, 1983.
———, and Karl Reichl, eds. *Prosimetrum. Crosscultural Perspectives on Narrative in Prose and Verse*. Cambridge: D. S. Brewer, 1997.
Harris, William V. *Ancient Literacy*. Cambridge, Mass.: Harvard University Press, 1989.
Haslam, Michael. "Homeric Papyri and Transmission of the Text." In *A New Companion to Homer*, edited by Ian Morris and Barry B. Powell, 55-100. Leiden: Brill, 1997.
———. "Papyrus #4452: Commentary on *Iliad* XIX." In *The Oxyrhynchus Papyri* 65, edited by Michael Haslam, et. al., 29-44. London: Egypt Exploration Society, 1998.
Havelock, Eric. *The Muse Learns to Write. Reflections on Orality and Literacy from Antiquity to the Present*. New Haven: Yale University Press, 1986.
———. *Preface to Plato*. Cambridge, Mass.: Harvard University Press, 1963.
Heiden, Bruce. "Major Systems of Thematic Resonance in the *Iliad*." *SO* 75 (2000): 34-55.
———. "The Three Movements of the *Iliad*." *Greek, Roman, and Byzantine Studies* 37 (1996): 5-22.

Henderson, Dave. "Tradition and Heroism in the Middle English Romances." In *Oral Poetics in Middle English Poetry*, edited by Mark C. Amodio, 89-108. New York: Garland, 1994.

Hexter, Ralph. "*Latinitas* in the Middle Ages: Horizons and Perspectives." *Helios* 14 (1987): 69-91.

Hill, John M. "Middle English Poets and the Word: Notes toward an Appraisal of Linguistic Consciousness." *Criticism* 16 (1974): 153-67.

Hoekstra, A. *The Sub-Epic Stage of the Formulaic Tradition: Studies in the Homeric Hymns to Apollo, to Aphrodite and to Demeter*. Amsterdam: North-Holland Publishing, 1970.

Holland, William. "Formulaic Diction and the Descent of a Middle English Romance." *Speculum* 48 (1973): 89-109.

Holman, C. Hugh. *A Handbook to Literature*. 3rd ed. Indianapolis: Bobbs-Merrill Company, Inc., 1972.

Holthausen, Ferdinand. "Zu dem ae Gedichte von Ælfreds Tode (1036)." *Anglia* 50 (1939): 157.

Honko, Lauri. *Textualising the Siri Epic*. Folklore Fellows Communications 264. Helsinki: Academia Scientiarum Fennica, 1998.

Hooper, Nicholas. "Edgar the Ætheling: Anglo-Saxon Prince, Rebel, and Crusader." *ASE* 14 (1985): 197-214.

Howe, Nicholas. *Migration and Mythmaking in Anglo-Saxon England*. 1989. Reprint, Notre Dame: University of Notre Dame Press, 2001.

———. *The Old English Catalogue Poems*. Anglistica 23. Copenhagen: Rosenkilde and Bagger, 1985.

Hymes, Dell. "Breakthrough into Performance." In *Folklore: Performance and Communication*, edited by Dan Ben-Amos and Kenneth S. Goldstein, 11-74. Mouton: The Hague, 1975. Reprinted with revisions in his '*In vain I tried to tell you*': *Essays in Native American Ethnopoetics*, 79-141. Philadelphia: University of Pennsylvania Press, 1981.

———. "Breakthrough into Performance Revisited." In his '*In vain I tried to tell you*': *Essays in Native American Ethnopoetics*, 200-59. Philadelphia: University of Pennsylvania Press, 1981.

———. "Ways of Speaking." In *Explorations in the Ethnography of Speaking*, edited by Richard Bauman and Joel Sherzer, 433-51, 473-4. 2nd ed. Cambridge: Cambridge University Press, 1989.

Irvine, Martin. "Medieval Textuality and the Archaeology of Textual Culture." In *Speaking Two Languages: Traditional Disciplines and Contemporary*

Theory in Medieval Studies, edited by Allen J. Frantzen, 181-210. Albany: State University of New York Press, 1991.

Janko, Richard. Homer, Hesiod and the Hymns: Diachronic Development in Epic Diction. Cambridge: Cambridge University Press, 1982.

———. "The Homeric Poems as Oral Dictated Texts." CQ 48 (1998): 1-13.

———. The Iliad: A Commentary. Vol. IV. Cambridge: Cambridge University Press, 1992.

———. "The Iliad and its Editors: Dictation and Redaction." CA 9 (1990): 326-34.

Jensen, Minna Skafte. "Dividing Homer: When and How Were the Iliad and Odyssey Divided into Song?" SO 74 (1999): 5-91.

Keith, W. J. "Layamon's Brut: The Literary Differences Between the Two Texts." MÆ 2 (1960): 161-72.

Kellogg, Robert. "Oral Narrative, Written Books." Genre 10 (1977): 655-65.

Kelly, Douglas. The Arts of Poetry and Prose. Typologie des Sources du Moyen Âge Occidental, fasc. 59, A-V.A.2*. Turnhout: Brepols, 1991.

Kendall, Calvin. The Metrical Grammar of Beowulf. CSASE 5. Cambridge: Cambridge University Press, 1991.

Kiernan, Kevin S. "Reading Cædmon's 'Hymn' with Someone Else's Glosses." Representations 32 (1990): 157-74. Reprinted in Old English Literature: Critical Essays, edited by Roy M. Liuzza, 103-24. New Haven: Yale University Press, 2002.

Kindermann, Heinz. Theatergeschichte Europas. 10 vols. Salzburg: O. Müller, 1957-1974.

Kirk, Elizabeth D. "The Anatomy of a Mourning: Reflections on the Pearl Dreamer." In The Endless Knot: Essays on Old and Middle English in Honor of Marie Borroff, edited by M. Teresa Tavormina and R. F. Yeager, 215-25. Cambridge: D. S. Brewer, 1995.

Kirk, G. S. "Homer and Modern Oral Poetry: Some Confusions." CQ 10 (1960): 271-81. Reprinted in his Homer and the Oral Tradition, 113-28. Cambridge: Cambridge University Press, 1976.

———. "The Homeric Poems as History." In The Cambridge Ancient History, 3rd ed., edited by J. B. Bury, S. A. Cook, and F. E. Adcock, II.2, 820-50. Cambridge: Cambridge University Press, 1975.

———. "Homer's Iliad and Ours." PCPS 16 (1970): 48-59.

———. The Iliad: A Commentary. Vol. I. Cambridge: Cambridge University Press, 1985.

———. "Objective Dating Criteria in Homer." *MH* 17 (1960): 189-205.
———. *The Songs of Homer*. Cambridge: Cambridge University Press, 1962.
Kirshenblatt-Gimblett, Barbara. "Toward a Theory of Proverb Meaning." *Proverbium* 22 (1973): 821-7. Reprinted in *The Wisdom of Many: Essays on the Proverb*, edited by Wolfgang Mieder and Alan Dundes, 111-21. New York: Garland, 1981.
Kitto, Humphrey D. F. *Poiesis: Structure and Thought*. Berkeley: University of California Press, 1966.
Kotzor, Gunter. *Der altenglische Martyrologium*. Munich: Bayerische Akademie der Wissenschaften, 1981.
Lakoff, George. *Women, Fire, and Dangerous Things: What Categories Reveal about the Mind*. Chicago: University of Chicago Press, 1987.
Lamberton, Robert. "Homer in Antiquity." In *A New Companion to Homer*, edited by Ian Morris and Barry B. Powell, 33-54. Leiden: Brill, 1997.
Lapidge, Michael. "Aldhelm's Latin Poetry and Old English Verse." *CL* 31 (1979): 209-31.
———. "The Hermeneutic Style in Tenth-Century Anglo-Latin Literature." *ASE* 4 (1975): 67-111.
Lass, Roger. "Phonology and Morphology." In *The Cambridge History of the English Language*. Vol. III, 1476-1776, edited by Roger Lass, 148-55. Cambridge: Cambridge University Press, 1999.
Leclercq, Jean. "L'Idéal monastique de saint Odon d'après ses œuvres." In *A Cluny, Congrès scientifique. Fêtes et cérémonies liturgiques en l'honneur des saints Abbés Odon et Odilon, 9-11 juillet 1949*, 227-32. Dijon: Société des Amis de Cluny, 1950.
Lees, Clare A. *Tradition and Belief: Religious Writing in Late Anglo-Saxon England*. Minneapolis: University of Minnesota Press, 1999.
Lehmann, Paul. *Die Parodie im Mittelalter*. 1922. 2nd ed. Stuttgart: Anton Hiersemann, 1963.
Lerer, Seth. *Literacy and Power in Anglo-Saxon Literature*. Lincoln: University of Nebraska Press, 1991.
———. "Old English and its Afterlife." In *The Cambridge History of Medieval English Literature*, edited by David Wallace, 7-34. Cambridge: Cambridge University Press, 1999.
LeSaux, Françoise. *Laȝamon's Brut: The Poem and Its Sources*. Arthurian Studies 29. Cambridge: D. S. Brewer, 1989.
Levinson, Stephen C. *Pragmatics*. Cambridge: Cambridge University Press, 1983.

Lindahl, Carl. *Earnest Games: Folkloric Patterns in the Canterbury Tales.* Bloomington: Indiana University Press, 1987.
Lohmann, Dieter. *Die Komposition der Reden in der Ilias.* Untersuchungen zur antiken Literatur und Geschichte 6. Berlin: De Gruyter, 1970.
Lönnroth, Lars. "Hjalmar's Death-Song and the Delivery of Eddic Poetry." *Speculum* 46 (1971): 1-20.
Lord, Albert B. "Cædmon Revisited." In *Heroic Poetry in the Anglo-Saxon Period*, edited by Helen Damico and John Leyerle, 121-37. Kalamazoo: Medieval Institute Publications, 1993.
———. *Epic Singers and Oral Tradition.* Ithaca: Cornell University Press, 1991.
———. "Homer and Huso II: Narrative Inconsistencies in Homer and Oral Poetry." *TAPA* 69 (1938): 39-45.
———. "Homer and Other Epic Poetry." In *A Companion to Homer*, edited by Alan J. B. Wace and Frank H. Stubbings, 179-214. 1962. Reprint, London: Macmillan, 1970.
———. "Homer's Originality: Oral Dictated Texts." *TAPA* 84 (1953): 124-34.
———. "Oral Composition and 'Oral Residue' in the Middle Ages." In *Oral Tradition in the Middle Ages*, edited by W. F. H. Nicolaisen, 7-29. MRTS 112. Binghamton: CMERS, 1995.
———. "Perspectives on Recent Work in Oral Literature." In *Oral Literature: Seven Essays*, edited by Joseph J. Duggan, 1-24. Forum for Modern Language Studies 10/3. Edinburgh: Scottish Academic Press, 1975.
———. "Perspectives on Recent Work on the Oral Traditional Formula." *OT* 1 (1986): 467-503.
———. *The Singer of Tales.* 1960. Harvard Studies in Comparative Literature 24. 2nd ed. Edited by Stephen Mitchell and Gregory Nagy. Cambridge, Mass.: Harvard University Press, 2000.
———. *The Singer Resumes the Tale.* Edited by Mary Louise Lord. Ithaca: Cornell University Press, 1995.
Louden, Bruce. *The Odyssey: Structure, Narration, and Meaning.* Baltimore: Johns Hopkins University Press, 1999.
Lowenstam, Steven. "Talking Vases: The Relationship between the Homeric Poems and Archaic Representations of Epic Myth." *TAPA* 127 (1997): 21-76.
Ludwich, Arthur. *Die Homervulgata als voralexandrinisch erwiesen.* Leipzig: B. G. Teubner, 1898.
Lumiansky, R. M. "The Function of the Proverbial Monitory Elements in Chaucer's *Troilus and Criseyde*." *TSE* 2 (1950): 5-48.

MacCana, Proinsias. *The Learned Tales of Medieval Ireland.* Dublin: Dublin Institute for Advanced Studies, 1980.

———. "Prosimetrum in Insular Celtic Literature." In *Prosimetrum. Crosscultural Perspectives on Narrative in Prose and Verse,* edited by Joseph Harris and Karl Reichl, 99–130. Cambridge: D. S. Brewer, 1997.

Machan, Tim W. "Editing, Orality, and Late Middle English Texts." In *Vox intexta: Orality and Textuality in the Middle Ages,* edited by A. N. Doane and Carol Braun Pasternack, 229–45. Madison: University of Wisconsin Press, 1991.

Magoun, Francis Peabody, Jr. "Bede's Story of Cædmon: The Case History of an Anglo-Saxon Oral Singer." *Speculum* 30 (1955): 49–63.

Martin, Richard P. *The Language of Heroes: Speech and Performance in the Iliad.* Ithaca: Cornell University Press, 1988.

McGillivray, Murray. *Memorization in the Transmission of the Middle English Romances.* Albert Bates Lord Studies in Oral Tradition 5. New York: Garland, 1990.

Mehl, Dieter. *The Middle English Romances of the Thirteenth and Fourteenth Centuries.* New York: Barnes and Noble, 1969.

Merkelbach, R. "Die pisistratische Redaktion der homerischen Gedichte." *Rheinisches Museum* 95 (1952): 23–47.

Meyer, Wilhelm. *Die Oxforder Gedichte des Primas (des Magister Hugo von Orleans).* 1907. Reprint, with new pagination, Darmstadt: Wissenschaftliche Buchgesellschaft, 1970.

Mieder, Wolfgang. "Proverbs." In *Encyclopedia of Folklore and Literature,* edited by Mary Ellen Brown and Bruce Rosenberg, 525–8. Santa Barbara: ABC-CLIO, 1998.

Miller, William Ian. *Humiliation, and Other Essays on Honor, Social Discomfort, and Violence.* Ithaca: Cornell University Press, 1993.

Mills, M. "Havelok and the Brutal Fisherman." *MÆ* 36 (1967): 219–30.

Milroy, James. "*Pearl*: The Verbal Texture and the Linguistic Theme." *Neophilologus* 55 (1971): 195–208.

Morghen, R. "Monastic Reform and Cluniac Spirituality." In *Cluniac Monasticism in the Central Middle Ages,* edited by Noreen Hunt, 11–28. London: Macmillan, 1971.

Morris, Ian. "The Use and Abuse of Homer." *CA* 6 (1986): 81–138.

Murko, Matija. "The Singers and their Epic Songs." *OT* 5 (1990): 107–30.

Murphy, James J. "The Teaching of Latin as a Second Language in the Twelfth Century." *Historiographia linguistica* 7 (1980): 159–75.

Murray, Gilbert. *The Rise of the Greek Epic*. 1907. 4th ed. London: Oxford University Press, 1967.
Myres, J. N. L. "The Last Book of the *Iliad*." *JHS* 52 (1932): 264-96.
———. "The Pattern of the *Odyssey*." *JHS* 72 (1952): 1-19.
Nagler, Michael. *Spontaneity and Tradition: A Study in the Oral Art of Homer*. Berkeley: University of California Press, 1974.
Nagy, Gregory. *The Best of the Achaeans: Concepts of the Hero in Archaic Greek Poetry*. Baltimore: Johns Hopkins University Press, 1979.
———. "An Evolutionary Model for the Making of Homeric Poetry: Comparative Perspectives." In *The Ages of Homer*, edited by Jane B. Carter and Sarah P. Morris, 163-79. Austin: University of Texas Press, 1995.
———. "An Evolutionary Model for the Text Fixation of Homeric Epos." In *Oral Traditional Literature: A Festschrift for Albert Bates Lord*, edited by John Miles Foley, 390-3. Columbus: Slavica, 1981.
———. "Homeric Scholia." In *A New Companion to Homer*, edited by Ian Morris and Barry B. Powell, 101-22. Leiden: Brill, 1997.
———. "Homeric Questions." *TAPA* 122 (1992): 17-60.
———. *Homeric Questions*. Austin: University of Texas Press, 1996.
———. "Irreversible Mistakes and Homeric Poetry." In *Euphrosyne: Studies in Ancient Epic and its Legacy in Honor of Dimitris N. Maronitis*, edited by I. N. Kazazes and Antonios Rengakos, 259-74. Stuttgart: F. Steiner, 1999.
———. *Pindar's Homer: The Lyric Possession of an Epic Past*. Baltimore: Johns Hopkins University Press, 1990.
———. *Poetry as Performance: Homer and Beyond*. Cambridge: Cambridge University Press, 1996.
———. "Response: Aristarchean Questions." *BMCR* 98.07.14.
———. "Review of M. West, *Homeri Ilias*." *BMCR* 00.09.12.
Nagy, Joseph Falaky. *Conversing with Angels and Ancients: Literary Myths of Medieval Ireland*. Ithaca: Cornell University Press, 1997.
Niditch, Susan. *Folklore and the Hebrew Bible*. Minneapolis: Fortress Press, 1993.
Niles, John D. *Beowulf: The Poem and Its Tradition*. Cambridge, Mass.: Harvard University Press, 1983.
———. *Homo Narrans. The Poetics and Anthropology of Oral Literature*. Philadelphia: University of Pennsylvania Press, 1999.
———. "Understanding *Beowulf*: Oral Poetry Acts." *JAF* 106 (1993): 131-55.
Nolan, Barbara. *The Gothic Visionary Perspective*. Princeton: Princeton University Press, 1977.

North, Richard, and Tette Hofstra, eds. *Latin Culture and Medieval Germanic Europe. Proceedings of the First Germania Latina Conference held at the University of Groningen, 26 May 1989.* Mediaevalia Groningana 11. Groningen: Forsten, 1992.
O'Brien O'Keeffe, Katherine. "Body and Law in Late Anglo-Saxon England." *ASE* 27 (1998): 209-32.
———. "Heroic Values and Christian Ethics." In *The Cambridge Companion to Old English Literature*, edited by Malcolm Godden and Michael Lapidge, 107-25. Cambridge: Cambridge University Press, 1991.
———. "The Performing Body on the Oral-Literate Continuum: Old English Poetry." In *Teaching Oral Traditions*, edited by John Miles Foley, 46-58. New York: MLA, 1998.
———. *Visible Song: Transitional Literacy in Old English Verse.* CSASE 4. Cambridge: Cambridge University Press, 1990.
Okpewho, Isidore. *African Oral Literature: Backgrounds, Character, and Continuity.* Bloomington: Indiana University Press, 1992.
Ong, Walter J., S.J. *Orality and Literacy: The Technologizing of the Word.* 1982. Reprint, London: Routledge, 2002.
———. "Orality, Literacy, and Medieval Textualization." *NLH* 16 (1984): 1-12.
Opland, Jeff. *Anglo-Saxon Oral Poetry: A Study of the Traditions.* New Haven: Yale University Press, 1980.
———. *Xhosa Oral Poetry: Aspects of a Black South African Tradition.* Cambridge: Cambridge University Press, 1983.
Orchard, Andy. "Both Style and Substance: The Case for Cynewulf." In *Anglo-Saxon Styles*, edited by Catherine Karkov and George H. Brown, 271-305. Albany: SUNY Press, 2003.
———. *The Poetic Art of Aldhelm.* CSASE 8. Cambridge: Cambridge University Press, 1994.
Orwell, George. "Politics and the English Language." In *George Orwell: A Collection of Essays*, 156-71. 1946. Reprint, San Diego: Harcourt Brace, 1993.
van Otterlo, Willem A. A. *De ringkompositie als opbouwprincipe in de epische Gedichten van Homerus.* Verhandelingen der Koninklijke Nederlandse Akademie van Wetenschappen, Afd. Letterkunde, no. 51.1. Amsterdam: Noord-Hollandsche Uitg. Mif., 1948.
Page, Denys Lionel. *The Homeric Odyssey.* 1955. Reprint, Oxford: Clarendon Press, 1966.

Parks, Ward. "Song, Text, and Cassette: Why We Need Authoritative Audio Editions of Medieval Literary Works." OT 7 (1992): 102-15.
———. "The Traditional Narrator and the 'I Heard' Formulas in Old English Poetry." ASE 16 (1987): 45-66.
Parry, Adam. "Have We Homer's *Iliad*?" *Yale Classical Studies* 20 (1966): 175-216.
———, ed. *The Making of Homeric Verse: The Collected Papers of Milman Parry*. 1971. Reprint, Oxford: Oxford University Press, 1987.
Parry, Milman. "Ćor Huso: A Study of Southslavic Song." In *The Making of Homeric Verse: The Collected Papers of Milman Parry*, edited by Adam Parry, 437-64. 1971. Reprint, Oxford: Oxford University Press, 1987.
———. "Homeric Formulae and Homeric Metre." In *The Making of Homeric Verse: The Collected Papers of Milman Parry*, edited by Adam Parry, 191-239. 1971. Reprint, Oxford: Oxford University Press, 1987.
———. "Studies in the Epic Technique of Oral Verse-Making. I. Homer and Homeric Style." In *The Making of Homeric Verse: The Collected Papers of Milman Parry*, edited by Adam Parry, 266-324. 1971. Reprint, Oxford: Oxford University Press, 1987.
———. "Studies in the Epic Technique of Oral Verse-Making. II. The Homeric Language as the Language of Oral Poetry." In *The Making of Homeric Verse: The Collected Papers of Milman Parry*, edited by Adam Parry, 325-64. 1971. Reprint, Oxford: Oxford University Press, 1987.
Pasternack, Carol Braun. *The Textuality of Old English Poetry*. CSASE 13. Cambridge: Cambridge University Press, 1995.
Pearsall, Derek. *Old English and Middle English Poetry*. Routledge History of English Poetry 1. London: Routledge & Kegan Paul, 1977.
Petrey, Sandy. *Speech Acts and Literary Theory*. New York: Routledge, 1990.
Powell, Barry B. *Homer and the Origin of the Greek Alphabet*. Cambridge: Cambridge University Press, 1991.
Raaflaub, K. "Homeric Society." In *A New Companion to Homer*, edited by Ian Morris and Barry B. Powell, 624-48. Leiden: Brill, 1997.
Radner, Joan N. "Interpreting Irony in Medieval Celtic Narrative: The Case of *Culhwch and Olwen*." *Cambridge Medieval Celtic Studies* 16 (1988): 41-59.
Ramsey, Lee C. "The Sea Voyages in *Beowulf*." NM 72 (1971): 51-9.
Reece, Steve. *The Stranger's Welcome: Oral Theory and the Aesthetics of the Homeric Hospitality Scene*. Ann Arbor: University of Michigan Press, 1993.

———. "The Three Circuits of the Suitors: A Ring Composition in *Odyssey* 17-22." OT 10 (1995): 207-29.

Reiff, Arno. *Interpretatio, imitatio, aemulatio: Begriff und Vorstellung literarischer Abhängigkeit bei den Römern*. Ph.D. diss., University of Cologne, 1959.

Renoir, Alain. *A Key to Old Poems: The Oral-Formulaic Approach to the Interpretation of West-Germanic Verse*. University Park: Pennsylvania State University Press, 1988.

Reynolds, Dwight F. *Heroic Poets, Poetic Heroes: The Ethnography of Performance in an Arabic Oral Epic Tradition*. Ithaca: Cornell University Press, 1995.

Ridyard, Susan. *The Royal Saints of Anglo-Saxon England: A Study of West Saxon and East Anglian Cults*. Cambridge: Cambridge University Press, 1988.

Rigg, A. G. "Golias and Other Pseudonyms." *Studi Medievali*, 3rd ser., 18 (1977): 65-109.

———. *A History of Anglo-Latin Literature, 1066-1422*. Cambridge: Cambridge University Press, 1992.

Robb, Kevin. *Literacy and Paideia in Ancient Greece*. New York: Oxford University Press, 1994.

Roberts, Brynley F. "*Culhwch ac Olwen*, the Triads, Saints' Lives." In *The Arthur of the Welsh. The Arthurian Legend in Medieval Welsh Literature*, edited by Rachel Bromwich, A. O. H. Jarman, and Brynley F. Roberts, 73-95. Cardiff: University of Wales Press, 1991.

Robertson, Elizabeth. "'This Living Hand': Thirteenth-Century Female Literacy, Materialist Immanence, and the Reader of the *Ancrene Wisse*." *Speculum* 78 (2003): 1-36.

Rollason, D. W. "The Cults of Murdered Royal Saints in Anglo-Saxon England." ASE 11 (1983): 1-22.

Rubin, David C. *Memory in Oral Traditions: The Cognitive Psychology of Epic, Ballads, and Counting-out Rhymes*. Oxford: Oxford University Press, 1995.

Ruijgh, Cornelis J. *L' élément achéen dans la langue épique*. Assen: Van Gorcum, 1957.

———. "D'Homère aux origines proto-mycéniennes de la tradition épique." In *Homeric Questions: Essays in Philology, Ancient History, and Archaeology*, edited by Jan Paul Crielaard, 1-96. Amsterdam: J. C. Gieben, 1995.

———. "Le mycénien et Homère." In *Linear B: A 1984 Survey*, edited by Anna Morpurgo Davies and Yves Duhoux, 143-90. Louvain-la-Neuve: Cabay, 1985.

Saenger, Paul. "Silent Reading: Its Impact on Late Medieval Script and Society." *Viator* 13 (1982): 367-414.

———. *The Space Between Words: The Origins of Silent Reading*. Stanford: Stanford University Press, 1997.
Saville-Troike, Muriel. *The Ethnography of Communication: An Introduction*. 1982. 2nd ed. Oxford: Blackwell, 1989.
Sayers, William. "Early Irish Attitudes toward Hair and Beards, Baldness and Tonsure." *Zeitschrift für celtische Philologie* 44 (1991): 154-89.
Schaefer, Ursula. "Two Women in Need of a Friend: A Comparison of *The Wife's Lament* and Eangyth's Letter to Boniface." In *Germanic Dialects: Linguistic and Philological Investigations*, edited by Bela Brogyanyi and Thomas Krömmelbein, 491-524. Amsterdam Studies in the Theory and History of Linguistic Science 38. Amsterdam: Benjamin, 1986.
Schein, Seth. "The *Iliad*: Structure and Interpretation." In *A New Companion to Homer*, edited by Ian Morris and Barry B. Powell, 345-59. Leiden: Brill, 1997.
Schelkle, K. H. "Cento." In *Reallexikon für Antike und Christentum*, edited by Theodor Klauser, 2:972-3. Stuttgart: Anton Hiersemann, 1950-.
Schmaus, Alois. "Ćor Huso Husović." *Prilozi proučavanja narodne poezije* 5 (1938): 131-6.
Schofield, W. H. *English Literature from the Norman Conquest to Chaucer*. London: Macmillan, 1921.
Scott, Anne. "'Do nu ase þu sedes': Word and Deed in *King Horn, Havelok the Dane*, and the 'Franklin's Tale.'" Ph.D. diss., Brown University, 1988.
Scott, John A. *The Unity of Homer*. Berkeley: University of California Press, 1921.
Seaford, Richard. *Reciprocity and Ritual: Homer and Tragedy in the Developing City-State*. Oxford: Clarendon Press, 1994.
Sealey, Raphael. "From Phemius to Ion." *Revue des Études Grecques* 70 (1957): 312-55.
———. *Women and Law in Classical Greece*. Chapel Hill: University of North Carolina Press, 1990.
Searle, John. *Speech Acts: An Essay in the Philosophy of Language*. 1969. Reprint, Cambridge: Cambridge University Press, 1988.
Sharpe, Richard. "Latin in Everyday Life." In *Medieval Latin: An Introduction and Bibliographical Guide*, edited by F. A. C. Mantello and A. G. Rigg, 315-41. Washington, D.C.: Catholic University of America Press, 1996.
Sheerin, Daniel. "Medieval Latin: *In media Latinitate*." *Helios* 14 (1987): 51-67.

Sheppard, John T. *The Pattern of the Iliad*. London: Methuen, 1922.
Sherratt, E. S. "Reading the Texts: Archaeology and the Homeric Question." *Antiquity* 64 (1990): 807-24.
Shipp, George P. *Studies in the Language of Homer*. 1950. 2nd ed. Cambridge: Cambridge University Press, 1972.
Sims-Williams, Patrick. *Religion and Literature in Western England 600-800*. CSASE 3. Cambridge: Cambridge University Press, 1990.
Smithers, G. V. "The Style of *Hauelok*." *MÆ* 57 (1988): 190-218.
Sorabji, Richard. *Aristotle on Memory*. Providence: Brown University Press, 1972.
Spearing, A. C. *The Gawain-Poet: A Critical Study*. Cambridge: Cambridge University Press, 1970.
Stanbury, Sarah. *Seeing the Gawain-Poet: Description and the Act of Perception*. Philadelphia: University of Pennsylvania Press, 1991.
Stanley, Eric G. "*The Judgement of the Damned* (from Cambridge, Corpus Christi College 201 and Other Manuscripts), and the Definition of Old English Verse." In *Learning and Literature in Anglo-Saxon England: Studies Presented to Peter Clemoes on the Occasion of his Sixty-Fifth Birthday*, edited by Michael Lapidge and Helmut Gneuss, 363-91. Cambridge: Cambridge University Press, 1985. Reprinted in his *A Collection of Papers with Emphasis on Old English Literature*, 354-83. Publications of the *Dictionary of Old English* 3. Toronto: Pontifical Institute of Mediaeval Studies, 1987.
———. "Laȝamon's Antiquarian Sentiments." *MÆ* 38 (1969): 23-37.
———. "Rhymes in English Medieval Verse: From Old English to Middle English." In *Medieval English Studies Presented to George Kane*, edited by Edward Donald Kennedy, Ronald Waldron, and Joseph S. Wittig, 19-54. Woodbridge: D. S. Brewer, 1988.
Stanley, Keith. *The Shield of Homer: Narrative Structure in the Iliad*. Princeton: Princeton University Press, 1993.
Steiner, Deborah. *The Tyrant's Writ: Myths and Images of Writing in Ancient Greece*. Princeton: Princeton University Press, 1994.
Stenton, Frank. *Anglo-Saxon England*. 1943. 3rd ed. Oxford: Oxford University Press, 1971.
Stock, Brian. *The Implications of Literacy: Written Language and Models of Interpretation in the Eleventh and Twelfth Centuries*. Princeton: Princeton University Press, 1983.

———. *Listening for the Text: On the Uses of the Past.* Baltimore: Johns Hopkins University Press, 1990.
Sutton, Dana F. *Homer and the Papyri.* www.chs.harvard.edu/.
Tannen, Deborah. *Talking Voices: Repetition, Dialogue, and Imagery in Conversational Discourse.* Cambridge: Cambridge University Press, 1989.
Taplin, Oliver. *Homeric Soundings: The Shaping of the Iliad.* 1992. Reprint, Oxford: Clarendon Press, 1995.
Tatlock, J. S. P. *The Legendary History of Britain: Geoffrey of Monmouth's Historia Regum Britanniae and its Early Vernacular Versions.* Berkeley: University of California Press, 1950.
Taylor, Andrew. "The Myth of the Minstrel Manuscript." *Speculum* 66 (1991): 43-73.
Thomas, Richard F. *Reading Virgil and His Texts: Studies in Intertextuality.* Ann Arbor: University of Michigan Press, 1999.
Thormann, Janet. "*The Battle of Brunanburh* and the Matter of History." *Mediaevalia* 17 (1994): 5-13.
Townsend, Julie. "The Metre of the *Chronicle*-verse." *SN* 68 (1996): 143-76.
Tracy, Stephen V. *The Story of the Odyssey.* Princeton: Princeton University Press, 1990.
———. "The Structure of the *Odyssey.*" In *A New Companion to Homer*, edited by Ian Morris and Barry B. Powell, 360-79. Leiden: Brill, 1997.
Trudgill, Peter. *Sociolinguistics: An Introduction to Language and Society.* 1983. New 3rd rev. ed. London: Penguin, 1995.
van der Valk, Marchinus. *Researches on the Text and Scholia of the Iliad, Part Two.* Leiden: Brill, 1964.
———. *Textual Criticism of the Odyssey.* Leiden: A. W. Sijthoff, 1949.
de Vet, Thérèse. "The Joint Role of Orality and Literacy in the Composition, Transmission, and Performance of the Homeric Texts: A Comparative View." *TAPA* 126 (1996): 43-76.
Vitz, Evelyn Birge. *Orality and Performance in Early French Romance.* Woodbridge: D. S. Brewer, 1999.
de Vries, Kelly. *The Norwegian Invasion of England in 1066.* Woodbridge: Boydell Press, 1999.
Wackernagel, Jacob. *Sprachliche Untersuchungen zu Homer.* 1916. 2nd ed. Göttingen: Vandenhoeck u. Ruprecht, 1970.
Waldron, R. A. "Oral-Formulaic Technique and Middle English Alliterative Poetry." *Speculum* 32 (1957): 792-804.
Wardhaugh, Ronald. *How Conversation Works.* Oxford: Blackwell, 1985.

Watson, Jonathan. "Affective Poetics and Scribal Reperformance in Lawman's *Brut*: A Comparison of the Caligula and Otho Versions." *Arthuriana* 8 (1998): 62-75.

———. "The Minim-istic Imagination: Scribal Invention and the Word in the Early English Alliterative Tradition." *OT* 17 (2002): 290-309.

———. "'Óðinn's Storm': A Case Study in the Literary Reception of Old and Middle English Oral-Derived Verse." Ph.D. diss., Indiana University, 1998.

West, Martin L. "Archaische Heldendichtung: Singen und Schreiben." In *Der Übergang von der Mündlichkeit zur Literatur bei den Griechen*, edited by Wolfgang Kullmann and Michael Reichel, 33-50. Tübingen: G. Narr, 1990.

———. "The Date of the *Iliad*." *MH* 52 (1995): 203-19.

———. "The Rise of Greek Epic." *JHS* 108 (1988): 151-72.

———. "The Textual Criticism and Editing of Homer." In *Editing Texts: Texte edieren*, edited by Glenn W. Most, 94-110. Göttingen: Vandenhoeck & Ruprecht, 1998.

West, Stephanie. *The Ptolemaic Papyri of Homer*. Papyrologica Coloniensia 3. Köln-Opladen: Westdeutscher Verlag, 1967.

———, with Alfred Heubeck, and J. B. Hainsworth. *A Commentary on Homer's Odyssey*. Vol. I. 1988. Reprint, Oxford: Clarendon Press, 1992.

Whiting, B. J. *Chaucer's Use of Proverbs*. Cambridge, Mass.: Harvard University Press, 1934.

———. "The Nature of the Proverb." *HSPL* 14 (1932): 237-308.

———. "Proverbs in Certain Middle English Romances in Relation to Their French Sources." *HSPL* 15 (1933): 75-126.

———. *Proverbs, Sentences, and Proverbial Phrases From English Writings Mainly Before 1500*. Cambridge, Mass.: Harvard University Press, 1968.

Whitman, Cedric H. *Homer and the Heroic Tradition*. 1958. Reprint, Cambridge, Mass.: Harvard University Press, 1967.

Williams, Ann. "Land and Power in the Eleventh Century: The Estates of Harold Godwineson." *Anglo-Norman Studies* 3 (1980): 171-87, 230-4.

Williamson, Craig, ed. and trans. *The Old English Riddles of the Exeter Book*. Chapel Hill: University of North Carolina Press, 1977.

Windeatt, Barry. *Oxford Guides to Chaucer: Troilus and Criseyde*. Oxford: Clarendon Press, 1992.

Winterbottom, Michael. "On the *Hisperica famina*." *Celtica* 8 (1968): 126-39.

Wolf, Alois. "Medieval Heroic Traditions and Their Transitions from Orality to Literacy." In *Vox intexta: Orality and Textuality in the Middle Ages*, edited by A. N. Doane and Carol Braun Pasternack, 67-88. Madison: University of Wisconsin Press, 1991.

Woodhouse, W. J. *The Composition of Homer's Odyssey*. 1930. Reprint, Oxford: Clarendon Press, 1969.

Wormald, Patrick. "*Engla Lond*: the Making of an Allegiance." *Journal of Historical Sociology* 7 (1994): 1-24.

Wright, Roger. *Late Latin and Early Romance in Spain and Carolingian France*. ARCA Classical and Medieval Texts, Papers and Monographs 8. Liverpool: Francis Cairns, 1982.

———, ed. *Latin and the Romance Languages in the Early Middle Ages*. University Park: Pennsylvania State University Press, 1996.

Wyld, H. C. "Laȝamon as an English Poet." *RES* 6 (1930): 1-30.

Yolen, Jane. *Commander Toad in Space*. 1980. Reprint, New York: Scholastic, 1993.

Zesmer, David M. *Guide to English Literature from Beowulf through Chaucer and Medieval Drama*. New York: Barnes and Noble Books, 1961.

Ziolkowski, Jan M. "Classical Influences on Medieval Latin Views of Poetic Inspiration." In *Latin Poetry and the Classical Tradition: Essays in Medieval and Renaissance Literature*, edited by Peter Godman and Oswyn Murray, 15-38. Oxford: Clarendon Press, 1990.

———. "Cultural Diglossia and the Nature of Medieval Latin Literature." In *The Ballad and Oral Literature*, edited by Joseph Harris, 193-213. Harvard English Studies 16. Cambridge, Mass.: Harvard University Press, 1991.

———. "The Highest Form of Compliment: *Imitatio* in Medieval Latin Culture." In *Poetry and Philosophy in the Middle Ages*, edited by John Marenbon, 293-307. Leiden: E. J. Brill, 2001.

———. "The Medieval Latin Beast Flyting." *MJ* 20 (1985): 49-65.

———. "Mnemotechnics and the Reception of the *Aeneid* in Late Antiquity and the Middle Ages." In *Style and Tradition: Studies in Honor of Wendell Clausen*, edited by Clive Foss and Peter E. Knox, 160-75. Beiträge zur Altertumskunde. Stuttgart: Teubner, 1998.

———. "The *Occupatio* by Odo of Cluny: A Poetic Manifesto of Monasticism in the 10th Century." *MJ* 24-25 (1989-1990): 559-67.

———. "The Prosimetrum in Classical Tradition." In *Prosimetrum. Crosscultural Perspectives on Narrative in Prose and Verse*, edited by Joseph Harris and Karl Reichl, 45-65. Cambridge: D. S. Brewer, 1997.

―――. "Text and Textuality, Medieval and Modern." In *Der Unfeste Text. Perspektiven auf einen literatur- und kulturwissenschaftlichen Leitbegriff*, edited by Barbara Sabel and André Bucher, 109–31. Würzburg: Königshausen & Neumann, 2001.

ABOUT THE CONTRIBUTORS

Mark C. Amodio, Professor of English at Vassar College, writes on Old and Middle English literature and oral and literate poetics. His recent books include *Writing the Oral Tradition: Oral Poetics and Literate Culture in Medieval England* (Notre Dame, 2004) and *Unlocking the Wordhord: Anglo-Saxon Studies in Memory of Edward B. Irving, Jr.* (Toronto, 2003; co-edited with Katherine O'Brien O'Keeffe).

John Miles Foley is W. H. Byler Endowed Chair in the Humanities and Curators' Professor of Classical Studies and English at the University of Missouri, Columbia, where he also directs the Center for Studies in Oral Tradition. Among his major publications are *Immanent Art* (Indiana, 1991), *The Singer of Tales in Performance* (Indiana, 1995), *Homer's Traditional Art* (Penn State, 1999), and *How to Read an Oral Poem* (Illinois, 2002). In press are an experimental edition-translation of Halil Bajgorić's performance of a South Slavic epic, *The Wedding of Mustajbey's Son Bećirbey* (2004) and *The Blackwell Companion to Ancient Epic* (2006). He has recently developed a series of internet tools for studying oral poetry, among them an e-companion to *How to Read an Oral Poem* and an e-edition of the South Slavic epic, at www.oraltradition.org.

Lori Ann Garner has published articles on Old and Middle English literature and oral traditions in *Neophilologus*, *Studia Neophilologica*, *Western Folklore*, and *Oral Tradition*. She is also a contributor to *Teaching Oral Traditions* (MLA, 1998), and the *Routledge Encyclopedia of Narrative Theory* (forthcoming). She is currently a Lecturer in the Department of English at the University of Illinois, Urbana-Champaign where she teaches courses on oral traditions, the history of the English language, and descriptive grammar.

Tim William Machan is Professor and Chair of the Department of English at Marquette University. He has published widely on medieval language and literature. His books include *Medieval Literature: Texts and Interpretation* (MRTS, 1991), *Textual Criticism and Middle English Texts* (Virginia, 1994) and, most recently, *English in the Middle Ages* (Oxford, 2003). His edition of the *Sources of the Boece* is forthcoming from the Chaucer Library.

Daniel F. Melia has taught in the department of Rhetoric and the Program in Celtic Studies at the University of California, Berkeley since 1972. He received his Ph.D. at Harvard University where he was a student of Albert Lord's. His recent publications include "Orality and Aristotle's Aesthetics and Methods, Take #2," "Congruent Desires: Medieval and Modern Reconstructions of Irish and Welsh Literary Artifacts," and "On the Origins of *LU*'s Marginal .r." He is also co-editor of *Sources and Analogues of Old English Poetry*, Vol. 2, with Daniel G. Calder, Robert E. Bjork, and Patrick Ford (Boydell & Brewer, 1983).

Joseph Falaky Nagy, Professor of English at the University of California, Los Angeles, is the author of *The Wisdom of the Outlaw: The Boyhood Deeds of Finn in Gaelic Narrative Tradition* (California, 1985), and *Conversing with Angels and Ancients: The Literary Myths of Medieval Ireland* (Cornell, 1997). He is currently the editor of the *Celtic Studies Association of North America Yearbook* (Four Courts Press).

Katherine O'Brien O'Keeffe is Notre Dame Professor of English at the University of Notre Dame. Her work focuses on the literary culture of Anglo-Saxon England, with particular emphasis on the textual evidence for early medieval subjectivity and on cultural transmission. She has most recently edited the C-text of the Anglo-Saxon Chronicle for the joint project, *The Anglo-Saxon Chronicle: A Collaborative Edition.*

Alexandra Hennessey Olsen is Professor English at the University of Denver, where she teaches courses in Old English, Middle English, and Linguistics. She is the author of numerous studies on Old and Middle English, including *Speech, Song, and Poetic Craft: The Artistry of the Cynewulf Canon* (Lang 1984), *New Readings on Women in Old English Literature* (Indiana, 1990; co-edited with Helen Damico), and *Poems and Prose from the Old English* (Yale, 1998; with Burton Raffel).

Contributors

Steve Reece is Associate Professor of Classics at Saint Olaf College. He has published a wide range of articles on Homer, oral traditions, historical linguistics, and the teaching of ancient Greek. He is the author of *The Stranger's Welcome: Oral Theory and the Aesthetics of the Homeric Hospitality Scene* (Michigan, 1993). He has recently been awarded a Woodrow Wilson Fellowship for his monograph on early Greek etymology, *Homer's Winged Words: Junctural Metanalysis in Homer in the Light of Oral-Formulaic Theory*.

Jonathan Watson is Assistant Professor of English at Manchester College. His most recent work on Old and Middle English poetics has appeared in *JEGP* and *Oral Tradition*. In 1993-94, he studied as a Fulbright Scholar in Iceland, and in 2001, he participated in the NEH Seminar: "Anglo-Saxon Texts and Manuscripts" in London. He earned his Ph.D. from Indiana University.

Jan M. Ziolkowski, Arthur Kingsley Porter Professor of Medieval Latin at Harvard University, has focused on the literature of the Latin Middle Ages. He has written some eighty books and articles as well as fifty book reviews. The books encompass critical editions of Medieval Latin texts (such as *The Cambridge Songs; Jezebel: A Norman Latin Poem of the Early Eleventh Century* [Garland, 1994]; and two of poetry by Nigel of Canterbury), a book on intellectual history (*Alan of Lille's Grammar of Sex: The Meaning of Grammar to a Twelfth-Century Intellectual* [Medieval Academy, 1985]), a book on literary history (*Talking Animals: Medieval Latin Beast Poetry* [Penn, 1993]), and collections of essays written by himself and others (*On Philology and Obscenity: Social Control and Artistic Creation in the European Middle Ages* [Brill, 1998]).